AF787618

REINVENTING LIBRARIES WITH FUTURE TECHNOLOGIES

REINVENTING LIBRARIES WITH FUTURE TECHNOLOGIES

Dr. Dattatray Narayan Phadke
Dy Librarian IIT Bombay (Retd.)
Consultant Librarian
Pillai College of Engineering
New Panwel, New Mumbai

Ess Ess Publications
New Delhi

REINVENTING LIBRARIES WITH FUTURE TECHNOLOGIES

Copyright © by Author

All rights reserved. No part of this book may be reproduced in any form or by any electronic or mechanical means including information storage and retrieval systems without permission in writing from the publisher, except by a reviewer, who may quote brief passages in a review.

While extensive effort has gone into ensuring the reliability of information appearing in this book, the publisher makes no warranty, express or implied on the accuracy or reliability of the information, and does not assume and hereby disclaims any liability to any person for any loss or damage caused by errors or omissions in this publication.

ISBN : 978-93-87698-77-2

Price : Rs. 1850/-

First Published 2020

Published by:
Ess Ess Publications
4831/24, Ansari Road,
Darya Ganj,
New Delhi-110 002, INDIA
Phones: 23260807, 41563444
Fax: 41563334
E-mail: info@essessreference.com
www.essessreference.com

Cover Design by *Patch Creative*

Printed and bound in India

Contents

Preface

As the library and information science field always works hand in hand with information technology(IT), almost every new development in IT has to influence the functioning of the libraries. The pace of IT development is so fast that every librarian and LIS professional would like to keep track of each and every advancement of IT and its applications in library management in order to equip themselves with the use of the new technologies in library automation. The span of library automation is so wide that it has become difficult to discuss its all components together in one single book. Considering this I have separated component of Library Computerisation and has simultaneously published the independent book on it namely, **Advances in Library Computerisation** (Ess Ess Publications, New Delhi). In present book I have concentrated only on Library Information Technology. This book is the results of my efforts made on understanding how the present and future technology would be reshaping and reinventing the library world and what the challenges the library management would face in the coming future.

The gathering of relevant information becomes difficult since all the advances are published on the internet in terms of experiments or case studies under the broad title of, "Future technologies in future libraries". Secondly, such information is pouring on the internet platform so fast that it becomes difficult to list them completely, so I have tried to collect all the available information on the banner, analysed it consolidated the contents and prepared a manageable list. Looking into long list of future technologies it was only possible to discuss a few of them in independent chapters and take a review of all the other developments in the concluding chapter.

The discussed topics relating to information technology in library are as follows:

- Internet Technology and its future generations (Chapter one)
- Internet Security (Chapter Two)
- Development of Digital Library (Chapter Three)
- Metadata (Chapter Four)
- Data Mining and Data Warehousing (Chapter Five)
- Library Electronic Security Systems : Products and Services(Chapter Six)
- Management of E-Resources : Collection Development (Chapter Seven)
- Use of Web 2.O Tools in Library (Chapter Eight)

- Open Source Technology and Open Access Resources (Chapter Nine)
- Semantic Web (Chapter Ten)
- E-Publishing Technology in Library (Chapter Eleven)
- Cloud Computing (Chapter Twelve)
- Big Data (Chapter Thirteen)
- Introduction to BIBFRAME: Future Cataloguing Format (Chapter Fourteen)
- Green Library (Chapter Fifteen)
- Future Technology in Future Libraries (Chapter Sixteen)

Following new technologies have been briefly reviewed in the concluding chapter:

Future Technologies for Reinventing Libraries

Virtual Reality; Augmented Reality, Big Data, Blockchain Technology; Internet of Things (IOT), Drones and Robots, Library Utensils, ,Library Mobile APPs, Digital Interface for Printed Book, Intelligent Library Guide and Bookmarks, Maker Space Programmes, Applications of Artificial Intelligence in Library, Data Harvesting, Biometrics, Digital Signature & smart cards for authentication, Digital Preservation and 3D printing

Emerging Terminologies

Repositories : ROAR,DOAR-Open DOAR,SHERPA,SHERPA-RoMeo ,

Internet Terminologies : HTTP,FTP,URL,URI,RDF ,RDFs and PROTÉGÉ

Cataloguing Protocols and Standards : ISO-2709,Z39.50,Z39.71,Z39.2

Bibliographic Formats : ISBD,MARC-21,CCF,RDA, FRBR and BIBFRAME

Data Harvesting

Social Mobile Analytics and Cloud (SMAC)

Intrusion Detection Systems(IDS)

With this exhaustive coverage of library information technological themes and with a review on future library technologies, this book presents a good first-hand source of information for the librarians for adopting future technologies in their quest of reinventing their libraries and coupled with new array of terminologies it has also become a good encyclopedic compilation for the library professionals and students to keep themselves up to date in the latest developments in the field of library and information science field and also for preparing competitive exams like NET/SET and in shaping and brightening their professional career.

I consider it my moral duty to express my gratitude to all those whose written material, mostly available in public domain has been referred or indirectly used in presenting my take on future technology in future libraries. I am grateful to the bloggers, professional home page owners, authors of books, contributors of journal articles whose material has been referred in terms of definitions, figures, tables or images with due acknowledgment. I am also grateful to **Ms. Amber Billey** the former Metadata

Librarian at Columbia University Libraries, currently Systems and Meta Data Librarian at Bard College Huston. While writing a chapter on BIBFRAME I had mail correspondence with her and I got valuable explanation about BIBFRAME project and its status at her place.

I would like to express my gratitude towards Mr. Sumit Sethi, Chief Executive, Ess Ess Publications, New Delhi and thank him and his team for enthusiastically considering publishing this book at a short notice and extending all the cooperation in this regard. Thanks are also due to Mr. B P Juwale of Universal Prakashan, Pune for his cooperation and consideration.

I express my gratitude towards my family members for sacrificing their family life while I was busy in accomplishing the task of writing this book for the benefits of the readers.

I hope that readers would appreciate the contents of this book, read it patiently and look for more information on the themes discussed in the book to widen their knowledge base in library and information science.

— Dattatray Narayan Phadke

Introduction

The book, **"Reinventing Libraries with Future Technologies,"** attempts to cover almost all the currently available advances of information technology and its use in library automation. The book would be useful for working librarians and library professionals in refreshing/upgrading their knowledge about the uses of advanced information technology tools in library. For students, it would help in filling the gap between LIS school curriculum and the current requirements of IT skills/expertise needed in getting good placements. It is expected that LIS students would extensively use this book while appearing for SET/NET exams. While reading the book, readers would get a feel of encyclopedic nature covering all the latest information technology tools available at international level and their use in library automation. As far as one of the important components library automation viz Library computerization the author has independently published a book on, **Advances in Library Computerization** recently. The present book would act as a guide and would certainly inspire librarians in planning, modernizing and reinventing their libraries in the light of future technologies.

The book is divided in 16 chapters, giving practical aspects of use of IT in libraryas follows:

Chapter 1 : Internet Technology and its Uses in Library Management reviews all the aspects right from evolution of internet technology along with its historical background to various generations of internet. Then it presents the technical side of it. It further refers modern trends of data transmission like WIFI, LIFI, microwave devices useful in getting internet connectivity plus it has also described types of browsers and finally gives account on how internet can be used in library functioning.

Chapter 2 : Internet Security covers all the threats posed in use of internet and mentions the methods to protect our internet activity with use of tools like fire wall, anonymisers, remailers and encryptors.

Chapter 3 : Development of Digital Library, which is a very important aspect of library automation, much discussed today. After initially presenting conceptual & evolution of digital library with its background, it discusses about DL software, resources of digital library. It has further given detailed account on digitisation process.

It further highlights managerial aspects of digital library and finally presents development of digital library practically with use of Greenstone and DSpace (Open Source Softwares).

Chapter 4 : Metadata, initially elaborates the concept of metadata, then on its types, expectations of metadata and about metadata structuring. Then it discusses various metadata schemes and finally describes Dublin Core metadata scheme in details along with its elements.

Chapter 5 : Data mining of Data Warehousing first clarifies the related concepts like data mining, data warehouse and data warehousing. Then it goes into actual process of data warehousing and data mining along with use of statistical packages and data mining tools.

Chapter 6 : Library Electronic Security Systems: Products and Services discusses first about importance of security in library then presents available electronic security systems like:3M Electromagnetic and RFID Security systems along with their usage details and about their equipments, consumables and other machinery. It has provided detailed account of RFID the smart security system along with its importance in library management. The chapter concludes with the use, of CCTV surveillance system in library.

Chapter 7 : Management of e-resources : Collection Development highlights importance of e -resources collection development with proliferation of e-resources in library. It then discusses all aspect of e - resources collection development like selection, acquisition, pricing, access and licensing. It has also covered on having open access e - resources in the library. Finally it described a few well known e - resources and their importance in library.

Chapter 8 : Use of Web 2.0 Technology Tools in library gives an account of evolution of various generation/ stages of internet technology e.g. web 1.0 web 2.0 and the future of web technology e.g. Web 3.0. It then presents the ideas of O'Reilly about web 2.0 technology with its characteristics. In conclusion it introduces all the tools available under web 2.0 technology e.g. RSS feeds, weblogs, wikis, streaming media, instant messaging, tagging, social networking, bookmarking, flicker, mesh-up and podcasting etc.

Chapter 9 : Open Source System and Open Access Resources first gives conceptual background of both the terminologies ,then it discusses role of open source initiative (OSI) and open access initiative (OAI) in promoting these concepts.

Chapter 10 : Semantic Web Technology discusses all together a new theme, Semantic Web Technology as imagined by Tim Burners-Lee, the pioneer of Internet in terms of open link data. It finally presents future scenario of internet technology, where free open linked data sets would be available on web and people could use them by interlinking as per needs.

Chapter 11 : E - Publishing Technology in Library gives the account of e - publishing technology with its concept and about e - publishing tools. It finally highlights how library would be able to publish its own e - journals on special subject as an alternative to commercial e - publishing.

Chapter 12 : Cloud Computing Technology gives conceptual background of cloud computing technology and its need in organising computing needs. It then describes various types of cloud computing services, like IaaS, PaaS, and SaaS. Then it describes different types of clouds and finally it provides knowledge on application of cloud computing with special reference to Amazon (AWS) and its use in library computerisation.

Chapter 13 : Big Data :A short introduction presents the technical details of Big Data Technology along with need of software like Hadoop and big data analytics which are useful in handling large data sets.

Chapter 14 : On, **Introduction to BIBFRAME : The future cataloguing Format/ standards.** This chapter has introduced the very new concept of BIBFRAME as taken up by Library of Congress with a view to provide the alternative to old MARCE format. BIBFRAME has given us a new way to make our library catalogue data visible on web by using open linked data technology. The chapter has reviewed all the developments of BIBFRAME.

Author hopes that the above chapter wise introduction would help in creating curiosity in the minds of reader to read them and would further inspire them to read more materials on these topics.

Chapter 15 : on **Green Library.** This chapter invites attention of librarians and managers towards future role of library in convincing society the importance of sustainability, becoming eco-friendly and working towards protecting the environment. Adopting green concept in building construction is more or less on the verge of stabilizing. The libraries also are now gradually planning in adopting the green concept in building new libraries or in renovating old ones. Greening libraries ideally it a difficult project but many libraries have not only successfully adopted the green concept but have become flagship green libraries and set as examples. Author has discussed many innovative features of green library.

Chapter 16 : Future Technologies in Future Libraries : In this chapter author has presented review of all the future technologies which would be seen in future libraries. Some of them are as Virtual Reality, Big Data, Augmented Reality, Blockchain Technology, Drones, Robots, Intelligent Library Guide and Bookmark, Internet of Things (IOT), Digital Interface for Printed Book and Makerspace Programmes, Application of Artificial Intelligence in library, Biometrics, Digital Signatures and Smart cards for Authentication, Data harvesting, Digital Preservation and 3D Printing.

Emerging Terminologies

Repositories : ROAR, DOAR-Open DOAR, SHERPA, SHERPA-RoMeo,

Internet Terminologics : HTTP, FTP, URL, URI, RDF, RDFs and PROTÉGÉ

Cataloguing Protocols and Standards : ISO-2709, Z39.50, Z39.71, Z39.2

Bibliographic Formats : ISBD, MARC-21, CCF, RDA, BRFR and BIBFRAME

Data Harvesting

Social Mobile Analytics and Cloud (SMAC)

Intrusion Detection Systems

1
Internet Technology : It's Use in Library Management

1.0. INTRODUCTION

Initially when internet was invented by Tim Burners-Lee, it was thought that perhaps it could be used either for communicating confidential information in the war field or for exchanging scientific information. Subsequently it was also felt that only rich or industrialists could afford to use internet facility. However, today internet is easily available for common man and is useful for all age group people. It is not only an affordable but has been proved very much useful plateform. In educational system, internet is taught right from primary level and any educational program does not end without providing internet skill training to the students. We see youngsters frequently talk about internet terminology and about how to achieve internet expertise which is useful or rather essential in their day to day work or professional life. We have seen in recent past existing of cyber cafes in almost every lane and we find now each house is equipped with internet connectivity. People do online railway reservations from home, they trade shares online or they buy thing from online stores. We see people invariably listen to online music programs or talk with near ones through teleconferencing or on Skype.

As such internet has captured our daily life but the way and extent kids in foreign countries use internet for social networking is really astonishing for all of us. However it is yet to be spread in developing countries like ours, but it is expected that not today but tomorrow it would happen. Internet means wonders of information technology. Library management and information technology walk with hand in hand. Library is the place where internet is used most. With this background we are going to revive, in this chapter our knowledge about internet from introduction to its advance use.

1.1. INTRODUCTION TO INTERNET

Internet is sometimes understood as a network formed with millions of computers in the world. However, it may be a vague understanding. If we want to define it properly it could be done in short as "Network of information resources spread world wide". A beginner may have a question in mind about where the internet exists? Is it on earth? it is in sky? or at underground? The answer is, it is not in sky or underground it is around us on earth's surface, except in case when satellites are used for communication. If we want slightly deeper knowledge then it can be termed as it is the collection of web pages. We would find crores of web pages are written and uploaded on internet and it works like the Tale of Alibaba's caves, where one by one doors are opened in order to reach the treasure of information. It works exactly like that, we travel from one web page to another interconnected web page. We may be curious to know how many computers participate in the internet network. Although efforts are on to count them out, but is very difficult. The most important thing about internet is that there is no owner for it. Only a few institutions work for controlling it. The internet is dependent on telecommunication media which is owned by private or semi government organisations.

1.2. INTERNET : TECHNICAL BACKGROUND

Now let us try to know about the technical side of the internet.

1.2.1. TCP/ IP

In an internet environment all the participating computers communicate with each other with certain protocol known as Transmission Control Protocol- Internet Protocol or it is known in short as TCP - IP / IP. It is a technical discipline which makes communication on internet possible. In the past this protocol was to be externally adopted but it comes these days as built in with your PC in its control system. You only need to configure it while setting it up your PC once in the beginning. Internet works with a client server relationship, where the server is the source of information (or giver) where as the client is an information receiving computer. When the client machine gets connected with the server and sends query, the server sends the relevant files or available services to the client, user at the client end receives them and makes use of them. It hardly matters where the server is located, it may be at any remote place in the world so getting connected to it through a client located at other remote place is achieved in a very easy manner. Internet Technology has made it simple for us.

Now with the internet we can avail many facilities like :

- Electronic Mail or e - Mail
- Information exchange through file transfer (FTP)
- Access to information sources
- Membership in internet user group.
- Computer - computer dialog
- Multimedia search
- Instant and continuously updated information from news websites
- Online purchase opportunities
- Internet banking

- Access to online e-journals, e - databases or e - books

Of course accessing these services on internet is bound by the respective access protocols. These are softwares and they try to co-operate with each other to provide you seamless connectivity and continuous information flow.

1.2.2. World Wide Web (www) Technology

World Wide Web or in short www is an internet domain server system. This system collaborate with various types of protocols available with the servers worldwide. These protocols include e-mail, F.T.P., and news. In addition www has its own protocol e.g. http or Hyper Text Transfer Protocol, Which makes it possible to access any website containing hypertext links. With http protocol and www domain we can open and access any website with the address which begins with www. We therefore see www words in the beginning of every address of internet based website. Above technicalities has made internet use as simple as possible. Web systems, multimedia technology and further advanced programs and web language jointly make internet an intelligent information tool.

We have by now understood that www is the main system domain which is capable to communicate with different protocols. Now let us try to know about http://. Internet is fully dependent on hypertext concept. Hypertext means the facility to get connected with the next webpage through a hyper texted word on the front page. It could be a word or graphics like link, figure, text string or clip which are hyper texted. It provides us the facility to click them and go to the next or further web pages.

We have understood about www and http. Now let us understand how the web pages are actually written. Are they simple text pages? No, they are not simple text pages but are written using special language like HTML or Hyper Text Markup Language. All the pages are written using HTML language but when they are presented to us for viewing we see them as simple text page with in between blue words or links created by hyper text language. When we click on them it takes us to the next page. This way from front page to next page from that page to further page we take a journey in the home page. HTML is a speedily progressing web language. Similar to HTML, there are other languages and style sheets which help us to see web pages in a better looks and feel. Among them are, Java, Java script, CSS (Cascading style sheets) or VB++ and PHP

With www we see files, script on home pages. Web system with multimedia streaming we see presentation of information like the virtual real world. Now a days these web pages are found interactive rather than the old type which were static in nature. Today we see web pages in combination of script and multimedia but days are not far when we could see television or listen to radio programs through web technology. Moreover, it happens today also.

1.3. BENEFITS OF INTERNET

With connectivity to internet not only we get treasure of information available for free but are benefitted in several ways, which mainly includes availability of email facilities. Overall the benefits of internet are listed as :

- **e-mail :** Facility to communicate with anyone in the world
- **News Group :** You can get membership of news group on your internet website which facilitates to us discussion and sharing with people working on subject similar to us.
- **Chat :** You can establish contact with your friends, colleagues or relatives and chat online from anywhere for any time.
- **You can read e-resources** subscribed by your library comprise of collection of e - Journals e - books and databases.

1.4. HISTORICAL BACKGROUND OF INTERNET

Foundation of internet was laid by US Defence Department sometime around 1967 when US Defence Advanced Research Department established a project known as ARPA to explore newer ways to use science and technology for defence purpose. ARPANET came into existence in 1969.

Under ARPANET all the computers at the three universities e.g. California University, Santa Barbara University and Stanford Research Institute plus Utah University in the periphery of Los Angeles were considered to form the network. Subsequently many other universities participated in the network. Basic and prime purpose of ARPANET was exchange of information to get ready to combat possible nuclear attack on US but it was further decided to use it for educational and research activities also. The work of engineers, scientists and computer experts of ARPANET started then was constantly going on up to recent time.

In 1970 the first protocol about free exchange of scientific information was available for use. By 1980 websites relating to e - mail, use mail and news related information service started emerging on internet. Academicians in universities and libraries started networking, facilitating communications among them and sharing the knowledge and discussions. Their library catalogues were networked making referral kind of information exchange possible.

These developments made searching information comparatively easy. In 1991 Minnesota University uploaded its own homepage names Gopher. This made browsing files, pages on internet with simple means. All these developments were happening on DOS platform till then and windows with multimedia were yet to be emerged.

In 1991 World Wide Web (www) came into existence along with www protocol, the inventor was Tim Burners-Lee. It was a victory of his efforts with his team associates at European Particle Physics Research Lab. With Lee's initiative CERN European Organisation for Nuclear Research, Switzerland was established. CERN brought the first web server. Lee used next-cuber for this. 1980 - 1990 was the period for invention to implementation of www. During the period Lee built EWQUIRE named personal data base of people and software models. With Lee's help CERN could prepare Hypertext Transfer Protocol

By Christmas of 1990 Tim Berners-Lee had built all the tools necessary for working with HTTP 0.9 and were made available. Hypertext markup language HTML was invented. Thus the first web browser (www web editor), the first HTML server software (CERN http) and first web page which describes www project came into reality. The browser could access Usenet news group and TTP Files also. However, the browser had limitation as it was not universal. Nicola Pellow created a very simple text browser which could run on any computer (line mode Browser). In order to encourage the use of www Bernd Poller Mann had put CERN Telephone Directory on web which was found easy to search for phone numbers.

While carrying out the research the web page was lost but subsequently it was retrieved by Paul Jones (UNC - Chapel Hill) in May 2013. CERN had once again published the first web page online in 2014 to the world viewers as a memory of www development.

We know that with hypertext concept web pages are linked with each other to form one set called home page. Tim Burners-Lee while he was the Director of World Wide Web consortium had played a pioneering role in bringing internet in reality. Many experts from Universities and Software Companies were closely associated with the consortium. This Consortium keeps a control on web technology.

Initially National Science Foundation, NASA and Energy Department of USA were jointly working for this project and were exchanging ideas and information and USA was funding for it. Initially the business people were not using this facility. Subsequently internet developed in a speedy manner. Purely private nature Websites started emerging on internet. Delphi Institute started providing internet facilities to its members without depending on government support. Initially in June 1993 the number of websites was just 130; within one year the number went up to 30,000. By 1998 the number of websites reached to 32 Lakhs. In September 2014 the strength of websites marked 1billion as confirmed by Net Craft in October 2014. This statistics confirms quantum of development in internet technology.[1]

The irony is that nobody controls the internet; neither there is an owner for it. Who so ever has a computer and an internet connectivity hardware can create his/her website and uploads it on internet, we only need to pay www consortium and membership fee to get space on the internet.

In Tim Berners-Lee's point of view he had dreamt to create space where information collection created for all, by which everyone can exchange his ideas and views freely and universal availability was the main motto behind the internet development. Hypertext concept has facilitated us to get ourselves connected with any website in the world, maybe it is personal, regional or government level, may be website is fully developed is up-to-date or it may be incomplete.

Developing website is not found difficult these days. We may not even need to have full knowledge of HTML or other web languages. Content Management Systems (CMS) have further made it easy to develop web pages where readymade template pages are available.

1.5. INTERNET CONNECTIVITY AND ESSENTIAL THINGS

We can connect our computer to internet in the following ways :

Subscription to Internet connection : Now a days there are several companies or network who provide you internet connectivity by paying their subscriptions. Company provides internet license/ internet account. They further provide you login ID and password. Initially one can get connectivity with limited download limit in terms of GB (1GB - 40 GB.....) and that too for limited time (1 month, 3 months or one year) but now we get internet with unlimited connectivity.

Getting Data Connection : As soon as you exhaust the download GB limit you cease to get internet. In another mode you can get unlimited mode for certain period e.g. without GB limit. The speed of the connection is also an important factor in getting connection. Speed can be from 512kps to 10 or 20 MB. With higher speed you can use internet comfortably else it takes a long time to open the page of desired web site.

This is about getting internet account; next question is through which medium you can get connectivity or what set up you need to get yourself connected with internet.

1.5.1. Communication Medium or Device

We need very first thing what communication medium you choose to have to get yourself connected with internet. It depends on the device you use to get internet. There are different devices as

1. Desktop PC or Laptop
2. Mobile Phones, Tab, iPod, iPhone etc.

Let us assume you have a desktop and need communication medium. There are different means to achieve this :

1.5.1.1. Through Internet Cable

In this mode we get or buy services of cable operators which provides cable connection where a line/wire cable is connected to the PC or laptop. Incoming cable comes from a network server which is connected to internet network may be through landline and thus you get connected to internet. Once you get a cable connection you need to subscribe to internet data connection or a license.

1.5.1.2. Through Telephone Connection

Nowadays everybody uses telephone connection available either from PSU companies or private companies. We use telephones for making voice calls. This medium of communication can also be used to internet Connection. There are various ways to get internet through telephone lines. They are as follows :

Basic Device	Medium	Modulator
Computer	Telephone	Modern
PC having Internet Programming	Telephone with Broad band	
PC with internet	Cable	LAN-card
Laptop	Wireless	Wireless
All sorts of devices	Wireless	WIFI

With telephone type internet connectivity we get in the following ways.

1.5.1.2.1. Dial up mode

In this case we can either make voice call or get internet. We need telephone wire connected PC, through a modem by registering you can get dialup connection.

1.5.1.2.2. Broad Band Mode

In this case telephone calls and internet connection can be used simultaneously. We need here same telephone wire connection to PC and caller plus modem or router.

1.5.2. Router/ Modem and LAN card

In previous paras we have read names of devices we use to get internet connectivity like modem router and LAN-card. Now let us understand about them.

1.5.2.1. Modem or Routers

Modem or Router is one of the most important tools in telephone technology which helps us in getting connected to internet network. Their function is modulation or demodulation. When signals flow in cable wires they are in analog mode. When we connect cable or wires to use PC and try to use data signals, the signal needs to be demodulated. In a PC we use digital signal. Modem or Router does the function of converting analog signals into digital ones or vice a versa. Routers are fixed outside the PC and are connected to an external cable wire and to the PC.

Modems / Routers are used to transmit signals. The capacity of modem / router depends on how much data is transmitted in what time duration. It is measured in KBPS or MBPS e.g. kilo bytes per second or mega bytes per seconds. Normal modems uses are of following types.

14 kbps = 14,000 bytes per second

28 kbps = 28,000 bytes per second

56 kbps = 56,000 bytes per second

512 kbps = 5,12,000 bytes per second

Higher capacity modems transfer data in terms of MBPS (Mega bytes per second)

1.5.2.2. LAN card

LAN card is a hardware device fixed inside the PC and it has various capacities depending on its speed. LAN card is the door to network from a computer. A computer requires LAN card to do network activities like Internet network, printer for connecting computers to each other. There are various types of LAN card or PC MCIA cards in laptop there are different ways to connect LAN cards i.e. Via USB port, some via PC Port inside the computers or some are embedded inside the computer. Most laptops have Integrated LAN cards for both wired and wireless networks. A PCI card goes inside PC computer. The card shows an Ethernet port. This is the spot where you plug in a network cable. LAN cards are governed by protocols i.e. Ethernet Card with Ethernet protocol. A fiber cable would have a different cable plug in and would work like with wide area network protocol. Ethernet port or a LAN card looks like a phone jack. Typical internet cable or network cable is the plug in that goes into LAN card or the network interface controller (NIC). So far we have understood how we get connectivity either through cable or wire and that too for a desktop PC. Now let us see how we use internet in mobiles.

1.5.3. Using Internet on Mobiles

Like telephones we use mobiles for calling friends, relatives and others. This is a voice communication, when we wish to use mobiles or smart mobile phones for getting internet connectivity we need to have the following set up :

1. By Getting Data Connection : We can get data connection from the service provider who provides you voice calling facility. In this case you can choose ways like limited connectivity i.e. facility to get connected on internet and download the data or browse the websites. It is in terms of GB and for certain time limit e.g. days or months. Another way is to get unlimited facility to use internet. Internet speed is another factor that comes into the picture e.g. with what speed you get internet facility. It is measured in terms of KBPS or MBPS. It speed is more one can get access to websites quickly or it takes long time to open the website and carry out internet work. Nowadays a new technology has emerged where in we can also make voice calls using internet data connection.

So far we have seen how we can get internet connectivity in devices like desktop PCS or in mobile handsets and about what devices are needed to access the Internet. However as communication technology has progressed we get newer and newer ways means and media to have internet connectivity. Nowadays there are technologies by which we can connect all the devices like PC, mobile, tab, laptop and I-pads etc with one single medium and e.g. wireless mode or WIFI. Now let us try to understand in detail about the wireless networking.

1.5.4. Wireless Networking

Wireless communication technology has become an integral part of several types of communication devices. It is possible now for users to communicate from remote areas. The devices used for wireless communication are cordless telephones, mobiles, CPU units, zigbee technology, wireless computer parts and satellite television. One wing of wireless communication technology is wireless networking. This technology is found very much in internet connectivity. There are several products developed in wireless networking and they are nowadays much are in use. We are going to understand about these products one by one.

1.5.4.1 WIMAX

These are wireless broadband systems which offer fast web surfing without getting connected through cable or DSL. Example of wireless broadband is WIMAX. It has the potential to deliver data, wherein transfer rate is more than 30 MB. However many provider do not maintain this rate of speed. WIMAX is also one of the versions of 4G wireless available in phones as sprints 4G Technology.

1.5.4.2. WIFI (Wireless Fidelity)

WIFI is a form of low power wireless communication used by many electronic devices such as laptop or smart phones. In a WIFI setup a wireless router serves as the communication hub. Due to low powered transmission their networks are extremely limited in range which allows user to connect only within proximity to router or signal receptor. It has now become most common in home networking applications and also in providing portability without any need of cables. WIFI network needs to be secured with a password for maintaining security and for avoiding misuse. It is easy for integration and convenience with mobility and expandability.

1.5.4.3. Bluetooth Technology

Bluetooth technology allows one to connect to different electronic devices wirelessly to a system to transfer and sharing data is the main function of Bluetooth. Cell phones can be connected to hands free earpieces, wireless key board, mouse, television, mike/mic, to laptop with the help of Bluetooth as it helps in transmitting signals from one device to other device. Bluetooth technology has many functions and it is used most commonly in wireless communication environment. is the symbol of Bluetooth connectivity.

Features

- Blue tooth technology uses radio waves to communicate between devices and most of these radio waves work with range of 50 feet.
- Bluetooth uses low powered signals with a maximum range of 50 feet with sufficient speed to enable to transmit the data among the devices.
- In order to establish connection pairing process is carried out which identifies all the available devices in the area. It also prevents interference of radio signals from non paired Bluetooth devices in the same area.
- It uses minimum power when it is needed thus saves battery life.

1.5.4.4. ZigBee

ZigBee is a wireless communication method designed to fulfill the needs of low powered wireless sensor and control network. It can be used almost anywhere as it is easy to implement and requires little power to operate. Zigbee sensor system has been developed to help in communicating data with simple structure compatible to sensor.

ZigBee has the following features.

- It is designed for low power consumption.
- ZigBee is used in commercial environment where sensing and monitoring are required.
- It uses very low power which helps in saving battery life,
- ZigBee provides flexibility to do more with reliable wireless performance with minimum battery operation

1.5.5. Types of wireless Data Transmission Devices

Wireless technology allows electronic devices to communicate in air without having connected through cables by using radio frequency signals. There are varieties of wireless data transmission devices and with greater mobility. These devices play a very important role in voice and internet communication. Now let use try to understand about them.

1.5.5.1. Wireless Routers

Wireless routers accept incoming internet connection and sends data as radio frequency signals to other wireless devices which are in proximity or range of router. The network setup with router device is sort of Wireless Local Area Network (WLAN). Routers are available with built in security features which help in protecting connected devices with the routers from infectious data such as viruses. Generally routers are used in homes to get internet connectivity to computer, smart phones, tablets, iPads and laptops.

1.5.5.2. Wireless Adapters

Wireless adapters are a kind of hardware which are installed inside the computer which enables wireless connectivity of a computer which does not have built in wireless adapter, as without an adapter it will not be able to connect to router in order to get internet connectivity. Some computers come with adapters in their mother board. Where as it is also possible to install adapter as standalone wireless devices to provide wireless capability to the computer where built in device is missing.

1.5.5.3. Wireless Repeater

Wireless repeater is a device which takes part in wireless networking which helps to extend the range of a wireless router. Repeater receives wireless signals from router which is further amplified, the strength of the signals and re-emits them. It is used by placing a repeater between the router and the computer connected to the router.

1.5.5.4. Microwave Devices

Nowadays microwave finds to be one of the effective types of wireless data transmission which transfers information. There are two method in this:

Satellite Method : In this mode data/ information is transmitted via a geostationary satellite which would be over 200 miles above the earth. The stations on the earth can send and receive data signals towards and from satellite ranging from 11GHz and with speed of 1mbps to 10 mbps.

Terrestrial method : Here two microwave towers having clear sight between them are used ensuring that there is no obstacle to disrupt the line of sight. It is used for privacy purpose; in such case frequency of data transmission for terrestrial systems are of 4GHz to 6GHz or from 21 GHz to 23 GHz with speed of 1mbps to 10 mbps.

1.5.5.5. Infrared (IR)

Infrared media is also used for data transmission which transmits data signals through light emitting diodes (LEDs) or lasers. Basically Infrared is electromagnetic energy which flows, having a wavelength longer than that of red light. It this case data signal current travel through obstacles in infrared system, however can be inhibited by light. One type of IR transmission is the point to point system in which transmission is possible between two points with limit to a range and line of sight. In this system the frequency would be 100 GHz to 1000 GHz i.e. 1THz and with speed of 100 kbps to 16mbps. Another method of data transmission with IR includes the broadcast system. Data transmission unit (reflective material) amplifies the retransmitted data signal to several other units. In this case frequency would be 100 GHz to 1000 THz with speed of 1MBPS.

We use other wireless devices like radio or wireless phones (cordless phones) using radio waves. Even GPS systems works on these principles.

1.5.5.6. LIFI (Light Fidelity)

Continuing our discussion of IR data transmission let us know how LED light could be used for data transmission. Like WIFI it is called LIFI. In UK it is already been achieved that data can be transmitted by using led lamps with speed of 10 Gbt /s and the technology is called as LIFI. Researchers used micro LED light bulb to transmit 3.5Gbt via each of the three primary colours e.g. red, green and blue which makes up the white light.

LIFI is the energy technology which used specialised LED lights bulb providing low-cost wireless internet connectivity.

In this technology data can be transmitted at the rate of 10 gigabits per second. LIFI is a light fidelity in which visible light spectrum is used as the source of wireless data delivery. The inventor of this techniques is Prof. Herald Hass from the University of Edinburg, who worked on the concept of visual light communication for over 10 years and proved that the semi conductor properties of LED light has the potential for lighting fast data transmission.

Presently he is working with a company called, Pure LIFI which is the leader in many ways in visual light communication. Their products include LI-flame the world's first bi-directional visible light communication system and LI-flame which can create equivalent of a wireless network by turning LEDs into wireless access points, allowing user to move from one light source to other light source without interrupting the flow of data. LI-flame is also being developed as a mobile unit the users can attach to their laptop or smart device.

We have so far clearly understood how our PC is made capable to receive internet by configuring it with TCP - IP / IP. Then we understood how we get internet connectivity for various devices like in PC, laptops or in even mobile handset. In spite of all the above things we need important things in our devices to use internet in a comfortable environment e.g. internet software or we need good browser to view internet websites on our devices. Now let us find out about the browsers and try to know the different types of browsers available today.

1.6. INTERNET BROWSERS

There are a few essential things which we need when we wish to get connected with the internet or want to surf internet and browse various website to get information. Browser is one of those essentials. Once your PC is configured with TCP / IP or internet protocol and once you have opted to get internet connectivity and connection, one can enjoy internet access, provided you have suitable browser downloaded and installed.

1.6.1. What is internet browser?

A web browser commonly known as browser is a software application or program which you can use to access the internet and view web pages on your computer. Browser is useful for retrieving, presenting, book marking and transferring information resources on the World Wide Web (www). All websites which are governed by http (hyper text transmission protocol) e.g. under the domain or www are available under internet can be accessed through the browser. Desktop and browsers translate HTML and allow reading text, view images and play videos online. Normally people select a particular browser that is faster and more secured. If one wants to compare browsers then they could be compared on the following characteristics :

- Speed of compatibility
- Features
- Security and
- Help and support

Let us see what we expect in each of these characteristic :

Speed & compatibility : Ease of use; initial start up time (seconds). Average startup time (seconds); Navigation time (seconds); mobile browser app and synchronization.

Features : Tabbed browsing, book marks, integrated search engine, add-ons, save tabs, customization options, zooming facility, find on page function, password manager, auto fill, automatic updates, seamless download manager, mouse gesture, voice interaction, open source development and parental control.

Security : Under security we expect pop - up blocker, clear data, anti spyware/antivirus, anti fishing, Private Personal mode.

Help and Support : We expect here online knowledge base, user guide, user forums, FAQS, tutorials, e-mail support and telephone support.

All the above characteristic talk about ideal browser and each and every browser cannot have all these expectations and naturally we choose one which could fulfill the above maximum expectations. There are various operating systems and we can group them depending on their compatibility. We see the following operating systems like

- Windows, windows 10, windows-7, vista & XP
- Mac-OS
- Android
- iOS
- Open source: Linux, Fedora etc.
- CentOS

As on today there are nearly 80+ browsers which are compatible with one or the other operating systems. We are going to know about a few of them in the following paras :

We can list the browsers depending on some parameters or category.

- Major Browsers : Opera, Firefox ,Safari and Google Chrome
- Cross Platform : Mozilla browsers
- Windows browsers : K- Meleon
- Macintosh browsers : Omniweb
- Linux browsers : konqueror and icab and Epiphany

All these browsers support the following technical features :

- Tabbed browsing
- Modern web pages with HTML, CSS, SSL and java script
- Cookies Management
- Plug-ins and java
- Add of popup Blocking
- Download Managers
- Integrated Search
- Favorites/ Book Mark and import

In the same categorisation as above let us know more about them

1.6.2. Major Browsers : Opera, Fire fox, Safari, Google chrome

1.6.2.1. OPERA

Opera was originally released in 1996. However it has won the war with other browsers. It has been constantly innovating and it is now available as a full-fledged internet suit with web, e-mail, news and chat with a lot of features.

OPERA-26 was released on 3rd Dec.,2014 :Opera is also used as mobile web browser (Opera Mini) in addition to Android and iOS. It is a java capable device. There are two modes e.g. desktop opera like opera mini or opera cost. Opera browser and opera mini which could be freely download from site http://www.opera.com.

1.6.2.2. Safari

Safari is Apple's favorite browser for Mac; It is very popular in Apple product users. It emerged predominantly when Microsoft stopped developing it for Mac PCs. Safari is known for its elegance, speed and as default browser for Mac products. It is also used as browser on iphone, iPod, and iPad. Safari could be downloaded from the site apple.com. Latest version : iOS 11.3 was released on 30th March 2018.

1.6.2.3. Google chrome

Google chrome is the advanced version of basic browser we use e.g. Google. In 2008 Google rethought its assumption about its browser and brought out chrome with enhanced performance for web application. Chrome uses the website engine like safari and is available as the default web browser on android mobile phone platform. It is freely available for downloading from the site : www.google.com on the web to even low end mobile phones.

1.6.2.4. Firefox

Mozilla Firefox has been the most successful alternative as web browser. It is the flagship product of Mozilla. It has been originated from the old browser Netscape Firefox and is known for characteristics like design, secured and for extensibility. The Mozilla thunder bird mail and news client is the perfect companion choice, works on windows as well as on open source O.S.

A mobile Firefox is available for Android and Maemo for Apple iPad and iPhone. Firefox home syncs your Firefox history, bookmark and tabs to your phone browser. Firefox could be down loaded for free from site http://www.mozilla foundation.com

1.6.3. Linux / UNIX Browsers : Konqueror, Epiphany

Conqueror : This browser was developed as an open source platform like Linux and UNIX. This browser is for KDE - Desktop. It is highly customizable browser. It was selected by Apple for Safari. Konqueror is highly integrated with the KDE application such as kontact / K-mail or e - mail and Aggregator for RSS feeds. It can run under GNOME or similar desktop environment

Website : www.konqueror.org

Epiphany browser is known for its speed and simplicity. It was developed as off shoot of Galleon. It now uses web kit like safari and chrome. It is provided as default browser for GNOME desktop and also runs on other environment.

Website : www.wiki.gnome.org.

Microsoft Browser : Internet Explorer

Internet Explorer : We just cannot forget this age old browser. Initially when other competition was yet to emerge there were mainly two browsers available e.g. Netscape and Microsoft Navigator. Netscape got further developed and many new browsers emerged and MSN was converted to Internet Explorer

Internet Explorer : It was the most popular browser once upon a time developed by Microsoft. However, use of Internet explorer decreased through the years. However, its version-II had features some useful things and as such its use is increasing. It is faster, has cleaner interface, security is upgraded. It has new tab isolation features. It also has features like one box for both addresses and web search , has download manager. It supports HTML, CSS-3 and SVG. Its newer version was formally released on 17th October 2013. Latest is Explorer - 12 which could be useful for Windows - 9 when it comes.

1.6.4. Cross Platform Browsers

- Mozilla - Sea Monkey, K Meleon
- Omniweb and icab

Mozilla-Sea monkey : Originally it was created as on open source testing ground for

Netscape. Mozilla implemented many of the features that have made its browser Firefox popular. Although development was concentrated on Firefox it continued its development in the form of sea monkey. In addition to Firefox and sea monkey, Mozilla's Gecko engine is the basis for a number of platforms specific browsers such as K-Meleon for windows, sea monkey e.g. all in one internet application suit. It was jointly developed by Netscape and Mozilla. Sea monkey version 2.39 was released in 2015 November.It is available for download at www.seamonkeyproject.org.

K-Meleon version 75.1 2015 : Before Firefox emerged, K - Meleon was launched which was meant for Window's platform. Its strengths are speed and customizability. Website: www.keneteon browser.org

Omniweb: This browser was created for Macintosh computer. It was the first web browser released for Mac OS X. Omniweb focuses on power features. Its version 4.5 is being used for Apple products web cove technology. It uses same engine used by safari with innovations.

Website: www.omningroup.com

i-Cab : It was the first publicly available browser to pass the Acid-2 test. icab3 was the last modern web browser built for Classic Mac OS since 2008. I-Cab 4 and later version use the webkit engine and are OS X - only. i-Cab for mobile is also available. Its free limited edition is available and its full version is available for $ 20 or C 15 for i cab pro. Website www.icab.de

Latest version 9.0 or i-cab mobile was released in 2015. I-cab 5.6.2. is now available.

1.7. KNOWLEDGE & SKILLS REQUIRED IN USING INTERNET

We have read every thing about Internet from introduction to its technical details. We know that www is an internet server system which facilitates browsing different types of websites. It cooperates with hyper text concept and thus different home pages based on their protocol could be browsed through the internet. WWW supports hyper text protocol known by its short string http:/ / www and every website name follows after these words.

With the help of browsers we start on websites which are equipped with graphics, pictures, sound video or animation. Browser presents a very good picture of any website and thus we enjoy browsing them. We have understood that in order to get connectivity to internet we need wired or wireless connections and devices like modem or routers. After having the adequate knowledge about internet we still need to have some knowledge and skill about how to make use of internet effectively. What is that? Now let us know about it in the following paras.

Whenever we wish to visit any web site we need to know its correct address. Before finding ways or means to know web addresses first let us try to know the structure of any website. Let us take an example of any website say website of Times of India as. http://www.timesofindia. indiatimes.com Let as try to analyze this website address as:

http	= It an is internet protocol
www	= It is a world wide web host
timesofindiaindiatimes	= Name of domain server.
.com	= Indicates it is a commercial website

Let us closely see the characteristic of this address. It is also called URL (Universal Resource Locater). What we see http:// www are the common words in any website address. The symbol is specific and mandatory. After this entire website is written in lowercase letters and that too without any space. **.Com** truncation indicates the type of website and .com means it is a private and commercial website. There are other different extensions after (dot) at the end of every website as:

- gov = Government Website
- edu = Educational Website
- net = Network website
- mil = Military Website

About website address one should be clear that it needs exact address of website and any error in writing browser fails to understand it and it will respond as "no website is found with the string entered in search window". Then how to remember the exact address of each and every website or is there any help available to search them. Now let us try one way and do some practical.

Assume that you have started a computer having internet connectivity and also having data connection to use the internet. Your PC would have opted for one of the browsers and on opened screen there is an icon of the browser. Now let us click it and get browser screen on your monitor. Try to observe browser screen carefully and see what things and facilities are seen there. Now assume that you do not remember the correct address of the desired website you wish to enter in search window. Try to see words (buttons) arranged in line above the search window like :

Left side: Back forward stop Refresh Home, Search, Favorites, History etc.

⟵ ⟶ ⊗ [H]

Now let us click the search button. There we would get search helps with words like - go, msn, AltaVista, web help or web crawler. You can choose any one of them and enter key word of the website of which you need to know the address. Once we click you would you get list of links pertaining to your keywords. After going through the list you can very well find out specific web site. It you click the link of that website it is inputted in the search window and after clicking search button you can get your website.

In another way when we know the address of the website, we can enter it in search window. Please note that the correct site address is required to get and open the site. While this is happening in case if browser keeps searching the site you may see moving icon on top left corner and also down on the task bar which also indicates that the browser is getting connected. Once it is done, the task bar would indicate word "done" and you would see website is completely opened.

While looking at the site you would see some words in blue colour. These words are hyper texted words, means when we take cursor there arrow sign gets converted into sign of hand. The meaning of it is that there is a link in that word and if you click on it takes to next page of website. This way one can travel further from page to page. If you click back button (ß-) on your left top corner it brings you back page by page. This way you can come back to your original page. There would also be some button on top in a horizontal line which helps you to visit specific part of that website. This was in nutshell how you can experience web surfing. It is said that web searching or internet searching is an intellectual skill. Skills required are mainly of entering the right word to get right site quickly. Otherwise technical matters are not difficult.

Let us see the list of commonly visited websites.

http://www.timesofIndia.indiatimes.com

http://www.amazon.com

http://www yahoo.com (yahoo.co.in) for India

http:// www.google. com (google.co.in) for India

http://www.economictimes.com

Whenever we go on browsing sites, those site addresses are preserved and if you click drop down sign (V) at the end on search window one can get list of those sites previously visited. Same way you can click history button to see your internet work day by day. You can save any particular site in favorites list by clicking favorite button and by confirming it. The entire site matter you can download/save by clicking file button and further clicking save button. There are various ways to save the pages e.g.html or in text form or as PDF. By giving file name you can save it first in downloads and then in documents.

We have seen various extensions of web site such as .com, .edu, .gov etc. There you would not see country codes of USA. However if any website belongs specifically to country other than USA then there needs to mention country code in the extension part such as:

http://www.bbc.uk

http://www.iitb.ac.in (IIT Bombay)

http:// www.nic in (National Information Centre)

http:// www.gov.in (Govt. of India)

When we refer search facility on any web browser you would get list of search tools and you use one of them to search website URL address and finally get it and browse the site. However, there is a great helping tool which helps us to find out number of links pertaining to any word and that is called search engine. Now let us try to know about search engine in the next para.

1.8. WEB SEARCH ENGINE

Search engine is a software tool which is designed to search for information on World Wide Web. It helps to provide list of links pertaining to words entered in browser search window. The information could be mixed of links, images or related files or even adds. Search engine always maintain an up to date data or called data mining in their index. Search engines also maintain real time information by running an algorithm on a web crawler.

Before 1993 the World Wide Web was entirely indexed manually. It was a list of web server edited by Tim Berners-Lee which was hosted on CERN. Subsequently NASA announced news under the title "What is new?" There were many such experiments in 1994. Crawler based Search engine known as web crawler came out. It allowed users to search for any word in any web page. It followed with inventing many search engines including Magellan, AltaVista and Yahoo!. In 1998 Google announced the idea of selling search terms. Around 2000 Google search engine became prominent. In the same year yahoo started providing search services. Microsoft first launched MSM Search engine in 1998. It rebranded its search engine with the name Bing launched in June 2009. On July 29, 2009 Yahoo! and Microsoft finalized a deal in which Yahoo! Search would be powered by Microsoft Bing technology. As on today there are 30+ search engines available in the world.

How web Search Engine works : Any web search engine gets its information by web crawling from site to site. The spider checks for the indexing components for each website as title, page content, heading or its metadata in HTML metatags. These components are associated with its domain name and HTML based fields. This index database is made available for public for search queries. A query from user could be a single word or multiples of it. Index or search engine helps to find information relating query as quickly as possible. If the search engine index has the same names or words, it lists down the links. The list of links is arranged depending maximum words found in index. If user enters 4 words then on top there would be a link pertaining to all four words, subsequently link corresponding to 3 words and then for 2 words and so on. All the above is about simple search, which is available as default. In addition most search engines support the use of Boolean operators AND, OR and NOT in order to help users to refine their queries. In this case engine looks words or phrases exactly as entered. Some search engines provides some advanced features called proximity search where distance between keywords is also considered.

Usefulness of a search engine depends on the relevance of the result set given back. We might get millions of web pages. However, most search engines employ methods to rank the result to provide best result first.

Most search engines are commercial ventures supported by advertising agencies to get revenue and thus some of them allow advertisers to have their listing ranked higher in search results for getting money. Those who do not accept money for their search result make money by running search related ads along your right side of the regular search engine result and search engine gets money every time someone clicks on one of these ads.

Now let us know what way search engines are preferred in the work. Following is the list of market share they hold. The Google is the world's most popular engine as seen in the list.

Search Engine	Market share as on Sept. 2015
Google	69.24%
Bing	12.26%
Yahoo!	9.19%
AOL	1.11%
Lycos	0.00%

In addition to the above popular search engines there are other types or customized search engine groups such as.

- Bias search Engine
- Search engines who customise search results and provides filter bubbles as in Islamic search Engines.

1.9. USE OF E-MAIL

E-mail is a very useful facility which has come to us as a gift from Internet technology. Raymond Tomlinson in 1971 invented e-mail at Arpanet technology. E - Mail is invariably used for exchanging messages, files, photos etc. Moreover there are several e-mail sites which e - mail facility provides free of cost such as:

e-mail

Google-Gmail

Yahoo!

Rediffmail

Hotmail etc.

We can find out web addresses of these by searching on Google. One can choose any of such free e-mail site and register. When you open such site it would expect you to enter your ID and sign if you are already register or know the ID and password. If not, then you can click to register. Once you give all the data asked in the form within no time you can get you login ID and password. Once you confirm the things you can start using the e - mail facility for sending messages or to forward files, photos etc as attachment. Most of the e - mail boxes provides the following facilities ,which are mostly common among all mail boxes :

Inbox : List of e-mails received from others. The e - mails which are still to be read are shown as highlighted other read mails are saved in Inbox.

Sent : List of mails sent so far.

Folder : One can make various folders depending on your choice, preference and classification. They are named once and can be used to store the received and sent mails by moving them to respective folders. Once they are moved to the folder they are removed from the Inbox.

Draft : One can create a mail but not sent it then it is stored in a draft folder till it is sent. Once mail is sent then it goes to sent box and removed from the draft.

Compose : This is link available for sending /forwarding mails outside. Once you click compose you get a blank screen to write message along with the following things or actions e.g.

To : To mail ID to whom mail is to be sent.

CC : This facility is for forwarding same mail to someone else by writing e-mail ID

Subject : To write subject of your mail.

Send : After completing all the above things you can finally click "send" to forward the mail.

One can create a signature by writing your name, designation, address and contact number. This is done once by going to settings and saving the same. Then in every mail it appears automatically. You can also do beautification or present it in desired font or add emoticons/emoji signs of different moods to make them live. The mails which are received in your mail box, you can do several things with them e.g.

Delete

Move to folder

Label

Mute

Report as spam

Print Mail

Make as unread

In addition you can do further things like.

Reply : To sender to address, this comes by default

Forward : To other people by writing e-mail IDs

All deleted mails go to bulk or trash folder. They remain there for some time.

On front page there would be a link to come out of mail (Logout). When you open the mail box next you need to enter your ID and password to open the mail box. If you desire, you can nowadays with Google- Gmail you can view your incoming mails sorted by default as :

Primary, Social Networking and Promotional, which helps you use your mails conveniently.

List of e-mail IDs is automatically created as you do your mail work. You can make addition to address book by entering names and mail IDS. The mails received from already listed address with you are mostly categorised as the primary mails else they are categorised as either social networking or a promotional. With one mail box your can create different mail boxes and mail box provides you with facility to Manage Your Accounts.

If you have different key boards in your computer or in smart phones which pertain to different languages then you can write your e - mail message in a desired language and send it.

1.10. OTHER IMPORTANT THING ABOUT INTERNET

The internet we use is the beginning version of internet technology. However, there are different generation of internet technology as it has evolved as it became further advanced. Let us now try to know them.

1. Web Generations : As internet or web technology has been developed it has constantly and consistently improved and progressed. These improvements, up-gradations and progresses could be categorised into different generations as.

Web 1.O, Web 2.O and Web 3.O. Note after decimal point it is not zero but a character "O"

The advances in internet technology in terms of generations were required as:

- Unstructured data of resources and things were not usable for average users
- Exponential growth in internet data traffic and handling of multimedia.
- Need of virtual and mobile internet facility
- To manage online video or 3D and high definition transmission.

Now let us try to understand some more details about the Web Generations

1.10.1. Web 1.0

It was known as dot.com or first generation of web which began with hyperlinks between web pages. They were of personally owned title or of kind of portal. They were mainly static in nature and not having dynamic feature in it such as user generated content with frame sets and labels to positions or with alignment on page. Web pages did contain text / graphics, images and with other multimedia contents/ files hyperlinks were used to navigate between web pages.

However web 1.O lacked in context, interaction, scalability and thus no user data was available.

1.10.2. Web 2.0

It is the second generation of web which focused on the power of community. It allowed information sharing with a social media and inter operability. Contents were generated by user and not by only web master in virtual Community Environment. It was possible to search for information through key board and make data available. However web 2.O generation lacked in personalization, up to mark portability and inter operability. Web 2.O provided tools and utilities like social networking sites blogs, Folksonomies video Sharing (Flicker) Sites, Mashups, Web applications, Instant Messaging and hosted services and wikis

1.10.3. Web 3.O / Semantic web

This web generation was more logical which used natural languages so that software agents could read and use them to share and integrate. It is a collection of data resources which are interconnected and can talk in the same Language. Now with 3.O generation it was more simplified with semantic web; it makes search engine much smarter and moreover search engine to understand who are you and what you have been doing and where you would like to go next. In other words machines taking part in web are smart enough to understand what is what and about relation among the words. (Like Ram, Dashrath or Sita.)

It is like asking for personal assistance through agents which would find a shop within 100 miles, which are open 24X7 and if any contact details are available then it would facilitates to add them in my address book automatically. We can see the features of these web generations in a tabulated from as (Table 1.1):

Web 1.O	**Web 2.O**	**Web 3.O**
Read only contents and static HTML Web site	User generated contents and read write web	
Push Technology	Share Technology	Live Technology
Pushed web text graphics based flash	Two way web, Blogs wikis, Socials Networks, Sharing, podcasting video, Personal, Publishing 2D portal	The real time co creative web Croming, 3D Portals MUVES avatar, Representation, Interoperable Profiles, Integrated games educated and business all media in and out of virtual words
No security Required	Security Necessary	Security Required
No user communication	Yes user Communication is Present	User Communication is Present

Table 1.1

Future of Internet Technology : Future technologies of internet beyond Web 3.O have also been imagined as:

Web 4.O- would be a Mobile Web. Tim Berners-Lee gave an inspired TED talk in 2009 on this new open linked web. He views that although web 4.0/web 5.O is still in developing mode and true shape is still forming.The first signals are in that web 4.O/web5.O will be about a linked web which communicate with us like how we communicate with each other (like personal assistant). Web 4.O/web 5.O is called "symbolic" web .This will be very powerful and fully executing.Whereas web 5.O will be about (emotional) interactions between humans and computers. The interactions will become daily habits for a lot of people based on neuro-technology. For the moment web is emotionally neutral means web does not perceive the user's feelings and emotions. It will be changed with web 5.O as emotional web. One example of this is www.wefeelfine.org which maps emotions of people .with head phones on, users will interact with contents that interact with their emotions or changes in facial recognition.

1.11. TYPES OF INTERNET TECHNOLOGIES (INTERNET, INTRANET AND EXTRANET)

If we look at terms Internet, Intranet & Extranet apparently they look the same and one may get confused while using them in the absence of knowledge about them. In information technology point of view they are distinctly different and we should know about them as they are pertaining to use of internet technology. With this need in mind let us try to know about them one by one.

1.11.1. Internet

Through the present chapter we have gained fare knowledge about internet. If we try to revise the same we find that internet means a collection of web pages. The main protocol behind it is TCP / IP on which it works. Web pages are written in HTML or java like web languages and are uploaded on internet. It uses hypertext technology (in short http://) We normally consider web pages under domain world wide web and www makes it possible to browse most of the web pages whose address invariably begins with www with the support of web browsers like fire fox. We surf the web pages on internet. We use search engines in order to find web pages from the internet pertaining to search terms. In other words we look for the server which has information you are interested in. Actually we try to know the IP address of the server as each computer on the net is identified by its IP. Generally IP address looks like http://209.37.27.100 where mostly numerals are used, only for us it is presented in words by the browser. If browser is able to find IP of web page and if it is able to trace the web page we can see the site else it would say site is not accessible or "Site is not found." Normally websites which are freely available for browsing are categorised or available as the Public Domain Sites. Such sites in public domain are easily accessible. So the internet and the collection of public domain sites which we access freely is entirely called the internet. Internet is an infrastructure base or tool and internet is further used as platform to access commercial sites mostly through subscription except open access resources. Now let us try to know about similar sounding term "Intranet"

1.11.2. Intranet

Intranet is a local form of Internet. It is established in an institution which is limited to its campus. It is a network through cable running from building to building and accessible anywhere on the site. Here the technology is the same as internet. It is collection of web pages, only difference is that WebPages making intranet network are not uploaded on the internet and as such it is not accessible for the outside world. They possess the typical address where www domain letters are missing in address e.g. http://etd.iitb.ac.in. It is address of electronic theses and dissertations (ETD) based digital library of IIT Mumbai, which is accessible only to the students and faculty of IIT Mumbai. Intranet network is kept secured from the outside world through the use of Firewall security technology. Internet search engines also do not analyse or index intranet sites and hence they are reachable or searchable on internet. Library OPAC and other contents can be browsed on such network by campus users. Now on the contrast let us try to know about Extranet.

1.11.3. Extranet

Extranet could be called as extension of intranet. Intranet sites are accessible on local network only. Due to use of firewall control no one can access the intranet from outside. However, an intranet user could be given a facility to access intranet from outside world. This facility means the Extranet. The facility is about giving access to Intranet users from outside of the intranet by giving them special authentication (log in ID and password) which makes the user to allow breaking the firewall security with a special permission. This is also applicable to use LDAP login to access local e - mail server from outside the campus by allowing with special access privilege.

1.12. PULL AND PUSH TECHNOLOGIES

As Internet use is being popularised in the society, newer and newer Internet based products are being developed and marketed. Pull and push are such internet based products which are becoming popular. We are already familiar with pull type product. It is nothing but searching information from web servers through search engines or some other information we register and obtain. Push product is comparatively different. We always come across messages and information attached with the message. Such delivery of messages keeps coming in your mailbox unless you unsubscribe and stop them. The reason for this is while registering in mail box form you unknowingly (*) tick marks some of services or products pertaining to your interest. Secondly you also give your acceptance that you have no objective if mail box shares this information to the third party ad agencies. Considering your registered interest corporate companies keep on sending information to your mail box and you do not have any control on them, whereas in pull category you have full control on it. In commercial point of view push kind of internet products help companies to earn money. Pull kind of technology is very simple but push category of technology is specially developed to fulfill commercial interests. Now let us know about the technology behind push kind of products.

Push Technology : Push technology is comparatively a new technology. Push technology facilitates posting of information into users desktop constantly. It could be of graphics, audio or video hyperlinks or scrolling type of data. This is done mostly through FTP rather than through e-mail because of limitation of e-mail communication. While broadcasting information to user's computers is only commercial point of view which includes advertisements or product information. This system is called pulling with getting any conformation or consent from the users. So it keeps on delivering. However such service requires pre registration. Many a time unknowingly users tick marks the interest which results in delivery of such information.

Let us now understand types of information services given under pull and push mode of internet technology.

Examples of "pull" Technology

- In online book shop to select books and add into cart.
- Browsing websites of e - journals or news papers
- Choosing audio or video clips on online music sites and listen or download

Examples of Push type of information delivery

- Delivering updated editions of e - books to subscribers to his desktop.
- Keep on delivering issues of subscribed journals to subscriber's computer
- Posting information to desk top of user about health, sports, travel and educational programs keeping commercial purpose in mind.
- Receiving selected programs from cable TV or radio network online to users end computer
- Alerts or flash messages about warning from government to people keeping security and safety in mind.

We may conclude that in pull type, internet services are within control of users and they have full right to select the service, where as in case of push type service right to send/ post information to users is fully in the hands of companies, once user directly or indirectly consents the mode. It is expected that considering this situations commercial companies come out with newer and newer internet product to achieve their commercial purpose unless users are alert and careful while responding to such product adds on internet. Now let us try to know pull and push concept diagrammatically (Diagram Nos. 1.1 and 1.2).

Pull concept

Webpage	For each request search	
News	⟶	Web
Movies	⟵	User
Date	one web page is available	

Diagram 1.1

Push Concept

Channels		
Magazine	Data provides ⟶	Continuous posting to User
Advertisements	control postings ⟶	
Data		

Diagram 1.2

1.13. PORTAL, VORTAL AND SUBJECT GATEWAY

As a result of speedy progress of internet, pouring of information on this platform is tremendously increased. We try to get scholarly information but as the information much proliferated it is found difficult to get such information in the flood of information of scholarly nature. We need specific kind of information with high information value in it. We also need picking and selecting tool to collect information. We need the information presented in a desired manner suitable to users. We also need a special kind of searching tools to search information from collected sources. We also need sufficient customization in user's point of view and with main source having several links relating to various angles of the main subject area. Considering all these innovative qualities in one web tool efforts were taken to redesign special kind of web tool to get quality, scholarly and highly valued information by using advanced internet tools. The result of this endeavor is portal, vortal and subject gateway. Now let us try to understand them in detail in the following paras.

Portal, Vortal and Subject Gateway : Many researchers need quality and scholarly information, they expect selected personalized and value added information. On this back ground the new tools Portal, Vortal and subject gate way have emerged.

A web portal is generally one specialized designed website which brings information together from diverse sources in an uniform way. As compared to normal website portal bears special characteristics in presenting information. It consists of integration of different services, systems and application. For users it is the most customised form which provides space for personal use. Its information services are highly valuable and are in value added form. Portal provides connectivity to other useful web sources so it becomes easy for subject expert to use. In portal by using web technology specialized information is provided. Portal facilitates searching information in different forms and from various digital sources by using special and advanced search engine or an interface which provides additional external links relating to the subject. Portal is not just an information tool depending on the web technology but it provides information in various angles as well as in integrated forms; moreover it is an ideal set up to get rich information with added value. The normal web sides could be termed as horizontal or standard portals and they are meant for common people where as portal is meant for highly specialized people.

Vortal : Vertical form of portal is called vortal. Scope of vortal is not useful for general public but for specialized group which is related to specific industry. It contains integration of related information sources which are most customised and to personalized nature. As compared to normal portal, vortal contain highly valued information, where emphasis is on specific or to the point information and with at most security.

Subject Gateway : Another qualitative level of portal is called subject gateway. Australian Subject Gateway describe it as an internet based innovative program by which it aggregates selected information of specific field from various high level resources added with various related links.

In Subject Gateway there are two parts of portal where the first part gives information structure along with titles of information sources called front end where as in other part e.g. back end provides available links to the related subjects. In another words subject gate way is a way of presenting various information sources in a specific area along with their location and availability with the help of internet technology. It provides a collection interface relating with many related information resources. It is a special kind of portal where information sources relating to specific field are searched keeping subject structure of front end of subject gateway in mind. Information sources relating to subject area are not taken as they are from internet but the information is repacked in a desired manner. Sources are selected by applying quality parameters so that the finally selected sources would be on specific minute subject containing highly specialized information added with value. Subject gateway contents are continuously refined and made up to date by adding new resources and by deleting old and obsolete ones.

While designing portals, emphasis is given on its contents rather than community. It facilitates with specialized and innovative search systems. Advanced technology is used in presenting information. For users it is found to be highly customised. It contains information of high level and they are designed to satisfy specific and special group of people.

Portal try to handle information in different than normal way, such as in old system, information flows from publisher to library patron where as in portal it is from Publishers

⟶ Aggregator ⟶ Patron

⟵ Patron ⟵ Publishers

There is one example for subject gateway

J-Gate is a product of Informatics Ltd. Bangalore, which tries to aggregate information from content pages published in various scholarly journals and present it in subject wise manner.

Type of Portals : Considering specialized subjects purpose, scope and specialized user group there are various types of portals as

Horizontal portal

Commercial portal

Government portal

Library of publishing portals

Portals are designed with specific purpose in mind where emphasis is given on customizability, efficient and effective search, controlled share-ability, privacy and security.

1.14. USE OF INTERNET IN LIBRARY MANAGEMENT

Impact of Internet on our daily life is clearly evident today. Our professional activities and even our daily life activities like in doing railway and air reservations, payment of our electricity, telephone or even tax bills use of internet have made it easy and transparent than before. In educational activities too computer literacy, e-learning and internet skills have become essential. We may not use it in our family life except in social networking we make maximum use of internet in our daily life and its use is increasing day by day. Searching information on Internet may be superficially and easy but in reality searching important and valuable information is a really skillful task. In library and information curricula incorporating subject of internet has become significant. Especially in obtaining useful information, handling obtained information and providing it pin pointed to users one needs to be up-to-date in use of information technology or the internet. The main reason is that information technology field is developing and progressing constantly and consistently. Newer and newer information resources are emerging. Exploring each and every resource and finding information has become challenging task today. Nowadays in library computerisation is being adopted on a large scale to carry out day to day housekeeping functions. In modern times and in information technology age it is rightly done otherwise libraries world remain behind in time race. Not only in housekeeping activities but today by using computer and internet, libraries are doing wonderful job of providing advanced and up to date information services to their users and they would continue to do so. Public, academic, school or research/ special libraries world not be exception to this trend. Now we are going to review how libraries are making use of internet in providing information services in addition to carry out their basic functions.

As far as effective use of internet technology in library management is concerned at the first instance we look for the intelligently developed and presented library web page, then the OPAC and the next is development of digital libraries. Initially search services are made available within the institute's intranet but gradually they would be naturally made available on internet. One should note that making internet facility available to readers is not the prime objective of the library else library may turn into a cyber cafe. Many Libraries still do this but it should be avoided as it would divert the main purpose of the library. It is necessary however that library professionals should get internet facility in serving their readers in a better way. It depends how the professionals are making use of this facility. It could be searching a topic of research then it is okay but if they are using internet for browsing news sites or viewing live cricket matches or listening to music or using it for e-mail work or for chatting then it would be an unproductive use of the internet. All these things are concerned with entertainment and it is not a library professional activity, moreover it would be a misuse of internet. One can make use of internet in more effective way. With this point of view in mind let us try to understand how it is done in real sense. In library management internet finds use in acquisition, in technical processing, in serials control, in circulation so also in providing reference service and providing information services in many ways to library users. Now let us see it one by one.

1.14.1. Use of internet in Acquisition

In acquisition part of library, things are planed in such a way that one can find about new publication to and new arrivals from publishers or find availability books or to know their distributors and finally buy books required by the readers. Especially about books published in foreign countries we need to know things like their bibliographical details. In acquisition section one needs to consult tools like Books in Print while buying new books. In the above cases library can use internet very effectively. How it could be used let us see as :

- Nowadays all the bibliographic tools are available online. It is always economical to subscribe them online rather than buying them physically and storing on shelves.
- We can find publishers; their addresses, contact details and agents very quickly on Internet.
- One can find out availability of books with the publishers or in local market (If one knows the publishers) with their editions, binding(hard and soft copies) and their prices.
- Now a days we find nearly 30 - 40 online book shops available on internet and librarians could buy needed books by ordering online with them. One can make payments online through internet banking or through credit cards As such the entire process of purchasing books is done in a few minute and in paperless way. Even individual readers can also by book online if library makes this facility available to them on their websites.
- Readers can read reviews of books to be purchased. They can go through content pages and see images of books to be bought through use of Internet.
- Library can find out information about non book materials like printed or non print materials, about availability of patents and standards and they can buy them online.
- One can know availability of government publication and resources through Internet.
- LMS are yet to explore incorporating model of buying book electronically or online from the local market through e - purchasing. By using Internet libraries can very well introduce e - bidding system to purchase books, which is the most transparent system to purchase books without wasting time in buying them through manual quotation system.

List of website useful for acquisition

- www. amazon.com
- www.harnesandnoble.com
- www.bookfinder.com
- ww.bookganga.com

Websites of publishers and distributors

- BIP - www.bowker. com
- BNB - www.bl.uk
- IBIP - www.booksinprint.com
- ISBN Directory - www.degruyter.com
- Intl. Books In print-www.isbn-international.org

Subject guide to books in print

- www.amazon.com

Out of print book in print

- www.abcbooks.com

1.14.2. Use of Internet in Technical Processing

Normally Library Technical processing section involves the following task .e.g.

- Classification (DDC, UDC or LC)
- Subject heading (LCSH,SHE etc.)
- Cataloguing

Classification & cataloguing work is done considering local needs and consistency. These functions always require guidelines. It is therefore better if one uses internet in these activities so that the tasks become easier and it can also helps to maintaining consistency. For example one can make use of online or electronic classification system and subject heading sites. Especially when library takes up retrospective data revision or conversion, it is possible to download catalogue entries using Z39.50 type of catalogues e.g. catalogue of Library of Congress. With such facility one can build library database. Let us use some useful websites useful in the above task.

- Library of congress catalogue
  www. catalog.loc.org.
- worldCat : www.connexion.oclc.org
- National Library of medicine
  www.locatorplus.gov
- Dewey Decimal Classification(DDC) www.oclc.org
- Library of congress subject Headings(LCSH)
  www.id.loc.gov

- UDC Online -www.udc-hub.com
- Library of congress online catalogue Z39.50
  www.loc.gov.z39.50
- Online colon classification
  www.iskoi.org.

1.14.3. Internet in Library Circulation

In library circulation activity, internet finds use especially in inter library lending. One can also find availability of books in other libraries by using union catalogues on internet. Searching material on WorldCat gives us an idea about availability of needed book in nearby libraries. Library can explore availability of books through e-mails. Also library can provide facilities to users like renewal of memberships, online reissue of books. Library can also communicate with readers to remind them about overdue materials with them and for informing availability of needed books or about activation of reserved books. Library can also facilitate users to download various forms relating to circulation activity. Library can even facilitate issue of e -books online to readers. In order to enable library users to access online resources on reader's laptop on tabs by creating wifi zone in the library, whereby people can search the library catalogue (OPAC) and can use facility to reserve books online anywhere on campus. Accessing digital library online is very useful facility for the readers.

1.14.4. Use of Internet is Serials Control

Serials control section of library always needs tools to find out information about serials or periodicals published worldwide including bibliographic data about serials and journals e.g. about their publisher's addresses, ISSN numbers, types of serials, subscription details, distribution of journals and about frequency of journal issues. Instead of using printed tools like ULRICH now it has become easy and convenient if online form is available. Nowadays most of journals are published online along with their printed editions. To subscribe e-journals and to provide their access to users in library or on campus is one of the widely adopted and important activity of serials control section. As such this is done on internet platform very well. Normally each journal publisher provides content pages of each published issue of journal which is available online free and library very well could plan some information services by availing this publisher's facility. In addition by using RSS Feeds library can arrange providing content pages of journals to be received by users in their mail box by registering online on behalf of readers. Irrespective of whether library subscribes the journals or not, this information could be made available to library users. For arranging exchange of scanned copies content pages of needed journal and articles libraries can effectively make use of e - mail to explore such inter library pan arrangement or electronic document delivery system.

Ulrich - www.ulirichweb.com

Google scholar - www.scholar.google.com

http://chrome.google.com

- Directory of Online open access journals: http://doaj.org.

Normally most of the online internet resources are made available to users through library websites and websites are accessed on internet or intranet. The internet plays a valuable role in library services.

1.14.5. Use of Internet in reference and library information services

Before internet came in use, reference librarian used to give reference service to readers by using printed reference sources. In Internet age, online reference sources are used to provide information services. Even in Selective Dissemination of Information (SDI) which is a personalised service and the reference service based on projects, internet can be effectively used. In this situation consolidated list of reference information sources are newly made available through digital library. Digital library is created within the library and through it sources of information and made available to readers. Libraries these days provide full text and bibliographic commercial resources by providing their links on library website. It was only possible by using internet for the same. Let us have a list of full text bibliographic and bibliographic resources which are made available to users by using Internet technology :

Full Text Resources

- Science Direct
- Emerald Full text
- IEEE (Journals)
- IEE (Journals)
- Nature
- Springer-Verlag
- AMS Journals (American Mathematic Society)
- IOP Electronics Journals (Inst. Of physics)

Bibliographic Sources

Ei-village - Engineering Index

Eivillage- Inspec

Scifinder Scholar

MathsScinet

Chemical Abstract(CA)

In addition in anticipated type of reference and information services about future conference abstracting services, online standards and patents are possible to be rendered by the reference section of the library.

Nowadays Virtual Reference Service is also being provided by reference section to the readers. Under the virtual reference service online software like Question Point (OCLC) is being used in providing reference service (at pre announced time schedule). Readers ask reference queries through chat portal. Reference librarian provides information through available digital resource (or by using Worldcat) and provides information links in reply. With this he can satisfy many readers at one time and satisfies them immediately or in subsequent sessions. The reader in this case need not visit library as they can contact reference librarian from any corner of the institute or on internet through chat link on library web site.

In addition all the above tasks library can also effectively use internet for interlibrary cooperation or tasks relating to participation in the library network (Local Regional, National or International) with the use of Internet. Thus internet has been available for library as a boon to library management.

Useful websites are as :

OCLC = www.oclc.org

British Library = www.bl.uk

DELNET = http://delnet.nic.in

INFLIBNET = http:// www.inflebnet.ac.in

1.14.6. Important Information (Web) Sources for library

1.14.6.1. LISTA and DOAJ

LISTA : Like LISA which is priced and subscribed abstracting sources there is free source available called LISTA Library Information Science Technology Abstract. EBICO Publishing co is providing it on EBSCO Host platform.

DOAJ : Library normally subscribes journals which are supposed to be peer reviewed or scholarly journal which are subscribed by paying huge amounts. This category of journals are listed in impact factor based journal report (Annual) prepared by Thomsonreuters.com (JCR). However, there are several open access quality journal available free of cost. The list and links of such journals (Subject wise) is made available by DOAJ Directory of Open Access Journals. Such journals could be made available to readers online through library website.

1.14.6.2. Library Consortia-INDEST & INFONET

Library Consortia : Now consortium concept is used in library management also. The concept is that where libraries are working in more or less same subject area come together to form the consortium under which they purchase books or subscribe journals (mostly e. journals) collectively. Consortium concept is supported by many publishers. In consortium multiple copies of books are purchased and multiple copies of journals are subscribed together as it benefits the publishers due to business promotion. For library with every multiple buying of a book or each multiple subscription of a journals good discount is given in order to keep interest of libraries alive and at the same time publisher's business would not hamper as there is trend of cutting journal due to cut in library budget. Libraries in turn share the benefit collectively. There are various library consortium available in India. Let us know about them.

Indest : Indest is consortium established to equip elite institute libraries with necessary e - resources. These Institutes are IITs, IIMs and IISc Bangalore which are called INDEST core snstitutions/ library group. Considering their areas of fields MHRD provides e - resources (e – Journals, e - Databases and e - books) to these institutes free of cost means IITs, IIMs need not have to pay from their pockets. List of such resources gives us an idea how exhaustive information support is available to faculty, students and researchers of these institutions.

List of INDEST Resources :

ABI / Inform

ACM Digital library

ASME Journals

Capitaline

Compendex or Inspec

IEL Village

Euromonitor

IEL online (All IEEE and IEE journals)

Indian standards

Mathscinet

Nature

Prequest Science journals

Science Direct

Springer link

Springer-Kluwer

Now in Addition to IITs, IIMs and IISc Bangalore the INDEST consortium services are also made available to AICTE (Engg. Colleges), but they need to pay respective consortium subscription amounts towards the resources they choose to have.

Infonet Consortium : Like Indest there is another consortium called Infonet. Infonet consortium is pertaining to UGC based university libraries. Infonct is developed in phases, at initial phase only selected 50 university libraries were considered. Due to progressive development now nearly more than 200 university libraries have inter linked in Infonet consortium. Under UGC Infonet consortium emphasis is given to get e - journals and e - data bases related with fields like Arts, Humanities, Social Sciences, Computer Science, Mathematics and Statistics. The online information resources to be received by university libraries under infonet consortium include names as:

- American chemical Society
- American institute of physics
- American chemical society

- Annual Reviews sciences
- Blackwell Publishing group
- Cambridge University press
- Elsevier science
- Emerald
- Mathscinet
- J-Store etc.

2
Internet Security

2.0. INTRODUCTION

In information availability point of view, internet is known to be an excellent and useful source. Secondly, as a platform or base for external information sources internet is an advanced information technological tool. Right from ARPANET i.e. from its take off stage till today the internet has been constantly and rapidly evolving. Newer and advanced features and facilities are consistently added in its fold. It has become advanced than before. Today's internet technology is more advanced and newer form than yesterday's. The evolving stages of internet are clearly visible in its generations like Web 1.0, Web 2.0, and Web 3.0. In order to make internet more advanced, scientists are constantly doing research and taking lot of efforts on it.

Use of internet has tremendously increased. In day to day life also it is becoming not only important but an essential tool. Right from entertainment to carrying out major and complex financial transactions, internet is being preferred by the people at large. In all most all the professional field internet finds its applications. Similarly in library and information field also it is effectively used in handling and providing information to the readers. Internet it also used to access e-resource as a platform. We see a lot of enthusiasm and passion to make use of internet. Every professional is eagerly and honestly trying hard to earn internet using skills at the earliest to catch a pace of its development.

We use internet for fruitful or constructive purpose. However, there is also the other side of it i.e. some people try to use internet for destructive purpose only. As we see makers or developers of internet there are also some people who work to destroy it or make nuisance or creates threats in use of internet. As such internet technology is not at all any more safe today. On one side although we see good progress in internet technology, while on other side we see more and more threats to disrupt its use. It has, therefore, become essential to make note of these threats and take security measures to maintain its security and integrity. In order to make libraries and library professionals aware of these facts, as users of internet in a large scale to access the information, this chapter on "Internet Security" has been added in the book. We enthusiastically use internet for personal use or for business purpose, and it is a fact that while doing so insecurity of internet may put our transaction into a great risk. The question then comes in mind, whether there is any solution to this or are there no solutions to this, the answer to this is certainly affirmative and relieving us from these dangers and worries. There are software tools like Firewall, Anonymisers or Encriptors and Remailers to secure work on the internet safe. We are going to know about all such tools available to make use of internet risk free and safe. However, before that we are going to understand the state of internet confidentiality and then we would discuss the internet security issues.

2.1. CONFIDENTIALITY OF INTERNET

Significance of Firewall : In internet usage, constituent parts are :

1. User's client machine for searching information.
2. Web resource server which provides information to user.
3. Internet technology &
4. Communication Media

While searching information on internet packets of uploaded queries from client machine and downloaded information from server travel back and forth through telecommunication medium. At any moment these packets come in contact either with internet destroyers, with internet virus or with defective computers which could be vulnerable for security threats.

Internet creators never thought that there would be any security threat to the internet technology. However, everyone is scared about internet security today , about security of individual's identity on web or about security to our business or financial (confidential) transactions. In the absence of any security protection, internet destroyers or so called hackers are present all over on the internet network map observing our internet use and eagerly looking for an opportunity to attack and damage the systems. It happens so quickly and silently that one does not even know when they own the control on your computers and internet work. It happens due to continuous flow of communication signals of systems which are not capable to notice or detect the threats coming across in their communication way. However, even if there is a serious threat there are ways and means to tackle the damage, to find out such dangerous scripts / programs and destroy them to make systems safe. The technology tool to take care of security threat is known as Fire wall.

2.1.1. Significance of Fire wall

Fire wall is a software which keeps a close watch on the internet communications and identify if there are any dangerous scripts in the flow of communication and if found, works to stop them. So they are stopped from coming into your computers.

Nowadays most of the operating systems come with free installed fire wall format. However, in case of windows the situation is different and worrisome, as it does not have the system to stop dangerous entities or virus coming through communication flow. Moreover, windows platform is the most vulnerable to disclose your computer identity or your confidential data to the outside internet world, which is quite dangerous. In order to prevent this and protect your system from virus if becomes essentially to adopt additional firewall system. It is therefore, always necessary to keep your IP address and your personal login ID and passwords secured.

2.2. RISK OF COMPUTER IP ADDRESS

Your computer is always under threat due to its IP address in the internet world. Whenever we surf on internet or we try to search information it is known to the outside world. However ,we do not understand this. Not only everything is seen to the outside world what we do on internet but details like your computer's IP address and its related details like name of your system or your location on internet is also known to the world. Search engines not only remember your search key words but also knows IP address of your computer. Another factor comes in picture while we do our internet search known as cookies. Cookies are floated by advertising companies which convey your search details to them. Cookies keep on adding your search details in the profiles stored on our computer files. Cookies websites being strangers are unknown to us and we do not know how to handle them. Their existence is seen in pop up screens suddenly coming on your monitors. Even if we close the internet or computer they do not disappear. Whenever, we restart computer and internet next time they again appear and keep showing popup screens to attract you, as they know IPs of your computer. This puts security of your computer into danger. In such situations it becomes necessary to stop messages and clips coming in through cookies. In order to achieve this we must maintain confidentiality about IP address of our computer safe and secured by using anonymisers.

In the internet environment computers are easily infected due to virus. Whenever we download information or whenever we exchange information, unless we take proper care, internet virus worms are bound to come along with information packets. Such virus worms come into your system and they stay there. They not only try to destroy files in your computer but they also get spread through mail communication to other computers and try to spread its destruction action further. There are antivirus softwares which can keep your computers away from such dangerous virus. Especially in windows based system it is strongly advised to always have such antivirus protection. When we start using internet it is better if we have antivirus packages, try to scan your PC time to time for any virus threat and update these antivirus softwares so that it can protect your computer from newly emerging virus worms.

2.3. DANGERS AND RISK IN USING YOUR E-MAILS

We all agree that e-mail is a gift to human kind by the internet technology. We use e-mail facility to exchange messages; greetings as well as we exchange documents, photos and music files as attachments through our emails. E-mail IDs facilitates us to participate in user groups, forums, mailing list and also participate in group chatting. We get e-mail facility by registering ourselves with one of our favorite mail boxes. While registering we accept their terms and conditions also. In a way we authorise them about contents of our messages or our confidentiality. Once we register with mail box we unknowingly disclose our personal details about your work or business and naturally our mail IDs made available for storing in public data storage. E-mail authorities are also free to distribute your details to marketing or promoting agencies on which we do not have any control and it remains open to outside world for years together. As a result we keep receiving promotional or spam kind of mails. After knowing this situation every one may like to protect our personal details from making it public. There are means to do it and it is the use of Remailers.

2.4. RISK INVOLVED IN DOING (ONLINE) CONFIDENTIAL TRANSACTIONS ON INTERNET

While using internet we face another dangerous situations especially when we make confidential correspondence through internet, or we purchase things online or make online payments or we use internet banking facilities to transfer our funds or we trade shares online; we invest money online, or even we search online resources. In all the above modes of working on internet we are bound to record our personal details, and we also record our bank mandates or credit card details. While doing the same we need to disclose our login password, client IDs and transaction IDs. There are fare chances unless, concern institutions impose security protection that all these details could be known to public or they could be liable for retrieval by miscreants and there are chances that these details could be misused by them. There is also a threat that you might face considerable loss due to misuse of your confidential details by destructive elements or by fraud people or agencies.

It is therefore, always advisable for those who use internet frequently or otherwise to take utmost care while disclosing your confidential data on the internet site. It is also necessary to make sure that whether the websites on which you are going to use for any financial transactions follow internet privacy policy or not and if one is not sure about it then it is always better to keep yourself away from such unsecured portals, who knows those sites themselves try to encourage misuse of your details by thefts and hackers.

In addition to risk factors, in using internet there are other technological issues also. The type of communication technology used in internet network is also important. Normal coaxial copper wired are prone to risk where as in optical fiber network it is difficult to break the security. However, there is a solution to these problems and that is the encryption.

In summing up the above discussion, we may conclude that today's internet is not safe to use. Whatever equipment we use for internet one should make sure that our user environment would be properly secured for its security then only we can maintain our confidentiality and privacy safe. We should see that the network is encrypted and we use computers which are in anonymised environment, so that no one from outside world have control on our internet user authentications. Having discussed the various threats in using internet through your PCs or with the help of communication systems, now we are going to discuss the tools and softwares to be used to ensure security and privacy of Internet

2.5. INTERNET ANONYMISERS

Internet anonymizers are such website which helps us to maintain web browsers protected and confidential to outside world of hackers. For protecting our e-mail there are remailers available for us. We understood that anonymizers provide us safe and secured internet connectivity. These systems surf the websites on your behalf and provide the desired information on your browsers. Due to anonymisers your internet work and the details of what information you have searched are kept confidential and nobody from outside can find or search it.

For internet security the first internet anonymiser was available as "Anonymises.com" in

1957 developed by Lance Cottrell. Cottrell was a renowned privacy advocate. Cottrell also had developed very useful remailer called "Mix Master" to protect e-mail communication. In order to have safe and secured information communication on war field, Cottrell had taken lot of efforts while he was working on Kosovo Privacy Project of Defense Dept.

There are other anonymisers which are useful to protect internet and e-mail work as:

Anonymize.net

Anonymous.org

Mute-mail.com

obome.deultimat_anonymity.com

proxify.com

surfol.com

These are useful websites relating to anonymisers

Google proxy services

yahoo web software privacy

stayinvisible.com

Easy Proxy - by OCLC

Other anonymiser resources are as:

alt.privacy.anon-server

(The anonymisers protect user's privacy on the web)

2.5.1. How Anonymisers work

Once your internet PC is connected to anonymiser site, it searches the website and the information you are looking for and at the same time it does not allow to disclose your computer IP and details and it keeps away your computer identity from the hackers. We have seen while normal internet work through the search engines, outside agencies or hacking elements or cookies can easily find out your computer IP and other details. With the use of anonymiser like IP-infonet work, tool.com, 404 research or lab super length the process of knowing your IP stops.

There are two types of anonymisers

1. Networked anonymisers
2. Single point anonymisers

2.5.1.1. Networked Anonymisers

Normally when you work in the intranet environment then before you reach to an expected website you are channelised through a series of computer net like:

Computer A – Computer B – Computer C and internet website

The information searched also travels back through same channel and in the reverse direction same way like website → Comp. C Comp. B → Comp. A and your computer which happens due to intranet proxy. While using anonymisers for securing signal to reach your computers from outside is made difficult. For this more than one connecting modes are used. Secondly, between the communication of query uploaded by you and signals received from web site, purposely a communication break for a few milliseconds is created. This makes difficult to know what you have searched from outside. So also an artificial imbalance is created between the search query and its related details. The security is also achieved by anonymisers by searching different websites simultaneously. These creates confusion for the hackers or other miscreants to pose danger to privacy of your computer or your work, which results keeping your internet work safe and risk free. The possibility of use of anonymisers and their services is more in case of large organisations where such internet security is very much essential. The first networked type of anonymiser was called as "Zero Knowledge System". However, this company was closed and was renamed as EFFSTOR Company which was available for adoption; it made it possible to provide security to multi-server network system design to acquire system confidentiality feature in the systems.

2.5.1.2. *Single Point Anonymiser*

We have seen that with the help of anonymizer your internet web browsing work is protected. In doing so your communication with various web sites and communication we receive from those web servers is kept confidential for outside web world. In networked type anonymizers it provides maximum protection to your work and systems as compared to single point anonymisers, although their protection level is lower than networked type anonymizers, but finally somehow security is achieved, so both these type of anonymisers are useful. In these anonymizers there is a common methodology. The anonymisers analyses the entire website you are searching in the list of links and each and every hyper link is anomymized to make them anonymized links, which helps in protecting our net surfing and also in keeping IP and details of our systems and computer safe. Most of the anonymizers try to anonymise all transfer protocols and internet services. In doing so we need to work in encrypted mode, which is most necessary in creating protective environment.

2.6. REMAILERS

As anonymisers helps us in protecting our internet work and our system similarly re-mailers provide protection to your e-mail communications. With re-mailers, your email messages, communication, sending and receiving is kept safe and confidential. It keeps your e-mail ID confidential from outside hacker world. Not only your messaging is protected but due to encryption method no one can read messages from your mailbox unauthorizely. The first re-mailer had a name Penet.fi. There onwards many re-mailers became available for adoption, but Cypherpunk and Mix Master were well known among them. Cypherpunk is type one category of remailer in which PGP method of Encryption is used. In these types of remailer, security needs to be provided to each and every node. Whereas Mix Master is type - 2 category of remailer in which right from composing till the message is delivered to other site e-mail mail box security is provided in the entire process. Remailers keep your e-mail IDs safe and confidential. Remailers try to break our messages into equal number of packets which makes hackers to feel that all packets are same which makes them to analyse the messages difficult and thus the messages are delivered safely to the destinations. In doing so deliberately the imbalance is created in message communication by using method of store wait and send.

The various types of available Remailer websites are listed as :

- Google - Anonymous Mailers
- Anonymous Remailers - FAR
- Remailer statistics
- Mix Master -Remailer statistics
- Yahoo - Anonymous mailers
- Anonymous Remailer Information
- Frog Admin - Remailer Statistics
- Type II(Mixmaster) Remailer list

2.7. ENCRYPTION

In order to keep the privacy of security of communication between two systems or individuals encryption mode is used. These days advanced encryption methods like - Public Key Cryptography or PKC is one of such cryptographic systems. In this type, the individual can meet high level transaction without meeting but through mathematical coding. This coding helps achieving trueness of transactions. Now a days many banks use PKC type descriptors while providing very secured internet banking facilities to their customers. Customers can do financial transaction for buying things for transferring funds from their bank accounts with the protective cover of PKC. In this method the customer is advised to download particular software which bank uses to maintain the security in transactions. Customer through his / her computer is connected to his bank accounts where in the software first recognises the IP details of his computer then issues web pin to be entered (for that particular computer) in the input through SMS on his/her register mobile. Once the transaction is complete he/she is advised to close the screen which helps in avoiding any possibility of misusing the facility. Not only this, the customer is sent a message that you had done an online transaction on the date and time and get confirmation that whether he / she actually used the internet banking, if not then he/she is advised to contact the bank, so that any fraud case could be quickly found out.

Under encryption there is a software called Pretty Good Privacy (PGP) which is also used for online internet transactions. Use of Digital Signatures is also used as an alternative to encryption methods.

2.8. INTERNET HACKERS AND CRACKERS

We know that hackers and crackers always exist on internet either individuals or in a group. Hackers basically are supposed to be very intelligent programmers, who are expert in finding bugs in any program quickly. However, nowadays we see them as bad or spoiled faces. Today hackers are known for their destructive activities like hacking the websites and stopping its functioning, or cracking security of a high level system, cracking login and passwords and misusing them for extracting money from bank accounts. They are also known for devising and spreading virus programs which destroy the systems and hard disks. They are also called crackers. Original hackers were honest and useful for mankind. Richard Stallman, John Dropper and M C Anne are the names of well known true and honest hackers for their good constructive work.

2.9. COOKIES

We have already understood a bit about the cookies. We always notice them again and again while surfing the internet in the form of popup screens, which attract your attention towards them in such a way that you would be tempted to click it and forget your original work and reach some unexpected destination. Cookies is an important part of ad business. They look for people search information which has some similarity with products of advertising companies. Cookies are smart programmes which are allowed to be operative by the search engines. They try to collect your search details along with your computer IP and other details and store them in the backup. Such data is then shared with advertising companies. They do not disappear even when you logout or switch off your PC. Whenever you come again on net the websites cookies recognise your existence on web and again start streaming pop up screens in your webwork. Unless you disable they would come again and again on your screen. Sometimes they create nuisance for net surfer and may trap you in an embarrassing situation or even put you in loss by making you panic. Cookies are more vulnerable in windows environment as cookies are stored in MS explorer in cookies folder. Through documents and settings path they are stored in folders. In Firefox Mozilla browsers also they are stored in cookies folders. Although we apparently find that cookies are helping you in searching the information and in optimising your information search. However, it sometimes creates threats to your security on web. Many cookies distribute or share the information to other websites without your knowledge. Your details like personal identity, your IP address and your activities on web are shared to people or sites unknown to you. It is dangerous to allow your browser to store the cookies on unknown websites without your knowledge. Many web security systems always advise customers to disable cookies while doing your confidential work in security point of view.

Ref : Internet Security http://www.livinginternet.com/i/is.html (Accessed on 19th June 2016.)

3
Development of Digital Library

3.0. INTRODUCTION

Post Second World War and after invention (1452) of Gutenberg's Movable Printing press, flow of printed literature increased exponentially. Subsequently this followed with inventions of newer and rugged alternative media as information carriers. They include inventions of micrographics, magnetic, cinematography and digital or optical media. Looking into the speed of the development it has facilitated availability of newer and more sustainable formats of knowledge communicators as compared to paper. It was felt that perhaps the future libraries would be "Paperless" as predicted by Lancaster in 1970. However, it did not come true but libraries were greatly influenced especially by digital media and started acquiring digital collection along with printed ones, which gave them a new name as hybrid or multimedia libraries. Thus traditional library collection got a new component in its fold. Electronic library, Virtual Library or e - Library terms were synonymously used to describe the new component of modern library.

Normally Electronic Library or e - Library or even virtual library are the advanced versions of traditional library which came into reality by consolidation of all the e - resources and putting them into use through a single interface for the readers. The great advantage was to have facility to use the e - resources even without actually coming to library through internet or extranet. Yes! this greatly facilitated users to get these resources at their convenient point of time and place. All these developments led to emergence of another new concept called Digital Library. Library in the present status seems to be more associated with hybrid library. It comprises of tradition library collection, an electronic library comprising of mostly available commercial and non commercial web based digital resources along with digital library containing digital collection developed locally by the library. Development of digital library or so called institute repository has its importance and significance in library innovations. Moreover, development and advancement of digital library technology facilitated to have such integration with a definite framework which has led to emergence of the modern digital library systems to manage and provide mechanism to access the digital contents gathered at library with addition of this new feature as a part of ICT development. Digital library is now seen existing in mostly every modern library. Digital library development has been seen since last one and half decade. It has not only influenced each and every librarian but it has also become essential for the library professionals to take a note of digital library and try to acquire certain degree of expertise in developing digital libraries. Having this need in mind the author felt it is necessary to devote present chapter to narrate digital library development right from the concept to actually establishing the digital library.

3.1. DIGITAL LIBRARY : CONCEPT, DEFINITION AND CHARACTERISTICS

3.1.1. Digital Library: Definition

Digital library(DL) can be described as collection of digital documents or objects. Development of digital library is discussed at length in US literature. Almost every large and a bit advanced type of library would like to have digital library in its portfolio. DL technology have facilitated establishing digital library in order to have bibliographic control on documents in electronic format so also store them in full text form. By definition, characteristics and use makes the digital library distinct from the traditional form of library. Up till now library was emphasising on presenting e-resources collection with the banner of electronic/digital library to its users. Nowadays we handle digital format or digital data in variety of ways where we try to handle information in digital environment. Considering this there are some mis-concepts in understanding digital library fundamentals. We would learn about them while discussing the conceptual background. Now let us try to see some definitions of Digital Library, which will bring some clarity in our understanding about the concept.

Such definitions which would bring clarity in our current understanding the concept of Digital library are – Smith (1) defines it as a – "digital library is organised and focused collection of digital objects" It is much more than just randomly assembled collection of digital objects although it retains several qualities of traditional library. They are more collection focused, more community focused and having quality of long term availability of digital documents.[1]

Following definition given by the Digital Library Federation tells us the essence of the digital library as -

"Digital Libraries are organisation that provides resources including the specialised staff to select structure, offer intellectual access to interpret distribute, preserve the integrity of, and ensure the persistence over time of collections of digital work so that they are readily and economically available for use by a defined community or a set of communities".[2] The definition stresses the fact of digital library meant to provide access to digital work for a long time irrespective of status or form of information technology, as it also captures metadata of digital form of the document. We find the term digital library is used synonymously with electronic library or virtual library. There are elements which are identified as common to various definitions such as:

1. Smith, Abbey : Strategies for building digital collection Washington DC : Digital Library federation council on library and information resources 2001 available on http://www/clir.org Library perception.
2. Digital library federation, Register of digitised books and serial publications (www.digilib.org/collection)

- The digital library is not a single entity
- It requires technology to link the resources of many.
- The linkages between many digital libraries and information services are transparent to the end users
- To provide universal access to digital library is the goal
- Digital library collections are not limited to document surrogates. They extend to digital artifacts that cannot be represented or distributed in printed formats

We understand here that catalogue entry of digital document and the document both are available at the same place in digital library.

William Arm, tries to conceptualise the digital library in an informal definition as: "a digital library is managed collection of information associated with services where the information is stored in digital formats and accessible over a network"[1]

A crucial part of this definition is the management of digital information. A stream of data sent to earth from a satellite is not a digital library. However when same data is organised systematically becomes a digital library collection. Most people would not consider a database containing financial records of one company to be a digital library, but would accept collection of such information from many companies as a part of digital library. Digital libraries contain diverse information for use by many different users. Digital libraries range in size from tiny to huge. They can use any type of computing equipment and any suitable software. The unifying theme is that information is organised on computers and made available over a network with procedures to select the material in the collections to organise it and to make it available to users and to archive it.[2]

IFLA has been promoting the idea and development of digital library across the globe with the goal of bridging the digital divide making the world cultural and scientific heritage accessible to all. IFLA/UNESCO has brought out manifesto of digital libraries. In the manifesto it defines digital library as :

"A digital library is an online collection of digital objects of assured quality that are created or collected and managed according to intellectually accepted principles for collection, development and made accessible in a coherent and in a sustainable manner, supported by services necessary to allow users to retrieve and exploit the resources."

While stressing the need of digital library as a part of library system, IFLA says that: "A digital library forms an integral part of the services of a library applying new technology to provide access to digital collection. Within a digital library the collections are created, managed and made accessible in such a way that they are readily and economically available for use by a defined community or set of communities". About collaboration of digital libraries IFLA says that, "a collaborative digital library allows public and research libraries to form a network of digital information in response to the needs of the information society. The system of all partners in a

---

1. Arms, William Y. Digital Libraries Cambridge, Mass MIT press C 2000 in our library system as
2. Berkeley Digital library SUNSITE

collaborative digital library must be able to interoperate. A digital library complements digital archives and initiatives for the preservation of information resources."

While framing and promoting mission of digital library development IFLA furthermentions that :

"The mission of digital library is to give direct access to information resources, both digital and non digital in a structured and authoritative manner and thus to link information technology, education and culture in a contemporary Library services."[1]

The efforts taken by IFLA in promoting digital library for the world users are really appreciable. However, studying global perspective of digital library is very vast at the moment. The current chapter therefore needs to limit its discussion to development of digital library or an institutional repository. The working definition of digital library used by the CDLM (CDLM = Classical Digital Library Model) is as:

"A digital library is a collection of electronic knowledge resources developed and maintained in order to meet the totality of information needs for a given user population".

While stressing the need and purpose of digital library production Guide of the Kentuckian Digital Library says that: "A digital Library is an organised collection of selected digital resources created to support scholarship research and teaching through the use of appropriate technological standards a digital library is created to facilitate permanent access to and resource discovery of selected digital resources".

While giving his version of definition of digital library, Terence Smith says that,

"Digital library is the controlled collections of information bearing objects (IBOS) that are in digital form those may be organised accessed, evaluated and used by means of heterogeneous and extensive set of distributed services that are supported by digital technology"[2]

3.1.2. Digital Library : A conceptual background

In previous paragraphs we referred some of the definitions of digital library and got a clear idea about it. Now let us try to review the mis-conceptual background of it. First let us see how digital library is vaguely conceptualised for the following things:

- Library Networks
- A file or folder contents
- Scanned copies of pages of a book
- Scientific database
- Online resources like e - journals, e - books and e - databases
- A computer facilitated with internet connectivity

---

1. IFLA/UNESCO Manifesto for Digital Library http://www.ifla.org/files/assets/digital.libraires/documents/ifla/unesco.digital.library.manifesto.pdf (accessed on 18th June, 2016)
2. Smith, Terence R: Metadata information environment of digital libraries D Lib Magazine, July- Aug 1996

- Collection of softwares
- Computarised catalogue of a library
- Library website with links to collection of e - resources
- Collection of clips of digital audio or video
- Digitized movie or a film

However, in true sense none of the above could be termed as digital library. So let us try to know real time concept of digital library. In digital library collection documents are stored but in their digital formats only. Such collection is accessed on internet. The collection of digital documents is organised with the help of digital library software to facilitate search of the digital document in it. The types of software used are as Greenstone, Dspace, e - print and so on. In addition to use of software in digital library there would be related kind of metadata software. The metadata thus stored in them takes care to facilitate use of digital documents for a longer time irrespective to changes which would come in digital formats. In digital library there is an emphasis on content management.

3.1.2.1. Comparison of Digital library with traditional library

At this juncture one would like to compare concept of digital library with that of traditional library. We know concept of our traditional library has been emerged even before 25 centuries. We know the importance of a library. It is recognised as a social institution which stores knowledge in terms of resources, documents and book. Before the invention of printing press it contained various artifacts with carvings and engraving information on them. Subsequently, libraries started getting books, journals and reference books in their collections and it was saturated mostly with printed materials.

As time passed we find that multimedia forms were invented, like microforms, magnetic media and finally optical or digital media. New forms in printed materials also emerged like non book material. All these new media and formats impacted publishing of literature and all of them influenced libraries to acquire literature in various medias and formats.

After printed material era was at its saturated level, libraries started adding materials in non print formats also and as a result we see the today's nature of library becoming a hybrid one. We however still see new literature in printed format but we also see various non book printed materials and not only in printed form but we also see various non book printed literature like e - journals, e - books, e –databases, magnetic journals, videos, DVDs, video journals and CDs etc.. However if we try to compare the hybrid version of traditional library we find that all printed collection is on shelves, all non print collection is also on shelves where as online resources like e – journals, e - books and e - database are on library websites. As such entire collection is consolidated in a library through the catalogue or OPAC.

It we see the constraints of traditional library where we find that it faces a lot of difficulties in handling various formats and types. Readers also face lot of difficulties in reaching these variety of collection and finally there is no way to preserve the multimedia collections for the longer period. As the digital or offline formats get older and become obsolete as time passes and with information technology changes or with IT upgradations.

Online resources are bound with time constrains as well as lot of copy-right restrictions in freely accessing them. In comparison there are definite solutions to all the above constrains in the form of Digital Library.

One good thing we see with today's modern library that they provide computerised catalogues to reader which facilitate easy search of library material through modes like intranet or web mode on the library website. There are online paid resources also available on the library website. In spite of all these library developments, need of digital libraries is strongly felt and we see they are gradually emerging in every such modern library.

The development of digital library is the initiative and creation of library. It is also managed systematically which involves scientific development of digital resources, management of these resources and finally efforts are taken in providing the digital resources to the users in a most easy way. With this backdrop let us compare digital library with that of traditional library.

Comparison of Digital library with Traditional library : If one wishes to compare digital library with that of traditional library then it could be on the following issues :

Traditional library

- The emphasis is on actual and physical collection
- Library catalogue directs readers towards physical object - a book
- While searching the material there could be two possibilities
  - — The physical book is on the shelf or
  - — It is issued out and reader has to wait for it.
- With the help of library people get social or educational benefits.
- Library which may be hybrid type could provide print as well as digital information services.

Digital Library

- In digital library most of the constrains and difficulties in using information carries are removed as :
- In digital library readers find catalogue entry and actual document at the same place along with its metadata. Only one common or supplementing thing we find in traditional and digital library is that the information retrieval tools used in traditional library are also essential tool of digital library; secondly in information retrieval system document and its surrogate are very important entities. Thirdly exact matching has great significance and in digital library importance is always given to exact matching of these two. In traditional library emphasis is on catalogue entries oriented search but in digital library it is metadata oriented search, which is obviously more comprehenssive. (Table No. 3.1)

Comparison of digital library and traditional libraries is further tabulated as follows as presented by Berkley Digital Library Project.[1]

---

1. Trivedi Mayank : Digital Libraries functionality, usability and accessibility.Librarian Philosophy and Practice 27.05.2010

Traditional library	Digital Library
Print or Partially digital collection	All resources are in digital form,
Stable with evolution	Dynamic of ephemeral
Individual objects are not directly linked with each other	Multimedia and fractal object are well linked with each other internally,
Flat structure with minimal contextual metadata,	Scaffolding of data structure and richer
Scholarly contents with validation, process	More than scholarly contents with various validation process,
Limited access points and centralised management	Unlimited access point distributed collection and access control,
Physical and logical organisation correlated	Virtual, physical and logical organization
One way interaction,	Dynamic of real-time dialog,
Free and universal access	Free as well as fee based

Table 3.1. Comparing Digital Library and Traditional Library*

3.1.2.2. Comparison of digital Library with www

- On World Wide Web or on internet information is not scientifically managed where as in digital library it is done scientifically
- Most of search engines provide the search based on keywords available with their indices, where as digital library provides more or less exact information as per search terms used by searcher by considering entire digital document digit by digit

3.1.3. Digital library : Characteristics, Goals and Benefits

3.1.3.1. Digital library Characteristics

Although there is a lot of confusion over the digital library concepts, technology of digital library has emerged with its significance and characteristic. Digital library characteristics could be listed as :

1. Digital library could be seen as digital mirror of traditional library collections like digital/ electronic print and other types like audio, video, graphics, animation etc.
2. Digital library owns and controls actual digital documents with its metadata index and it is not just surrogate of collection.
3. Digital library is an organised and well capable structural set up which takes care of longevity

* Courtesy - Berkley Digital Library Project cited by Trivedi Mayank

and access to digital contents irrespective of future technological up gradation.

4. Digital library is not a standalone entity, it evenly links digital document located outside its periphery through use of internet technology.
5. Digital library provides prompt and efficient access to large number of distributed digital collection having linked and integrated internally.
6. Digital library maintains digital documents and provides access to them over unlimited period due to their metadata inclusion. It accommodates many formats with their availability in multi lingual span.
7. Digital library can compass all the processes and services which are offered by traditional libraries which gives feel and touch of traditional library.

3.1.3.2. Benefits of Digital Library

Digital library signifies its difference with traditional library in many ways and characteristics. It provides many benefits to users as.

1. DL improves access through internet and they can be virtually accessed from anywhere and any time which are tied up with physical location and operating hours like in traditional library.
2. Digital library widens access to meet simultaneous access needs of user to a single document. It is capable to serve larger reader population due to its virtual characteristics
3. Digital library improves information sharing due to inclusion of metadata and information exchange protocol. As such digital libraries can easily share information among each other and helps in enhancing access to users.
4. Finally the most significant benefit of digital library is preservation as digitally converted physical document do not subject to physical deterioration was happening with the paper based media. Digital version can be easily handled, copied or down loaded. Thus Digital Libraries contribute to a great extent for persuasion of special and rare documents and the artifacts available in library collection.

3.1.3.3. Goals of Digital Library

Digital Library meant to work for the following mission and goals as envisaged by IFLA in order to fulfill the digital library mission as depicted in their manifesto :

- Supporting digitization, access and preservation of library's core collection having concern with culture, scientific and historical heritage.
- Providing access for all users to the information resources collected by libraries while respecting their intellectual property right.
- Creating interoperability among different digital library systems to promote open standards and access
- Supporting the pivotal role of libraries and information service in the promotion of common standards and best practices.

- Creating awareness of urgent need to ensure permanent accessibility of digital material.
- Linking digital libraries to high speed research and development network
- Taking advantage of increasing convergence of communication media and institutional roles to create and disseminate digital content[1]

3.2 EVOLUTION OF DIGITAL COLLECTION

If one looks into the real purpose in developing digital library in digital age we see the following important aspects :

- Preservation of rare and deteriorating knowledge treasure in printed form through digitising them.
- Creation of digital resources as per need of users.
- Availability of information in its natural flow.

When we try to go into evolution pattern of digital library we get the same inference in history as below :

11th century manuscript of "Beowulf" an epic poem describing the heroic adventures of Scandinavian Warriors is said to be one of the most precious treasures of the British Library. It was donated to the British Museum in 1700 while it was in almost destroyed state in a fire. It kept on further deteriorating over the next century due to handling by the researchers. However its further degradation was halted in mid of 1800, when it's each page was mounted on protective frame, although it was much damaged by the time. In 1993 The British Library initiated a project named "Electronic Beowulf" project in order to capture, enhance and preserve this cultural artifact in a digital form. These efforts facilitated in capturing the manuscript in the existing form. Moreover it facilitated readers and scholars to access it from anywhere for study and research.

This gives an example how ancient libraries, museums and archives were trying to preserve the rare & valuable collections of concern to cultural history of knowledge and making them available to the next generation through digitization.

Digital image technology is now so advanced which gives opportunities to these social institutions to preserve irreplaceable artifacts.

Another example was about Dead Sea Scrolls written as old as in 2nd century BC as they have been recovered from caves. These parchment scrolls have been recovered fifty years ago. They were also in degraded condition due to exposure to weather. The attempts were done to obscure the text and casing parts of writing in order to transfer to adjacent parts of the scroll. Specialized cameras and fitters of Eastman Kodak which were basically used for space programs were used to capture image of the fragments of scrolls. The process of preservation has helped to view the character in normal light which were not otherwise visible previously. This has facilitated researchers to undertake research to reconstruct new parts of text on the scrolls.

This innovative technique has facilitated students, researchers, information scientists and

---

1. IFLA / UNESCO Manifesto for Digital Libraries

even common public to access many of world's rarest artifacts right at their desk converted to a digital form, including from Gutenberg Bible to paintings of Monalisa. They could be browsed now on internet at any time and from any location in the world. Not only images of printed rare books but audio recordings of historical speeches or exotic bird calls, video clippings from televised TV programs, geospatial data and photos are also being delivered directly to the desk of students and researchers in digitized form.

All these developments have led to emerge an idea of digital library creation in the libraries and to promote research in this field, which has accelerated scholars, research without limiting only to physical access. In 1990s many digital library projects were undertaken in US and UK.

The overall research in development of digital library represents the trend as follows: US National Science Foundation (NSF) and UK's Joint Information Systems Committee (JISC) initially sponsored the research. The project was further expanded in 1999 to an international level which finally led to formation of JISC/ NSF International Digital Library Initiative.

The objectives of this program (which had 3 years tenure) are as follows:

- To consolidate collection of information which was not otherwise accessible or usable because of technical barriers, distance, size and system fragmentation or other limits
- To create new digital library technology and understanding to make it possible for a distributed set of users to find, deliver and exploit such information to evaluate the impact of this new technology and its international benefits. With these initiatives many other groups also become involved in expansion of digital library technologies such as EU -Association Computing Machinery (ACM), The Institute of Electrical and Electronics Engineers (IEEE), the International federation of Library Association (IFLA) The American Library Association (ALA), the coalition of Networked Information (NI) and Digital Library Federation (DLF). These developments have also impacted the development of library automation software resulting LMS vendors to introduce commercial product for developing digital library. These experiments led to introduce the products which aimed to facilitate educational institute to install digital libraries and maintain them easily as per industrial standards available like (2002 – 2007) NSF – JISC. Digital Libraries in the class room projects (1999 – 2001) NSF JISC Digital Library Projects.

This trend is divided into two time phases e.g. 1994 - 1999 at NSF phase - I project where as in 1999 - 2004 was of phase 2 project. The land marks seen in the period from 1990 to 2005 as:

1991 – World Wide Web released

1995 – Commercial internal access providers emerged. At this juncture debate emerged about the concept of digital library, about what really constitutes the digital library. There have been many definitions in support of digital library's concept such as: "from Electronic catalogue which describes physical items in a brick and mortar to an advanced multimedia environments housing all digital collection. H. T. Thomas Hickson from Cornel University felt that it is time to erase line between physical and digital library as a major portion of library system now a days are supported with information technology. The Internet also has shown credible impact on library modernisation.

The libraries are managing large systems and they are very well delivering bibliographic information through use of their system. Bernie Hurley- Director of library technology of U.C. Berkeley puts his comments while comparing digital library with that of traditional library as,- digital libraries are different in that they are designed to support the creation maintenance, management access to and preservation of digital contents. Hurley feels that the research underwent at U.C. Berkley and other large research libraries to be noted as the **first generation of digital library** development and once the specifications are set commercial products could be designed and marketed.

Sun Microsystems defines digital library as- "the electronic extension of functions users typically perform and the resources they access in a traditional library, these information resources can be translated into digital form, stored in multimedia repositories and made available through web based services. It is seen that the emergence of digital library prompted the growth of e-Learning which is seen as the virtual alternative to traditional school attendance. It is believed that as student population increased, choice to opt for off-campus or distant learning looked as a alternative lifelong learning. It is therefore, expected that library must evolve to match this new educational concept, wherein students naturally try to search for other ways to conveniently locate information resources from anywhere and any time.

Subsequent to this digital library conceptual development and after establishing its basic idea digital library began to appear on the campus of universities in UK & USA in 1990s. The research of experiment began in Computer Science department with funds from the government. Campus librarians however were not much involved in this phase. Computer Scientists were concentrating mainly on digitization technology, metadata schemes, data management techniques and digital preservation techniques. Daniel Greenstein, the then Director of Digital Library Federation and the Head California Digital Library characterised this phase of development as- **the second generation digital library.** With the availability of advanced knowledge and technology it was prompted to set aside these experimentations and look for still advanced technology. This was characterised as **the third generation of digital library**. In this stage philosophy was focusing on creating digital collection through modular system architecture instead of fully integrating digital material into library's collection. This modular approach liberated the idea of digital library giving it independent from physical library. Thus it led to implement digital library in creative way with the involvement of library to take a central role in digital library development. Use of digital library was thus facilitated serving a large and diverse audience with partnership of information technology group and library. This further resulted in development of campus wide standards, which established new relation and integration with education enterprise. It further facilitated to meet students requirement for access to library resources.

With the advancements of internet access to information increased tremendously. Now it was not required to go to library to have the material or wait to get it on interlibrary loan for certain time. Now patron instead expects instant access to all information resources from any location and at any time from any device. This was the prime objective of digital library to fulfill. Now digital library is in a present position provides advantages such as:

- To gain access to the holdings of libraries worldwide through automated catalogue.

- To locate both digital and physical version of scholarly document.
- To optimize material search simultaneously on internet through commercial data base and also in library collection.
- To save search results and use it for next time in order to save time or to refine the search
- From already obtained search result to facilitate to click useful search terms to get additional information.

All these capabilities and advantages are available from desktop or from other web enabled devices. In addition the users could also customise their information queries to reflect the individual needs and preferences.

All the above developments brought much clarity in the concept of digital library by presenting its key components as:

1. Initial conversion of content from physical to digital from
2. Extraction and creation of metadata or indexing information of digital document to facilitate searching and locating as well as administrative and structural metadata to help in object viewing, management and preservation of digital document irrespective of its technical (IT) characteristics
3. Storing of digital contents and metadata in an appropriate multimedia structured digital repository. These digital repository would also consider handing irrespective of intellectual properly right in order to provide free flow of information. If required e – commerce functionality would also be provided in order to handle accounting and billing.
4. It would ensure user rights and client service to the browsers including searching digital content and necessary work flow.
5. Content delivery via FTP and streaming media.
6. Patron access to be provided through the browser or dedicated client.
7. To support private and public network content.

As such digital library technology development is seen in two ways:

1. Development of digital library as a part of library management systems as seen in case of like VTLS or Koha
2. Development of digital library on a standalone technological structures or DL softwares like DSpace or Greenstone, where emphasis has been on open source type of softwares with one view to make digital libraries as the most economical way. Then software is further aligned with metadata softwares in order to take care of data markup or technology.[1]

3.3. NEEDS OF DIGITAL LIBRARY

Considering the present constrains of age old library systems and limited life of printed collection housed in them, readers would certainly look for an alternative to the traditional library

1. Digital Library Technology Trends by Sun Microsystems Inc. 2002.

systems. In librarian's point of view preservation of rare and valuable collection should be given top priority by converting it into digital collection. This major need have prompted to have digital libraries to think of preservation, converting library's most used collection in digital form which facilitates making it permanently available to users with convenient access by using advances of library information technology. So the development of digital library is the need of present and future. There are other certain reasons for creating digital libraries along with traditional library systems. These needs are discussed in the following points.

1. Limitations of print media : We find accumulation of mostly printed literature in library collection. Libraries try their best to preserve such collection. However there are limitations on durability of paper based literature. It is bound to deteriorate as it gets older with time. Each library certainly has rare and valuable books with them and they cannot afford to lose them with time neither publishers guarantee to preserve them and make them available permanently. As such the responsibility and challenge come on libraries to preserve them for the future user generations. There is a need to convert such rare and important documents to a durable medium. Photocopying them is not a good alternative as that also has age limitations being paper based. Now the time has provided with a reliable medium i.e. digital medium. The libraries need to adopt this technology for preservation of their valuable collection. While adopting the digital technology for preservation special care needs to be taken. Just frame by frame digital imaging would not serve the purpose but it need to use proper digitization technology, so that each digit or letter could be digitized so that the contents world be recognised and used for years together through digital technology.

2. Need of preservation of literature available in different formats : Libraries not only face challenge to preserve only printed collection but preserving collection in non print form such as audio, video and cinematographic Collection through digital conversion is more challenging as it requires higher level of digitization techniques. Libraries also stock non print collections like artifacts, paintings collections of museums and archives, play articles, models and photographic collection. Libraries need to take a lot of efforts to preserve these variety of formats. Many a times such collection of artifacts face damaging due to improper handling by researchers. The libraries therefore need to find permanent solution to these problems by considering preservation of these collections along with rare printed collection and preserving and organising them in the digital library.

3. Need of having single platform for using literature available in different languages: We know literature is published in many national and international languages. Libraries also maintain collections available in various languages. In addition country like India there are various regional languages and this variety is also reflected in library collection. Literature in various languages can also be preserved by using digitization technology. However providing one platform to use the entire digitized collection is certainly a challenging task. Digital Library technology provides a proper solution to this problem.

4. Difficulties in Using Literature published on Internet : Since Internet technology is available to provide information in digital form, we might feel that internet could be good platform to use digital collection, as e - journals, e - databases or e - books are available through the internet platform. However we must note that internet provides scholarly literatures or literature having reference value is mainly from commercial publishers. There are lot of constrains, limitations and commercial conditions in using such information. It depends whether library makes proper monetary arrangement to make internet base literature available for longer period or not(for perpetual access). There comes an affordability problem for libraries in maintaining and preserving such literature even though it is available in the digital form. Of course all the literature published in e-journals or e - books may not have permanent information value but certainly there is a good portion of literature especially scientific literature which needs to be preserved for unlimited times. Publishers try to publish soft form along with printed form including journals, databases or e- books and libraries do acquire them with a view to provide convenience to the readers to read them anywhere any time. However, other than convenience and ease literature published in digital form on internet does not ensure its preservation for a longer time in future. It may create major hurdles for researchers; the libraries therefore need to find some way to preserve such literature. The literature available on internet is not properly organized so they need digital libraries where organising digital collection is done properly.

5. Need of producing literature through local intellectual assets : Every library tries to create a collection using available resource structure and within constrains. If one considers cost of journal literature or cost of e- resources it becomes difficult to provide literature of scholarly reference value to their patrons. In such situations it is always advisable for academic institution to tap the intellectual assets available within the institute with individuals, scientists, technologists and academics in producing their own literature for the use of students and researchers. Very useful literature could be produced locally by sharing the intellectual knowledge base existing in each institution. It may include class notes; computer programs, problems and solutions, video, audio lectures, various syllabi, exam papers and full length research articles contributed by research students, faculty, scientists, engineers and research guides. All such locally obtained literature could be organised and made available on campus through a digital library.

3.4. COMPONENTS OF DIGITAL LIBRARY

Normally digital library framework consists of following components:

1. User Interfaces
2. Search system
3. Handle system
4. Repository
5. Digital library architecture
6. Digital Library software

Let us understand them in bit detail.

User Interfaces : Here we need two types of interfaces one is for end users who browse digital library the other interface is required for digital librarian or for the system administrator who manage digital collection.

Search Systems : Design of digital library assumes that there would be many indexes and catalogues. Those could be searched to discover information before retrieving it from repository. These indexes are managed independently with the support of wide range of protocols.

Repository : Repository stores and manages digital objects and other information. The interface for this is called Repository Access Protocol (RAP). The repository consists of.

1. Data
2. Metadata
3. Meta Objects
4. Identifiers or handles

Data is collection of digitized, borrowed or acquired digital documents. They may be textual documents, images, audio or video clips. The place where all these different kinds of digital documents are stored is called a depository. (or a repository)

Metadata : It is data about data which describes the contents and attributes of any particular digital item in the digital library. It describes the digitized item in terms of bibliographic metadata and format of document in terms of computerised descriptions which is called Meta objects.

Identifiers or Handle systems : Repository would have identifiers for each document on internet they are also called handles

Digital Library Architecture : In digital library data, metadata and meta objects are considered. Data are like library materials but only in digital form. Metadata is bibliographic data like catalogue entry about the document in traditional library where as meta objects that provides references to a set of digital objects which lists all converted versions of the specific digital item.

Operational Systems Architecture : At operational architectural level it is important how information flow is managed through the systems components. Digital library is a collection of different system and resources connected through a network and integrated within one interface most likely a web interface. These resources may reside on different systems and in different data bases. However for user they appear as one single system. It is therefore necessary to have information interoperability in search and retrieval in digital library systems through a middleware. Digital library therefore needs some common standards to facilitate cross domain search and retrieval. Digital Library software tries to comprise all the above components in one entity. Digital library softwares are pre-structured with all these components which provide users ready to use platforms.With these brief details of digital library components we would understand more about various digital library softwares.

3.5. DIGITAL LIBRARY SOFTWARES

We have seen that digital library software is one entity which carries out all the function of digital library in a user friendly manner. Digital library softwares are specialized softwares used for building, maintenance or for running digital libraries/ institutional repositories. There is no difference between digital library and institutional repository in their functionality point of view. There are good number of digital library softwares available today such as :

- Alfresco Software
- Biblical Software
- Digital commons
- Dspace
- E-Print
- Exo platform
- Expanded books
- Fedora common
- Greenstone (Software)
- Image Ltd
- International Image
- Interoperability Frame work
- Intra Text
- Invensio
- Islandora
- Knowledge Tree
- Logos Bible software
- Olive Tree Bible
- Software
- OPUS (Software)
- Pleade : EAD
- SABDA
- Simple DL
- Sobe KCM

Out of this long list of DL software we world try to know about the following a few in an elaborated way :

- Dspace
- Greenstone
- E-Print & Fedora Commons

3.5.1. Dspace

Dspace is an open source repository software package typically used for creating open access repositories for scholarly as well as for published/unpublished digital content. Dspace at one hand shares features overlapping with content management system and document management systems where as it also serves a specific need as a digital archive system adopted for long term storage, access and preservation of digital contents. If we see its historical evolution process its first public version appeared in November 2002. It is a joint venture between development from MIT and HP Labs. The user group meeting held in 2004, interested group of institutions formed the Dspace Federation. This group further took over the governance of future development of this software with adoption of Apache foundation's community development model. Subsequently in 2004 July Hp and MIT jointly formed the Dspace foundation, a nonprofit organisation as its user group base grew larger. In 2009 another collaboration took the shape between two related projects i.e. Dspace foundation and Fedora Commons Organisation which continued their not-for-profit activities called Duraspace. Currently Dspace software and its user community receive guidance from Duraspace.

Dspace uses technology described as a set of cooperating java web applications and utility programs which maintain as asset store and an associated metadata store. Its web application provides interface for administration deposit search and access. Asset store of Dspace is maintained on the file system similar to storage system. The metadata including access and configuration information is stored in a relational database and supports the use of post SQL and Oracle database.

Dspace is currently supporting to two primary web interfaces. JSPU which uses JSP and java servlet, APL and XMLUI based on Apache cocoon using XML and XSLT. Holding of Dspace are made available via web interface but it also supports the OAI-PMH V2.O and is capable of exporting METS (Metadata Encoding and Transmission Standards) package. Dspace supports to common inter operability standards used in institutional repository environment such as Open Archive Initiative.

Protocol for Metadata Harvesting, SWORD open search and RSS, more recent versions of Dspace also support faceted search and browse functionality using Apache server.

Dspace DL Software runs on variety of operating systems like Linux, Solaris, UNIX or windows where as Linux is the most commonly used platform for Dspace.

Dspace is used for the following six good reasons all over the world such as :

1. Large community
2. Free
3. Customizable
4. All institutions types
5. Out of the box
6. Any digital contents

It is available at the site www. dspace.org

Dspace uses Dublin Core metadata software to manage its metadata.

Dspace currently possesses a considerable large clientele base and has characteristics of facilitating support as :

- Latest Release - 6.3 (27 June 2018)
- Bugs and Features Enhancement
- Add-ons and extension
- Software Development
- Contributors
- User group meetings

3.5.2. Greenstone Digital Library Software

Brief : Greenstone is a software for building and distributing digital library collection. It facilitates organising and publishing such collection on web or on removable media such as CDs/DVDs or USB Flash drives. This software has been produced by the New Zealand Digital Library project at University of Waikato and further developed and distributed with the cooperation of UNESCO and Human Info NGO. It is an open source multilingual software issued under GNU General Public License.

The aim of Greenstone software is to empower use, especially in university libraries and other public service institutions to build their own digital libraries. Emphasis of this software is to disseminate information among communities and institutions in the field of education, science and culture around the world and specifically in developing countries.

Fact sheet : Greenstone is not a digital library but a tool to build digital library. The software facilitates organising digital collection and publishing it on web in the form of fully searchable, metadata driven digital resource. Other than network version it can run on standalone PC. Greenstone has received IFIP award in 2004

Technical Details

Versions : There are two versions of this software i.e. Greenstone-3, which is a complete redesign and implementation of the original digital library software developed back in 2000 Greenstone 2. This new version is backward compatible. An import Greenstone - 2 collection has also been provided in Greenstone Librarian Interface (GLI) to assist such transition or migration. Greenstone - 3 is written in Java and it takes advantage of many new web technologies such as XML transforms (XSLT) and Java Authentication and Authorisation Service (JAAS). This upgradation has made software highly customizable and extensible in the functionality in delivering the benefits. In contrast Greenstone - 2 was written in C++. Greenstone - 3 is highly recommended to download but at the same time prompt services are available for Greenstone - 2 adopted by libraries in the past.

Platform : Greenstone is an open source category of DL software which runs on all versions of Windows, UNIX/Linux and MacOS-x platforms. For default window installation no configuration is required and end user can easily install it on their personal PC or laptop. Institutional user can run it on main server where it interoperates with standard web server software (i.e. Apache for Greenstone - 2 Tomcat for Greenstone - 3) an experimental version is also available for Android operable on user's smart phone.

Interoperability : Greenstone is highly interoperable using contemporary standards. It interoperates a server that can serve any collection over the Open Archives Protocol for Metadata Harvesting (OAI- PMH) and Greenstone can harvest documents over OAI-PMH and include them in the collection. Any collection can be exported to METS and Greenstone can import documents in METS form. Any collection can be exported Dspace in batch import program and any Dspace collection can be imported into Greenstone

Interfaces : There are two interfaces, one for reader and other one for librarian or admin person. Admin or supervisory interface is a Java based graphical interface which facilitates, gather material, enrich with metadata, upload them and maintain it further. Greenstone-3 provides built in facilities to browsers.

Languages : Greenstone's unique strength is its multilingual nature. The readers interface is available in 60 world languages which include most of Indic (Regional language)

Metadata formats : User can define metadata interactively within the librarian interface. These metadata sets are predefined such as :

- DublinCore (Qualified and unqualified)
- RFC 1807

- NZGLS (New Zealand Govt. Locator Service)
- AGLS (Australian Govt. Locator Service)

New metadata sets can be defined using Greenstone. Metadata set editor plugins are used to import externally prepared metadata in different forms and plug-ins exist for : CSV, XML, EXIF, MARC, CDS/ ISIS, Procite, Bibtex, Refer OAI, Dspace and METS.

Document Formats : Plug-ins are also used to import documents. For external documents there are plug ins for PDF, Post script, Word, RTF, HTML, Plain text, Latex, Zip archives, Excel, PPT, Email and Source Code. For multimedia contents there are plug-ins for images (any format including PNG, JPEG, PEG - 2000, GIF, TIFF) MP3 audio, 099 orbit audio and generic plug ins that can be configured audio formats MPEG MSDS etc.

Greenstone : Greenstone has a very broad base of clientele. It is distributed on Sourceforge since November 2000. On an average every month around 5000 downloads are done. The total download number till June 2015 is 949156. Platform wise it is Windows 76% Linux - 13% Mac - 8% . It is being used nearly in 170 countries.

For downloading latest version of Greenstone one can visit site at www.sourceforge.net / projects/greenstone

3.5.3. Other Digital Library Softwares

3.5.3.1. Fedora Common

Brief : Fedora is a robust modular open source repository system for management and dissemination of digital contents. It is especially suitable for digital libraries and archives both for access and preservation. It is also competent for handling very large complex type of digital collection of historic and cultural materials as well as scientific data. Fedora has broad user base spread worldwide that includes academic and cultural heritage organizations, universities, research institutes, university libraries, national libraries and govt. agencies. Fedora software development project was led by Fedora leadership group and is developed and maintained under the banner as Duraspace i.e. not for profit organisation which ensures durable persistent access to digital data. Fedora is being used in over 300 institutions worldwide.

Fedora (Flexible Extensible Digital Object Repository Architecture) was originally developed by the group of researches of Cornell University as an architecture for storing, managing, and accessing digital contents in the form of digital objects inspired by Kahn and Wilensky framework. Fedora defines a set of instructions for expressing digital object asserting relationships among digital object and linking behaviors (i. e. services) to digital objects.

Global Fedora repository project Community is made up of registered sites, sponsoring organisations, service providers, and code contributors, common needs, use cases, and collaborations on software developments have been always under consideration. There are additional tools, applications, and utilities that augment the Fedora repository including the Hydra, Islandora and Avalon platforms have been made available for community members. Fedora ensures long term access to digital resources. It is flexible to accommodate all types of digital content. The examples of Fedora used for digital collections like e – resources, digital libraries, archives, digital preservation, institutional repositories, open access publishing, documents management, digital asset management etc.

Fedora user profile includes organisations like :

- Columbia university: Academic Commons
- Stanford University Libraries
- Repositories-Smithsonian Institution: SI-Dora
- D.G. National Library of Medicines
- University Prince Edward Island, Island Archive project
- University of Virginia - LIBRA

Current Release of Fedora is 4.7.4 released on 01-08-2017

It is available for download at the site www.fedoracommons.org /download which is distributed by Dura space at Winchester MA USA

3.5.3.2. E-Print

Brief : E - Print is a free open source software package for building open access repositories that are compliant with Open Archives Initiative Protocol for Metadata Harvesting (OAI- PMH)

It shares many of the commonly seen features in digital document management systems but is primarily used for institutes repositories and scientific journals. E - Print has been developed at the University of Southampton, School of Electronics and Computer Science which have been released under GPL License.

E - Print was created in 2000 as a direct outcome of 1999 Santa Fe Meeting which became an eventual base for OAI-PMH. E-print software was enthusiastically received which became the first and most widely used free open access institutional repository software which has inspired further digital library software to develop.

E-Print version 3 was officially released on 24th January 2007 at the open repository conference.

Technology : E - Print is a web command line application based on the LAMP architecture which is written in Perl language. It is run under Linux, Solaris and Mac-OS–x, Windows MS version was released 17th May 2010

Version 3 introduced plug-in architecture for importing or exporting data converting objects and user interface widgets

For E-print configuration involves modification of configuration files written in PERL or XML. The appearance of E - Print is controlled by HTML templates, CSS style sheets and inline images. e - Print is shipped with English translation however needs to be translated to other language through language specific XML Phrase files. Presently translations in Bulgarian, French, German, Hungarian, Italian, Japanese, Russian, Spanish and Ukrainian of e - Print are available. The software is in use worldwide for the last 15 years and available as not-for-profit principles E - Print is available (Version v3.3.14) for downloading at site : www.eprint.org/uk

3.5.4. Characteristics of Digital Library with Digital Library Softwares

Use of the above referred digital library softwares has made digital library development easy and more productive and with some initial training of digital library software, digital library developer or any LIS professional would be certainly in a position to develop their digital libraries for readers use. The special characteristics exhibited by digital library with DL Softwares are listed as below:

1. Digital Library can be searched through internet browsers in order to get the information
2. It works on windows, UNIX or Linux platforms
3. Digital Library presents the information in concise as well as in full text form.
4. Searchers can modify the retrieval as they need
5. Catalogue of digital collection is automatically generated out of metadata
6. Available metadata can be used to optimum level.
7. Capacity of information handling can be increased as it needs
8. It can accommodate digital documents available in most world languages and it can be searched in those languages too.
9. It organises variety of collection as text, audio, video form, pictures and photos, animations, and artifacts
10. It possesses the capacity to handle data in gigabytes
11. Since information is searched through authentication (User login and Password). It is safe and secured
12. It accepts new information, can facilitate removal of old information.
13. Its contents can be published on CD - ROMs
14. It provides multi-way search facility.
15. No worry about the copy right of contents and hence contents can be downloaded.
16. It justifies to get what you intend to get.

3.6. SELECTION CRITERIA AND RESOURCES FOR DIGITAL LIBRARY

We have so far understood the concept, definitions and evolution of digital library. Now we also have an idea about the various characteristics of digital library and finally we have significance of the various DL Softwares which provide the structure to build the digital library. Digital library is generally built locally as per needs of library and its users. It does not come in a readymade form so we need to think about the selection of resources one can put in it. Before we take this issue let us know the broad purposes for which digital libraries are created and what type of literature can be included in them. We can view digital library resources broadly in the following two categories :

1. General type of Literature : Collection of digital documents having temporary information values consisting of documents concerned to academic or educational interest and which can be replaced, improved, proved or removed subsequently :

- PPTs
- Question Papers
- Chapters of books
- Class Notes
- Problems and Solutions
- Diagrams
- Submissions
- Projects
- Video Lectures
- Discussions
- E - Mail Contents
- Pre-Prints

2. Digital Libraries created with specific propose : In this category there could be more sub categories such as collection of digital documents having permanent information values like

- Digitized rare books (Copy right settled or beyond copy rights years)
- Archives having historical value
- Museum artifacts
- Documents belonging to ancient period
- Models (Digitized)
- Paintings (Digitized)
- Audio and Video documents but in digital form
- Photographs - digital
- Lectures of historical values

3. Institutional Repositories : In other sub category we can consider digital documents which have research values. These are generally called institutional repositories. Institutional repositories are the digital libraries which are created to support the aims and objectives of the institution or they are created with some definite purpose in mind. Such repositories are normally accessible on the campus or the intranet for the definite audience within the purview of the institutions. The materials in such repositories consist of mostly grey literature which has not been published or at the stage just before their publishing. They could be listed as:

- Preprints of Teaching Staff or Scientists
- Working papers

- Thesis and dissertations
- Research and Technical Report
- Conference proceeding (held on campus or not commercially published)
- Departmental or research center newsletters and bulletins
- Status Reports
- Committee Reports or Memoranda
- Statistical reports
- Technical reports
- Technical documents
- Surveys

All the above types of literature forms a part of informal scholarly communication process and contributors would not mind in sharing their contents with a point of view to attract the comments on them or just to find if any repetitive literary activities are occurring so that duplication could be avoided.

When we consider resources of any digital library we must note the main characteristic of the digital library that it contains collection created locally of which there are no copy right issues. The individuals who contribute to digital library normally share the copy right of contents for circulating the submitted material among the group of people interested to browse them.

Thus digital libraries are not created out of documents which have been commercially published, else it would be violation of publisher's copy right. Documents like scholarly journal papers, published thesis and dissertations, e - books or even open access materials. At the most one can include the abstract of such material (with the permission of author / or publishers) by giving link of the publishers website from where the particular papers could be downloaded by making necessary payment or one can access it in full text provided the institute is subscribing that e - resource which is available on their campus intranet IP range or accessed through official login password.

3.6.1. Selection of Material for Digital Library

Planning of any digital library development involves the following decisions

- Objectives.
- Scope
- Policy for the type of digital document to be incorporated

The next is to search and select resources for the digital library. Where the resource for digital library to come from. One of the above three major ways may be considered such as :

- By converting available literature in library to digitized form
- By obtaining documents which are already in digital form
- Incorporate digital document from the internet

Now let us discuss the feasibility of these

3.6.1.1. Converting Existing Library Collection to Digital Collections

If one thinks to consider digitizing library's entire collection then it may not be feasible looking into huge quantum of library collection, so one must think whether such the task is really needed. Secondly, even if the library decides to do it, it would be illegal unless the copy right of each and every book / document is purchased or settled which looks just next to impossible, as it involves requirement of huge funds, which is beyond the capacity of the library. The library therefore needs to set some priorities of taking up digitizing of the existing materials of the library such as:

1. Only rare or out of print or valuable deteriorating collection of which copy right tenure is over or for those rare books library can settle the copy right to be considered
2. To consider collection heavily used by the readers. Such material could be bought with their digital ownership cost by paying any cost affordable to the library.
3. To consider comparatively less used material.

It would be always feasible and justified if the library chooses to digitize collection mentioned at no. 1 and 2.

3.6.1.2. Creating Literature out of local intellectual assets

After considering the initial and priority source of digital collection i.e. digitally converted rare valuable and deteriorating printed collection for inclusion in digital library. Now we would move further to explore further sources of digital collection which is created out of local intellectual assets of the institute. Such digital collection is always beneficial for the library as it has the essence of originality, secondly it is available without any copy right liability as the same is given and shared enthusiastically for free distribution of knowledge to the students or knowledge seekers. Such literature has intellectual importance so also has educational material creation scope. However, care needs to be taken while inclusion or uploading that so called created material has not been copied the text from any other published source. Normally digital literature created locally out of local individual's contributions is of the following categories :

1. Educational material concern with educational course requirements as listed earlier like educational aids or classroom supplementary material provided for further reading or for self study by the students and researchers such material may not have permanent information need or value.
2. Collection of literature consisting of preprints, working papers, reports, discussion documentation etc.

Such material has the same purpose of sharing the contents with colleagues or with peers to promote discussion or to seek comments from the group working in the same field. Such material could have certain research value.

3.6.1.3. Considering Digital Literature available on Internet

People normally have wrong notion that each and every piece of material available on internet is free to download or available for inclusion in the digital library. However, it is not so, each of such material do carry digital copy right so it is always worthwhile to seek prior permission, if anyone wishes to copy/download and include it in digital library then duly endorse the same with acknowledgement in the material. Such material however needs further editing and correction plus one need to create bibliographic or digital metadata of their contents. It is not ethical to copy e-books e-papers or e-journals available on internet and include them in digital library but one can provide metadata and abstract of them along with provision of website link so that searcher uses such literature directly from the respective website.

3.7. DIGITIZATION OF PRINTED MATERIALS

3.7.0. What is digitization?

Digitization is a computerised process to convert printed material to a completely digitized form. It involves many steps including scanning and OCR. However, just scanning a printed page does not mean the digitization.

3.7.1. Converting printed literature to Digital form

We have seen that converting available rare and valuable printed collection which would otherwise be destroyed in the course of time due to limited life of paper and preserve such literature for future is one of the important step of development of digital library. So the librarians need to understand the process of digitization closely. In digitization process the printed material is first scanned, saved in a computer and then digitization process is carried out on it. The digitization process is somewhat time consuming and costly but it is worth considering for the cause of preservation.

Digitization process involves two major steps i.e. scanning and OCR. In scanning first the image of printed material is prepared, whereas with OCR or Optical Characteristic Recognition the scanned image of printed page is properly converted into a digitized form. Many people carry misconception of digitization as only scanning of material. They scan printed pages and make them available to readers and they call such collection as digital library. However, by now we know that it is not true. Post OCR also there are further steps of indexing digitized material and provide the facility to search a word or string of words from the digitized material. Giving ability to search a word or letter from the digitized page is very important and it is the characteristics of digitization. One cannot have this facility just from scanned image of print pages. OCR tells whether the page is completely digitized or not if not then how much % it has digitized. This depends on how much printed form is converted into scanned image. Now let us understand the steps of digitization in detail.

3.7.1.1. Scanning

In a scanning process with the help of scanner we convert printed page to a computerised image. It is just a photo image of printed page. The important unit of scanning process is "pixels" or dots which are in black and white colour in case of black and white image. They would be in different colours in case of colour scanning of coloured printed page. Most of the scanners have both the capabilities of scanning in black and white or in colour image. We therefore need to decide first before scanning of any page whether to use colour scanning mode or just black and white. Next step is to choose resolution. Resolution means to consider the number of pixels in one linear unit. i.e. in one inch, the following table (Table No. 3.1) gives an idea of the different images created by different equipments in terms of their resolutions :

Types of Equipment	Resolution DPI	Strength of bits
• Fax Machine	200 × 100 or 200 × 200	1
• Laser printer	600	1
• Scanner	300 × 300 or 600 × 600	1, 8, 24
• Laptop monitor (DPI = Dots per inch)	92 × 92	8, 16, 24 or 32

Table 3.1. Images from Different Equipments and their Resolutions

Quality of scanned image depends on how many dots/pixels are in one inch. Let us first understand some basics of scanning.

Scanning involves three basic steps.

1. Place the original printed black and white or colour page on the scanner plate
2. Open your scanning software and tell it to make the scan (scan it)
3. Save the resulting image to your computer (in correct file format) so that you can print it, mail it, post it on web or use it for digitization.

Scanning Elements

Depending on the final product one would want to set your scanner to capture the best balance between file size and image quality. There are 3 basic settings to be adjusted for scanning the original.

1. Resolution : Digital images are stored in pixels/dots of lights with colour value. Resolution is measured in number of dots per inch (DPI) and it indicates the amount of details available in the final image. Higher the resolution the more detailed image it is. So to determine the minimum resolution it is necessary to capture the significant dots present in the source document.

- **Web pages :** Most computer monitors display at the resolution in the range of 72-96 dpi so 96 is the good resolution to use for scanning it on web.
- **Printing :** Printers have limitations on resolution. A good thumb rule is to scan at a resolution that is 1/3 of your printed output i.e. scan at 200 dpi and a 600 dpi for laser printer. However, if you wish to print the image on high quality printer, then you may need higher resolution.

2. Bit Depth : This is the number of bits / pixel or the number of colours that the scanner would capture or show. Greater the bit depth the better is the colour and dots of the picture. There are 1, 8, 16, 24 or 32 bit depth types

- **Black and white :** A-1 bit scan will capture only black and white.
- **Colour printing :** A-4 bit scan will capture 16 colours and a 8 bit scan will capture 256 colours, 16 bit scan would get over 65000 colours and 24 bit scanner will capture 16.8 million colours.
- **Web colour:** Monitors usually have a bit depth in the range of 8-24 grey scale like colour. Higher the bit depth more the shades of gray will show.

File formats : There are several file formats in which you can save your scanned image. The most used formats are as

- **GIF :** This format is used typically for drawing ,clip art, graphs or diagrams.
- **JPG :** This format is used for photos or higher quality colour drawings which are put on web or to be sent on mail.
- **TIFF :** This format is also used for photos which use less compression process means, there would be no loss of details as it could be in JPG format. File size would be larger so one should only use the TIFF format in case of printing high quality image. When we try to create digital image for putting it in digital library we think whether it is clear for reading. Thus we need scanning quality by which try to produce the image which is most nearer to the original documents. The important things are file size and quality of image and resolution is to be selected accordingly.

3.7.1.2. Optical Character Recognition (OCR)

If one wishes to digitize printed page in real sense then one must do successive OCR of the scanned image of the document. OCR means "Optical Character Recognition". In OCR process attempt is made to recognise each and every letter of the scanned image and the process does not consider the pixels of the image. There are various softwares with which OCR process is carried out. First automatic OCR is done by the software device and in subsequent steps it is done manually to understand or recognise those letters which machine fail to recognize. In order to digitize a page or document then OCR needs to be done 100% or to a maximum extent. To do OCR manually is a time consuming process. In OCR a dumb image of document is converted into fully digitized or to an intelligent page. It is assumed that it is necessary to have image quality of documents created with minimum of 300 (DPI) dots per inch which means it must possess font of 10 or above. Page having font 9 or less then its resolution should be between 400-600 DPI. The success of OCR depends on how quality of scanning is done. If the original document is in normal font and clean image is created with suitable resolution then it is possible to do 99.9% OCR of the document. If there is only one mistake in 2000 letters then it is called OCR of higher level.

Normally first OCR is done automatically with OCR device then it is done manually by two persons to correct the mistakes of automatic scanning. If the quality(perfection) of OCR is less than 95% then it is called a defective OCR. Inclusion of Latin letters or special letters or symbols, Roman letters, highlighted letter, pictures or tables brings down the quality of OCR as without the support of OCR software it becomes difficult to correct such errors of automatic OCR process. In manual OCR correction process works in interactive mode of OCR software used. It helps in searching mistakes accurately and also while doing clean up image this facility helps in saving time required for correcting the errors. There are various steps in interactive OCR process such as:

- Image acquisition or checking
- Clean up
- Page analysis
- Recognition
- Saving

Now let us know about these sub processes of OCR

Acquisition : In this step a scanned image of a document is accessed and installed in OCR software. It is the general step in any OCR software which is called TWINE.

Clean up : In this step image in cleaned by removing unnecessary stains or dots by using filtering process.

Page Analysis : In this step a layout of entire page is considered. This is done either by OCR machine or by manual method. The process divides page into text, heading, table, title, pictures, footer and photos which are marked in squares and their order is drawn in such a way that it starts with header and ends with footer. Special care is taken for tables and its contents which are normally done manually. In this process most of the things are made recognisable in the computer.

Recognition : In this process emphasis is given in recognsing each and every letter of the document. This considers the letter fonts also. In order to make it feasible all fonts, scripts, symbols and special letters available with software are used while recognising letters. Sometimes use of encyclopedia is also made. Lower and upper case of letters are also taken into account. Difficulties are faced in understanding joint letters which are available in languages other than English like Indic or regional languages. If the letter is very difficult to understand then alternative letters are put in place of old letters. The secret of success of OCR depends on how much recognition is successfully done.

Checking : Next to recognition is the checking step where errors are tagged/ coloured with different colours. Letters not recognized, not possible or there are no clues found in encyclopedia are arranged in the order of status many a times spell check or zooming facilities are used in recognising error letters.

Saving : Saving is the last step in OCR process. Page completely processed with OCR is saved in a file in an appropriate format like HTML, RTF, MS word or PDF.

Other Related Features in Digitization

Since scanning is the most important step in digitization it needs to be done carefully and accurately. In order to do it effectively page and pages of document/ book are separated for scanning. In case of rare and fragile documents having archival value it becomes difficult to do this as pages are in brittle condition and it may result is further damaging the document in handling. In such case a carefully microfilming is done first and then scanning is carried out to keep original document safe. OCR in digitization is found expensive and time consuming. It is therefore necessary to do proper planning of digitization project considering quantum of work. At the same time there is need of financial planning, if necessary libraries need to look for donors or sponsors to carry out the work. Since digitization process involves a lot of mobilization of technology, equipment, software expert and skilled manpower it is always advised to do proper planning considering all aspects in order to make it success. Digitization is good medium to convert rare and valuable library collection and such project gets lot of support looking into the cause of sincere efforts on the part of library of preservation of literature or the human knowledge.

3.8. MANAGEMENT OF DIGITAL LIBRARY

We have covered some important aspects of Digital Library Development like use of digital library softwares and then about the resources to be incorporated in it. Now onwards we are going to discuss about the managerial aspects of digital library development

3.8.1. Planning of Digital Library

Planning of digital library involves organising various tasks relating to creating a digital library collection, developing strategies to handle theme, identifying required resources and formulating timeline to complete this task. If the institute needs a considerable larger digital library then a feasibility study may be conducted to assess all of its aspects in order to seek approval from the authorities. The planning of digital library considers the following things.

1. The first stage of planning digital library collection development is to ascertain the need or purpose of digital library. There could be several things which initiate such development as:
   (a) For preservation of rare delicate and valuable collection by digitizing and putting them on web.
   (b) To improve the access to heavily used materials through digitization.
   (c) Putting collection on web having temporary information needs like clipping, news extracts or question papers or teaching materials.
   (d) Creating special collections like faculty publications/published journal articles or Organising Electronic theses and dissertation collection for the use of researchers or Project reports and collection of Gray literature
2. To define various sources of digital documents such as :
   - Rare books
   - Internet resources
   - Readily available digital sources
   - Resources created with involvement of local contributions
3. Defining key features like nature of the collection i.e. static or dynamic. Whether to provide access on intranet or on internet. Policy about sharing the materials with other organisation and digital library networks.
4. Deciding organising features like :

(a) Funding basic or recurring

(b) Human resources for development of digital library

(c) Maintenance of digital library for post establishment period.

(d) Selection of DL software and metadata software

3.8.2. Functional components of digital library

Digital library involves the following functional components:

1. Initial conversion of printed literature to the digital form (digitization)
2. Searching of metadata and indexing information useful from the digital documents and entering it in a form fed provided by the particular DL software. Once they are fed users can use them for searching
3. Storing digital content and its respective metadata in an appropriate multimedia depository available DL software set up. The respective depository consists of right management capabilities to access document within intellectual property rights as recorded in DL establishment. It require e - commerce functionality which would also be provided as per DL set up policy.
4. Providing services to clients for browsing including repository querying and work flow.
5. Providing contents through FTP or streaming media.
6. Providing access through the browsers or dedicated clients.
7. Supporting private or public network.

Let us visualize functioning of digital library as shown in Fig. 3.1

The Flow Digram of Digital Library Functioning

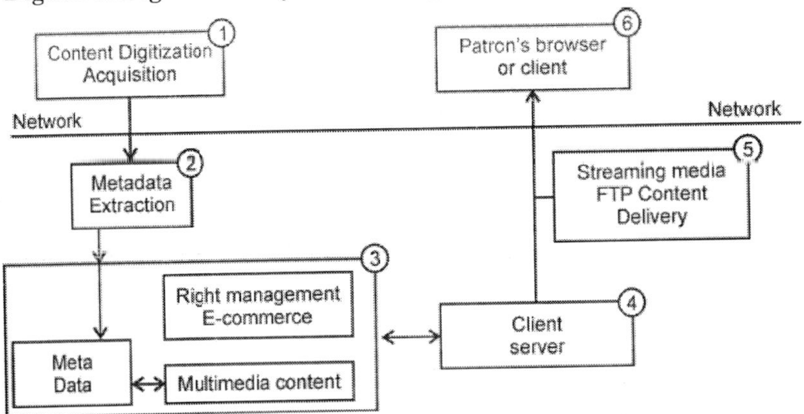

Fig. 3.1. Flow Diagram of Digital Library Functioning

3.8.3. Digital library Architecture

Digital Library is built using building block i.e. components like digital objects. They are the ways of structuring information in digital form. Some of them are metadata which also include unique identifier called handle. However, information in digital library is structured far from simple and they have many parts, a complex internal structure and arbitrary relations to other work. Thus several digital objects are grouped together. They are known as a set of digital objects.

Materials in digital library information are divided into different categories. i.e. text with SGML, Markup, world wide web objects, computer programs, digitized audio video objects. For each category rules and conventions describe how to organise the information as digital objects. User interface would be aware of the rules and conventions applying to certain categories of information would able to interpret the structure of sets of digital objects. Since user interface recognises how material is represented, it can provide users with suitable access to information.

Components of digitals library Systems : In a digital library framework there are different computer systems to exist which is displayed in the Fig. 3.2. The network i.e. internet connects them:

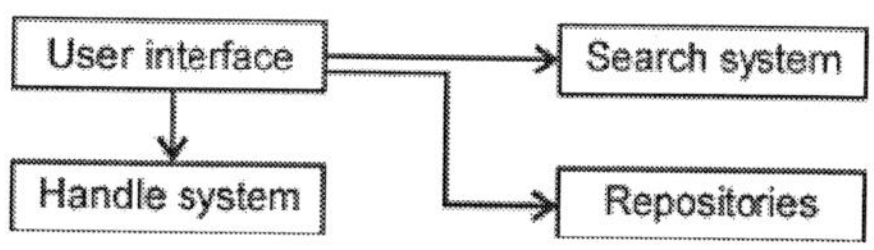

Fig. 3.2. Digital library Framework

User interface : The system has two interfaces one is user of the digital library and other for librarian or system administrator, who manages the collection. Each user interface possesses two parts i.e. internet browser and client services which provides inter-connections between the browser and other parts of the systems. Client service allows users to decide where to search and what to retrieve.

Repository : Repositories store and manage digital objects and other information. Repository have interface called the repository access protocol. Features of the interface are to recognise rights and permission that need to be satisfied before a client can access a digital object

Handle system : Handles are general purpose identifiers which can be used to identity internet resources, such as digital objects over a long period of time and to manage material stored in any repository of database.

Search systems : Design of digital library assumes that there would be many indexes and categories which can be searched to discover information before retrieving it from the repository. The indexes are independently managed and support a wide range of protocol.

The information architecture is based on three simple concepts, data types, structural metadata and meta-objects.

A data type describes the technical properties of data such us format or method of processing. Structured metadata is the metadata that describes types, versions, relationships and other characteristics of digital material. A Meta object is an object that provides references to set of digital objects. Meta-objects is the list of handles or other digital objects.

Each item of data has all associated data types. Type specifies that the data has a certain format i.e. data is in the JPEG, which should be processed in a specific way and with specific organisation i.e. Section of text has been marked up with SGML tags.

Handles are given to individual items of intellectual property. Meta objects are used to aggregate digital objects. Handles are used to identify items listed in meta objects.

3.8.4. Content Management in Digital Library

Digital Libraries have emerged for handling of management of digital document collection. Handling process starts from acquisition to storing to searching to delivering required documents to users. The document collection includes multimedia objects like text, audio, video and animations. Thus it requires new methods with all aspects of multimedia data management. Digital libraries need to use all modern network and server technologies with a view to provide services of better quality.

When we try to establish digital library through any available software like Dspace or Greenstone we hardly need to do anything specially to manage the contents of digital collection as the software itself takes care of every aspect of content management. At the initial stage of digital library development when readymade softwares were not available everything was done to achieve to make digital library technology functional. However, it is worthwhile to look into the process which gives us opportunity to visualize the process of content management as it happens in digital library software set up. While discussing this author refers a pilot DL Project which was in development in 1998 in Poland by Polish National Broadband Network POL - 34. The content management foundation was used with the available software resources. The architecture of the content management system was like as follows (Fig. 3.3) which was in the following flow diagram.

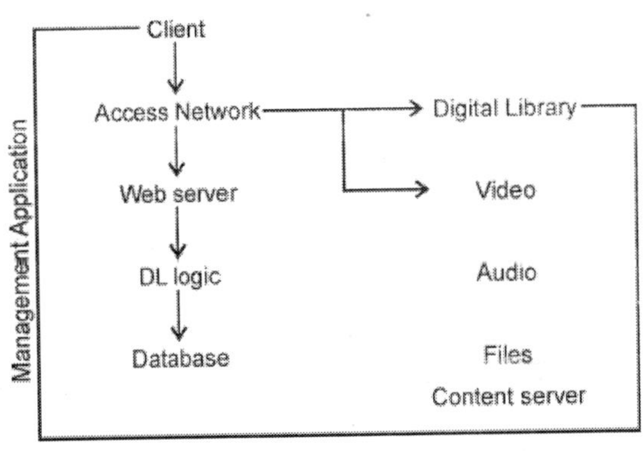

Fig. 3.3. Digital Library Flow Diagram Courtesy Polish Broadband Network Project

The DL uses inter-component communication network to connect its components. These components are places on a different host. The communication among all the components is based on the standard or proprietary protocols. The main components of the systems are :

1. Metadata management application (DL logic)
2. Content servers for storing and serving multimedia objects.

3. Web server to present digital library contents
4. GUI management application for content load and management

The important and main components of the system would be the Oracle database which stores all metadata. It describes the library content and user privileges. DL logic was hosted using server stored procedures written in PL/ SQL. The DL logic here means rules imposed on the library and documents structure, user privileges and searching capabilities. The procedures are the interface used for the components accessing metadata.

In order to store multimedia objects different types of server specific to the type of objects are used such as :

- Oracle video server for storing digital video objects.
- Progressive networks Real Audio server for storing audio objects.
- Oracle web application server for sorting all other files based on the objects.

Among these the last one is an application for presentation and searching of library documents through web interface which is written in PL / SQL. Based on metadata stored in database forms are generated for searching contents as well as web pages presenting library contents. A graphical three dimensional interface using VRML facilities could be developed which allows simple and fast browsing through library structures and contents.

The main components of DL installation are GUI application which supports user with functional interface to library contents, which is written in Java language with graphical features. This component supports only the content load and management. The application uses system access control rules, and handled in the database which allows restricted access by a particular users to their respective library bunch or group of documents. This allows for distributed content management where each user interested in publication can be granted his / her own branch of library for which the contents he / she is responsible. This application allows the accessing and loading for new documents. The document can be viewed by putting together objects of different types (text, image, video or audio) and by defining the structure of the documents manually dividing them in to chapters and pages containing selected objects. The objects are described by simple metadata such as author, title and key words. With the above search definition the documents are displayed by using HTML editor which is stored on a local disc. After pointing its localization, document is analysed by the application. All objects included in the document are described by metadata and sent to content servers and data badges are fixed in such a way that they point to new physical location of used objects. The document is then presented using its own HTML, the application user SQL net protocol and JDBC driver for communication with database. However, the contents have to be placed on different servers depending on the type of document. In case of the Real audio server and the web application standard FTP protocol is used to transfer the contents on to them but video server requires an agent to copy video files to real-time system and tag them.

In spite of all the above capabilities, content management development as a result of ongoing research, there are challenges before the designers like how to allow sharing of contents of digital libraries and bring more quality in functioning of digital libraries, which requires further capabilities as :

- Distributed library and inter-compatibility.
- Quality of service - new way of presentation of multimedia objects as per user needs.
- Performance and resource management
- Access control

Considering the above innovations and future requirements some suggestions have come forward as :

- Component based system design for allowing more flexibility in extending Library functionality by simple additions of new components.
- Using CORBA middleware for internal component and external communication and IDL for component interface definition
- Using RDF standard as consistent way of storing exchanging and organising library and documents metadata.
- Use of L - DAP based directory services as a central place for user authentication for easier integration with other IT systems
- Using model describing particular content server's performance and agents monitoring and reporting servers load for performance management and admission control.

3.8.5. Handling Copyright of Materials

In the first step we have discussed the conversion of existing printed material for incorporation it in digital library. As far as copy right is concerned there could be different types of materials such as:

1. Materials of which copy right has already be exhausted.
2. Material of which copyright still exists

In the first case there would not be any problem in converting and adding such material to digital library. Moreover, converting such material is done purely for preservation so it is a good act where as in the later case we need to search for the individuals or the institutions who have the copy right and one must negotiate to settle it either paying compensation or by seeking due permission for conversion and adding them in to digital library. Without doing this step it would be violation of copy right.

While developing digital library one can own the material which is already in electronic format and add it in digital library. It is comparatively easy, only while submitting description metadata is to be created.

Considering electronic material available on internet for adding it to digital library is not wrong. However, before doing it one should seek necessary permission to do so and by acknowledging appropriately, such material need to be edited and necessary metadata needs to be created. Providing web address of such material is always worthwhile.

In repository type of digital library normally while submitting documents the respective author fills the metadata and at the same time he / she voluntarily provide his copy right to the digital library, then there would not be any question of claiming or violating the copyright.

3.8.6. Bibliographic Control in Digital Library

We see in traditional library system there would be catalogue for searching the material by the users for the required material. In doing so the searcher gets details such as: Title, author, editor, edition, imprint and the location code e.g. call no. These details are enough for the reader to locate the book or other literature available on search. Computerised library catalogue provides easy and quite comprehensive facilities for searching the materials. There would also be advance search facilities in library OPAC. However, details give only the description of material and not the actual material. In contrast, in digital library bibliographic details and actual material both stored at the same place. Thus it is more comprehensive than traditional library search. Secondly, since the entire material is available in a fully digitized form each page or word is searchable in digital library, which is not possible in case of traditional library search. Not only this, all types of material available could be searched with a single search action i.e. a book, PPT or a paper. In digital Library there is linking in documents having some common relation. Digital Library provides various ways of searching materials such as:

- By Bibliographic details author title.
- By metadata fields
- Handle address or by
- Keyword search or search by a word.

Since normally if the author is submitting his material then he creates metadata of his own document which is certainly elaborated and comprehensive.

3.8.7. Search Medium in Digital Library

We have seen that as compared to tradition library, digital library has many ways to search the digital collection. Great advantage is that reader need not have to go to digital library; moreover digital library goes to the reader. Most of digital libraries are accessible on internet and reader can access it from where ever they are, provided they have a right to access it. In digital library special and advanced technology or protocol is used for search facility e.g. CORBA- Common Object Request Broker Architecture Protocol.

Although the digital libraries are available through internet where only authorized users are allowed to access the material through registration or authorization which ensures necessary protection to digital contents of digital library.

In digital library readers are provided another useful facility e.g. digital watermarking as it is available while reading an e - books.

There is a great advantage for libraries to exchange bibliographic data online by way of another protocol e.g. Z39.50 which facilitates downloading entries of digital material by matching for the required documents.

Digital Libraries are accessible on the intranet or internet as per policy of the digital library. The new concept of networking digital libraries is also emerging however; we need to wait to see this advancement.

3.9. BUILDING DIGITAL LIBRARY

3.9.1. Digital Library with Greenstone Software

3.9.1.1 About Greenstone

Greenstone is a pack of software used for building and distributing digital library collection. Basically it is not a digital library but a structured set of tools for building digital library. Greenstone provides a special setup to develop digital library with dynamic nature. It is an innovative way of organising digital documents and publishing them on the internet in the form of fully searchable metadata driven digital Library. The greenstone software has been developed with the support of UNESCO and Human Info NGO in Belgium. It is on open source type software having capacity to handle multilingual digital collection. It is issued under the terms of GNL General Public License. It is downloaded from their website http://www.greenstone.org

3.9.1.1.1. Technical Features

Greenstone platform runs on all versions of windows and UNIX / LINUX or Mac OS - X platforms. With widows platform it does not need any configuration being a default facility and one can routinely install it even on personals laptops or workstations where as institution can run it on their main web server and for this they can use standard web server i.e. Apache.

3.9.1.1.2. Interoperability

Greenstone software is highly interoperable with existing available standards. It can interoperate with servers which can serve any collection over the Open Archives Initiative Protocol for Metadata Harvesting (OAI - PMH) and Greenstone can harvest documents over OAI - PMH and can include them in its collection. And also any collection can be exported from it to METS and Greenstone can ingest documents in MET form. It can export collection to D - Space Software based digital library or exporting collection from Dspace to greenstone is also allowed.

3.9.1.1.3. Interfaces

Greenstone has two interactive interfaces i.e. interface for readers and interface for librarian. End users access collection of digital library through reader's interface which operates on normal web browsers. Librarians interface however operates on Java based graphical interface which makes it easy to gather materials for a collection/ downloading it from web /network source to enrich it.

3.9.1.2. Downloading and installation of GSDL Software

GSDL Software can be downloaded from the site:http://www.greenstone.org Then we required java 2 runtime environments which can be downloaded from http:// filehippo.com.

We also require:Image magic available from http://www.imagemagic.org and Ghost script which is available from http://www.cs.wise.edu/Àghost All above things are to be downloaded first and then installed appropriately.

Installation : One needs to have java 2 run time environments first to install GSDL. Then with it one can install GSDL. The latest version (Currently Greenstone 3 is available as 3.08) There are respective versions available for windows, Linux /GNU and Mac OS. One can also choose local mode of installation. Further once needs to install image Magic and Ghost Script softwares which are required for building image collection and to advanced conversion to PDF and post script documents respectively. One can further choose default option available from installation wizard.

3.9.1.3. Building up collection

Building GSDL collection is done through using librarian's interface which allows one to collect documents, assign metadata and build the documents into digital library set up. For doing this following steps are required.

1. Gather Documents
2. Enrich documents by adding metadata
3. Design collection for its appearance and access
4. Format the interface of the digital library
5. Create the collection or convert it in to CD - ROM

Start with New Collection : First one can collect basic collection in digital library and further add new collection path as start

Start → Programs → Greenstone

Greenstone librarian interface involve new collection link from file menu. Fill the name of collection by giving a title and its brief description about contents in respective column in pop up window. Choose new collection from the base/ dialog box and click O.K..

Document formats : For textual documents plugins are used to ingest them such as :

PDF, Postscript, world, RFF, HTML, Plain Tex, Latex, Zip Archives, Excel, PPT, E-mail version source code, Media wikis.Whereas for multimedia documents following plug ins are available :

Images (any formats including GIF, JIF, JPEG, TIFF) MP3 Audio 099 Vorbis

After having known important features of greenstone software in a short way now let us go step by step in developing collection in Greenstone digital library (GISDL) and also to develop search indexes and browsing classifier.

GSDL - Steps for building collection : The main objective here is to collect or download digital documents, organized them into a suitable collections and make the collection accessible to end users. We would go through steps of building digital library in windows operating systems. By adding respective metadata, designing for readers interface and publishing gathered collection over intranet/ internet.

Collection Building : For collection building and designing normally one need to interact with librarian's interface which is hosted on the same computer. Collection can easily be copied or shared among different greenstone installations. It is possible to provide right to authenticated user to manage collection from remote server. One can choose an applet version of librarians interface available on greenstone platform.

3.9.1.4. Metadata formats

User can predefine metadata formats within the librarian's interface metadata interface. Following metadata formats are preferred :

- Dublin Core (Qualified & unqualified)
- RFC - 1807
- NZGLS (New Zealand)
- AGLS (Australia.)

However with Greenstones metadata set editor new metadata sets can be defined. Plug-ins are used to ingest externally prepared metadata in various formats. Plug-ins are available for: XML, MARC, CDS- ISIS, Prosite, Bib-Tex, Refer, OA, DSpace, MET etc.

3.9.1.5. Gather the Documents

Once gathered panel becomes active one can go further to gather required documents from computer storage by browsing folders to drag the required documents in right hand pan or copy paste it individually or sets of documents available in the folders. Software would direct you to choose the required plug-in if not included by clicking add plug-in button.

3.9.1.6. Enriching Documents with Metadata

In the following step one could enrich those documents by adding their metadata. Individual documents are selected and respective metadata such as title author ,subject are filled. For doing this there is "Enrich" button which brings panel to do the things. Left side there would be collection of document/ files. One by one file could be clicked and respective metadata could be enriched.Since Dublin core metadata software is used in greenstone with each metadata filed you would find DC word prefixed. Such as title, creator, subject Key word, publishers, contributors, date, language etc.

3.9.1.7 Designing collection and Documents plug-ins

Designing the collection : For designing collection one has to use design menu. It consists of many facets which are shown at left of screen

Noting Document plug-ins : Depending on format of document, respective plug-ins are need to be recorded for converting it into greenstone archive format. Names of all plug-ins are listed there and exactly respective need to be picked up.

3.9.1.8 Creating search index

Next step is to assigning plug - ins i.e. creating search index. Idea is to note fields or metadata which are expected to be considered for searching and browsing for the documents. So choose the respective Meta fields. Here content text is made as default selection, which is not to be changed as the entire digital contents is considered for searching. In creating search index previous index is to be removed and new search index in created by clicking button "Add index". Browsing classifiers for collection is generally done by choosing required metadata fields such as title, creator, or subject key words. The System provides browsing classifier as per metadata field names such as DC–Title, DC – Creator. Instead of them one can create browsing classifies as it would be convenient for the browsers. This action has two steps i.e. 1 .to remove already existing browsing classifiers for respective title and 2. assigning new browsing classifiers. These actions can be completed by clicking respective add button or menu links.

Setting page display format & build collection : This is the step to choose a general appearance of front page of digital library or insert relevant picture on the screen or icon. They could be selected from a pixel list available in the system itself. It is not a mandatory step but choosing picture for digital library gives better look and feel. One can also skip this step and can go to next major step i.e. Build the collection.

Build the collection : After successfully completing all the above preparatory steps one can lead to the next major step i.e. "Build the collection". This is done by going to create panel wherein build the collection is located, so one can click it.

After completing the process of building the collection, the very next step is to see the preview of page design to cross check the actions considered and the actual outcome of them. At this stage one can see the front page of digital library with a button "select the collection" with clicking on it the page facilitates searching collection by (i.e. provided by default)

- Search Index or by
- Choosing required browsing classifier

3.9.1.9. Converting Digital library to a CD - Rom e.g. offline mode

This is done by choosing a button on left side in the file Edit menu named : "write CD / DVD image". This facilitates wider distribution of digital library among the users. One can give a name to CD converted digital library, once the data is exported to DVD the action to be completed by clicking close button.

3.9.2. Building Digital Library with DSpace Software

3.9.2.1. A Brief about Dspace

Dspace is an open source software used to build digital libraries. It is a static kind of software as compared to dynamic one i.e. greenstone software. Dspace is a joint project of MIT Libraries and HP laboratories. It is a digital asset management system which allows institutions or their libraries for collecting, archiving, indexing and disseminating the scholarly or intellectual content among the community. In designing Dspace is combinations of technologies used, which is primarily used to collect bibliographic information for describing articles, papers, theses and dissertations. Dspace is conveniently adaptable to different community needs. Dspace supports in the operability between systems and it adheres to informational standards for metadata formats. Since it is open source type software Dspace can be customized to the extent of its capabilities. The main characteristics of Dspace documentation are as follows:

(i) In is service model for open access and for digital archiving for perennial access

(ii) It provides platform to build an Institutional Repository and thus collection build is retrievable on the web.

(iii) Dspace helps to make available institutional based scholarly materials in digital format. Such collection would be open and interoperable.

(iv) It helps to preserve literature in digital form for the years together.

3.9.2.1.1. Functional Features

Dspace has been designed to operate as a centralized institutional digital library service. Its function involves participation of different communities within the institution such as departments, labs, centers or schools, which would have their own separate areas within the system. Members of these communities deposit their digital contents directly via a web user interface designed to make this possible in a simple way. Alternatively a batch mode importing or bulk mode loading the contents is also available.

For each community one could also appoint as reviewer, who reviews and edits the submissions, if necessary before its inclusion in the digital repository or one may reject it by giving valid reasons. Dspace system indexes the metadata submitted along with documents as per access privileges planned while designing system. The functionalities of Dspace digital library are listed as:

(i) Data modes for basic organisation are defined.

(ii) Metadata of different types stored by the system

(ii) System stores information about uses having different level rights.

(iv) Providing full public access is not possible or it is risky hence systems different levels of authorization function are included in the system.

(v) System should allow accepting incoming materials

(vi) Work flow as per community needs is spelled out

(vii) Handle system is used to assign globally unique persistent identifies for archiving objects (items)

(ix) In order to give wide & free access to contents metadata of contents is wide open archives exported. Initiative protocol for Metadata harvesting (OAI -PMH)

(x) Facility RSS Feeds or alerts for inclusion of new materials should be provided in user's interest.

3.9.2.1.2. Data model

Dspace bound digital library organisation works on the following data model (Fig. 3.3).

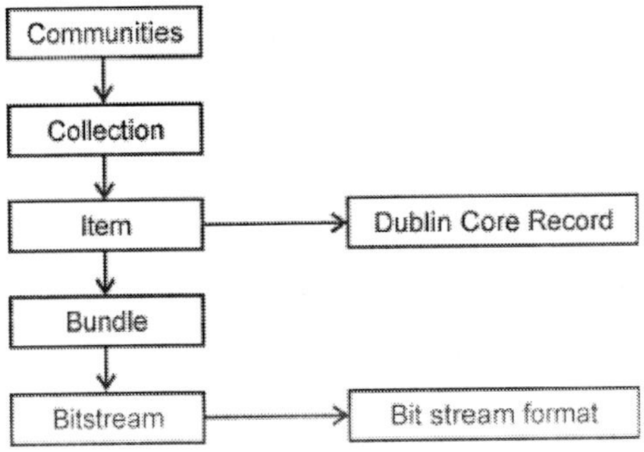

Fig. 3.3

Communities can contain sub communities. Collection can contain items and item contains metadata and bit-streams. Examples

Communities : College of Engineering,

Community : Department/ faculty

Collection : ETDs,Conference papers, PPTs etc.

The data in Dsplace is organised in such a way that each Dspaces site is divided into communities. They typically correspond to a laboratory, research centre or a department. Communities contain sub communities. Communities contain collection which is groups related contents. Each collection is composed of items which are basic archival elements of archive. Items are further subdivided in bundles of bit streams. They are simple or bits usually in the form of ordinary computer files. Bit-streams are somehow closely related and organised into bundles, for example HTML Files and images that composed in a single HTML documents. Let us tabulate these concepts as follows :

Object Type	Examples
Communities	Dept. of computer Sc. Nanotechnology Research Centre
Collection	Computer programs Nano Research report
Item	A program A Research Report
Bundle	A group of HTML docs. and images bitstreams making up an HTML document
Bitstreams	Single HTML files a single image file or a source code file
Bit-Stream format	Microsoft word version6.0 JPEG encoded format

Bitstream format has special significance in Dspace. Each bitstream is associated with one bitstream format as digital document preservation services are an important aspect of Dspace. For every bitstream its specific format of the file is captured from the user who submits the documents. In Bitstream format data is very important as it helps in invoking the file in future whenever user need to refer the same.

3.9.2.2. Metadata Types in Dspace

Metadata is a very important aspect in digital library. It plays multiple roles in using digital collection right from accessing contents to preserving them. Dspace holds three types of metadata i.e. descriptive, administrative and structural metadata.

1. Descriptive Metadata : Each item has one qualified Dublin core metadata record. Institution can easily change this. Dspace maintains a registry of elements and qualifiers. Similarly other type of metadata i.e. MARC records could also be held in serialized bitstream. Communities and collection have simple descriptive metadata held in DBMS.

2. Administrative Metadata : This includes preservation metadata provenance and authorization policy data which is held in Dspace's relational DBMS scheme. Provenance metadata is stored in Dublin Core records. Additionally some other metadata like bit-stream, byte size and MIME is replicated in Dublin Core records so that the data is easily accessible outside Dspace.

3. Structural Metadata : This includes information about how to present an item or bitstream within an item to the end user such as maintaining textual data with relevant images within the document.

4. Data About System Users : In Dspace document discovery and retrieval are used anonymously. However, System users expected strictly to be authenticated to perform various functions such as document submission for getting e - mail notification or for doing administrative tasks. System users are grouped according to task they perform.

Dspace preserves data about each user such as :

- E - mail address
- First Last names
- Authentication details such as Login and P.W.
- Information about user notification of alerts
- Information about whether user is self registered or institutional admin has registered the user.

Users are given various authorizations depending on their right to use the system as :

Read : Searching or browsing by using associated metadata

Write : Right to only modify the metadata with an object and not to delete the same

ADD : Action of adding an object item to collection. For submitting an item user to have add permission

Remove : Rights to remove object from collection

Workflow : Rights to participate in system work flow actions associated with collection including right to reject the submission.

3.9.2.3. Work flow in Dspace

While installing the Dspace the nature of workflow is set as policy of institutional repository as defined and work flow process is started. So there could be one or more human reviewers to check and review the submission. There could also be approvers. There would be authors or writers to submit the documents and finally there would be system admin who upload or merge the documents into the repository collection. The work how once defined is applicable to each and every submission. The admin creates communities, sub-communities and collections and the system is thrown open to public.

In an actual work flow process as documents are submitted, reviewer gets e - mail communication and document is passed further for approver if the status is accepted else if the document is to be rejected then marked to admin person who them communication according. Communication about all accepted and approved documents is sent to admin. In case there are no reviewer/approver then those steps are skipped and thus all the submitted objects are merged with the repository through admitting them directly without any check. Once all the reviewer approver steps are crossed successfully by the submission then administration left with following actions. (Chart No. 3.2)

Work flow step	Actions
1	To accept submission for inclusion or reject submission
2	To edit metadata of submission as fed by user but cannot change the document can accept or reject
3	To edit the metadata of the submission then merge documents to archive but may not reject it

Chart 3.2. Dspace work flow Actions

3.9.2.4. Handles

Every writer or researcher require a factual point of reference to their submission to facilitate them quote in their list of articles. This point of reference is called handle. Such web address needs to be permanent on internet. The Dspace creates persistent identifier for even item as far as item is merged to repository along with their community and collection details. Dspace uses CNRI handle system to create identifiers or handles which is communicated to writer built in work flow process. It is the responsibility to maintain handle details once assigned and communicated to users.

Example :

hdl:1721.123/4567 or

http:// hdl.handle.net/1721.123/4567

3.9.2.5. Search and Browsing facility

One can search the digital content in Dspace DL in a number of ways:

1. Via external reference i.e. handle
2. By searching one or more key words
3. By searching through metadata created search links/ indexes

Web User interface : In Dspace system user interface is built on Java servlet and java server page technology. It allows end users to access Dspace via their web browser. User interface consists of:

- On line help
- Community and collection home pages, recent arrivals in the collection as well as subscribing and depositing controls.
- Searching and browsing menus.
- Item pages with basic metadata associated. Full Dublin Core and bitstreams contained in an item could be accessed from this page
- Admin section consisting of pages intended for use by the administrator.

3.9.2.6. Dspace system Architecture

In Dspace architecture the main code of Dspace is implemented in Java and run on any UNIX like systems such as Linux or HP UX.Several third party open source systems are also used like:

- Post grey - SQL - It is an open source relational database systems
- Jakarta tomcat Java servlet container
- Apache HTTP Server for optional SSL and X 509 certificate support
- The main Dspace system is organised into three levels and each of them consist number of sub levels as shown in the following chart

Dspace levels sub levels

Level - 1

Application Layer
- CNRI handle Server (Plug – in)
- Web UI
- OAI - Metadata providing service
- Batch item importer
- Item Exporter

Level - 2

Business Logic Layer Dspace Public (AP)
- Search, Browse APl, Handle manager, History Recorder
- History Recorder, content management, APl, Work flow manager
- E - person / Group, Manager, administrative tool kit, Authentication

Level - 3

Storage layer		
Storage APl	-	RDBMS Wrapper
		Bitstream storage manager
JOBL	-	Postgre SQL

3.9.2.7. Steps for Downloading and Installing Dspace

1. Preparations for Dspace installation : software requirements

- Java SDK
- Apache Ant
- Apache Tomcat
- Postgre SQL
- Dspace

2. System Requirements

It needs computer running on 32 or 64 bit Windows :

How to check this : Open system by clicking

Windows Vista Windows

Start → Control panel → system and maintenance here you can see the system type

For windows XP

Click : Start → Run → General Tab

System details are displayed as

for 64 bits : windows XP professional X 64 edu

Version (year) appear under system

for 32 bit : Version Operating system Windows XP professional Version (year) Appear under system

3. Installing steps : Prior to installation make sure that the following softwares have been downloaded and saved. You need to install then prerequisite software for Dspace 1.5 x and higher, check the window installation section. It the section i.e. the system documentation for the most recent prerequisites, as they sometimes differ based on the versions of Dsapce you are going to run :

- Java SDK V1.5+ (or latest) formant to work properly one should ensure that Java-Home is set.
- Postgre SQL 8.X for windows. It comes with a window installer app. one should make sure that ODBC + JDBC options are selected as well as the admin III tool.
- Apache Maven 2.0.8 + Unzip it whenever you want to install it and (path to apache maven) \bin to your system path

- Apache Ant 1.7.X just unzip when to install and add path (Path – to – Apacheant)\bin to your system path
- Jakarta Tomcat 5.X+ this come with windows installer app and it is easy to do.

General Installation Steps

- First get the Dspace software by downloading online from the source forge and save it somewhere (winzip would do this) or can grab a SVN checkout.
- Next ensure that postgre service is running and then run PG Admin III (Start) Postgrey → SQL 8.x → PG Admin III → then connect to local database as the postgre user and create a "login Role" (User) Called Dspace with the password "dspace" One can however set own login details as:
- Create database called dsapce owned by the user dspace with UTF - 8 encoding
- Then update path in (dspace source)\dspace \config \dspace.cfg Use format flasher / for path separator or one can use drive letters i.e. Dir = C: / Dspace
- Create the directory for the Dspace installation e.g. C:// dspace .Build Dspace in normal fashion from (Dspace source) dspace run: mvn package
- Then install Dsapce to your specific location. From (Dsapce Source) / dspace target\ dspace\ version dir run:ant fresh - install
- Create then an administrator account e.g. assuming c :\dspace is where your dspace installation is c:\ dspace\ bin \ dsrun org. dspace. administer. Create administrator (Then enter the required information)
- Copy the war web application files from c:\ dspace \ Webapps to tomcat's webapps dir, Which should be like c:\ program files \Apache software foundation \ Tomcat \ Web apps.
- Then start Tomcat Services
- Browser http:// local host: 8080 / Dspace

One should see the Dspace home page with the above steps. One can perform actual installation of Dspace. However one may note the following steps again for installing Dspace. Creat an empty directory in C: drive where actual configuration program files and data files of dspace world reside C: / Dspace

Extract all the contents of Dspace 3.0 - src. Release zip to one folder (eg Dspace) and copy entire folder to your c: / drive as c: / dspace - 1.7.0 src release. Zip. Once the files are unzipped go to c:/ dspace / dspace - 3.0 src release dspace / config.

Then windows Dspace.cfg and open it in notepad and change the following parameters. Use forward slashes for path separators

- Dspace. dire = c :/ Dspace
- Dspace name = Dspace Repository
- Mail server = mail. your institute. ac. in
- Mail from address = admin@piit.ac.in

- Feedback. recipient = admin@piit.ac.in
- Mail admin = admin@piit.ac.in

Note for starting tomcat service if it is not already running then follow steps as Control panel → administrative Tools → Services → Apache Tomcat 7 and click on start.

Point your browser to

http:// local host:8080/jspui

or

http:// local host:8080/xmlui

We would be thus successful in installing dspace

Next steps are for creating:

- Communities - sub Communities
- Collections - can contain items
- Items - Contains metadata and bitstream files

Steps for creating communities

1. Logic
2. Click communities of collections under browse
3. Click on create communities
4. Give community a name and add a short description
5. Upload logo files
6. Click finish

Sub communities are created under communities as they are required to follow the same steps to do this

Steps for submitting items

1. Log in
2. Chose the desire community/ sub community
3. Select submit a new item
4. Describe the item in terms of respective metadata
5. Then browse and upload the respective file (Bitstream)
6. Correct if necessary
7. Grant the license

There are mainly two types of user who use the system.

User = who would have definite role in the system

Groups = Who share the submissions

Steps to create users and groups

1. Select people (Under administrative access control)
2. Click create a new e - person
3. Add name of the new person's name with contact details (E - mail)
4. Create e - person

Groups

1. Choose group
2. Select create new group
3. Give it a name
4. Use "search members" to add e - people the new group
5. Click "add next to" to e - people you want to add to the group
6. Click to save

Work flow steps

- When there is no work flow action submitted items are straight made available directly otherwise there would be task as :
- Workflow step - 1

  Accept / Reject
- Work flow step - 2

  Accept / Reject / Edit Metadata
- Work flow step- 3

  Edit metadata

DSpace Work flow Diagram (Fig. 3.4)

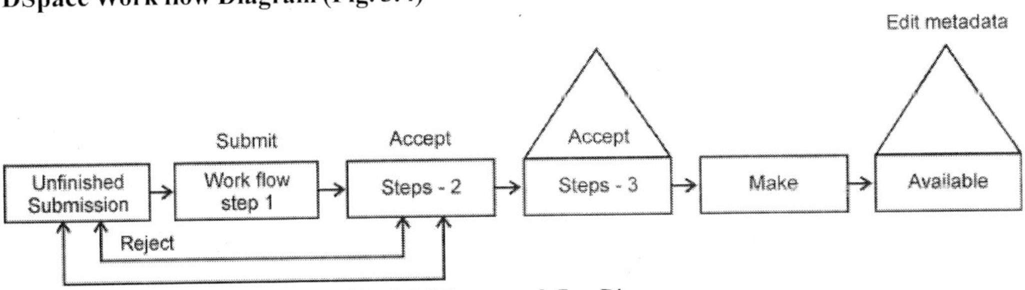

Fig. 3.4. DSpace work flow Digram

Work flow steps for collections

How to create work flow

1. First select community and collection which is to be edited
2. In the context box select, edit collection
3. Edit collection metadata

4. Choose the assign role tab
5. Assign e - people and / or groups to the role that are relevant to the collection and the work flow you have selected.

Metadata Structure

Descriptive Metadata

Qualified Dublin Core limited expansion to the other format

Submission forms

Customizable in configuration file

Editing metadata

Can be done after submission

Adding metadata

Can be done after submission

Metadata Registry

Create new metadata fields

Item Template

Assign default values

Steps for removing items

Withdraw or Delete

Withdraw

Remove item from view

Do not show in search Recoverable

Delete

Unrecoverable Handle is not reused

Can be done by a repository administrator

1. Navigate the item to be removed /deleted
2. In the context box choose link Edit this item
3. Select withdraw or select permanently delete

Finish the action.

Authorization steps

Communities click Authorizations
(Through Admin Access)
↓
Click community required
↓
Choose add a new policy

↓

Or Edit Existing policy

↓

Grant Permission to the group

↓

Choose the group

↓

Choose save

Collections

Choose collection

↓

Edit collection

↓

Choose to "Assign Role" tab

↓

Choose e - people group for whom the role is assigned

↓

Choose save

Dspace Backup

Once Dspace digital library is created and documents are added it is always advisable to have system to store the backup in order to meet the eventual situation. The action steps to take back up are as:

[Dspace - Source]

[Dsapce]/ asset store]

[Dspace] / config

- Program file / Apache software foundation / Tomcat / Web apps
- [Dspace] / history and [Dsapce] log if you want to preserve / active records
- Postgre SQL especially / Usr / Local / PgSQL / data (Or where the data dir is)

3.10. WORLD DIGITAL LIBRARIES

In this chapter we have dealt with the various aspects of development of digital library from introduction to installation. Author hopes that the readers have got a fair idea about digital library. While continuing the theme now we would try to know about various digital libraries existing all over the world and available to provide free access to global users. There are of course thousands of such libraries all over. However, we are going to know about some of them including those available in India :

World Digital Libraries

1. World Digital Library
2. Million Book Project

3. Project Gutenberg
4. E - LIS : International open Archive (E - print in library and information Science)
5. World Digital Library wikipelia.inc
6. Digitals Book Index : World Virtual Library
7. INDEST : Indian National Digital Library in Science and Technology
8. Library in Engg. Science & Technology
9. Librarians digital Library (LDL)
10. Digital Library of India : IISc (Bangalore)
11. Digital Library of India C-DAC (New Delhi)

Let us know in brief about them.

World Digital Library : It is organised jointly by Library of Congress and UNESCO. It comprises of rare books, manuscripts, maps, photographs and other important documents. It is collaborating with libraries, archives, museums, educational Institutions and international organisations around the world. Further details can be accessed at : www.wdl.org

Million Book Project : Objective of this project is to create a free to read searchable collection of one million books, primarily in the English language available to everyone over the internet. It is a huge task accomplished by scanning books and indexing their full text. It is being created with the funds from Carnegie Mellon University. Details could be accessed at their site: www.cmu.edu

Project Gutenberg : (Free e - books project) Gutenberg project offers over 50000 free e - books. One can choose among free e- pub books, free kindle books, download them or read them online. No fee or registration is required. It has mobile site also. More details at site http://www.gutenberg.org

E - LIS (E - prints in library and information science) Established in 2003 E-LIS is an international digital repository for library and information science. E - Lis is a kind of multilingual cultural e - repository. It is a key to open access of all repositories visit . www.elis.org

(World) Digital Library : Wikipedia the free encyclopedia

It is a digital Library is a special library with focused collection of digital objects that can include text, visual materials, audio, video stored in electronic media. visit the site http://en.wikipedia.org wiki.world

Digital Book Index : Digital Book Index provides links to more than 1,65,000 full text digital books from more than 1800 commercial and non commercial publishers, universities and private organisation out of which nearly 1,40,000 books, texts and documents are available free.

See the site www.digitalbookindex.org

INDEST : It is Indian National Digital Library in Engineering. Science and Technology. It is a consortium oirganised by all IITS, IIMS, and IISs Bangalore comprising of all e - resources available for the users of these elite institution. It is organised at IIT Delhi and funded by MHRD, Govt.of India

Indest Consortium : http://paniit.iitd.ac.in

Librarian's Digital Library (LDL) : This digital library is devoted to the field of library and information science organised presently known as : Open DOAR - Digital Library organised Indian Statistical Institute, Bangalore. Open DOAR is an authoritative directory of academic open access repositories

Website: www.opendoar.org

Digital Library of India : There are two digital Libraries with this name one is organised by IISc Bangalore and other is organised by C - DAC New Delhi.

International Children's Digital Library : It is a library for the world children. It is organised at University of Maryland USA website : http://en.childrenlibrary.org i.e. imparting education among students.

REFERENCE LIST AND ACKNOWLEDGEMENT

1. Brainbridge, David et al (2004): Greenstone digital library developer's guide. New Zealand Digital Library Project, New Zealand
2. Dspace Digital library software

   Kaushal Giri and Nilesh Shewale

   PPT - Part of course PG Diploma in Library Information Technology

   PIIT New Panvel.

   www.pgdilit.piit.ac.in / ppt / Dspace%20 installation.PPT
3. Installation Dspace prepared by Mark Diggory modified by Bram Luyten Dec. 15 http://wiki.duraspace. org/display/DSDOC4X/installing Dspace
4. Loots, M. et al (2001) From paper to collection. New Zealand Digital Library Projects, New Zealand.
5. Morete, Pablo and Rose, John: Creating Digital Libraries Based on CDS / ISIS Databases. (Downloaded from World Wide Web)
6. Rajsekharan K. and Nafala K. M. - Building up a digital library with greenstone: A self instructional guide for beginners.

   Library & information Div: Kerala Institute for local Administration
7. Robert Tansley, Margret Branschosky and Daniel Chudnov - Digital Repository system Dsapce institutional current functionality. Proc. of the 2003 Joint conf on Digital Library, JEES (JSDL - 03)
8. Witten, Ian H and Brainbridge, David (2003): How to build a digital library. Amsterdam, Morgan Kaufmann
9. Witten, Ian H and Boddie, Stefan (2004): Greenstone Installer's Guide. New Zealand Digital Library Project, New Zealand
10. Witten, Ian H. et all(2006) Greenstone User's Guide. New Zealand Digital Library project, New Zealand.

4

Metadata

4.0. INTRODUCTION

So far we have conceptually understood the information technology and its constituent parts and also understood about the application of information technology in various needs. While doing so we have touched upon several aspects of IT like database development, preservation and search facilities step by step. Subsequently we got an idea about database management systems (DBMS) and in the next step we tried about the quality aspects of database creation and about its standardisation. Although we have considered most of the new concepts in the information technology we still find newer and newer concepts keep on emerging due to the speedy progress in the field. In this chapter we are going to know about one such newly emerging field i.e. about Metadata and its new product called Dublin Core Metadata systems.

Metadata concept is closely related with digital library development as digital library technology has emphasized creation of metadata of its collection; hence it has gained much significance these days. First of all let us have the introduction to metadata.

4.1. WHAT IS METADATA?

In simple term metadata is defined as "Data About Data". However, these words fail to give us more details about it. Like definition of internet it is not so simple to understand. Out of these definitions we get some idea that it is a new category to explain the data. If we try to go into more details we find that it could be about data sets or it could be a thing or description of resource. If we still pursue its meaning further we find the information about how data was created, who created it, where it was created and what was its format? All these details tell us about in detailed description of metadata. Many a times we feel that metadata tells us that it is a factual / physical status of data or data about digital collection.

Metadata is created both, manually as well as through metadata programme tools. The basic concept of metadata is not so new to us but description about its format and its technical structure is certainly new to us. When we handle any information its data structure is always considered, for example when we think of catalogue data created for books etc., it is also one type of metadata and we call it as bibliographic data. It is used to create database of library collection. The same data is used in collection organisation and also used as collection searching tool. These days when we create metadata in digital environment we need to describe its format or about its mark up additionally and try to record them in metadata structure. The main reason behind this is because the information technology is constantly progressing. Computer technology which is a part of it is also going through innovation and it is the main tool used for preserving the documents and its data. The metadata therefore is mainly concerned with the fact that the data we are creating today, should be able to use it after a gap of time. Even if technology changes in the course of time we should be able to use it without any difficulty. The metadata considers the provisions made today in order to preserve digital data for ever. Once we broadly understand the concept of metadata we can look into further clarification as: we can describe digital document or data in three different ways e.g. definition, structure and administration. When we try to describe electronic document we try to enhance the quality of data. We may take example of a web page. While describing metadata of web page we need to consider in which web language it is written, which tools were used for its creation and where to go to know additional things about the web page. Describing data in this way we simplify specify things which would be useful to use the data. Additionally it takes care of overcoming difficulties faced in using the data after a long time perhaps when technology is completely changed. The recording of additional data attributes certainly help us under such situations.

4.1.1. Definition of Metadata

If the metadata term is to be defined it would be as - Metadata means presenting additional information sets about the data which were not recorded up till now i.e.

1. Information tools used to create data / document
2. Purpose of document
3. Date of data creation
4. Name of author/ creator
5. Location of document available on net
6. Data standard used

Another definition of metadata as per techterm.com is as:

Metadata describes other data. It provides certain information about item's content for example an image may include metadata that describes how large the picture is, the colour depth, image resolution the time when the image was created and data about tools used to create it.

Metadata means about data although Meta prefix means beyond or after it is used to mean about in epistemology.

Considering about the information sets it could be further explained by another example. In describing metadata of text document one can consider additional data/ information as length of documents (no. of words), name of the writer, date of publishing, document form and format details would be additional information about the document. Method of registering metadata has been in use quite early times. In library cataloguing class number assigned for a book as per DDC classification scheme gives additional information about the subject of a book. Secondly use of catalogue card of size 5 X 3 and presenting information sets about the book in a structured manner as per AACR - II style is also the metadata about a book which include data like title of book, author (full name), subject key word and review of a book are presented. In addition if library devices method of indicating exact location of the book on shelf and includes in catalogue entry could be additional information. Another example of metadata registration could be seen in the long form created by the US census data which was used in data mining method of identifying demographic pattern seen in the population map.

All the above examples gives historical proofs of use of metadata concept in the past as well as at present.

While looking into the historical background of metadata we find that "metadata" term was first used by an information scientist Philip Banley in 1968 and the concept was settled further. Since then use of metadata started in most of the fields e.g.in information management, information science, library science, information technology, Geographic Information Systems (GIS). In all these fields the concept of metadata has been considered as "data about data". In a discussion on metadata we frequently find terms like electronic documents, file data and objects. Out of these "object" term refers physical items like book, CD, DVD, map, digital image of artifacts available in museum, digital photo, document, programme file, database table and also entry in the computerised catalogue is considered as metadata. While registering metadata of digital photo file it is necessary to record owner's copy right details, camera detail which clicked the digital photo. In addition additional data about key word of photo contents which computer tools/ utility to be used to open and view the photo are to be recorded as metadata sets. Metadata about video film includes things such as contents of video, conversion transcripts, texts and details of scenes present in the video. In case of web pages data tags, key words are necessary in its metadata. Normally any search engine creates its index considering data tag given in web sites.

4.2. CREATING METADATA

Normally all things referred above are considered for recording in metadata. Metadata is created automatically by using designated software or each metadata is manually created by referring the document itself. As we have seen earlier metadata has more significance in digital library collection development. Normally, the author is allowed to submit his/ her digital document for inclusion in digital library. While doing so author himself/ herself records metadata about the submission manually along with bibliographic metadata. One needs to submit description of digital objects also while submitting document in digital depository.

Metadata recording in digital library development is otherwise normally done by the computer professional and details about document like when the file was created, who created it, who further revised it, size of the file, format of document (Plaintext, HTML REF, PDF, Word etc and the version) Language like VB, VB++ , C++ or Purl are automatically recorded as metadata recording.

4.2.1. Metadata structure

Metadata structure consists of two parts i.e. structural metadata and descriptive metadata. Structural metadata is about the containers and descriptive metadata uses individual instances of application data or the data content. For different types and formats of electronic document like document photo, Video, Webpage there are respective standards used to enroll the metadata. These standards favor for entering metadata of those respective formats, in which metadata standards and models, these two types of data structure are considered. For keyword registration there are various tools used such as controlled vocabularies, taxonomies or classification systems the source data dictionaries and metadata registers are used as alternatives to the standard.

4.3. METADATA TYPES

Metadata recording is concerned with data fields which have not been used up till now. In order to make provision to enter such data field there are various type of universally accepted models available. Experts have suggested the fields suitable for metadata.

For example Bretherton and Single has suggested two types 1. Structural Metadata 2. Guide Metadata. Out of which structural metadata type is meant for computer system related fields like for charts, tables or indexing lists format whereas guide metadata type is used as normal information searching tools for example key words, controlled vocabulary. Ralf Kimbol have also suggested similar types or metadata fields such as technical metadata (Internal) and business metadata (External) in addition to these also suggested on more type i.e. Process metadata.

On the other hand NISO (National Information Standard Organisation) has suggested three types for metadata e.g. Descriptive metadata 2) Structural Metadata and 3) Administrative metadata. Out of these the first descriptive metadata describes the information fields which are useful in searching the object e.g. title, author, subject, keywords and publishers etc. In structural metadata type, one can describe the format and in administrative type of Metadata fields are used to describe technical details of digital format such as the type of field, utility used to create document and the version of that utility. Administrative metadata type has further two sub types such as right management and data concerns with preservation of digital document e.g. preservation metadata. We have seen different metadata types. Now let us try to know how metadata is organised where inter relations of metadata elements are explained. Such as:

1. Hierarchical
2. Linear
3. Planner

In hierarchical scheme metadata elements are arranged one below the other i.e. parent child relationship order. In other arrangement scheme relation among metadata elements is shown as one dimensional way, in which each metadata element is treated as independent. However, in other type it could be a group of elements or core filed which are called linear arrangement. Dublin Core metadata scheme represents one dimensional data element type relation. Like this, two dimension metadata scheme is also considered.

4.4. WHAT METADATA DOES? EXPECTATION

Metadata does the task of description of information source at any level. As it described the whole source it can also describe a part of source. Example about images or figures included in a text document. As cataloguer tries to describe a compound or edited book where each chapter is catalogued independently in the same way metadata is also recorded. As IFLA has introduced the method of recording metadata for each information component while metadata recording is done. In such resources the recording of metadata of parts of document is done in resource itself or it is done separately. Generally metadata is recorded in H.T.M.L format since metadata stored along with source, hence possibility of losing it does not arise. Due to these specialised method of recording metadata source and metadata are always inter linked. In case, any revision is done changes are done in both i.e. original sources as well as in its metadata.

About metadata, it is always said that metadata is the key to ensure that resources will survive and continue to be accessible in the future. Metadata helps to present the source with its all parts. In one way it works like cataloguing, which also helps technically further in terms of

- Digital Organisation
- Digital Identification
- Inter operability
- Supporting to archiving and preservation

4.4.1. Digital Organisation

Concept of digital organisation is like, normal source in the digital form and its parts/ components are stored in a database and whenever it is required, the source and its components are presented is called digital organisation. In the present web technology age all these contents are stored in web language. Moreover, it is not necessary that they are stored at one place. Whenever needed they are brought from different locations on the web and presented. In this process metadata works like portal design and with dynamic web technology original source is linked with its parts. May be it would require some software efforts.

4.4.2. Interoperability

Metadata interoperability means with the help of metadata, information is described in such a way that various systems and computers both would understand it. Technically metadata recorded in one metadata scheme is also recognised by the other metadata schemes is called metadata interoperability. It would be possible irrespective of use of various systems, hardware or software or even different basic infrastructure is the speciality of metadata interoperability. In this diverse environment in order to understanding each other's metadata and the source makes it possible due to interoperability. So once metadata of a source is created with a particular type of metadata scheme as per metadata shared transferred protocol and cross walking rules it becomes possible to see the metadata of other schemes also. The interoperability works in two ways:

1. By searching cross systems
2. By metadata harvesting

Z39.85 Database protocol is useful in cross system search where as open archives initiative (OAI) technology is used for data harvesting for interoperability. In such cases the capability scheme needs metadata scheme of higher level. Metadata harvesting means retrieving useful data from internet resources.

4.4.3. Digital Identification

With the help of any metadata scheme it is possible to reach the original resource through metadata elements and their linkages on the net. This has been the main task of metadata. In the metadata environment the source is assigned a specific unique standard number so that it becomes easy to search the resource from the collection. Systems like Digital Object Identifier (DOI) or Persistent Universal locator (PURL) are used. Sometime location of original source on web gets changed and with PURL technology it is possible to locate it accurately. System can apply one or more identification numbers.

4.4.4. Archiving and Preservation

As information technology is speedily progressing and the technology available to handle digital collection is coming with newer forms, the digitized status of source might get changed. This has invariably happened in the past. Metadata has provided solution to this problem. With changed information technology it is possible to preserve old digital resource and make it possible to use it forever was main reason behind evolving different metadata schemes. It may so happen that today's created digital data gets useless after a course of time. Digital data is always fragile and it is likely that it might get damaged or become unserviceable. Even if there is a small change in the hardware it might become difficult to read the old digital documents. To overcome this problem was really challenging. With format migration technique and advanced hardware technology makes it feasible to meet the challenge.

In the process of archiving and preservation it becomes necessary to find the facts about from which environment the document is coming and in which environment it is to be sent or used. Suppose a document in PDF format was created, when we wish to use it in a new environment then it becomes important to know the version of PDF at the time of creation and which PDF version is currently in use. When we try to use document of old version we need to see how it reacts with a new version or hardware. It is necessary to seek the response by making some change in it. To overcome difficulties in reading old digital document in an upgraded environment archiving and preservation becomes necessary.

Most of the Metadata systems have associated with management of archiving and preservation. At international level there are guidelines available for such management. For example National Library of Australia, British Cedars project (CURL examples in Digital archives), Joint working group of OCLC, Research Library Group (RLG), PREMI (Preservation Metadata Implementation Strategies) designed by RLG where in OCLC and RLG have jointly provided guidance for metadata systems for preparing metadata sets, decoding data, storing, archiving and management of the same.

4.5. METADATA STRUCTURING

It is the prime objective of every metadata scheme to describe the source in terms of metadata elements. Each metadata element of the scheme is adequately defined, which is called semantics of the metadata scheme. In computer technology point of view, each metadata element has a designated data value which tells the information stored in that element. Most of the metadata elements specify their metadata elements and their values. In addition, the style of data recording in those elements is also spelled out. Examples : Main and subtitle, names first and next authors, capitalization preferences, word order or controlled vocabulary, dictionary, guidelines for content or syntax and rules for data entry in each data elements.

Most of the metadata schemes use mark-up languages like SGML, XML which are advanced version of HTML. With use of S.G.M.L language decoding information from metadata structure to convert it and fixing the specific tags becomes easy. Mark up technology is useful for encoding data and also decoding it.

4.6. METADATA SCHEMES AND THEIR DATA ELEMENT GROUPS

All the levels of advanced Information technology new processes/ Schemes have been emerged for storing and preserving digital literature. They are called metadata standards, metadata schemes or schemas. New metadata schemes are prominently discussed in LIS literature these days and they are further evolved due to research and development. Now let us try to know about them in short. Examples :

1. Dublin Core
2. Text Encoding Initiative (TEI)
3. Metadata Encoding and Transmission Standards(METS)
4. Metadata Object Description Schema (MODS)
5. Other schemes

4.6.1. Dublin Core (Concise details)

In 1995 discussion meet was jointly organised by OCLC and National Centre for Supercomputing Applications(NCSA) at Dublin City situated in Ohio. The outcome of this was framing of Dublin Core metadata elements. Since the meet was organised at Dublin it was named as Dublin Core. A long research was done on this and finally Dublin core metadata standards have emerged. Credit of this research goes to Dublin Core Metadata Initiative Institution (DCMI).

The original objective of Dublin core was to frame a data cluster so that any author can be described his work on web in terms of these metadata element. Like proliferation of printed literature now digital literature is also growing in an incremental way as such for libraries it was finding very difficult to catalogue them while including them in digital library collection. In order to overcome this difficulty Dublin core scheme carried out research in framing metadata elements structure and in preparing guidelines on using them. The scheme has presented the metadata element recording method in such a simple way that anyone without having knowledge of cataloguing is able to register them.

Initially group of 13 core elements was suggested and subsequently by adding two more elements group elements number reached 15. The Dublin core data elements are as :

1. Title	2. Creator	3. Subject	4. Description
5. Publisher	6. Contributor	7. Date	8. Type
9. Format	10. Identifier	11. Source	12. Language
13. Relation	14. Coverage	15. Rights	

Dublin Core has been widely accepted as the simple, useful and short way for describing digital source, which has been recognised as an international standard. All Dublin core data elements suggested under the scheme are optional and which are repeatable type. The scheme also suggests use of controlled vocabulary. A group of researchers is constantly working on it which presents standardised list of keywords. With a view to guide libraries a group of bibliographic experts is always available to provide consultancy. Due to simplicity of this metadata element the scheme is being used not only in libraries but outside libraries and its use is increasing day by day. for example: researchers, museum managers, musical composers etc. Several worldwide projects have chosen Dublin core metadata scheme to register metadata and describe web related sources. Out of which nearly 50 projects are linked to DCMI website. The use of Dublin core scheme covers wide range of fields from cultural heritage to mathematics and physical sciences.

4.6.2. Text Encoding Initiative (TEI)

Text Encoding Initiative(TEI) is an international (project) scheme to record metadata of literature available in electronic form. The scheme is useful to record metadata of literary forms like novels, poetry, etc. It is also useful for research in humanities and social science fields. In this metadata scheme there is a provision to record detail of literary work in it's built-in headers. It is done by using document type definition tag available in SGML mark-up feature. Along with DTD(Document Type Definition) feature TEI has been known as comprehensive metadata scheme. Sometime it could be complicated to understand but there is concise edition known as TEI - Lite is available for easy use.

It is assumed that the text recorded by TEI scheme is electronic version matches with printed text form. Due to the built in headers facility of TEI are invariably used in bibliographic data wherein electronic version of text can be linked with its printed version. Normally bibliographic details are similar to library catalogue which is linked with data elements in MARC form and further linked with MARC tags. In case if the library has full text documents framed in SGML then TEI can be used in cataloguing of digital sources. In some libraries there is a facility in cataloguing that one can reach MARC record via TEI or it could be reached to TEI via MARC records.

4.6.3. Metadata Encoding and Transmission Standard (METS)

In order to record metadata to describe digital objects which are complicated to describe metadata encoding and transmission, then standard scheme is used viz METS. It is a XML category of metadata scheme. In this scheme it is feasible to record descriptive and administrative data of digital resources plus it makes it feasible to record locations of files, digital documents available outside of digital library. Out of these structural types of data, recording is useful in management of pages of e - book and their order.

Digital Library Federation in its initial stage had recommended use of METS for recording administrative and structural data for describing digital literary works. METS metadata scheme consists the following seven divisions such as:

- METS header
- Description metadata for linking MARC like external structures
- File section
- Structural Map
- Structural Links
- Behavioural metadata etc.

4.6.4. Metadata Object Description Schema (MODS)

The MODS is another type metadata recording scheme. In this scheme for descriptive metadata recording selected tags of MARC - 21 structure has been used which is based on SGML language. In this scheme instead of numerical tags language based tags are used. A MODS has its unique existence in metadata schemes. MODS can collaborate with the structure of similar metadata scheme like Z39.85.

4.6.5. Other metadata schemes

In addition to the above described major metadata schemes there are several schemes used to record metadata elements of digital objects like :

- Encoded Archival Description (EAI)
- Learning object Metadata (LDM) IEEE 1484.12.1 2001 standard
- E - commerce indices and Onix
- Visual objects - CDWA and VRA
- MPEG - Multimedia metadata
- Metadata for Datasets etc.

4.7. DUBLIN CORE METADATA SCHEME (ELABORATED DETAILS)

We have understood in short about Dublin core in the previous para (No.4.6.1). Now we are going to have the detailed information about it in this section.

Textual Documents or document with comprehensive multimedia form can be described in terms of Dublin core metadata in a simple way. By which e-books, digital literature and objects e.g. video and audio clipping, images, textual document as well as documents in multimedia, or web form can be catalogued and their metadata could be registered in this scheme. The documents once described by Dublin Core metadata scheme it becomes easy to search and use the digital resources as Dublin Core has been recognised as an international standard to handle digital collection very efficiently. Many libraries and computer centers have therefore, adopted the scheme to record metadata. Dublin core scheme is based on resource description frame work which fits in XML category. International standard has published as ISO- 15836 where as NISO has revised its standard in 2007 as Z39.85

Dublin core scheme was initiated in 1995 at Dublin in Ohio district during discussion meeting held in Dublin city. In 2008 OCLC established Dublin core metadata initiative (DCMI) Organisation. Under this group a task force group is actively working with objective to bring awareness. It has been now widely received as a result organising user group conference workshops and by arranging several training programmes for the users.

4.7.1. Types of Dublin core metadata Scheme

Dublin core metadata scheme is available at two levels as :

1. Simple Dublin Core
2. Qualified Dublin Core

Let us try to know about these two levels

4.7.1.1. Simple Dublin core

Simple Dublin core contain 15 metadata elements such as :

1. Title
2. Creator
3. Subject
4. Description
5. Publisher
6. Contributor
7. Date
8. Type
9. Format
10. Identifier
11. Source
12. Language
13. Relation
14. Coverage
15. Rights

Out of these elements except a few, others are not mandatory but are optional. They could also be used repeatedly. DCMI provides necessary guidelines as well as subject key word dictionary is also made available. One can get details and explanation about it in Dublin Core Registry.

4.7.1.2. Qualified Dublin Core

Subsequent to announcement of 15 core metadata elements in DC simple edition revisions were suggested by DCMI through their continuous research and efforts. As a result Qualified Dublin Core, higher level metadata set has been emerged. Under this revision minute micro level metadata elements were available for use. In addition 3 new core elements were also added like Audience, Provence and Rights Holders, which were not in the simple version of DC. With availability of Qualified Dublin core its utility has further increased tremendously. Now it has given much freedom in selecting required metadata elements and entering data in them in an easy manner.

Dublin Core metadata scheme is available in terms of international standards as:

ISO: 15836:2009 (Feb)

ANSI / NISO Z39-85-2007

IETF RFC 5013: 2007 (Aug)

4.7.2. Dublin core metadata elements (Chart)

Now let us know more about Dublin Core metadata Elements in the following chart no.4.1

Sr. No.	Name of Metadata label	Explanation
1	Contributor -Repeatable and Not Mandatory URL http://purl.org/dc /elements/1.1/ contributor	Individual Responsible source creation (Person, Organisation, or service or Name of contributor
2	Coverage- Repeatable & not mandatory URL http://purl.org/dc/ elements/1.1/ Coverage	Geographic &Time period Scope e.g. Location, Time, period
3	Creator- Repeatable & mandatory URL http ://Purl. org/ac/ element/1.1./creator	Individual or organisation responsible for source creation e.g. person organisation or service
4	Date- mandatory if repeatable URL http ://purl.org/dc/ elements/1.1/ date	Time Date of source creation
5	Description – Repeatable and mandatory URL : http://purl.org/ac/ elements/1.1/ description	Source Description e.g. abstract contents etc
6	Format: Repeatable and Mandatory URL http://purl.org/dc/ elements/1.1/ format	File format size etc External form size or digital form
7	Identifier - Repeatable and mandatory URL - http://purl.org/dc/ elements/1.1/ identifier	Additional information about source, about availability
8	Language– Repeatable but not mandatory URL - http:// purl.org /dc/ elements/1.1/ Language	Language of source
9	Publisher - Repeatable and mandatory URL - http://purl.org/dc/ elements/1.1/ Publisher	Publisher's name

Sr. No.	Name of Metadata label	Explanation
10	Relation - Repeatable or Mandatory URL - http://purl.org/dc/elements/1.1/ Relation	Source related other details
11	Rights - Repeatable and mandatory URL - http://purl.org/dc/ elements/1.1 rights	Copy right ownership
12	Source- Repeatable but not mandatory URL - http://purl.org/dc/ elements/1.1 source	Origin of source, related volumes, part etc.
13	Subject - Repeatable and Mandatory URL - http://purl.org/dc/elements /1.1/subject	Subject of source class no etc
14	Title - Repeatable and mandatory URL - http://purl.org/dc/elements/ 1.1/title	Title of the source
15	Type -Repeatable and Mandatory URL - http://purl.org/dc/ elements/ 1.1/Type	Source type, file, medium, text etc

Note : Since every element has a separate web page, explanation is easily available

Chart 4.1. Dublin Core Metadata

Example of Assigning Metadata by DC

After considering elements as above elements of DC we would further understand them with an example (Chart 4.2).

Title	=	"Metadata Demystified"
Creator 1	=	"Brand Amy"
Creator 2	=	Daly, Frank
Creator 3	=	"Mayers, Barbara"
Subject	=	"Metadata"
Description	=	"Presents an overview of metadata convention in publication"
Publisher	=	"NISO Press"
Publisher	=	"the Sheridan Press"
Date	=	2003 - 07

Type	=	"Text"
Format	=	"Application/pdf"
Identifier	=	"http://www/niso.org/standrards/resources/metadata_ Demystified.pdf"
Language	=	"en"

Chart 4.2. Dublin core metadata recording example

4.7.3. Why to use Dublin Core?

Dublin Core is an internationally accepted metadata standard which consists of 15 core elements for describing digital source. Bibliographic & computer experts from libraries, museums, publishers and editors of textual materials have contributed in designing and preparing semantics of it. Data elements prepared by Dublin Core metadata initiative organisation have been approved by INSO and honored with international protocol of Z39.85

The characteristics of Dublin Core

1. Dublin core metadata elements facilitates us to register metadata and thus to preserve the digital collection.
2. The terminology and semantics built in which Dublin Core have been universally accepted metadata standards.
3. Due to its international status it is useful for worldwide cross culture and multi language recourse.
4. Since there is emphasis on core datasets adopting additional data elements is possible with its innovative nature it is ready to accept metadata sets of newly emerging digital documents.

REFERENCES

1. NISO: Understanding metadata NISO Press: 2004
2. National Archives of Australia AGLS Metadata Elements sets part - 2 usage guide
3. Bigley, Philips: Extension of programme language concepts Philadelphia University Science centre 1968
4. Bretherton, F. P and Single, P.T. Metadata Users view. In Intl. Conf. On very large data bases (VLBD) 1994 PP 1091 - 1994
5. Ralf Kimball Data warehouse life cycle New York Wiley 2008
6. Types of metadata University of Melbourne metadata \ http:// www.infod.unimelb.edu.an

5

Data Mining and Data Warehousing Techniques

5.0. INTRODUCTION

In Library Management study various research methodologies have been considered important for improving library functioning and services. In order to carry out analysis of user surveys various analytical techniques are used. In such analysis emphasis is given on library use study or user's study. Along with traditional method, statistical or computerised methods are also being used these days. In other fields especially industrial or commercial fields study on customer's behavior is given a great importance. In these fields use of little higher techniques like data mining and data warehousing are found more useful. Due to progress in computer technology such applications have now become easy. Application of data mining and data warehousing is growing in other fields also. Even this technique is also explored in library management to study library use and in user's behavior Considering importance of analytical techniques in various fields including library and information science we are going to discuss Data Mining and Data Warehousing in this chapter. Before we look into the specific applications of data mining and data warehouse, it is worthwhile to know, what data mining and data warehousing technique is?

5.1. DATA MINING AND DATA WARE HOUSING : CONCEPT AND SCOPE

If we look at the term "Data Mining or Data Warehousing," it reveals that in this analytical technique, data is used or database might be handled with some special technique. We know that between database and software a bridge of database management system exists, so we may guess that there may be some relation with DBMS or similar treatment to data. If we concentrate the word "Mining", we feel that the technique must be similar to process of exploration like done in mines. As in mining study of rock patterns or layers are studied, similarly in data mining also data patterns might be studied. With this understanding let us look into the actual concept of data mining and data warehousing. Since the data mining technique is largely used in industrial or commercial fields, let us first know the concept as used in these fields.

5.1.1. Data Mining

Data mining means by inter connecting different databases attempt are made to find out hidden patterns in them, which were never noticed before. In order to search data samples, based on data pattern from the databases which are stored in warehousing are used. In data mining exploration statistical techniques like Regression, Classification and Clustering methods are used. Now first let us try to know about "data mining" and then about "data warehousing".

5.1.2. Data Warehouse

Data warehouse means when the activities with involvement of database and software for performing specific transactions are carried out and after transactions are completed, data is removed from the system and stored into data warehouse elsewhere. In a normal way after completion of various computerised processes finally data is stored back into the same system database. However, when the data is no longer required in the system it should be removed and kept in data warehouse as all the processes/ transactions are completed in all the respects. The data thus stored in data warehouse is used for data mining for the purpose of finding patterns or data samples out of transactions or processes occurred in the past. Out of the stored back data bases some useful data bases are selected and specific data sample located and used for data mining analysis.

The above explanation reveals that for data mining analysis database from warehouse are used. Now after understanding about data ware house let us try to know about data warehousing.

5.1.3. Data Warehousing

Data warehousing means from the database stored in data warehouse selection of specific database suitable for data mining is done. In this process after selecting useful databases, their cluster or group is made and some process is carried out to make it usable for data mining. All these processes are collectively called data warehousing.

In data mining analysis it is expected to trace the hidden data patterns or data layers which were so far never been explored. Based on the existence of these hidden data patterns future prospectives of forecasting could be predicted. These forecasting helps to take decisions. Data mining analytical techniques are prominently used in industry and business fields. Data mining technique can reveal data patterns of the customer's behavior which were never understood or noticed so far.

These data layers or patterns are used to predict the future trend of business growth and accordingly growth of any industry or business is planned to achieve the growth targets.

Through the above paras we have touched upon concepts of data mining, data ware house data warehousing and in short about data mining analytical process. In reality these process are complex in nature but with the help of computing facility the expected results are achieved without much difficulties.

5.2. STEPS OF DATA MINING PROCESS

The major steps in data mining analysis are as follows:

1. To prepare data pattern/ sample : First the sample data pattern, based on which the hidden data layer or pattern is to be traced. Then pattern is to be prepared considering a specific problem. This is the first step in the process.

2. Data warehousing : Once target data pattern corresponding to problem is prepared the suitable databases are selected from the data ware house in which it is likely to get data similar to data sample and cluster of them is prepared. Once useful databases are selected, all the personal or confidential details are removed from them in order to make them anonymous to prepare improved database structure.

3. To select Algorithm : Now considering the target problem which was used to trace the data pattern a suitable algorithm is chosen. The main algorithm in this case are Regression and Classification. In regression method numerical data is handled. In this method data is handled in terms of quantity for example weight, speed or age, where as non numerical data is handled by in classification type of algorithm. In this case descriptive or qualitative things are handled such as colour, name, gender etc.

4. To select suitable software for analysis : Once the above three steps are completed, then comes the last step of data mining analysis. This is to choose the available analytical package, such as SPSS, SAS or S – Plus to analyse the data and present the conclusions/ results. Finally the results are used to provide solution to the problem which was selected for locating the data patterns in the first step in data mining analysis.

So far through the above paras we have understood the principle base of data mining and data warehousing concepts. Now let us try to understand how this technique is applied in the practical life. We are going to have a non business example e.g. Library management.

5.3. APPLICATION OF DATA MINING AND DATA WAREHOUSING TECHNIQUE IN LIBRARY MANAGEMENT

Discussion about the use of data mining and data warehousing in the library and information science was first initiated by Nicolson and others. While doing this the first use of term "Bibliomining" was also done by them. The reason for exploring this new concept was felt because when one tries to use technique of data mining in library and information field its result was heading towards the software and data bases. Actually search should direct towards behavior of library users. In order to have solution to this problem Nicolson & Staton decided to use slightly modified data mining technique known as bibliomining concept. While doing this they also found similarity with the concept of bibliometrics, which is used for exploring research on finding streams of scientific communication.

Up till now in studying relating to user group, emphasis was on using frequency evaluation and aggregate measure type of evaluation. However, in such evaluation useful several datasets/ streams or patterns were not found as they remained hidden. It is challenging to dig out such patterns. However, is possible by using data mining and data warehousing techniques. This makes it possible to understand specific needs of user groups and by which services they would be satisfied. It would be also possible to forecast about the future services and to take necessary decisions by using this new technique. Now let us try to know about how the concept of data mining and data warehousing is applied for study in library and information field.

In this process by applying statistical and pattern recognition tools on comprehensive data available in library systems it would be possible to predict the decisions about which library services need to be introduced. There are the following six steps in data mining process such as :

1. To identify area of the problem (in vision) and prepare data sample relevant to it.
2. To select databases relevant to targeted problem/data sample from the data warehouse
3. Create data warehousing
4. Select statistical data analysing tools
5. Choose data mining analytical tools
6. To prepare analysis report using traditional tools to present conclusion and prepare implementation plan.

Now let us discuss the above steps to understand them clearly.

5.4. STEPS OF DATA MINING AND DATA WARE HOUSING

5.4.1. To fix Target problem Area

The first step in data mining is to fix the problem and its scope. The problem area could be specific or general. The information about the target problem can be located and relevant data sample is prepared. While searching the information, it is decided first whether data mining can be done direct or indirect. Suppose library management wishes to decide to reduce the manpower in the library as library's budget has been cut. Naturally manpower on the circulation counter has to be reduced first which is going to impact on the facilities provided by the circulation counter and there would be cut in the services also. In this situation it becomes necessary to study how readers are going to face difficulties and inconvenience. This type of data mining could be of direct data mining. In case of indirect data mining example could be as, previous to this situation readers used to get messages as part of services directly to users in their department as such they need not have to come to library personally and their visits to library would tend to reduce. One can find solution to this problem via indirect data mining way.

While pursuing regional problem through data mining there would be need to use various tools. Searching sample of data pattern pertaining to a specific problem is not an easy task. It is necessary to use internal as well as external data together and one also needs to select comprehensive group of data bases as it is very difficult to get frequency or reoccurrence of a particular data pattern. It becomes therefore necessary to first prepare competent structure of data warehousing

5.4.2 Selecting databases corresponding to problem

Once the type of data mining has been decided and data sample to relevant to problem is identified, next step is to select databases corresponding to data sample from warehousing. One needs all types of data for example transactional, not consolidated data as well as normal data. In many problems one needs system based local data as well as the external information. In most of the systems once transactions are completed data gets deleted. In order to understand this let us see the following examples.

Example : Book issued by readers has been returned to library and it is recorded in the system. With this, issue and return transaction(cycle) is completed and the data about it automatically gets deleted. Second example is the reader reserves the book which he/she needs but it is currently issued to someone else, hence reservation data is created in the system. After some time previous reader returns the book to library which is also recorded in the system. The next reader immediately gets a message about it as his claim gets activated. He comes to the library and gets the books issued. With this reservation, claim activation and claimant getting the book the entire transaction(cycle) gets completed. Above are the examples of defective library software. In standard library software it does not happen i.e. transaction data is never lost even after completing it. In western countries for security reasons such transaction data is purposely removed from the main system and kept in data warehouse. Under any circumstances it is better to remove such data and keep it in data warehouse which helps in cleaning database and secondly removed data is stored in warehouse for further use. In data mining point of view automatically deleting such data from system or removing it purposely both are harmful which makes it difficult to get data for data mining analysis. Best way is to store it in data warehouse by removing personal or confidential details from the database or to make it anonymous. Such data is always useful for data mining.

As referred above for data mining one needs operational or transactional data from local databases so also one needs data from external type to support it. In library data about readers is stored in software database or it is stored in servers of the institute. For example reader's data, their respective transactional data, data about readers browsing from e - resources or from web sites on internet. The data even if it is of internal type sometimes it becomes difficult to retrieve external data about readers if it is available outside the system. Such data could be with departmental system or with the central system of parent institute.

Readers could also be concerned about their existence in social data society or in geographic location databases or in population or census data or it could be in pin code database etc.

So far we have understood that we can find out the answer to some questions by using the software data. However, with the help of data which is invisible or so for remained hidden in the system can be traced from combination of system data and other external databases which could be used to predict the future possibilities and by analysing it, solution to the problems could be found and accordingly the decisions to provide values added services to the user is taken if analysis conclusion suggest it. In order to locate such hidden data, data mining technique is used and such data can be used for studying the problems relating to reader's difficulties. As the problem is simple or difficult corresponding data mining process needs to be chosen. In the next para we are going to look in to the creation of data ware housing and about handling databases for it.

5.4.3. Creation of Data Warehousing

Once it is ensured that data/ database for data mining are available then next task is to select useful databases from the data ware house. Preparing cluster of databases it is a challenging task.

Databases selected for data warehousing need to be reformatted reformat in which steps like cleaning and anonymising are involved. The main purpose behind this is to remove individual and confidential details from the databases. Next step is to create improvised database cluster and convert old data in to the new cluster. Now let us see how it is actually done through an example. Librarian prepares a query pertaining to the current problem, collects the databases from data warehouse useful for data mining and they are inter-connected through common fields. This makes a cluster of databases. From this consolidated data, cluster of information of individual or confidential type are removed to make it anonymous. The database thus finally formed is flat type database, which is going to be used for data mining analysis. The database structure is now ready to receive the data in it. The data mining process suggest which data from the system the librarian should decides to preserve and transfer to data warehouse and which is to be omitted or destroyed as such data may not be necessary to keep in the system. Preserved data would be useful for data mining. Analysis requires removing individual detailed from it by filtering the same. Maintaining data with individual and confidential data in the software is risky as it could be misused.

We have seen how to take care about system data, similarly data of users using web based services is also needed to be handled carefully. It is risky to preserve information like log in IDs and passwords. In addition since users use e - resources through networked computers, it also contains details like IP addresses of machines. If we try to preserve such data as it is, then someone can misuse it for hacking or destructive purpose. It is therefore necessary to filter all such individual and system related details from transaction data by anonymising it. Now let us see how data anonymising process works through an example.

5.4.3.1. Data Anonymising Examples

We have understood the process of anonymising by which system data is cleaned for individual details before it is transferred to data warehouse. Let us learn the process through following charts (Charts 5.1 to 5.3) :

Chart 1. Readers data in the system

Borrowers Code	**Name**	**Type of Reader**	**Name of Dept.**
373	Prakash shah	Pre Degree Student	Mathematics
392	Mukund Bajde	Research Scholar	Hum. & Soc. Sc.
475	Krishna	P. G. Student	Comm.Engg.
593	Nalini Deshpande	Faculty	Computer Sc.

Chart 5.1

Chart 2. Issue Return Transaction

Book Acc No.	Subject	Borrower No.
10035	Computer Science	593
21007	History	392
09231	Communication	475
00533	Mathematics	373

Chart 5.2

Chart 3. Improved data after anonymising process

Book Acc. No.	Subject	Reader Type	Department
10035	Computer Sc.	Faculty	Computer
21007	History	Research Scholar	Hum. & Soc.Sc.
09231	Communication	PG Student	Engineering
00533	Mathematics	PG Student	Mathematics

Chart 5.3

If we see the last chart carefully then we notice that there are no individual/ personal details, certainly which does not create any difficulties in using it for data mining.

In similar way user's data about their internet browsing work also can be cleaned by removing individual credentials and the system IP address details. After these processes data base structure can be created for searching for data samples needed for data mining, such data contain so many hidden data sets which correspond to user problem and thus solution could be found out.

5.4.4. Selecting Analytical Tools

Once data ware housing process is completed means preparations needed for data mining analysis are done. Next task is to look for suitable data mining analytical tools. Data pattern needed for solving the problem is fixed and in the point of view of the problem the entire data is handled. While doing this expected data patterns are verified. At the end of analysis conclusion report is prepared. Sometimes system built provisions are also used for this purpose. These days library management systems(LMS) provide tool to retrieve data samples by writing a small script and after running script data samples can be searched needed for data warehousing process. There are tools available like Online Analytical Processing (OLAP) tools which also could be used.

5.4.5. Statistical Packages available for Data Mining

The main objective of data mining process is to search data patterns corresponding to an identified problem which is suitable for data mining for exploring the solution. For this several tools like statistical technique to artificial intelligence are used. As we have seen in the definition of data mining it is about gathering data samples which were hidden till now and which are matching with the target problem. In order to search such sample automatic analytical technique tools are used. In data mining process two broad categories of processes are involved – 1.to describe and 2.to predict. In the first category it is confirmed and fixed the availability of expected data patterns, where as in the second category based on the possibility data which could be possible but not visible is predicted

Nowadays readymade software packages suitable for data mining are available. Data obtained from data warehousing process is imported from the respective databases, analysed and for finding conclusions from analysis suitable tools are used. An algorithm suitable for the solution predicted is selected and used with analytical tools to arrive at a conclusion. The list of analytical tools is as follows:

1. SAS - Statistical Analysis software
2. SPSS - Statistical Package for Social Sciences
3. S - Plus
4. Oracle Data Mining Suite (Darwins)
5. Microsoft SQL Server
6. Free walk data mining suite - Open source type.

5.4.6. Implementing the conclusion

Once report of the data mining process (static report or decision report) is ready the conclusion it is once again tested with the original data base and credibility of conclusion is verified. It is ascertained whether conclusion or solution to the problem is acceptable. If it is not acceptable then the data mining process is revised by refixing the problem and matching sample and data mining process is carried out once again. However, if the decision or conclusion is acceptable then further task structure for decision implementation is prepared and it is implemented.

5.5. EXAMPLES OF USE OF DATA MINING TECHNIQUE IN LIBRARY MANAGEMENT

Concept of data mining and data warehousing is generally applied in industrial and business or corporate fields. It was first used in USA in 1990. In library and information field using this technique it has been possible now to study the user's behaviour more efficiently and it is possible to plan new services based on the conclusions accordingly. Although the process is a bit complicated but with the help of available packages and tools data mining process can be carried out in finding out solutions to the problems of users. Now let us review the example of use of data mining in library science field.

Example 1

Problem : To find a solution to the problem of readers less using of library during day time.

Action : It is possible to find a solution to this problem by use of data mining technique

In this process corresponding to problem one needs to search data pattern reflecting readers current habit of using library from the data warehouse which would match the problem. It is then necessary to go for data ware housing. While doing so one need to clean and anonymise the data by removing personal data. After this it would need to import data from comprehensive databases in the data structure prepared. It would also be necessary to look data giving circumstances outside the library, which is related with the problem. Then one needs to accept algorithm which is matching with the problem. Next step is to use data mining analysis tools to analyse the data. It would be then possible to get conclusion. At the end out of this process it would be possible to identify pattern about reader's usage of library in the entire year and 24X7 (especially about their issue or return transactions.) It would be also possible to know the defects in usage rate or reasons behind less physical use of library by the readers. After completing the process of data mining in the above case the conclusion was found as follows :

- Readers are very much busy in their work during weekdays as such they are not in position to come to the library.
- It was further concluded at the end of data analysis that during lunch, tea break and also on holidays rate of use of library by readers was seen increasing than other working timings.
- The not visualised possibility in the analysis was if the issue and return time are kept on extended evening time or on holiday use of library physically by users would certainly be increased.
- In response to the conclusion the decision was taken to implement revised timing as expected by users. It was implemented and the rate of use of library by readers was seen actually increased. This example is based on the actual situation experienced by the author at his working place.

Now let us examine the example retrieved from the literature.

Example 2

Problem : Library management observed that use of library during previous two months was drastically reduced.

This is the second example of application of data mining technique in library management. This is based on the reference from a case study appeared in a journal from a library abroad. In a city public library it was observed in a review by trustees that the previous two months library usage (especially noticed at issue counter) was drastically reduced. In view of this, library management was thinking whether library manpower could be reduced in order to conserve the library funds. The task of actually verifying facts behind the problem was assigned to the librarian. The action begins with to search for data pattern which is matching with problem from the data ware-house as the data was preserved there. After carrying out data mining analysis the reasons behind the problem was ascertained as below:

1. Use pattern of the library by most of other groups was found unchanged and no reduction in their use was noticed.
2. The use of library by children was found drastically reduced during previous two months

3. From social situation point of view when problem was analysed it was observed that there were book exhibitions organised by nearby schools and most of children were attracted by this event which eventually impacted use of public library by the children group was seen reduced.

4. When librarian presented the facts and conclusion it was decided that in future if such situation is observed beforehand then library would decide to divert the circulation counter staff to undertake annual administrative tasks like physical verification or shelf rectification or data conversion in order to utilise staff time properly, when there is likely that library use would be reduced drastically. The facts seen from data mining analysis out of data ware-housing are as follows:

   1. Only rate of usage by children readers in public library was seen reduced which we can call as description of the problem.

   2. Situation outside the library was that the book exhibitions were organised by nearby schools which revealed in decreasing use of public library by those children, who were going to attend the book exhibitions. This fact was revealed from analysis of social data out of the library.

After considering the above two examples it confirms that data mining and data ware- housing technique can be successfully applied in library management field also. It is felt that there is a need to implement the concept of data mining in a planned way which involves understanding concept of data mining by librarian, professionals and other staff, providing them necessary training, to analyse data in context of problem and find the solution and take decision to enhance library services to users and implement the same. It is also necessary to have favorable situation to create data ware housc, prcparc thc data warc housing from the data kept in it(in data ware house) and prepare data sample and analyse the data by applying data mining and ware housing technique to find the solution to the current problem. One would note that all these efforts are taken to improve the library services to the users.

5.6. CONCLUSION

In this chapter we have discussed the concept of data mining and data warehousing. About how this technique is applied in industry /business fields. Subsequently we explored whether this technique could be used in library management research. We understood the concept of data mining first, then about the steps of use of data mining technique, then about data warehouse, next about data ware housing and finally about analysing data by using data mining and statistical tools. At the end of the chapter we have understood about library management application by referring two live examples. In short data mining technique could be listed in the following steps :

1. According to data mining problem fix the target area
2. Search the data mining pattern matching with the problem.
3. Carryout data warehousing process once databases from data warehouse are selected, cleaned by removing person specific details.

4. Data imported from comprehensive data bases in the relevant data structure
5. Accept an algorithm matching with data pattern and the problem.
6. Analyse data by using data mining and statistical tools.
7. Draw the conclusion, prepare report, verify the result and make decision based on conclusions and implement it.

REFERENCES

1. Nicholson, S. (2003) The bibliomining process: Data warehousing and data mining for library decision making. Information technology for Libraries 22 (4), December 2003.
2. Nicholson S (2003) Avoiding the great data wipe out – Three.
   American Libraries, 34(9) P . 36, October 2003.

Websites (Accessed on 24th June,2016)

- Bibliomining. www.bibliomining.com
- Literature written by Nicholoson, S. on bibliomining
  http:// bibliomining.com /nicholson.

6

Library Electronic Security Systems : Products and Services

6.0. INTRODUCTION

Normally it is assumed that library computerisation means library automation. Library computerisation is certainly a progressive step in that direction. However, after library computerisation there are further issues of library automation. Further progressive steps of post library computerisation have already been exemplified by western libraries. Unfortunately in developing countries like India we do not think beyond library computerisation. Further progressive steps are initiated but with a snail's speed. Library's comprehensive computerisation, establishing library network, developing library web sites, establish digital library and providing innovative information services to users are the furthers steps of library automation. In library automation along with above things to achieve library security is also an equally important aspect to consider.

Security of library collections envisages preservation of rare books, security of library hardware, software & equipments, security of non print collection of library CDs, DVDs, and CD databases, diskettes, audio and video cassettes. If we seriously think about the present state of library we find that our libraries are not at all safe. We try to adopt some measures to protect the library but they are very meagre. In order to automate libraries, in real sense with advanced information technology tools are needed. There are lot of responsibilities of securing library as a whole on library staff and ultimately on librarian being the head of library. As compared to the past today the responsibilities have increased in many folds as such the library security is becoming today the most important aspect of library management. In order to ensure library security now many measures and techniques are available. It is true that they are expensive. However, when we think of accepting any technology more cost is inevitable, so it would not be wrong if we spend little more on library security. Moreover, whenever we accept any technology we give more importance to its effectiveness rather than to the expenses. In this chapter we are going to discuss library security aspects in detail along with its products and services.

These days, in library management special attention is paid towards achieving security for library. It is being thought that can we use electronic technology products for security? Library security is however a very vast topic. In library automation point of view, some points of security concern are invariably considered in library management especially relating to circulation and journal departments of library e.g. vigilance in stacking areas(books and bound volumes), vigilance at entry and exit gates and vigilance at some isolated pockets in library. These and other aspects closely associated with security have been concentrated in this chapter.

6.1. NEED OF LIBRARY SECURITY

Library security has special significance in library management especially in libraries where open access system is operational as it is more relevant in the current age. Security issues are mainly connected with behaviors of some miscreants in the reader group. We are however not going to engage ourselves in research of readers psychological mind set but certainly going to study how we can bring control on unethical acts of some of them. Need of library security is found more important in under mentioned situations.:

1. With growth in library collection
2. Adoption of open (Free) access system
3. Increase in rare books in collection
4. Increase in high cost books in library collection
5. Lacking of photocopying facility in the library

In such situations some people having the tendency of stealing any materials generally go for stealing books from a library. There are several incidences, which keep happening in the library, where library's security comes in danger such as :

1. Stealing books quietly from library
2. Throwing books from windows adjacent to stacks
3. Hiding books which are highly in demand
4. Tearing off pages from books, reference books and journal issues (pilferaging)
5. Improper handling of library materials and damaging them
6. Scaring and troubling other readers
7. Tempting library staff with money to help in stealing of books
8. Stealing valuable personal things of other readers from property counter like, money purses, mobiles, calculators, bags and umbrellas.
9. Library losses its property in natural calamities like flood, fire, cyclone accidents or due to terror attacks.
10. Hacking login-IDs and passwords of library system and making changes in databases and in issue and return transactions
11. Stealing valuable equipments like computers, printers, servers, scanners, stationary and consumables, peripherals like keyboards, mousses or even hard cash from the lockers.

12. Readers get trapped in library as they falls asleep while closing of library.
13. Indecently behaving with other fellow readers.
14. Bringing eatables and drinks in study or stacking areas
15. Stealing ID cards and issuing book unauthorized
17. Carrying weapon or explosives in library and indulge in terrorist activities.

All the above incidences although do not occur regularly or frequently do pose security threats to the library. Secondly, comparatively a very few individual are found participating in such acts. However, in security point of view all of them are certainly dangerous events. Library staff needs to be alert all the time. It needs consideration that if scientifically and property planned antitheft, anti-pilferage and-anti disaster management systems are adopted then they would certainly help in controlling such event to a greater extent. How to deal with such situations? What action is to be taken by the library staff with the concerned individuals? Do they need any special training in dealing with such situations? It generally happens that if an individual is caught in doing some wrong thing one is likely to become violent. It could create threat to the life of library staff who deals the situation. Considering this utmost care needs to be taken.

6.2. LIBRARY SECURITY : MANAGERIAL MEASURES

It is very difficult to make appropriate preparation to deal with every incidence listed above in anticipation. In the library's day to day functioning some measures are necessary to be done so that a definite mind set and approach of all library people would be set ,such as :

(a) Attitude and psychology of library staff.

It is certain that any personality whether belong to management or from security or could be a normal library attendant every one must be vigilant and alert about library security and such attitude or psychology needs to be adopted by everyone.

(b) In case of fire or any other natural calamity a quick responsive action is strongly recommended. The responses received in previous such events need to be reviewed and adequate training programmed on how to deal with the situations need to be organised.

(c) Preparing proposals to equip with necessary equipments and infrastructure to prevent losses in dealing the cases.

(d) To analyse previous incidences regarding security and review the preparatory measures.

(e) To control unauthorised entry to the library.

(f) All the windows ,ventilators or any openings should be covered with mesh to prevent throwing books or anything out of the library

From management point of view the following measures could be adopted.

1. Organising training programmes about security measures
2. Appointing competent persons to deal the security
3. Preparing guidelines and methodologies to deals with security.

4. To take inventory of library collections stores and equipments time to time to assess the losses.
5. Providing appropriate instructions to security staff depending on their levels

6.3. LIBRARY SECURITY TECHNOLOGICAL MEASURES

It is necessary to have adequate and strong measures in security point of view comprising of normal as well as electronic security systems in order to ensure entire library security. There is also a need to make provisions for necessary tools and equipments such as:

1. In order to control the entry at the gate it must be seen that only authorised people (readers and staff) would enter in the library through library entry gate. This arrangement needs to have installation like : smart card readers, metal detectors, magnetic censors and mechanical gates
2. In order to alert of emergency security threats sounding alarm a buzzer is required.
3. In order keep watch at the bays in stacking areas (books and bound volumes) and at all isolated areas if any suspicious individuals are indulging in damaging and pilferaging library materials close circuit TVs need to be installed.
4. During night hours arrangement of proper security lighting around the library building is necessary to enable strict security on movements of people by security personnel.
5. To have provision of emergency exit for people to leave library building in case of fire or any accidents.
6. In order to check stealing of book, journals, non book materials, computers and equipment, electronic or magnetic security systems are required.

6.4. LIBRARY ELECTRONIC SECURITY SYSTEMS

In western countries it is observed that libraries invariably make use of electronic and mechanical tools to control entries and book theft cases in order to provide security. These tools are becoming day by day modern and innovative. In addition newer technologies and tools are also emerging which are useful in providing security to the library. For library security there are special technological tools available today, which include the following ones :

1. Electromagnetic or magnetic security system
2. RFID security and inventory management systems.
3. CCTV Surveillance system

Now let us discuss how they are useful in maintain library security.

6.4.1. 3M Electromagnetic Security Systems

Electromagnetic or magnetic technology based security systems are available today. Now let us understand the concept behind this technology. Such technology is mainly used in departmental stores or in warehouse or as stores inventory management systems. The concept is like this, the things/ products which are to be secured (which are in packed condition) are applied with magnetic strips which are magnetised or sensitised with the help of a machine. All such things then are sorted and kept in shelves. In departmental stores customers pick the selected items which they intend to buy. They are taken to the billing counter and after payment the things are allowed to be taken out by the customer. This is done by keeping product packages on demagnetising or desensitising machine. At the exit gate there would be security gate having detecting mechanism. The products or things which are desensitised are to be taken through the security gate do not sound the buzzer or alarm. However, if anybody tries to take out anything which has live magnetic strip through the gate it would sound the buzzer or alarm indicating the thing is being stolen or taken out unauthorized, as the detecting machine very well sense the status. Thus such systems try to help in detecting the theft cases. This technology is also successfully used in warehouse or multi-storeyed hardware stores for tracking the movement of things and for maintaining their inventory. Nowadays, these technological tools are used to secure library collection from stealing or unauthorizedly taking them out. The products of electromagnetic systems are being manufactured by many companies especially from USA, Japan etc. Out of them 3M Company is the leading company. The technology is constantly being progressing and variety of products are now available in the market. However, since the products need to be imported from USA in developing country like ours the application 3M security systems is found somewhat expensive for our libraries and many a times it becomes unaffordable. In spite of the high cost the 3M magnetic security system is being adopted in many Indian libraries as a part of their modernisation plans. Libraries realise that by using this system it is possible to provide security to valuable collection of the library in making them safe from book theft and stealing incidences. However, it cannot be argued to have 100% solution to the problem by adopting magnetic security system.

6.4.1.0. 3M Security System : (Products, Equipments & Consumables)

3M is one of the most reputed companies in US which manufacture 3M security systems equipments, consumables and supply them worldwide. Basically the system is meant for providing security to groceries in the departmental stores. However, the company has been successful in promoting it for using it in the library as a safety measure. The system consists of following equipments and consumables such as:

1. 3M Tattle Taper (Magnetic Strips)
2. 3M Detecting system
3. 3M Sensitizing /Desensitising Machine
4. 3M self check out workstation

Now let us know more about these products.

6.4.1.1. Tattle Tapes /Magnetic Strips

It is a thin metal strip with width of half a cm and length of book size. These strips come with magnetic field activated on them i.e. in sensitized condition. The tattle tapes or strips come in boxes of 1000 each. Each of the strips comes covered with adhesive sticker type plastic foil on both sides. They come in two forms 1. To facilitate to fix it inside the book spine e.g. on binding surface called B-1 type and 2. For inter leaving in pages inside the book. The tattle tape strips are inserted with some skills called as B2 tapes. The Procedure is like this:

1. Open a book find a deep inter leaved opening which would be in the beginning or in second half portion of a book. Take a tattle tape remove adhesive plastic of one side hold it from both ends. Try to stick the tape inside pages as deep as possible and see that it is stuck properly by pressing from other side. Then remove the adhesive plastic of other side, close the book and press it a bit on binding side so that tattle tape would be stuck properly inside the pages. Now even if you open the book you would find it difficult to locate where the tattle tape has been fixed. These are B2 type strips. This is a widely accepted method of putting tattle tape inside the book. It remains for there lifelong period as binding side book is rarely cut for repairing and rebinding (Fig. 6.1 and 6.2).

Fig. 6.1. Method of sticking of B1 type 3M magnetic tapes
***Courtesy* : http://www.3m.com**

Fig. 6.2. Method of sticking of B2 type 3M tattles tapes.
***Courtesy* : http://www.3m.com**

2. There is another way of putting tattle tape especially for thick book if you put on height side of the spine. If one opens the book you would see gap between jacket cover and binding. In this case metal device of same width is available. Adhesive plastic on one side is removed and it is stick temporarily on metal strip to make it hold straight. The other side adhesive plastic is removed and device is inserted in the gap of jacket and binding. The metal strip is then pressed from spine side to make it stick on binding. The metal device strip is then removed. By pressing it from outside the tattle strip gets stuck properly on spine binding. This way stuck tattle tape also remains there lifelong until section binding is redone for repairing or during binding time.

As mentioned earlier tattle tapes come in sensitized/ magnetised state. The execution of sticking tapes is done in a planned way. Shelf by shelf books are removed, tapes are stuck in them and they are reshelved back as they were. In this way for entire books collection the tattle tapes are applied and thus entire book stock is brought under security cover. The life of tapes is forever and no further maintenance is required. Cost wise 3M magnetic system is the lowest amongst its higher version security system. Readers can see the following visuals figures which show the method of applying 3M security tattle tapes.

6.4.1.2. 3M Detection System

3M Detection system means an electronic gate. This gate is available with one way or two ways corridors. The main function of this system is to try to detect through sensors if any book is being stolen or being taken out unauthorizedly e.g. without having properly issued and being taken out of the library. In any such case system senses it and starts sounding buzzer alerting security person seating next to the gate, who could catch an individual red hand. The electronic gate is fixed in such a way that there would not be any other exit gate and everyone goes out from that gate only, even library staff need to follow this. There could be independent entry gate on the other side of it but both the ways should never clash or mix with each other. Such a system certainly helps to track the people to enter and exit under the surveillance of 3M security system. Figure 6.3 below gives an idea of the electronic gate.

Fig. 6.3. Image of 3M Electronic Security Gate
Courtesy : **http://www.3m.com**

6.4.1.3. 3M Sensitizing/ Desensitizing Machine

3M sensitizing machine is generally kept next to the issue counter. This machine does both the operation i.e. sensitizing and desensitizing with its toggle switch. When the direction of this switch is showing gate/ door means it is doing desensitizing when the direction is showing towards stacks indicates it is sensitizing. We know that when all the books kept on shelves are always in sensitized condition as they are shelved immediately after security tapes are applied. When the books are returned back by the readers, they are again sensitised and re-shelved on racks (invariably after sensitizing) so logically all the books on shelves are in magnetically activated or sensitises condition.

When such book is issued to any user in a normal way through computerised issue terminal, before the reader takes it out the issue counter staff should desensitize it on sensitizing machine available next to issue terminal. When reader takes such book out through detection gate the machine does not sense it as it is desensitized state hence it does not sound the buzzer.

Next time when readers comes to return the book to library return counter, staff returns the book in system and he also sensitizes book by keeping it on sensitizing machine. The book is then goes back to shelf in a sensitized condition.

The most important thing of the security system is that when any one removes a book from shelf and tries to take it out of library through electronic gate which is not issued and authorised to take it out the machine acts its right e.g. senses and finds that it is in sensitized condition and immediately sounds the buzzer alerting security about the book theft case and helps security to catch hold of the individual and reports to authorities about it.

Normally in library we find single machines for sensitizing and desensitizing operation due to its high cost. However, if library has heavy daily issue and return transactions then it is advisable to have two such machines one each for issue and return terminals respectively. There is an advanced version of this machine (3M 995) available which does multiple operations i.e. issue or return, barcode reading and desensitising together in one single attempt. Naturally cost of this machine is quite high. Readers can see the visuals of sensitizing/ desensitizing machine in following figure No. 6.4:

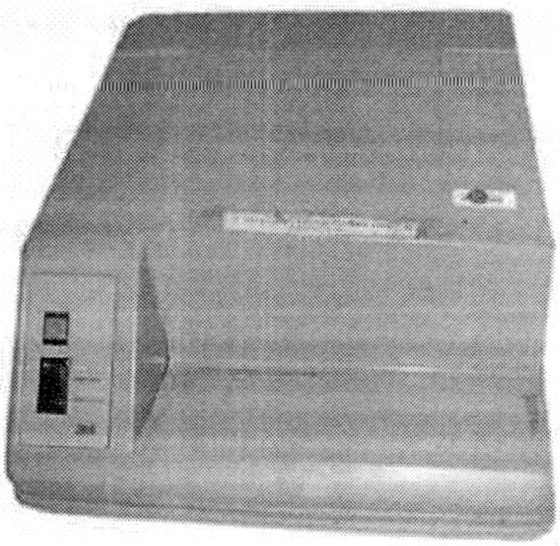

Fig. 6.4(a). Image of 3M Sensitizing Machine
Courtesy : **http://www.3m.com**

Fig. 6.4(b). Image of 3M Sensitizing and Desensitizing Machine (3M 995)
Courtesy : **http://www.3m.com**

6.4.1.4. 3M Self Checkout Machine

In the category of 3M security machines 3M self checkout machine is the most useful and sophisticated one. In the library where bar-coding of all the book collection has been done and all the books have been applied with 3M magnetic security tapes, then library can very well set this work station for providing self checkout facility without involvement of library staff for 24X7 by purchasing 3M self checkout system. This certainly helps reducing burden on counter staff of continuously attending issue/ return tasks and for the readers it is very useful as they need not have to depend on issue timings to get the books issued or to return the book to library without involvement of counter staff. This machine ensures adequate security and accuracy and at the same time helps readers to get books issued any time as long as library is open.

Fig. 6.5. 3M Magnetic Security System –Image of Self Checkout System
***Courtesy* : http://www.3m.com**

Readers may note that 3M security machines which we have seen before are not interfaced with library management software and they work independent of library software, whereas 3 M self checkout machine is fully interfaced with library software. In the operation of this machine readers are given some PIN like confidential code no. and only after matching the same it issues the books to the readers. This is how the machine works. It checks barcode of book, barcode of user, security no of individual while issuing books. The reader need to display the barcodes (books and of user) plus enters security code. Machine automatically reads both the barcodes, creates a issue transaction in reader's account, it desensitises book and all the operations are completed automatically within a few seconds. So that readers need not have to wait for long time. No human errors are involved and no man power is required in this task. However the cost of such machine is considerably nigh and libraries which could afford only can go for such machine. But it works wonderfully. Please see the images of 3M self checkout machines in Fig. 6.5 and 6.6.

Fig. 6.6. Image of self checkout machine actual operation
***Courtesy* : http://www.3m.com**

We realise that by using 3M Security system, products, machines and consumable it is possible to provide reasonable security to library collection especially to prevent theft cases. However, if the library decides to adopt 3M magnetic security system for entire library collection then it could be a costly affair for the library. Normally libraries go for only covering book collection to insure its security. Assuming that other materials are not either issued out of library or they are issued out with sufficient restrictions. The important thing in case of this system is that all the equipments and consumables need to be imported from USA and we need to pay price by converting US Dollars into rupees. If one considers prevailing conversion rates in developing countries, the total cost goes beyond library's affordability. However, large libraries that do not have funds problem certainly choose to go for it as a part of their modernisation plans. With a view to get an idea about the costing of all together adopting the 3M security system a rough estimate of cost for securing 1000 books with 3M magnetic system is presented as follows (Table No. 6.1) :

6.4.1.5. Estimates of Expenditure on 3M security system

Sample expenditure for 1000 books

S. No.	Name of Equipment Purchase	Number	Cost Rs.	With Bulk
1.	3M Detection with single corridor	1	5,00,000/-	4,50,000/-
2.	3M Sensitizing Machine	1	2,25,000/- (Rs.100000 Battery operated)	2,25,000/-
3.	Tattle Tapes	1000	7000/- @ Rs.7.00	6000/-
4.	Execution cost of inserting tapes in books	500	500/-	500/-
5.	Installation Charges		10,000	10,000/-
	Total Equipment cost			6,91500/-*
	Total costs excluding on equipment			6,500/-
	Cost per book			Rs. 6.50

* Cost the equipments and installation is onetime investment and it is spread for the entire library collection so once it is done cost of consumable is the only expenditure

Table 6.1. Estimates of Adopting 3M Security Systems for Library

The above estimates give an idea of adoption of 3M Security system. For the library collection more than 1000 books only consumable and execution cost needs to be considered. Addition details could be looked for in 3M's website www.3m.com We have tried to know about the electronic security system and particularly about 3M electromagnetic security systems. We understood the technology, its products, functioning and about the cost involved. This is not the only library security system available today as there are other systems available. 3M Electromagnetic system however, has its limitations. In this technology book is treated as an entity. System handles it like an entity is going out and coming in. However, the system does not decode its details. There are advanced systems available today which try to overcome all the limitation experienced with 3M which is known as Radio Frequency Identification System or in short RFID. Now let us try to know about it.

6.5. RFID (RADIO FREQUENCY IDENTIFICATION)

6.5.0. What is RFID?

Radio Frequency Identification in short RFID is a higher level electronic security system and supposed to be intelligent system as compared to 3M electromagnetic system. RFID is related with radio frequency technology and uses radio frequency devices. RFID tags used in this system are called smart labels, which take part in communication with local systems. RFID tag is a sort of small microprocessor which has invisible antenna and it emits radio signals. Normally in library when issue and return transactions are done barcodes of book and borrower cards are scanned to enter corresponding codes. RFID System also works in the same way but difference is that in case of barcodes one needs to read barcodes by scanner but in case of RFID radio signal emitted by tag are automatically recognised and read by the RFID reader and data input is done as these devices communicate with each other.

RFID frequency is a small frequency band of electromagnetic spectrum in physical science. A specific radio frequency is used for identifying objects attached with them. RFID devices and tags are also used for inventory management of goods, production and supply. RFID tags are pasted on products. Every tag has specific radio frequency by which it is identified. The tag emits its radio signals, with these signals it tries to communicate with nearby RFID readers and the reader also identifies it. Whereas in case of barcode we need to scan the barcode to read and identify to input. Thus RFID System reads data automatically and more speedily than barcode technology. As such RFID tags are found best alternative to barcodes and RFID System has emerged as smarter system than bar-coded system. In encyclopedias of library and information science RFID has been defined as: Identity of library materials which stored on a small tag or microchip, even if a reader walks with a book having RFID tag through the RFID zone book issue transaction is completed so it is so simple and quick.

6.5.1. Application of RFID technology In Library Management

If we try to compare 3M electromagnetic security system with that of RFID system we find that RFID is an advanced, intelligent and superior technology. With the emergence of RFID technology electromagnetic technology has turned to be older. In RFID when it is applied in library management it identifies books and other materials with their bibliographical data. With RFID technology we can do the following things:

1. Check out & check in
2. Self check out & check in
3. To take inventory of book stock
4. To navigate misplaced book
5. Detect book theft cases
6. Tracking movement of library material so also movement of readers (With RFID Card)

With the use of RFID technology library productivity increases by reducing errors in data input, to reduce the burden on library (counter) staff, which could also be utilized in providing other value added services.

In RFID we find joint use of radio signals technology and micro chip or computer technology. In microchip of RFID tag bibliographical details are stored and with the help of radio frequency wave details are automatically transmitted to the reader. When the item is issued the issue status is added to the existing details to the tag. When such book is taken out reader antenna at exit gate antenna reads it automatically with issue status and the book is taken out. When RFID System is used in library in addition to tags pasted on book one needs a RFID reader which is placed near the circulation counter. Thirdly at library exit sensor gate is installed which also has RFID antenna to sense movement of the materials. The sensor at the gate covers the area around the gate up to two feet. The width of gate is 4 feet, which considers two feet coverage of each gate. RFID technology not only ensures security to library from book thefts but there are several other advantages of it. Activities by using RFID in the library are listed as below.

1. Creating RFID tag for each book and sticking on them
2. With the help of RFID, reader does the issue/ return transactions
3. Readers could self checkout the material
4. Keep a watch on book thieves through RFID sensors
5. Return books through RFID drop box
6. Collection organisation, physical verification and finding misplaced materials by using hand held RFID scanners.

6.5.2. How RFID Technology works

We have reviewed the activities in library where RFID technology is adopted in its management. Now let us see in detail how RFID technology works. Use of RFID consists the following machines, portable tools and consumables:

1. RFID tags
2. RFID Reader
3. RFID Antenna Gates
4. RFID Handheld scanners
5. SIP-2 Servers

Now let us try to know from the following actions how RFID works in library.

Action No. 1 : Generate RFID tag for each book by using work station which gives RFID frequency to each book, and then add bibliographic data

Action No. 2 : Paste RFID tag at appropriate place on a book

Action No. 3 : When book bearing RFID tag is brought at the counter to check out, the reader at counter picks up the radio signal identity of book through communication between reader antenna and tag. Tag gets power as it comes in contact with reader and it starts emitting radio signals which are sensed by the reader. Since reader is interfaced with library software it gets the bibliographic data input. Book is issued to user and issued status with borrower details is saved back in tag through the radio waves.

Action No. 4 : When issued book is taken out from RFID antenna gate the sensor activates tag which emits radio signal giving book details plus issue status. The details are decoded. There could be two possibilities.

1. If the book is properly issued and issued status is decoded with borrower details the book is allowed to be taken out with Okay signal/ indicator.
2. In case if the book is being taken out without properly issued and issue status is not recorded,

system will decode the status of the book as theft case and buzzer would sound to indicate theft.

Action No. 5 : RFID Technology allows self issue facility when reader having RFID borrowers card and book bearing RFID tag moves through RFID circulation zone. The book is automatically issued to the reader and RFID tag is updated accordingly, which would allow the reader to take the book out of library through RFID Sensor gate by signaling okay.

Action No. 6 : Like self checkout RFID the system also allows reader to return issued books themselves by specially manufactured book drop box. The readers just have to drop the books in the drop box; system would sense the details, return the book and update the status in RFID tag attached to the book.

6.5.3. Constituents of RFID System

In RFID Technology the following machines, products and consumables take part.

1. RFID tags generating workstation
2. RFID tags for each book
3. RFID reader / sensor machine
4. RFID Antenna gate
5. SIP - 2 RFID servers
6. RFID self checkout circulation zone
7. RFID Handheld scanner to collect data during stock verification or for navigating misplaced material or to find a book in the library

Now let us try to know the technical details of RFID products

6.5.3.1. RFID tag

RFID tag is a microchip/ processor which bear paper cover. Normally once RFID tag is prepared giving it a radio frequency identity is stuck at the inside last cover of a book. Tag possesses built-in antenna. With the help of antenna tag communicates with counter reader and antenna at exit gate. It gets energy from the reader/antenna to activate and send the radio signals. All the bibliographical details are transferred to tag while the preparation of tag itself. Only subsequently issue/return status as the case may be is also transferred to tag at the time of issue and return.

Blank RFID tags are manufactured and supplied to libraries. They are filled with data and RFID frequency by having RFID work station. Since tag is a microchip which has minimum capacity to store data worth of 64 bites where as higher level tags can store data up to 1mb. Like CD-ROM tags perform read only WORM(Write Once Read More) or read and write function which enables to store variable information about circulation details. Each tag possesses specific radio frequency identification, which is used to identify book for issue, return, self issue, drop box, for physical verification or while navigating it. It can also be used to search book on shelf with the help of hand held RFID scanner.

Generally depending on the quality and costing there are two types of tags available :

1. Active Tag
2. Passive Tag

Active Tags are of higher grade / quality, their cost is also more. Active tags have their own built in power which facilitates sending radio signals on its own. Active tag facilitates data recording by WORM way and it could also be rewritten. Active tags can store data up to 1MB. Passive tags in comparison are ordinary type and they do not have their own power. When they come in the vicinity of either reader or sensor antenna they receive the power to get activated and send radio identification signals. Passive tags are comparatively cheaper. Active and passive tags survive lifelong but passive tags could get worn-out early. Function of tag is to store data and emit radio signal identification while communicating with readers or sensor.

RFID tag is nothing but an integrated circuit chip. RFID tag is known as smart label which has book accession number, bibliographic details and specific security code called EAS- Electronic Article Surveillance

RFID Tagging : Process of applying RFID tags to book and other library collection is called tagging. When decision is taken to adopt RFID technology by the library management the first step is to execute work of preparing RFID tags for every book and sticking them inside cover of each book. Since this is an ad hoc type of work but needs to be done quantitatively, it can be carried out by hiring additional staff. Normally tags are pasted inside of back cover where as video or DVD or cassettes have designated place to stick RFID tags.

6.5.3.2. RFID Readers & Sensor

RFID card readers placed at the counter, whereas sensor gates with antennas is installed at exit point. These are the main components of this system. The reader and sensors are equipped with other parts like radio frequency modulator, control unit and antennas as stated earlier. Readers are used for carrying out issue and return transactions, the same readers in the form of sensors are made available at the exist gates. Function of both these equipments is more or less same. Readers and sensors throw out radio waves for communicating with tags to read data available on tags. Readers and sensor are interfaced with library software through an additional server called sip – 2. Sip - 2 server stores circulation status of all the book collection at any point of time. Circulation status of every book is also stored on its respective tag. In RFID system, functioning and integration of reader, censor gate, tags and sip – 2 server is perfectly maintained, which is the success of this system. All these components help in smooth functioning of RFID system to carryout activities as mentioned below :

1. With the help of system terminal and RFID reader library staff carryouts issue and return Transactions
2. At the gate with the help of RFID sensors/ antennas, it is possible to prevent(catch) stealing of book
3. With self-check out and check-in counters readers get books issued without involvement of library staff, independently.

4. People use drop box facility to return issued book any time they wish to do so, even after library is closed.

6.5.3.3. Antenna

In RFID system readers and sensor possess built-in antennas in order to catch radio frequency signals sent out from RFID tags. Antennas of reader and sensor send radio signals which power the tags coming in vicinity of them. Communication between readers/ sensor and tags help to decode data stored on tags. If the book is issued to a particular reader accordingly status is also recorded on the tags so the system allows borrower to take it out. If anyone tries to take away book without proper issuing, sensor get the signal accordingly which senses that the book is being stolen which triggers buzzer to sound to alert the nearby security.

6.5.3.4. Sip - 2 Server

RFID system when adopted for library management it needs constant communication with library software. RFID system mainly needs user data, book data and circulation status of each book. RFID system needs a separate server called sip - 2 server which stores above data online. With RFID readers issue and return transaction are carried out, drop box and self check out systems also does the same function. The information or data of issue or return transaction carried out at these equipments is sent to sip - 2 server. The sip-2 server helps in controlling system at all above places e.g. counter, gate, self checkout terminal and drop box. The exact synchronising among all of them is necessary to function RFID system perfectly. So although library has library management system and its various servers, creation of additional sip - 2 server is a must for adopting RFID in the library. The problem faced by many libraries is that they wish to adopt RFID at a later stage of library computerisation and co - operation from LMS vendor in installing sip server becomes most important. If LMS vendor refuses to cooperate then it becomes difficult for the library to adopt RFID at a later stage. It is therefore advisable for librarian to consider and settle the issue of sip - 2 server at the time of adopting library management system for computerisation else adopting RFID at later stage becomes difficult.

6.5.4. Advantages of RFID Technology

As compared to other available security systems RFID technology is certainly advantageous in many ways such as:

1. Speedy issue and return : RFID system saves time required for doing issue and return transactions at counter. RFID reader reads data of books to be issued very quickly. Moreover it does not need to read tags of books to be issued one by one as it is done in barcode system. Even if many books are kept one above the other nearby reader/ machine, it reads data of all the books together at once. Normally counter staff needs to talk to the borrower while doing issue and return tasks in order to get necessary details. In RFID however, it requires minimum time for this. RFID System relives staff from work stress

2. Use of self checkout and check in facility : Since RFID system is the most secured electronic security system for library, it is safe to provide self check-out and check-in facility for the readers. There are various advantages with such facility as reader's library use gets enhanced. Readers can get books issued from self check out way as long as library is open which helps in reducing rush at the counter.

3. To bring efficiency in gate security : We have seen in use of 3M electromagnetic system to prevent book stealing from the library but we know that 3M system has limitations due to several loopholes in it. 3M system does not decode identity of books being removed from library. Comparatively RFID system is found to be more efficient as it decodes the identity of book including identity of individuals who try to steal book from the gate. In RFID, movement of books through gate is tracked and recorded. One can specifically find out which books were taken out, when and who has taken them out. RFID system additionally maintains statistics of use of library by the readers, keeping such statistics was not possible in 3M security systems.

4. Facility to return books through drop box : Normally in any library systems the work of book returning is done on counter terminals. Some libraries keep a simple box to facilitate readers to drop books in to the box to return books, especially it is useful when counter is not functioning or library is closed. However such books need to be removed and transported to counter to return them in the system. However RFID system facilitates to have intelligent drop box ,and as readers drop books to be returned in it are sensed by RFID sensor in drop box and they are actually returned to the system automatically, as it has built in RFID reader. Thus books dropped in drop box can go to shelf directly.

5. Use of RFID for physical verification and collection organisation etc. : In the process of adopting RFID in library, RFID tags for each book is necessary to be prepared by giving unique radio frequency (EAS)Electronic Article Surveillance code and by saving respective bibliographic data in it. Once the tags are pasted in books the collection is covered under RFID security and is available for all other application of RFID in library. With the help of secret code and radio frequencies many administrative tasks can be carried out for example.

1. Physical verification or taking inventory
2. Tracing misplaced books
3. To locate the place of book in classified order and on shelf

***Physical verification with RFID* :** Physical verification of library collection can be carried out in an innovative way with RFID. It is done in a very short time that too without removing books from shelves. A hand held RFID scanner is used for this purpose. By just moving scanner from left to right of each shelf the entire data can be collected and fed back to the system. So far physical verification was found tedious process to record head count by transporting books and scanning their barcodes was taking a few or more months but the same work could be completed by RFID method in a week's time.

RFID hand held scanner is found useful in finding misplaced books from shelves. This is done by feeding a particular radio frequency to the scanner. The RFID scanner is just moved on book shelf sequences and required book would be located at point where scanner starts beeping. Now after knowing the usefulness of RFID in managerial tasks now let us also know about the limitations of RFID technology.

6.5.5. Limitations of RFID technology

So far we have seen the positive side of RFID technology and seen the fruitful uses of this technology now let us understand the limitations and disadvantages of RFID technology.

1. Cost of RFID adoption in library is very high. Equipments like reader, sensor, RFID tag generation equipment are very costly, secondly consumable e.g. tags is also in the range of Rs.35/- to Rs.40/-. The libraries find it beyond their affordability and far from consideration.
2. Tags are subject to mishandling even if they are covered with aluminium foil its effects get nullified. Readers can remove tags or could damage them
3. Sensors with inadequate capacity fail to sense the signals accurately or completely.
4. RFID use in library may bring freedom of individual in danger as movement of readers (with RFID Id cards) is subject to tracking by the sensors.
5. RFID signals of two tags may clash with each other giving wrong signal and may create problems in library management
6. In order to avoid collision of two tags it needs alternative technical provision which results in increasing in cost.
7. RFID Technology is yet to be settled. It is also not fully supported with any international standards.

6.5.6. Standardisation for RFID Systems

Amongst library electronic security systems available so far RFID technology is found to be the best of all, accurate and works without any risk. Many libraries are adopting this technology. In spite of this there is lot of scope to bring improvements by standardising the same. There is a need to have RFID system fully standardised. International standard organisations have provided some standards for this technology. Organisations like Auto-ID centre and EPC Global have submitted specifications for RFID. In commercial and library management application High Frequency (HF) RFID is used. We can get details about the frequencies used as below:

Low frequency	High Frequency
Range 0.5 meter	Range up to 1.0 meter
Short range	Reading Accurate
Slow functioning	Quick Reading rates

The standards so far published for RFID are as follows:

ISO - 15693

ISO - 1800 - 3

Specifications for ISO - 15693 are as

- Physical Characteristics
- Signal Interface

- Transmission Protocol

6.5.7. Usage of RFID Technology

At international level RFID Technology is widely used. Especially in warehouses of industry it is being used heavily. As far as use of this technology in library is considered to be new and yet to be stabilized. The use of RFID in library has been widely appreciated globally. It is still in developing stage and it is expected that its capacity should be enhanced. It is also expected that its cost should also come down. At the moment equipments, products and consumables of RFID are manufactured abroad mostly in USA and as such in developing countries cost of importing this technology is very high, making it almost unaffordable for libraries to adopt. If the products of RFID are manufactured indigenously then perhaps it would become affordable to be adopted India in library functioning.

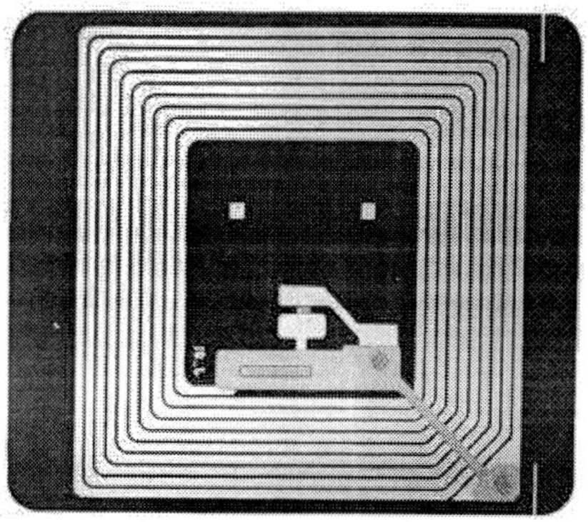

Fig. 6.7(a). RFID Tag
Courtesy : **http://www.3m.com**

Presently many companies are distributing RFID Products worldwide as listed below.

Bibliotheca, check point, 3M, Edutech, X- ident Technology, GMBN and Tagsys. Where as in India it is distributed by Vitaran, Pune

There is no big number of libraries or institutions using the RFID Technology in India in Library Management such as:

- NASSDOC, New Delhi
- University of Pune (Not fully operational)
- University of Jammu
- IIT Madras
- IIM Indore
- Bank of Baroda (Mumbai)
- IISc. Bangalore
- IIT Kharagpur
- IGCAR (Kalpakam) Chennai

6.5.8. Examples of Use of RFID in Library

Now we are going to see figures (from 6.7 to 6.10) showing images of use of RFID Technology in Library Operations as below :

Fig. 6.7 (b). RFID Tag Preparing Machine Image
Courtesy : **http://www.3m.com**

Fig. 6.7(c). Way how RFID tag is fixed in book
Courtesy : **http://www.3m.com**

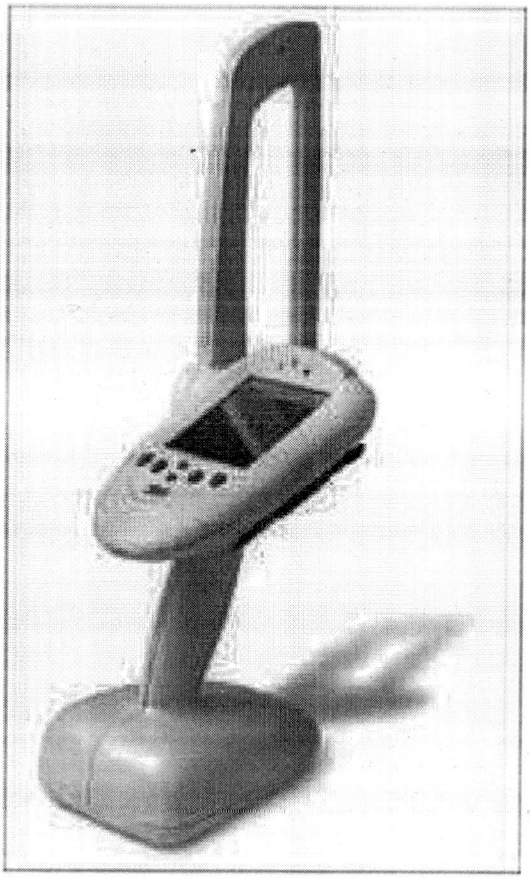

Fig. 6.8. RFID Hand Held Tracker/scanners
Courtesy : **http://www.3m.com**

Fig. 6.9. RFID Tracking Pads
Courtesy : **http://www.3m.com**

Fig. 6.10. RFID Book Return Box

***Courtesy* : http://www.3m.com**

So far we have studied how the electronic security systems are useful in providing security to the library. However, electronic security systems do not provide 100% security, as it helps only to prevent book theft cases or at the most gives solution to deliberate misplacement. There is a third security threat to the library i.e. pilferaging problem or in other words tearing of pages from books, reference books and from journal issues. There is however, solution to control pilferaging with use of Close Circuit TV. Now let us try to know about CCTV or library surveillance system.

6.6. CCTV - LIBRARY SURVEILLANCE SYSTEM

In the days of insecure environment life security is the most important. Places like cinema halls, shopping malls, hospitals, airport, temples, restaurants and parliament or democratic houses and at the places of social gathering need special security. Attacks of terrorist, human bombs are adding security threats to our life. We find that every where human security is found inadequate. It has become almost necessary to have the support of security system to support human security so that we could have some control on miss-happenings around us today. We see that there is lot of progress in developing technological security systems like close circuit TV (CCTV). These systems constitute web camera, digital video security or surveillance systems.

Nowadays close circuit TVs are also being considered for ensuring internal security in libraries. Since these days libraries have become readers centered and as such readers enjoy a lot of freedom due to adoption of open access system. However in such situations some miscreants try to misuse the facilities. We find stealing of book, misplace books deliberately or damage them or tearing of pages from valuable rare book, from costly reference books or from scholarly journals.

Libraries lose a lot of important materials in such unhealthy acts by some elements.

We have discussed how electronic security systems like 3M Electronic Security or RFID Security system are used in controlling book theft cases or misplacements. These systems are found useful, which try used to keep vigilance on library entry and exit gates. However, they are not useful in controlling pilferaging of library material. In this case CCTV surveillance system is found the most useful. Now let us learn about the CCTV surveillance System.

6.6.1. Close circuit TV Technology : Concept

Before we look into the use of CCTV for library security let us try to know the benefits and effectiveness of close circuit TV elsewhere through some examples:

Example 1 : In a convent or international school system we find use of close circuit TVs. There are audio speaker system operated from school principal's office to give instructions and notices in the classrooms to students and teachers Nowadays we find close circuit cameras are fixed in all class rooms in order to see what is happening in each class, how students are behaving or to see how teachers are teaching in the class. The school principal would have the facility to push the buttons and see the scenes of each class and record the things. Such systems are found useful in school management. As everyone knows that principal may watch them, it may create some kind of scare in the minds of students as well as in minds of teachers so their performance may improve.

Example 2 : This example is of police control room. Officers and police guards of crime branch use CCTVs for keeping watch on criminals or see people whose movements are found suspicious. Normally at most of the public places especially crowded places CCTV cameras are installed. They are fixed in such a way that they are hidden and no one would know where they are. Police department try to keep constant watch on such places through TV monitors which are connected to the cameras. If they find some suspicious people they are taken into custody for further enquiries. Places like jewelry exhibitions or big shops of gold ornaments or diamond shop are protected with CCTV system and the security system tries to keep constant vigilance on the movements of people inside such places. The things happening in front of cameras are continuously recorded and they are seen sequentially. If some robbery cases happen then individuals are held responsible if they are found participating in such event with the live proof of camera footage.

From the above examples we find that in example - 2 constant watch or TV monitors connected to each camera is kept where as in example-1 principal could see scene of one classroom at a time with some specific purpose.

However, it is difficult to keep a watch on criminals through all cameras humanly and it needs recording of footages. An arrangement to record each camera scenes independently is necessary and if need arises recording of each camera is examined by seeing footage recordings in order to get and clear idea about individuals involved in doing some criminal affairs.

Another thing we notice that the cameras fixed in example - 1 are clearly visible where as in example - 2 they are hidden and not at all visible so that the purpose for which arrangement is done is mostly fulfilled.

Now with the backdrop of the above referred two examples let us try to know how close circuits TV systems is organised in the library premises for security purpose. Normally close circuit cameras are fixed at the following points:

1. Library exit and entry gates
2. Library corridors and staircases
3. Book stacking areas including bays
4. Journals bound volumes stacking areas and bays
5. Corners and the places which are isolated from the general traffic
6. Reading areas
7. Issue and return counters

These are places where suspicious movements if any, could be seen and if it is necessary to keep watch on them through the close circuit TVs

If we compare cases discussed especially in example-2 we find major difference that places where cameras are fixed are hidden places and it is never disclosed about fixing of cameras. Where as in case of library generally a public notice is displayed at the entrance stating that:"For Security purpose CCTV Recording is done and you are under CCTV surveillance"

Such a notice displayed at the entrance certainly gives expected impact such as:

1. General readers accept the fact that for security purpose their movements are recorded on CCTV so they would not complain about it. If such a recording is done without information then many would feel their freedom is at risk.
2. It gives right message to the miscreants who try to involve themselves in bad acts which would be threat to library security and they are likely to caught red hand in cameras while doing some unsolicited thing. So it certainly leaves scaring impact on those people and it helps in reducing such events. However, those who are totally ignorant about it they are likely to be caught in the cameras.

6.6.2. Objective of Using Close Circuit TV Technology in Library

1. To keep a track on incidences like deliberate hiding and mis-placing of books and journal issues.
2. To look for incidences of pilferaging or tearing of pages from books and journals.
3. In case if the above incidences have occurred and the individuals are caught in camera then to produce the footages as a proof which would help in holding them responsible.
4. Readers and staff to make feel that they are in safe and secured place
5. Use recoded information for better library management
6. To see that close circuit tv surveillance system used for creative and fruitful purposes.

The information recorded by close circuit TV system need to be kept confidential and use it only for confidential purpose so that it would not put any highly educated individual and women in inconvenience. Many people try to oppose such recording and they can object to it. In this situation library should be ready with rules, and regulations and efforts should be made to convince readers about the ethical use of such surveillance systems.

6.6.3. Close circuit TV security functioning, equipments and costing

Generally in close circuit TV surveillance system cameras are installed at specific locations. Cameras are connected to monitors kept in control room through cabling. The system can consist of set up of minimum one camera and one monitor along with necessary other electronic components. In this system whatever is viewed in the range of camera is continuously displayed on TV monitor. It is necessary to keep constantly watching the monitor screen in order to record if any untoward incidence occurred. However, this is humanly not possible. There could be many cameras installed at different locations as it becomes necessary to control entire premises for security purpose. The cameras could be of different types e.g. stationary or moving. So also the pictures could be displayed in black and white or in colour and there are different respective technologies available.

In security point of view, each camera should be constantly on and providing continuous pictures viewed in its front. In library too, cameras are installed at many locations as required and for each camera view is to be continuously monitored. However, since it is not always possible to do so, recording of pictures received from each camera is preferred. In the past recording was done on video cassette on VCR machine, in that case also it becomes necessary to insert new blank cassette if previous one in filled. It also becomes difficult to do timely. Nowadays digital technology is used to continuously record the camera views. Digital video Recording technology is used for this purpose. There are advantages in going for digital recording than an old VCR cassettes recording method such as:

- DVR based recording can be preserved for long time
- It is easy to view DVR recordings and one can reach at any location quickly
- DVR recording and viewing can be done simultaneously
- DVR recording is clear and of high quality

Components of CCTV Security System : CCTV surveillance security system has following components

1. Video camera
2. Video Monitor
3. Recorder VCR or DVR
4. Cable to connect camera to recorder with other electronic components like server and amplifier etc.

Video Camera : Video cameras normally are of CCD (Charged Coupled Devices) type. Pictures received through camera lens are converted into electronic impulse which is transmitted to monitor and which is again converted into pictures. Size of the camera is measured in inches. Normally cameras are of 1/4-1 size. They come with resolution of 350-440 TVL. Higher quality cameras would have resolution of 480 - 500 TVL.See the image of camera in Fig. 6.11.

Fig. 6.11. Close circuit TV camera

Monitor : CCTV monitors are of LED type which are considered to be of good quality. However their cost is high.

Recorder : Nowadays digital technology is good for recording than of old VCR, which is becoming obsolete. DVR recorders are supposed to be the most suitable.

Actually adopting CCTV technology is a costly affair. However, in the large libraries it is found necessary and useful in these days in the situation where pilferaging is almost universal problem. In order to protect our valuable literature, especially in the form of scholarly journals or costly reference tools one cannot afford to lose them. CCTV can certainly help in preventing such incidences. If not adopted timely we would find that libraries would be having a large number of bound volume collection but important articles would have already been missing and lost forever. It is therefore advisable to make the investment to preserve our valuable collection timely and does not matter if it requires high cost.

The total cost of normal to high value CCTV cameras and other equipments would be from 25,000 to 50,000 and its related component costs are as follows:

1. Camera lens Rs 7500 - 12,000
2. Recorder - DVR type of recorders are bit costly and would be costing from Rs. 15,000 - 20,000. Library needs to bear the recurring expenses to the tune of 5 - to 8% for maintaining the CCTV surveillance system in the library.

REFERENCES

1. Boss R.W. RFID Technology for Libraries, Library Technology report Nov - Dec, 2003
2. Cooney, Elainam: RFID – Complete review of Radio Frequency Identification. Delhi, Thomson Learning 2007.
3. Kern C. Radio frequency Identification for security and media circulation in Libraries. Electronic Library 22, No 4 - 2004
4. Lindquist, Mats G.:RFID in Libraries: Introduction to issues paper presented at 69th IFLA conf. And council, Berlin, Germany, 9 Aug 2003
5. RFID Journal http: / www.rfidjournal.com Accessed on 17th April, 2016
6. Yu.shin.chiang, RFID implementation and benefits in Libraries Electronic Library 25 No. 1 (2007) 54-64
7. 3M Global Gate way www.3m.com -3M India Solutions 3mindia.co.in
8. Library security systems, Library security.co.Uk www.librarysecurity.co.uk
9. Library CCTV surveillance security cameras for public libraries CCTV Corporation www.cctvcorp.com

7
Management of E-Resources : Collection Development

7.0. INTRODUCTION

Advancement of internet and digital technology has facilitated publishing information in digital/ electronic form. After World War - II e.g. post Gutenberg's invention of movable printing press gave momentum to publish books in printed form. Now in present internet age publishing e –literature is also growing tremendously. With this availability of literature in e-format is increasing day by day. This has further impacted in growing e - literature in the library collection gradually. Today's library looks as multimedia or hybrid form. Now, E - Resources Collection Development" a new branch of collection development is emerging. E-Resources collection development is slightly different than the printed literature collection development. There are more responsibilities than difficulties. First is that the cost of e - resources is very high, secondly library need to make special technological arrangement for using e - resources. There are a lot of restrictions on use of these resources as one need to sign license agreement to make them available to the users. Nowadays most of the e-resources are published commercially; over and above readers do not prefer to read e - resources as compared to printed ones or they need some assistance in using e - resources. In this chapter we are going to discuss detailed information on this and on many more issues.

E-Resources collection development in library is a highly professional activity. Librarian plays a very significant role in organising e-resources collection. In author's view preparing e - resources collection development policy document is the first step in the direction, then only one can go for actual collection development. It would help in bringing quality in e- resource collection. The framing policy for this is absolutely necessary for it. Considering this need, while discussing issues relating to e - resources collection development the emphasis is given on how to prepare draft policy on E-resources collection development and it is expected that it would certainly guide librarian in actual developing of e-collection. Before we lay our attention to the core topic it is necessary to understand that e - resources collection development and incorporating digital literature in digital library are two different and independent issues. It is expected that while reading about e

- resources collection development the readers should not confuse with digital library development. Now let us start the discussion on e - resources collection development.

7.1. CHARACTERISTICS OF E-RESOURCES

In the beginning let us make it clear that the "electronic resource" and "e – resource" are synonymous terms as "electronic" word is represented by letter "e". As printed books, journals or reference tool are published same way printed literature is published in its electronic form. The rate of publishing of e - literature was initially less than publishing of printed literature. Nowadays due to availability of reading facility and due to its advantages, demand for e - resources is growing day by day so also the rate of publishing of e-resources has grown considerably. However, e - resource collection is yet to be stabilised. Some readers are still unhappy about e - literature form. Many libraries up till now were making literature available in both e. g. printed as well as e - form. However, the trend is changing as libraries are now going for only e - resources when the e-resources (e-journals) are newly introduced. Many libraries are discontinuing printed journal and going for only for e - journals as it saves cost of preservation of bound volumes plus it helps in saving shelf space. Now there is a new trend of buying e-resources collectively through consortium way, which further saves library funds as publishers offer discount on consortium buying.

If we want to look into the definition of e - resource it is like this," e - resource is such literature which could be read on monitors of computers or on different devices." E - Resource could be fully installed on a computer locally or it is accessed online from its server externally. Nowadays libraries are buying dictionaries and multimedia encyclopedias and making them available to the readers or they are subscribing online. Normally when library buys any printed resource it is almost owned by the library. However, when library buys any e - resource it is available only on lease basis and library does not own it. Once any e - resource is subscribed it becomes almost mandatory to renew the subscription every successive year in order to get uninterrupted access else the access is discontinued. Secondly, we cannot save a copy of e- resource for the future use. If the library stops the subscription then the publisher stops access for the library. However, some arrangement can to be made while subscribing e - resource, if the library wishes to have continuous access to e-resource archive (perpetual access) which needs additional payment. For some time e - resources were made available in two forms e.g. offline and online. The offline e - resources were made available in CD form. However, CD technology itself is on the verge of almost vanishing giving way to only online mode of e – resources. Offline resources were used by installing them in CD drives or in the form of mirror drive. Online resources are accessed on the computer but through internet platform.

There are however, several restrictions in using e - resources. Firstly, they are accessible to library's primary members, secondly they are available within the library building or at the most on LAN restricted i.e. within the premises of Institute which is called site license and thirdly library cannot share it's e- resource with any other library out of campus like inter library loan/ lending. E - Resource cannot be copied and saved or it cannot be sent through e - mail to anybody out of the institute premises.

There is a big list of non print literature. Out of these which are based on digital media are grouped as e - resource. Now let us try to know about the various types of e- resources.

7.2. TYPES OF E - RESOURCES

In this category almost in all field literature is published in electronic forms and there are various types within them:

1. Indexing and abstracting journals contain bibliographic details and the abstracts.
2. E - journals in full text form
3. E - books
4. Subject reference sources (bibliographic)
5. Subject reference sources (full text)
6. Census data
7. Geo referenced data bases etc.

In addition to the above types there are two types within them e.g. online priced and open access type(free)

Other than the above referred general types e-resources there are other e-resources like blogs, home pages, websites, hyper links, and digital libraries and e - resources available on the internet as a public domain. However, while discussing the topic of e - resources collection develop other than scholarly or academic type e - resources accessible on internet have not been considered. Institutions which publish e - resources mostly including are non - profit making organisation, professional organisations and private institutions.

7.3. E-RESOURCES (PRICED) ACQUISITION GUIDELINES

We are going to discuss the following issues relating to acquisition of e - resources.

1. E - resources selection criteria
2. E - resources selection process
3. Functionality and system use
4. Reliable access to e - resources
5. Involvement of vendors in acquisition
6. E - Resources licensing
7. E - Resources Pricing

7.3.1. Resources selection criteria

While selecting e - resources it is necessary to fix some selection criteria e.g.

(a) Whenever any new e - resources is to be included in a library the source should be in accordance with the institute's academic and research programmes, which would help in enhancing the quality and value of library collection.

(b) Selected e - Resource should satisfy heads of departments, other faculty and scientists of core and subsidiary or allied subject areas to a maximum extent

(c) Leaving archival type of e-resources, the e - resource to be selected should provide current and continuous updated knowledge of the subject.

(d) The subject content of e - resource should be published by the reputed publisher/ organisation and presented/contributed by expert, experienced and well known authors. The quality of literature is of professional or peer reviewed category.

(e) The resources published should exactly match with corresponding printed form of resources (if available in dual form) and it should be complete, means there should not be any publishing gap between printed and e - form resources. Secondly contents of e – resources should exactly match with that of printed and in respect of original text images, figures, charts and graphs.

7.3.2. E - Resources selection process

Since cost of e - resource is very high, its selection process should be scientific and with definite vision. It should be ascertained while selecting any e - source whether it has academic and information value. Whether it is universally accepted. For making selection of e- resource there should a special selection committee so that collective decision would be taken. Selected e - resource should have acceptance from all levels of user groups. In order to assess the recommendation of users to any e – resource it is necessary to provide all information to prospective users along with its demo and trail of resource access and then feedback may be obtained through surveye methods. Collected information may be analysed and e - resources which have majority of likes decision to select the same may be taken. Such process ascertains that selected e - resource would have definite and scholarly readership and it would be assured that selected e- resource would be optimally used. The e - resources should give positive impact on academic and research output of the institute then only e - resource collection development would be successful. It may happen that there are many e - resources available on the same subject scope then cost effectiveness and usage of e - resource may be compared while making proper selection. All such resources may also be exhibited to concerned users and feedbacks may be obtained which would be taken as supportive evidences while selecting e – resources. Experiences of other libraries about usage and effectiveness of a particular e - resource may be obtained ,shared and considered for decision making

7.3.3. E - Resource functionality and use of systems

With the availability, original literature source in an electronic form gets added value. In order to make it meaningful source using technology and systems must be user friendly. Some important features of it are as below:

1. To have introductory screen to describe the source
2. There should be online tutorial about how to use the source
3. Provision of "user help menu"
4. Appearance of pop-up screens giving interactive mean

With the above features using e - resources becomes meaningful, easy and interesting, with good search system, strong retrieval programme make the source more up to date, innovative and flexible.

In addition to simple search, indexing terms, title search the advanced search with boolean operators are used in order to make search easy and accurate. Availability of the sources along with controlled vocabulary would give a source the added values. In search there may be truncation or vicinity or nearby search facility.

Once user completes his / her search he / she should be able to save the search work in the source itself, which having facility to use it whenever it is further needed. User should also able to forward his retrieved information to the favored destination through FTP or one should also be able to down load it in a portable storage or to get a print copy. Once user finalizes his / her search strategy then he/her could be able to create an alert for future addition of information to the source which matches his/her search query so that whenever new information is added to the source user would get e - mail alert with details of new information. While searching the present source user should get links to extended sources which are similar to current source. Finally there may be system of customising search made in a bibliographic source connecting to corresponding full text sources available in the library.

7.3.4. E-Resources Access Issues

Access of e - resources is a tricky issue. Access of e - resources depends on what way and with what constrains the resource has been bought. Once any new e - resource is procured the access is made available to users. Access to e - resource is given in many ways.

Offline system : In the past e - sources were made available in an offline mode e.g. it was available through CDs which was received monthly as well as quarterly. In course of time library used to get accumulated with the previous CDs and as time passes full annual source which would be available in one single CD. Now this form is not prevailing and e - resources are available mostly in the online form.

Online System : E - Source access is made available now a days in the online form, where e-resource is provided directly from the publisher's server and it is continuously made available along with updates.

E - Resource either it may be online or old way offline; there are different modes of it in which it is made available which has direct relation with the costing of source. Library generally chooses the mode as per affordable of the cost. The various access modes are as below:

Stand alone : In this type e - resource is available on a single/designated (IP address) machine only. Such PC naturally would be kept in the library.

Multiple Accesses : In this case e - resource can be accessed on more than one machine. However, multiple accessed made is further subdivided depending on the cost from low to high e.g.

- Multiple Accesses from 2-5 simultaneous users
- Multiple accesses from 5-10 simultaneous users
- Full Network Access

e - Resource access could be available to "n" number of users in library building or with site license on LAN

Once one of the above modes is chosen the source could be accessed within the library building or it could be extended to the entire Institute's LAN which is called as site license.

If we consider availability of contents of the source then there would be further sub systems as:

(i) Only Bibliographic part with abstracts or

(ii) Full text source

The last option of access depends on the use and types as :

1. Only browsing and without downloading
2. Browsing & Downloading

Even after selection of e - resource access is made from one of the above modes and based on sub modes there is a last thing to consider in terms of computer technology. There are two methods how e - resource is made available to users in library or within the campus.

1. IP Filtering : E - Resources are made available to be used along with specific rights. No e-resource is allowed to access like a public domain in the local network as it is necessary to define in terms of IP address of machine only on which resource is made available. In case of IP filtering method while signing license agreement with the publishers specific IP addresses of machine(s) are necessary to be provided. There could be even range of IP addresses (dynamic IP) is given and the source is made available on all machines who's IP address falls within that IP address range. With this constrain the e - resource access is provided. As such e - resource access in any way is limited only to the site of the campus and it would not be accessed from outside.

2. Through authentication : Library always likes to have control over use of e - resources by the users on the campus. In order to check the misuse of e - resource the access made further individualised e.g. through login ID and password. This method is generally full proof as it gives further control on the use of e - resource as in case from any PC (Whose IP address is within range of IP given to publishers) is involved in sequentially downloading then the responsibility could be fixed on a person whose ID and Password is used to do so.

Normally methods of IP filtering and with authentication is found most suitable as it provides maximum access available, speedy search, saving the cost, less hurdles and less botheration on maintaining the system. However, password method is found risky as the users do not maintain its confidentiality and may share the passwords with others and password saving tendency puts resource access in danger.

While accepting e - resource it must be seen that the hardware and operating system environment is compatible and user friendly.

The most important thing is that purchasing e - resource and giving access to users in publishers point of view everything is transparent to them and subscriber has no freedom to do any corrections or manipulations in accessing the resource. The publisher's control and vigilance system is so powerful that they can easily know which source is used on which machine and by which user. If there is any misuse of resource anywhere in campus, publisher's system detects it first and knowing that they would try to alert the library authority. They initially give warning to stop the misuse or they finally discontinue the access and unless access issue is resolved amicably the access is not at all restored.

It is therefore necessary to make users aware about the conditions of access of e-resources. Moreover, if a usage policy is made available to the users by putting into display on the first screen and by getting acceptance from the user before getting started accessing e - source is always worthwhile as then onwards responsibility of use of resource entirely rests on the user him self / her self.

7.3.5. E - Resources Acquisition : Involvement of vendors

Need of help and involvement of vendor in buying and using e-resource is always advantageous. However, vendors should co-operate with library.

When library incorporates any e- resources it is always better to involve the concerned vendors as after buying the source we may need some help from them. Issues relating to this are as below:

1. Vendor who makes e - resource available should be reliable, reputed and established one.
2. In the process of selection of e - resource they should arrange to provide demonstration and trial access for the users.
3. After the e - resource is procured in the library, vendor should assist in organising training programmes for the users.
4. In case any technical problem arises in the post purchase period then they should help in solving it quickly, accurately and in a professional way.
5. Vendor should co - ordinate with publishers in providing e-resource usage report /statistics regularly.
6. In case due to mis-understanding, if any instance of misuse of the resource occurs and publisher discontinues the access of source to the library and its users then vendor should play a negotiating role to handle the problem in sympathetic way and try help library in restoring back the library access.

7.3.6. E-Resources pricing systems

Cost of e - resources is driven by many factors, mostly connected with different mode of access of it. Now let us understand costing of any e - resource in terms of the following points:

1. Whether e -resource is obtained in offline mode (in terms of CDs) or in online mode. However, offline mode is no longer available and most of e - resources are now preferred as online.
2. Whether library subscribes source as a standalone mode i.e. source is bought to use only on a single machine?
3. If library has opted for multiuser mode then how many users simultaneously would be using?

2 - 5 users?

5 - 10 users? Or

Full network version is opted?

4. Whether library choose to go for only browsing access e .g. without down loading or library has opted for unlimited access e.g. browsing as well as downloading to a limited extent as source allows.
5. If library goes for subscription of printed and its soft copy e - source together then publishers would consider some concession in e - resource subscription.
6. Normally any resource subscribed by the library would provide access for one year. In case if next year, the library does not continue to subscribe, then access gets discontinued automatically. However, if the library makes some arrangement while buying the source by paying additional fees which ensures the library to get archival access to e - sources subscribed for more time than the subscription period. The arrangement is termed as perpetual access.
7. The final point is about subscribing e - resource individually or as a member of any consortium. Publishers provide concession when libraries subscribe e - resources through the consortium. Consortium way of subscribing e-sources helps in saving funds.

7.3.7. E - Resource Licensing

We have discussed the various factors relating to getting access to e-resources by different modes and their corresponding impact on costing of e - resource. Basically those are the conditions on which library subscribes to any e-resource. License is a legal document depicting conditions and norms the library has accepted in procuring any e- resource. Library need to sign license agreement giving all those condition it has accepted in getting the e - resource. It is a two way agreement signed by a library authority and the publishers. In reality it is a one way binding on library to use the e - resource within the constraints and conditions specified in license agreement by the publishers. It leaves more responsibilities on the part of the library than on the publishers. It is therefore, necessary for the library to understand clearly text of such legal document and suggest corrections if necessary. It is also necessary to be careful by the library users not to violate those conditions any time else publisher stops the access of e - resource. In addition to those conditions library needs to specify list of IP address or range of IP machines on which source would be generally accessed.

7.4. E - RESOURCES ACQUISITION IN LIBRARY

After knowing access, costing and licensing details, now let us go through the actual process of e - resource acquisition. The first step in this direction is making decision about acquiring e - resource.

7.4.1. E - Resource Selection - Decision Making

The selection of e- resource and taking decision is a bit tedious and responsible process. Selection of normal printed literature is comparatively very easy. The reason in this case is the high cost of e - resource. Unless there is a provision of funds library cannot think about it. The responsible decision relates to its technical functionality, vendor's involvement, access right one needs to take careful decisions in choosing any e- resource It is certainly not a job of individual librarian so it is always better to have participation of expert people in taking decision. Moreover, it is better if library appoint a special purchase committee comprising of a group of experts. This way the responsibility gets divided and it does not leave any doubt about e - resource purchase decision. The committee could have the representation of the following personalities:

- Librarian, reference and special collection librarians
- Computer hardware, software and networking experts.
- Finance officer
- Consortia issue handling professional

The committee having the above experts would analyse the suggestions received from faculty and scientists and provide its decision time to time in the course of the year. It would also be ensured the provision of funds and it would look in to the issues like pricing, access, functionality, licensing carefully and gives its recommendations about going for e - resources.

7.4.2. Steps for E - Resource Acquisition

E - Resource Acquisition steps are as:

1. To acquire information about new e - resource useful to users from vendors and publishers and provide it to all concerned departs and users.
2. Invite suggestions on subscribing e - resource. Prepare list of useful e - resources and prepare questionnaire in order to get feedback from all concerned users in seeking approval of the authorities.
3. Analyse feedback received through the questionnaire. Prepare priority list of e - resources to be considered which have maximum demand to be short listed for taking further steps of decision making.
4. Through vendor get assistance in organising demos of resources and provide the trial access to the users in order to get feedback on actual browsing them by the users. Ascertain details regarding access of e - resource and the conditions under which resources is going to be acquired / made available to them and get their acceptance for it.
5. Prepare estimates of acquiring e-resources and to consider other expenses on their purchase.
6. Give all the data obtained through the above exercise to the purchase committee for information and consideration.
7. The special purchase committee would analyse the data, discuss all the issues and give its recommendation.
8. The text of license agreement document to be cross checked through a legal expert and to suggest correction in it to drop some of its clause which are not good in the interest of library.
9. Compare cost of e - resource with the consortium pricing and if there is considerable saving

by going through consortium way then to complete the formalities of becoming consortium member by signing the necessary MOU.

10. To forward formal e - resource subscription to publisher through the vendor. Pay the subscription amount, provide list of IPs to publishers on which e - resource would be accessed by the users.
11. Look for experience of subscribing particular e - resources from the other libraries who have acquired the source previously and try to know about services and usage report or consult consortium authorities while taking decisions.
12. The special purchase committee would ascertain whether purchasing e - resource fits in the e - resource acquisition policy of the institute.
13. Notify users about the availability of new e-resource once subscribed ,organise user training and appeal them for using the source to the optimum level so that the purpose of getting it is fulfilled and users are satisfied about it.

7.4.3. Dropping the old of unused E - Resources

The special purchase committee appointed for the recommending new e - resource can also suggest for removal of an old e - resource. In this respect the following criteria are taken into account:

1. E - resources which are not being used or which are not liked by majority of users can be removed.
2. If the technology of e - resource has become old which is not competent to be used on advanced platform can be discontinued.
3. If there are two e - resources which have same scope or which are overlapping one other and if by discontinuing one of them is going to save the funds.
4. The contents of e- resource have become obsolete and the information is not authentic can be removed.
5. Old offline resource which become difficult to use with new technology can be removed from the collection.
6. When there are difficulties in accessing the source or which goes frequently off and readers keep complaining then it is worth removing.

The e - resources which are from the above category could be decided to be dropped. Dropping un-useful resources saves recurring expenses and it gives opportunity for library to subscribe a new resources in replacement

7.5. SELECTION OF OPEN ACCESS (FREE) RESOURCES

These days there are several open access type of e - resources which are available free of cost, comprising of home pages, list serve or use group sources, government report and a good number of full text e - journals, e-magazines, e – books and online dictionaries/encyclopedias. If with addition of open access resource in collection is going to add value, if the information given in them is beneficial to academic programmes and if they have good scholarly value then it is worthwhile to add them in the e - resource collection of the library. However in selecting such resource some criteria must be considered as:

1. If any open access e - resource is published by a reputed well know publishers then it could be a good resource for a particular subject.
2. If such sources are being used by users in reputed libraries
3. If e - resource website is easily accessible, stable and it would be continuously available for use
4. If open access e-books and issues of e - journal have definite publishing schedule displayed on their web sites and are regularly updated.
5. If the design of e - resource website is attractive and it is widely acceptable by the readers, it is easy to use and it has site index and it has excellent search engine to search the information.

If any open access e - resource fulfills the above referred criterion then it is worth adding to library e - resource collection.

7.5.1. Open access e - resources to be avoided

There are quite a good number of open access resources available that does not mean each of them is good and non obligatory. Many of them could have some shortcomings. One should judge carefully whether they are authentic or is there any obligatory conditions in acquiring them? such as:

1. Open access e - resources which work for advertising companies or do sales promotion
2. E - source which give news type of information about an organisation.
3. The sources which are incomplete which are not suitable for academic programmes or which do not have any research value.
4. The open access web sites which try to ask for payments indirectly.

7.5.2. Copy right issues of open access e- resources

Whenever library procures open access type e – resources, it may be seen that while using the same users would not violet their copy rights. In providing such websites on campus through library website, library should complete the necessary formalities such as :

1. If the library wishes to adopt open access source for its users then its existence should be verified and library should acknowledge open access source which must be confirmed by the publishers.
2. While putting into use it may carefully be seen that the library does not display any indication of ownership of that site else it would be treated as violation of copy right.
3. There must be provision on the website to stop or unsubscribe the source at any moment.

7.6. PROCUREMENT OF E – RESOURCES: MANAGERIAL ISSUES

While any priced e - resource (Priced or open access) is included in library's e - resource collection then some managerial issues need to be fulfilled such as:

(a) Whenever the e - resource is put into use readers must be informed on what basis it is available to them such as:

   (i) Whether it is offline or online

   (ii) Whether library has accepted for site license or available as standalone

   (iii) Whether it has only browsing access or it is available as unlimited browsing and downloading.

(b) What way it is available to users

   (i) On IP address enabled and / or

   (ii) Through authentication i.e. against login ID and password.

(c) If e - resource is meant only to be accessed in digital lab. of the library then there must be arrangement such as:

   (i) A.C. Room

   (ii) Internet connectivity

   (iii) Power supply with UPS

   (iv) LAN Environment

The digital lab may be organised with a proper assistance of trained manpower to help the users and overs the usage .

7.7. E - RESOURCES USER TRAINING FOR USE PROMOTION

E - Resource is a special kind of source and certain information technology gadgets are required to use them. Considering bindings, restrictions and comparatively less response from the users it is necessary to put extra efforts so that readers would make maximum use of them. It is necessary to organise user training workshops and to work for the promotion of e- resources among the users. Especially newly admitted UG & PG students and newly joined faculty, scientists and researches should be given hands on training in their joining period by organising special training programmes. If such programmes are organised periodically or on certain date of every month so that users can attend then conveniently when they have free time. Especially the users who do not have previous experience and who are new to e - resources get confidence by attending such training programmes. All these efforts not only results in enhancing use of e - resources but it would also impact on research output by using the e-resources. If such programs are organised subject wise then with group interaction about the use of resources the programmes becomes more effective. If the programme comprises parts such as first introduction and then need based use of resources, brings a liveliness in them.

7.8. WELL KNOWN E - RESOURCES FOR LIBRARY

In this para we are going to have a short introduction of some of the renowned e- resources :

(A) Full text online resources

EBSCO

Elsevier- Science Direct

Emerald full text

(B) Bibliographic resources

Engineering village – Compendex

Engineering village - Inspec

Web of science

Scifinder scholar

Chemical abstract

(C) Standards or Patents

Indian Standards

Indian Patents

International Patents

Now we would have their short introduction as:

A. Full Text Online Sources

7.8.1. EBSCO Databases

This e - resource is meant for business field especially for business management institute libraries where it is most useful. This database contains articles from 3800 periodicals from business field. It's scope is related with literature published from twentieth century. Along with periodical literature the source also provides Business Thesaurus useful for business field. It also provides facility to search references from 1100 scholarly journals. Database covers full text articles from more than 3000 periodicals. In addition, it also provides PDF copies of articles published prior to 1985. Current literature is available since 1985. Subjects like marketing management, management information systems, accounting, finance, and econometrics and International business are covered in the scope of EBSCO. This resource also provide information relating to other fields.

Academic search elite : Most of the worldwide academic institutes depend on EBSCO's well known source - Academic Search Elitc. Elitc information source contains full text articles from 1833 periodicals most of them are in PDF form. Elite fulfills support literature requirement concern with academic courses, social sciences, medicines and Ethnic studies as these are the core areas of this source. It provides bibliographic details with the abstracts as well as full text literature.

For library and information science EBSCO publishes another very useful abstracting source e.g. - Library and Information Science & Technology Abstract (LISTA) on the similar lines of LISA.

EBSCO data base source is normally useful for the following types of Institutes like

- Colleges and Universities
- Hospitals and Medical Institutions
- Corporations
- Govt. institutions

- K-12 Schools
- Public Libraries

They can very well search information to various subjects in this source. Under college and university if one tries for information sources relating to library and information science it can be searched from the following database.

- Book Index with review.
- Information Science Technology abstract (ISTA)
- Library and Information Science Technology abstract (LISTA)
- LISTA Full text
- Library literature & Information science.
- Serials Directory

The website of this source is as: http://ebscohost.com/default.php

7.8.2. Elsevier Science Direct

Journal publishers like Elsevier Science and Academic Press have jointly brought out collection of journal articles, a full text source under the name "Science Direct." This source is well known for literature in the fields of Science, Technology and Medicines. Information from scholarly journals, bibliographic databases and literature from reference tools in their fields is made available in this source. In the scope of this comprehensive source contains 59 million abstracts, two million full texts and 1 million supportive literatures from 1500 scholarly journals, articles from these fields. For INDEST consortium libraries like IITs, IIMs and I.I.Sc. e - resources are freely available as sponsored by MHRD. This source provides full text literature from 2137 scholarly journals. The AICTE member libraries get full text literature from 225 journals from the fields like computer science, engineering and technology fields. Science Direct comprises of 2137 scholarly journals published from 1995 onwards of Elsevier science and Academic press jointly. Website: http://www.sciencedirect.com

7.8.3. Emerald full text

Emerald publishes scholarly journal literature for management and library and information & library fields with the name Emerald full text. The source broadly relates subjects like engineering, applied science and technology fields. To provide e - data bases for the fields of management and library science is the main objective of this source.

Out of contributions from the subject's experts from MCB University Press this source was first established in 1967. It takes the responsibility of making full text scholarly literature available in the fields like strategic management, change management and international marketing. Since 2001 it was renamed as Emerald Insight. For the academic and research this sources is found very useful.

Website http://emeraldinsight.com

B. Bibliographic Sources

7.8.4. Engineering Village : Compendex (EI - Village)

In earlier day Engineering Index used to publish in printed form subsequently its electronic version was published e. g. in CDs which was published offline as "compendex-plus" by Dialog. Its online version is known as EI village or Engineering village Compendex. This is the only comprehensive source in engineering field providing bibliographic index with abstract. Its scope is quite wide comprises of 5000 journals in engineering including conference proceedings containing nearly 7 billion references. It refers technical reports too. The core area of this source is applied science of engineering which concerns with subjects like Nuclear Technology, Bioengineering, Transportation, Chemical Process Engineering, Light and optical technology, Agriculture, Engineering & Food Technology, Computer data processing, Applied Physics, Electronic & Telecommunication, Control, Civil, Mechanical, Materials, Petroleum Aerospace and Automotive Engineering,this list shows its comprehensiveness. This source adds every year nearly 2,500 new records which are concerned with 175 engineering fields. The unique feature of this source is that it updates every week with new references, which reveals its up–to-datedness. It covers literature published since 1970 and beyond. However earlier data is also available

Website : http://www.engineeringvillage.org

7.8.5. Engineering Village - Inspec

Institute of Electrical engineering (IEE) publishes bibliographic index with abstract comprising of remaining fields (or fields other than engineering)The index is published with the name Engineering Village - Inspec which has its own inspec database. The source comprises of fields like physics, electronics, electrical engineering, computers and control with information technology. It concerns with references with abstracts of articles published in scholarly journals on physics, electronics, and electrical engineering and computer science. The citations listed in this source are of journals articles and conference papers. It also refers well known classic books, technical reports and research theses and dissertations. In this source there are 7.3 million records which relate with 4200 journals, 2000 conference Proceedings, books reports as well from Inspec database. INSPEC is now published with its main source e.g. EI-Village. From Inspec database it also provides online reference service on US patents, websites and standards. It covers literature since 1969 and onwards.

Website http://engineering village

7.8.6. Web of Science

The origin of this source goes to old Science Citation Index published by the Institute of Scientific Information (ISI) under the leadership of Garfield. The main emphasis of science citation index is to analyse who and how much the published scientific literature is used by others or in other words it concerns with citation analysis. With such publication it is possible to assess the impact of articles published by well known authors on science literature. Any authors gets an opportunity for inspiring others to use of his/ her articles in writing their articles by citing reference of the original author. Such impact is measured in terms of impact factor or H - Index. Getting certain impact factor or H - Index is an honor of the author.

The science citation or social science citation Index published earlier in printed form is now published in electronic form and online with the name "Web of Science". It is also known as "Web of Knowledge". Presently it is being published by Thompson Reuters in a commercial way. Web of science has the following sub-parts as :

- Social science citation Index
- Century of social sciences
- Arts of Humanities Citation Index
- Conference proceedings citation Index

Along with English this source is also published in other main languages. Web of sciences facilitates the following things:

- To prepare Citation Graph / Map
- Provides excellent citation analysing tools
- It also provides web based writing tools.

Websitewww://isiwebofknowledge/product-tools/multidisciplinary/webofscience

7.8.7. Scifinder Scholar & Chemical Abstract (Online bibliographic index with abstract)

This source is related with old printed source named Chemical Abstract (CA). Technically it has Z39-85 window's based interface which makes it possible to provide information from chemical abstract systems in a simple way. It has a coverage of chemical literature published since 1907 and onwards. Original Chemical Abstract source used to index articles, patents and standards published in chemistry field, however, now scifinder scholar covers CA as well as Medline-Databases. Articles and patents published in chemistry are further indexed on substance data, chemical reactions, chemical regulatory data, chemical suppliers, chemical formulas and biomedical literature which provide a comprehensive and up to date source. Over and above scifinder scholar online source is now not only limited to chemistry field but it covers other related field like Agriculture, Biology, Life sciences, Engineering, Food, Geology, Medical, Physics, Polymers and Material science. In spite of association of chemical abstract with scifinder scholar it is still published in original CA source [CA on CD or CA-online] independently.

Scifinder scholar has the following characteristics :

1. It is a unique source to get information from science field published in journals, articles and patents.
2. It refers nearly 10,000 journals from chemical science field
3. It covers patent data of nearly 59 patent authorities.
4. It takes us back to literature published from now to 1800

5. This is the biggest information source of organic and inorganic substances in the world
6. It captures articles published in the science field as less as in the last two days time period, published in any corner of the world

   Websites: http://www.cas.org/products/scifinder/index.html

   http://scifinder.cas.org

7.8.8. Indian Standards

Bureau of Indian Standards (BIS) publishes Indian Standards. It has its head quarter at Delhi. There are branches of BIS in all metro cities in India which makes standards available at local places.

Indian standards are now also available on CD s for only browsing purpose. CD comprises of 18000 Indian standards on it. This database is available against subscription which is updated after every two months. It has its own search engine which facilitates searching and browsing any standard on computer monitor. With standard no. and title. One can obtain the hard copy of it from BIS branches. It also helps in searching old standards. The list of broad subject of BIS standards is as: civil engineering, chemical engineering, electro chemical, food & agriculture, electronics, telecom engineering, production engineering, medical equipments, hospital equipments, management systems, mechanical engineering, petroleum, coal and related products, metallurgical engineering, water resources, transportation engineering, textile and standards for several consumer products.

Use of this source is available in the libraries of subscribing institutes. However, there are copy right restrictions on sharing them with other libraries or photocopying them.

Website: http://bis.org.in

7.8.9. Indian and International Patents

Indian Patent office is at Nagpur with its branch office in Mumbai and other metros. Industrial organisations apply patents for their products as well as designs and patent office awards the patents. Nowadays importance of patent information system is very much felt. Right from applying for patent to awarding it, needs lot of information, experience and legal expertise, which needs expert man power. There are agents as well as attorneys to assist in these matters. Patenting process also needs searching of patent databases of local and international levels. Indian Patent office provides the facility to search patents online through a comprehensive database and provides information services. This data base is also available on CDs which comprises the of following resources:

Ekaswa A - Database - Patents

Ekaswa B - Database patent applications files since January 1995 of notified oppositions

Ekaswa C - Data base patent applications published since January 2005 onwards. The cost of Ekaswa A and B database is Rs. 500/-

whereas Ekaswa-C on CD is costing Rs 1500/-

Website of Indian Patent Office

http:// www.indianpatents.org.in

International patent system : As per Patent Coordination Treaty (PCT) WIPO (World Intellectual Property Organisation) is providing assistance to patent applicants to seek patent protection internationally for their inventions. They also help patent offices with their patent granting decisions and facilitate public access to a wealth of technical or information relating to those inventions. The speciality of this patent system is that by filing one international patent application under (PCT), applicant can simultaneously seek protection for the invention in148 counties throughout the world.

WIPO is providing online source to search patents worldwide with the name- Patent-scope. With Patent-scope one can search nearly 56 million patent documents including 2.9 million published international patent and applications (PCT).

WEBSITES

WIPO- PCT: http:// www.wipo.int/pct/en

WIPO: Patentscope: http://patentscope.int/search/en/search.jsf.

8

Use of Web 2.0 Technology Tools in Library

8.0. INTRODUCTION

Up till now we have seen the various features of using information technology in the library. Normally when we complete library computerisation we look into further automation of library by using advanced information technology tools. As information technology is advancing further we find availability of newer and newer technologies for library automation. We read about them in library literature. However, it is challenging for libraries and ultimately to librarians to actually use the new technology in library management. Web 2.0 is one such new and advanced Internet technology tool emerged recently.

Web 2.0 technology has the background of web 1.0. It is said that web 2.0 is the advanced internet technology as compared to web 1.O.Using internet technology has brought revolution in library functioning. Nowadays every librarian and library professional is curious to know and use internet technology in library. In fact it has become essential for everyone to know and earn expertise in using internet. Internet technology has gone through many evolutionary phases to reach its current advanced stage e.g. web 2.0. Moreover, it is still evolving further to become more advanced. Web 1.0, Web 2.0 and Web 3.0 are those developing phases of internet technology. Unless we fully use these phases one would not be able to understand how they differ from each other or what their characteristics are. Libraries of western countries including public and school libraries are extensively using web 1.0 and also web 2.0. Not only knowing but users have earn expertise in using them. It would take little more time to see these technologies in our libraries. However, today we can certainly try to understand them. There is a good progress in using information technology in Indian libraries. However, the strength of librarians and library professional not having adequate knowledge and expertise of using advanced information technology is considerably large. Many of them are even not aware of it. So we need to do a lot to understand about the advanced internet technology e.g. about web 2.0. The scope of web 2.0 technology is very vast and it is difficult to accommodate it in one single chapter. However, the author has made an attempt in this direction. Although the topic of web 2.0 technology is not simple to understand but it is equally interesting too. It is expected that readers would at least have introduction of web 2.0 technology through this chapter which certainly would create interest and inspire them to read and know more about it.

8.1. INTERNET TECHNOLOGY - HISTORICAL BACKGROUND

Telecommunication technology has been greatly responsible for the emergence and evolution of internet technology as with the invention of telephony, telecommunication technology has developed speedily. Initially only voice signals were transmitted but now we see that voice, digital, video, animation, geographically referenced data and multimedia data are also easily transmitted without losing any data in the transmission. Packet switched switching system is the advanced stage of telecommunication technology. With such an advanced communication system communication between two computers also becomes feasible. The availability of such advanced communication medium has also helped in laying foundation of internet technology. With communication system we are able to retrieve information and data from the remote server through the client machine. This background development has proved to be a boon for development of internet.

There are various phases of development of internet technology. If we wish to look into its history, one needs to scan the period from 1957 to 1990. Arpanet concept is seen as origin of internet. In order to explore use of science and technology for defence purpose a division named Arpa was planned in 1967. The actual establishment of Arpanet took place in 1969. Under Arpanet initially all the computers of California University were connected to form a network. Subsequently computers from other universities also joined the network.

In order to face unclear attacks a strong information exchange system was felt necessary for which the Arpanet was made operational. Subsequently, academics, researchers, computer experts, engineers and scientist started using the Arpa network. In 1970 Information transfer protocol became available for use. In 1980 e-mail facility was also made available. At the same time web pages were designed. Libraries started uploading their computerised catalogue on the network. In 1991 Minnesota University established the first home page named "Gopher". With these developments it was possible to access files available on internet. In the same year a revolution came in internet technology with the invention of World Wide Web by Tim Berners Lee.

As such in real sense Tim Bernes-Lee is known to be the pioneer of today's internet technology. It was the success of research carried out by him along with other scientists of Particle Physics Laboratory. Under the same leadership the organisation called CERN developed the rules for exchange of information based on hypertext technique known as http (Hyper Text Transmission Protocol.) This technology has now become very much familiar to us. Under hypertext technology web pages were connected to each other through hyper texted words or links which could be accessed successively by clicking them. Home pages were formed with the collection of web pages. These home pages were uploaded to internet by giving them domain names. All the web page addresses begin with word www. When we put web address in browser window one can open and browse the website. Up to this stage it was termed as the initial time period of internet evolution. This stage onwards internet technology started progressing truly, which is termed as web 1.0 technology.

8.2. WEB 1.0 (THE FIRST GENERATION OF INTERNET)

After stabilizing the initial stage of Internet next step was availability of browsers e.g. MSN, NETSCAPE, Firefox, Fedora etc. for windows and UBUNTU which works on Linux. After having the browser, which works as friend or a guide in accessing internet. We need search engine like Google, Safari or Bing which help us in selecting specific website to browse. There are over 40 search engines. Information on internet is available with different categories of websites they could be grouped in following groups:

(A) Information providers (free)

1. News types of websites which are freely available
2. Websites for entertainment, sport or games
3. Websites of Libraries with their OPACs
4. Websites of universities, academic and research institutions plus govt. departments and e - learning sites.
5. Portals of industries, banks and portals of online shopping, e – commerce sites and web sites for trading, railway and air reservation sites.

(B) Information Sources (Priced) full-text and bibliographic

E - Journals

E - Books

E - Databases (Full text)

(C) Open Access

E-books & E - Journals

(D) Digital Libraries

Topics such as use of internet in library and development of digital library have been discussed in separate chapters in detailed in this book. With computerisation and with use of internet it brings quality in functioning and services of library. Librarians would understand significance of internet in library, if they fully utilise it in the library. Once they achieve expertise and competency in using web 1.0, it would not be difficult to use next advanced stage e.g. web 2.0 in library.

The discussion in the above paras takes us to the first stage of internet e.g. web 1.0. This age internet of was called "(Dot) .com" or "double click" age of internet. In the first stage of internet trend was that users used to travel to information. Where as in web 2.0 technology the trend is information is flowing to the users. Now after understanding web 1.0 technology let us try to understand what web 2.0 technology is :

8.3. WEB 2.0 : INTRODUCTION (SECOND GENERATION OF INTERNET)

Web 2.0 concept now has been fairly stabilized. Around 2004 Tim O'Reilly and Dale Dougherty, two engineers of O'Reilly Media Company first presented the concept of web 2.0 technology. It so happened in 1990 that the share market crashed and many dot.com industries suffered a huge loss. Considering limitations of dot.com technology need of new and strong technology was very much felt. In order to overcome short comings of web 1.0 new web 2.0 technology got emerged. The special characteristics of web 2.0 technology were that it was collaborative, more advanced than web 1.0 and most interactive. In Web 2.0 technology the line between developing and use was no more existing.

Definition of web 2.0 presented by Wikipedia in 2008 (The online encyclopedia) is like this, "web 2.0 technology is the advanced generation of internet comprising of the following tools e.g.

- RSS feeds
- Weblogs
- Instant Messaging
- Streaming media
- Wikis
- Social Networking
- Social Book Marking
- Tagging
- Mash-up
- Flicker
- Podcasting
- Start-up page
- Managing own search engines"

When we see the above long list of web tools available under the advanced internet generation, we realise that web 2.0 technology is certainly more advanced and rich.

In 2005 O'Reilly presented a paper in international conference on "What is web 2.0?", wherein he presented a comparative review of web 1.0 and web 2.0 technologies and explained the world about web tool which have been freshly incorporated under the web 2.0 umbrella. Based on his review a comparative list of services which were available under both the technologies web 1.0 and web 2.0 are tabulated as in the following tables respectively (Table 8.1 and 8.2).

Web 1.0	**Web 2.0**
Internet Technology & Services	Internet Technology& Services
Old technology	New and advanced technology
Individual homepages	Weblog
Online published Encyclopaedia	Wikipedia or wikis
Textual assignments	Use of streaming media
Tecsonomy	Focsonomy
E - Mail communication	Instant Messaging
O photo	Flicker
One way presentation	Interactive
Web master centered development	Collaborative Development
PC specific Usage	Online Universal Usage
Costly technology Tools	Free of cost web tools

Table 8.1. Comparative Review of web 1.0 and web 2.0 Technologies

New Technologies Available Under web 2.0 Which were not available in web 1.0
RSS Feed Social Networking Social Book marking Tagging Podcasting Start Page Managing own search engine etc.

Table 8.2. New Technologies available under web 2.0

Above two tables tell us all together about new technological tools available under web 2.0

If we look at the above tables we find that under web 2.0 more advanced tools than web 1.0 are available. Under web 2.0 many new and useful tools and concepts are available which were not existing in earlier technology. After taking comparative review of web 1.0 and web 2.0 technologies, let us look into the special characteristics of web 2.0 technology.

8.3.1. Characteristics of web 2.0 Technology

The characteristics of web 2.O technology are as follows.

- Web as a platform
- Collaborative intelligence
- Freedom from software loop

Now let us discuss them in detail

8.3.1.1. Web as a platform

Significant difference from older technology that we experience in using web 2.O technology is that whatever web technology or tool we need are available on web and we are going to use them on web itself. As against pervious situation in web 2.0 resources and your computer would not be different, so everything is available on web itself through our local PC as stepping in point. We need not have to download softwares, install them in your PC and preserve / maintain them in your server or PC. In the old environment we used to write a paper, send it to our friend for improvement or addition via e - mail attachment. In turn our friend needs to save the paper in a file in his PC, after editing he used to send it back to you via e-mail. You then have to download it to see and read. However, when we work with web 2.0 technology we need not have to do all these things. One can skip all these steps and do the work in a very easy manner. In this case you need to upload your draft paper once on web with some suitable web 2.O tool. Your friend can see the same on web. He can edit it by using word utilities available on web. After having the feedbacks from all a final collective paper would be ready for publishing. When we use web 2.0 utility our friend need not have to depend on different PCs. Whatever is collectively available all could see from anywhere from a remote corner and continue your work. This becomes as simple as it looks like. Only thing needed that all contributors should register for one single web tool and access the material by logging it with their passwords. One can also interface a database to the source collectively created on web. You can work from office or anywhere or even while on tour nothing comes in your way. In case if you feel worried you can keep backup of your work in your home PC.

8.3.1.2. Collective Intelligence

While describing web 2.0 advanced internet technology it is said that it is possible to use collective intelligence very easily. Moreover the web 2.0 technology emphasises doing many things collectively through the free access instead of keeping knowledge in custody of individuals. Under web 2.0 technology there are several tools for creating information source collectively (wikis). Another example in web 2.0 is that one researcher creates his/her own index for a library catalogue or for using an encyclopedia. The index thus prepared is also made available to other researchers working in the same field which makes it easy and convenient for all (Tagging). Not only this, with encyclopedia created by using web 2.0 technology tools (wiki) anybody can open the same and edit or improve it further. People can create an information source for the whole society (Social Networking). Someone can host a blog on web using relevant tool on a subject which is too latest and put it for discussion on the web. Interested people post their reactions and feedbacks to such blogs. Considering all these a comprehensive information source would be on the topic ready for other others to read. All these things become possible only by organising collective intelligence.

8.3.1.3. Freedom from software Loop

The third characteristic of web 2.0 technology is freedom from software loop. Now a days it is seen that difficulties faced in getting open source application software have considerably minimised. In case of proprietary type of softwares a commercial company manufactures software and makes it available to buyer after putting it to test. However, a customer when starts using the software they find so many bugs in it. With all these feedbacks and suggestions it comes back to the manufacturer for revision. However, this process takes a long time which keeps user waiting for improved software. With 2.0 technology we can have a solution to this problem as with web 2.0 software design circle works in a very different way. It works like this- once the software is given to the user it is made operational. If users find any bug while using it is reported to the software owner where they try to correct the programme error directly on the web online. In this way the software which is put into use remains with the user, its functioning does not suffer and the work of improving is done side by side. Such process saves time and efforts of both, users and the software manufacturer. The major revision or up gradation of software can also be done in this way. As such users get freedom from trapping themselves in a loop of software development process. In software development in web 2.0 environment there would not be a stage of Beta test mode.

While going through the above characteristics of web 2.O technology one might feel that all the points looks imaginary and it may not be the fact. However, there is no scope of having misunderstanding about web 2.0 as the things in web 2.0 are done so promptly with the use of advanced web language called AJAX (Asynchronous Java script and XML). In this new language tool we can find collective effects of XML, HTML,Cascading Style Sheet(CSS) and java script. With this advanced techniques of correcting bugs in programmes would be done very quickly without spending much time on it. Secondly, while handling web pages we would find them in a static form. Not only it would be possible to divide a web page if it is convenient, it would also be possible to incorporate fresh part in the websites or to bring changes in them. These things the user would also be able to do. In this entire process users can have full control over the webpage development. They can combine two different web pages in to one web resource by using web tool like Mashup.

8.3.2. Web 2.0 Technology as imagined by O'Reilly

We have seen that O'Reilly presented his idea about web 2.O technology in his paper on, "What is web 2.0?" at the international conference in 2005. The characteristics we referred above are based on seven points given in this paper. The points he discussed in his paper are like this:

1. Web as platform
2. Harnessing collective intelligence
3. Data is in the next Intel inside
4. End of Software release cycle
5. Lightweight programming models
6. Software above the level of single device
7. Rich user experience

O'Reilly has discussed the above characteristics of web 2.0 technology in his paper at length. Although the discussion in his paper could be complicated to understand however, it is worthwhile to look at a web map displayed by him in his paper, which seems quite knowledgeable and informative . See the same in Fig. 8.2.

8.4. FUTURE OF WEB TECHNOLOGY (WEB 3.0)

In this chapter we have studied about the various generations of web technology such as:

- Initial Internet Technology
- Web 1.0 technology
- Web 2.0 Technology

Now question comes to the mind what is next after web 2.0? However, now there is an answer to this question. Internet experts are already busy in inventing web 3.O technology. It is sure that web 3.0 technology would be more superior to web 1.0 or even web 2.0. It is expressed that web 3.O technology would work for us like our personal assistant or rather correct word like 'Agent'. Out of these three generations of web technology, web 2.0 technology was more memorable. Nobody would have believed that such an advanced internet technologies would come into reality.

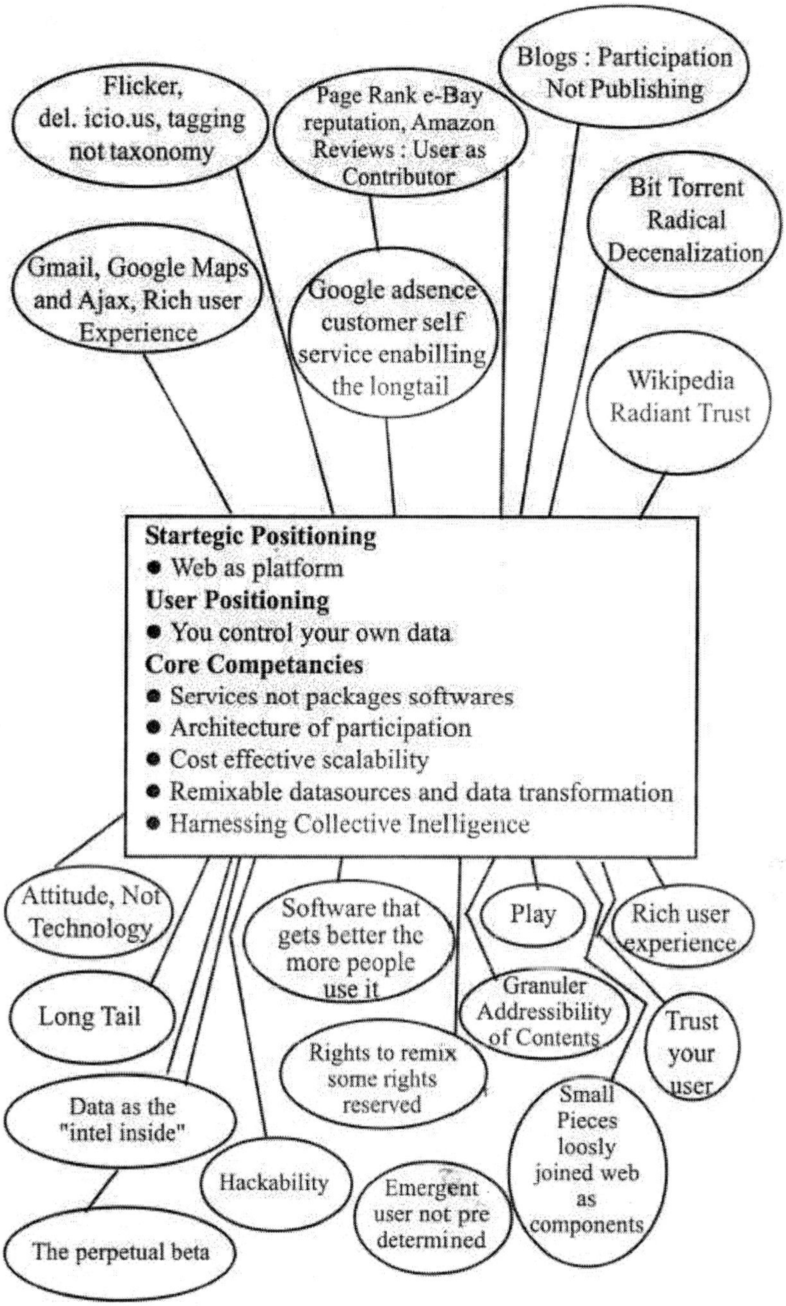

Fig. 8.2. web 2.O map
Courtesy : **Tim O'Reilly," What is web 2.O?"**
http://www.oreilly.com (accessed on 8th June 2016)

We have fully used web 1.0 technology. In this stage we were using the resources as they were available on the web. We did not have any freedom to make changes in them or incorporate any new information in it or try to improve them, which was possible in web 2.0 technology period. We remember amazon.com was the first web portal which allowed us to write online reviews on the books available there, publish them with the book for the information of other browsers. Web pages could connect groups of people with each other. Under web 2.0 available tools like social networking or my space(Facebook) or YouTube are the other examples of getting freedom on web to collaborate or interact with web sites. Today one of the powerful web tools to exchange the contents of information is YouTube. Web 2.0 has gifted us with the facility to keep receiving information alters from websites and blogs in the form of RSS (Really simply syndication) feeds. These days we see use of new tools like cell phone feeds, video game terminals or viewing internet programmes like YouTube on our television screen through chrome cast or Google stick -HDMI streaming device which converts normal television into a smart TV.

Now we are trying to understand web tools available under web 2.0 and use them. However, at international level people have long back adopted web 2.0 technology and now they are trying to understand how to use web 3.0 technology.

It is said that web 3.0 technology would work like our personal agent on web. Web 3.0 technology is also compared with a big-data. Now examples of using web 3.0 are being discussed in the professional literature. It is termed as complex search facility, for example suppose you wish to go for a movie with your family in a nearby cinema hall and subsequently also wish to have dinner in a nearby good hotel. You may be curious to know how much it would cost you? Whether cinema tickets would be available? It is said that web 3.0 technology would easily provide you answers to such complex questions that too very quickly such as :

1. Which movies are screened in which cinema hall, their timings and availability of tickets with cost.
2. Distance and time needed to reach there and availability of roads.
3. The list of good hotels nearby to cinema halls where one can go for dinner with table reservation facility
4. Distance and time to reach hotels and distance and time needed to come back home, availability of nearest road.
5. Total estimates for the above expenditure.

All that is needed in web 3.0 is just one question containing all component queries. The technology would answer it within no time. Web 3.0 technology would be so intelligent that it not only would work on the terms but it would understand their context about What is what? It would consider your need very intelligently and provide the satisfactory answers to it. However, it would take some more time to see actual utilization of web 3.0 technology in our practical daily life. Internet experts are working how all the sources on internet could be connected as it is envisaged in semantic web concept. Now after having the information on all generations of internet now let us try to know about web 2.0 related concept e.g. library 2.0

8.5. LIBRARY 2.0: CONCEPT

We see the impact of web 1.0 internet on library functioning. Since web 2.0 is still advanced technology and it is certain that it will not remain isolated from being used in library functioning and services. Considering tremendous utility of web 2.0 in library, librarians and library professionals are trying to understand it and earning expertise in using it in library management. Use of web 2.0 in library is being extensively discussed in LIS literature these days. If we want to explain the significant difference between web 1.0 and web 2.0 it could be said that the technology of web 1.0 was of static in nature, where as new web 2.0 technology is in its dynamic form. Let us try to understand this through an example from the library environment. When readers search the reading material of a library by using OPAC. In this process they enter a search query in OPAC search window, they get search result. However, when the library would adopt web 2.0 then there would be big improvement in this process. In web 2.0 environment when the same users try to search through OPAC the system would record their queries, the search results and also identify the searcher. When the same user would try to search material through OPAC next time , he/she would be prompted with his previous search queries and the saved search result, which is really significant in reader's point of view. Not only this, system would try to interact through response and alert with new information as web 2.O technology would understand the interest of the reader in using the library services.

Another example we can take from readers using e - resources in the library, whenever reader tries to browse e - resources they may face various difficulties. One may not understand what to do and whom to ask for helps as there would not be any interaction between reader/ searcher and the librarian in this process. However web 2.0 technology would smartly understands the difficulty of the reader. It would flash message under instant messaging system and offer necessary assistance to the readers about e - resource searching. Such help really makes readers very happy and he does not feel isolated or missing in the library systems. The above examples clears our doubt how web 2.O technology would be useful in library.

Library 2.0 is not any new concept but it has emerged in the form of using web 2.O technology in library. The process of using web tools available under web 2.0 in library functioning and service is collectively called **library 2.0**. The definition given by Jack M. Maness helps us to further understand this concept clearly - he says that "application of interactive collaborative and multimedia web based technologies gives to web bases library services and collection means library 2.0"

Now having understood web 2.0 technology in all respect, let us have the introduction of various web tools available under web 2.O technology.

8.6. WEB 2.0 TOOLS: AN INTRODUCTION

Web 2.0 has gifted us several wonderful tools which has made our life easy and at the same time made further advanced through the use of internet. The list of these tools is very long and still many more are emerging tempting us, which one to choose. In fact all of them are very useful for us as an individual or for institutions:

1. RSS Feeds
2. Weblogs
3. Wikis
4. Steaming Media
5. Instant messaging
6. Tagging
7. Social Networking
8. Twitter
9. Social Book marking
10. Flicker
11. Start page
12. Developing own search Engineer
13. Podcasting and Mashup

Now we are going to have a short introduction of each of them. We can understand these tools in a better way by using them in our practical life rather than just reading about them.

8.6.1. RSS Feeds

Nowadays we would invariably find an icon of RSS Feed on every web page prominently on the front page. The meaning of this icon and link is that the website provides RSS Feed service for the particular heading to the website visitors. When we click on RSS Feed link it would ask you to register your mail ID and choose the webpage about which reader expects to get regular alerts from the site whenever any new information is published under that link. The website takes a note of it and regularly posts the latest information to the web reader based on his / her choice. Once the reader registers for RSS Feed service, he would get updates regularly unless he stops or unsubscribes them. With every post there would be radio button (link) under "unsubscribe" and if you click it web site would stops posting any more updates.

By using RSS Feed a reader can create his own source of information as he would be getting several RSS Feed alerts from the different web sites as he has created RSS Feed alerts on them.

This service is very useful to the readers who read journal literature regularly. If they register for the content page of journal issues to be received as RSS Feed then the publisher would regularly post the same in their mail boxes as soon as they are published. This service is free and before going to the library reader can have updates on what he / she would look for during his/her next visits to the library. Reader can choose to register if his/her library is also providing RSS Feed information service to its readers.

8.6.1.1. Tools used for RSS Feeds

There are various tools available to create RSS Feed on any websites.

- Feedity

- Feed 43
- Feedyes
- Web RSS
- Pony Fish
- Dapper
- Feedmarket
- Page 2 RSS
- Feed Beater
- Feed Fire

There are two ways to create RSS Feeds for library services as :

1. By using blogger platform
2. By having Drupal content management system. (http://drupal.org) Or By using plone (http://plone.org)

8.6.2. Weblogs

Under web 2.0 another very useful tool is for creating "blog" or "weblog". Creating blog is a good opportunity to publish own literature or to create a tool to discuss new subject on the web. As such an individual or an institute can create a blog and publish it on the web. Such blogs are available for search by the interested readers. Once a blog is searched and link is saved in favorite then it is possible to visit the blog whenever one wishes so. The blog is not a tool to read it unilaterally but it is an interactive and contributory one. One can give comments on the literature read on blog and participate in the discussion. Visitor can post his / her literature on the blog similar to blog subject. Blog is meant for publishing author's own literature and his/her subsequent posts/updates plus the responses and comments received from others on the subject. With the original subject write-up and with further posts/responses it can become information source through the community contributions.

Blog is also called as "Online Diary". The blogger creates a blog, puts his material on the web and makes a beginning of the discussion on the subject and it grows further with the following comments, responses and feedbacks. Since the blog topic/ subjects are very new, it helps readers and researcher to get unpublished new literature on it. As blog grows the issues and comments are seen chronologically arranged on the sides of the main pages in the form of links.

The characteristics of blog are as:

1. Weblogs are personal
2. Information on blog is arranged chronologically
3. Information of blog is always up to date
4. One can get useful information on new subject. It also gives an opportunity for readers to participate in the discussion

5. Subject is the king of blog

Let us discuss the specialities of blog in elaborated way as :

1. Blogger creates a blog and begins the discussion of his choice. Readers to post their comments on the blog subject. With this original write up of blogger and responses posted by other readers, good amount of information is collected on blog. The entire information source becomes available for other new visitors.
2. Information on blog is presented in a chronological manner. Means latest response is seen on the top which follows with posts submitted subsequently. All these contents are listed in the form of links at sides of main blog page. The first is order in terms of days (today and previous days), previous month, and next following months of the year and subsequently it is arranged year wise.
3. Once any subject is presented on a blog it is constantly updated. The information available is as of now and as just submitted. So the blogs are referred for latest information and not for old information. Readers are constantly visiting blogs and submit their comments and responses which makes the blog an up to date source of information. One can create and alert to get new submission to the blog by registering with e-mail ID.
4. With a good presentation of a particular subject on the web weblog gets publicity. It gives an introduction as "a blog on a subject created by someone" for example: Blog of Phil Bradley

Blog is a web 2.O technology given most useful tool to us. There is a famous web tool available to create a blog e.g. Google's www.bloger.com. There is a web tool available which helps us in searching the blogs on various subjects. e.g. Google's Blog search :

http://blogsearch.google.com

Blogs are also created for institutions or for libraries in order to reach out to their readers. Through blogs libraries can provide useful information like library opening timings, list of newly added books, information about new e- resources - like e- books, services of library, readers programmes of library, virtual exhibitions, results of surveys about library needs and their feedbacks and so on about everything of library. Since the information or postings on blog are interactive and readers can post their views making the discussion live.

8.6.2.1. Web tools for Blog making

Blogs can be created and hosted using following tools.

- Blogger - http://www.blogger.com/start
- Live Journal - http://livejournal.com
- Type pad - http://typepad.com/index-2.html
- Movable type - http:// moveabletype.com
- Expression engine
- Text pattern http:// taxtpattern.com

One can also host RSS Feed facility on blog with the tool http://bloglines.com

8.6.3. Wikis

People are already using Wikipedia or the online encyclopedia and this new technology provided by web 2.0 is already known to almost every one. Actually the word "wiki" is a common noun and "Wikipedia" is a proper noun. Wiki is a new concept of building an information source by community collaboratively. As such any one can visit any wiki based source and can add his / her contribution to it. Importance of wiki is that the information on a new subject (unknown) could be created or one can improve or edit previously submitted material. There is an editor for every wiki source who controls it. It makes the information available on wiki qualitatively good. Wikis is also called as community study. Library can create its own wiki on new subject. Information on wiki could be made interesting by incorporating audio, video or animation along with text materials. Since many people contribute in making a wiki, it is read as a good information source on the subject.

8.6.3.1. Web tools used to create wikis

- **Never again :** Community portals
  http://neveragain. Epov.org/never_ again: community_ portal
- **Never again :** library portal
  http://neveragain - epor.org/library
- **Wikipedia :** http://en.wikipedia.org (For contributing new material there)
- **Wiki farms :** http://wikipedia.org/wiki-farms (wiki out sourcing tool)
- **Wiki spaces :** http://www.wikispaces.com
- **Blue wiki** (create a free wiki site) http://www.bluwiki.com/go/mainpage
- **Editme :** wiki web publishing other sources - jot spot, PB wiki, stick pad, wikia etc.
- **Wikimapia :** it is online editable map where one can describe any place on earth-http:// wikimapia.org

8.6.4. Streaming Media

Along with the textual material mixing of other multimedia in the school or college study material is called streaming media. It has been proved that if audio, video or animation media is used in the teaching material it becomes a live and effective. Streaming medias a tool in web 2.O technology, which is one of the powerful tools. Nowadays it is a new trend of educational technology to make assignments available on web especially in school library media programmes. Students make use of materials presented on flash programming screen cast/web cast as well as audio/ video screaming. Such programmes are of quiz or question answer type and along with it there would be materials to increase the information literacy competency of the students. Such programme could be made more effective with screaming media.

It is also proved that in providing library user education programmes use of streaming media is largely done. Instead of including just lectures, library tours with tape slides in them if they are mixed with media and kept on web it brings convenience and makes an effective tool in teaching library skills to the students. Programmes like computer assisted instructions & other various programmes on library user education if made available on web along with streaming media they can get good response from the students. Since in these techniques there is no direct contact with the teachers, students make use of such programmes like self study material. There could be layered programmes and student can successively complete the course module by module and achieves related skills. Such programmes help in promoting library material among the students.

8.6.4.1. *Web Tools for making streaming media*

For web casting and for making web streaming various tools are available such as:

(A) Main methods to create streaming media include:

Video in proper formats, Real networks, Real media, Microsoft's Windows media

(B) Steps of making streaming media.

1. **Acquisition**
   — Video on demand
   — Live web cast
2. **Encoding**
   — Real Networks
   — Windows media
3. **Transmission Resources**
   — Real impact, online video service
   — AV Labs, play stream
   — Audio-video web single real

8.6.5. Instant Messaging

People are already using messaging or chatting on e-mail portals. Most of the youngsters we see them chatting hours together through Google, Yahoo, Orkut or Face Book and the What's App which is a recently added tools.They are extensively used for chatting these days. Although these facilities have been developed under web 1.0 are mostly static in nature except What's App. Whereas under web 2.0 technology chatting is now fully developed. Till then one used to download the chat server for this. Web 2.0 gives chatting facility on web itself. Now this technology is more advanced than before. It has now added facilities like co-browsing, file sharing, screen capturing, data sharing as well as link sharing techniques which was not possible earlier. Now such an advanced instant messaging tool is available for various fields including in library management. Especially it is being used for providing reference service, which is called "virtual reference service". There are web 2.0 tools available and a links can be provided on the web site for such virtual reference service or instant messaging links could be made available on website, whereby readers can post their reference queries to the reference librarian, who would be available online on the link (At designated time). He instantly answers the queries by providing available digital materials or by providing links in answers. If it is going to take more time to answer then he could keep the chat on and subsequently provides the material to the readers. Like this he keeps chatting with many readers simultaneously and try to satisfy all of them. There are suitable online reference tools available which are also used in answering reference queries. Some sources are like readers can obtain answer through online FAQ (Frequently Asked Question) System. In addition to providing reference service instant messaging tools are also being largely used in libraries of western countries. OCLC has provided its own software called "Question point" for such services, which uses reference source of world-cat but their services are charged.

Most of the instant messaging utilities available under web 2.0 are available free of cost. Instant messaging technique is also used by students when they try to browse e-sources but have some difficulties and need some help from librarian. The help and assistance could be made available instantly at that particular point which is the speciality of this technology.

8.6.5.1. Web Tools Available for Instant Messaging

Other than Google, MSN or yahoo there are good web tools available for instant messaging which can be easily downloaded such as :

AOL - Instant message (AIM) -http://info.aol.co.uk/aim

There are some higher level web tools for instant messaging available like:

- Trillion- www.trillian.im
- Gain - http://gain.sourceforge.net
- Fire (For MAC systems) http://fire.sourceforge.net

Instant messaging tool for library management is also available such as:

http://I:success.org/index.php /librariansusing_im _reference.

Other IM web tools are as:

- http://blog.meebo.comp
- www.chatpatrol.com
- www.asknow.org

8.6.6. Tagging

The meaning of tagging is that while browsing websites or library catalogue one can create one's own searching keywords and plan one's own search/ browsing method. Tagging technique provides the facility to searcher while handling metadata or the web content as per searcher's own convenience. Any web source provides its set of key words or headings for searching in various subjects. In addition searcher gets freedom to add his own key works. This not only helps making information retrieval easy and effective but such added terms are available for use by the other browsers also, which is advantageous for all searchers who work in the same field. Libraries can make such facilities available such facilities in OPAC search, which could increase use of library OPAC.

8.6.6.1. Web Tools available For Tagging

- Furl or Spurl -www.furl.com
- Delicious - www.delicious.com(This source is very useful and interesting)

Taxonomy is the main principle used in library classification like DDC, LC and CC. It was old taxonomy which is now available as tagging in web 2.O. There are tools for folk Taxonomy or folksonomy available such as used in

- Drupal ,Joomla, flicker, YouTube, Revver and Google video.

8.6.7. Social Networking

Web 2.O technology's best available tool for community platform is the "social networking" in which effects of instant messaging, blogging, streaming media are collectively used to make it more effective. Through social networking it is possible to develop information collaboratively, social networking facilities are available mostly for individuals working in the same field, where they share their experiences to others so also share their own hobbies and feelings with others. In western counties a web tool named "my place" or mebo were mostly used not only by adults but also by children. Now it's new version "facebook" is most popular for social networking. Orkut was similarly available. Under social networking many groups are formed like private club, book reviewer, clubs or friends of libraries, business chambers, and departmental groups or residential associations.

Now a days in the library, readers can actively form reader's group in social networking to share experience of library use, which includes topics like library skills, skills in using various e-resources, success stories of information retrieval etc. Readers try to create their own profile on the topics of their interest and try to share same with other group members. Such communication and sharing in group can certainly result in effective use of library resources and services. In western countries such social networking is a common feature which helps them in self learning things.

8.6.7.1. Web tools available for social Networking

- Yahoo Group - http://group.yahoo.com
- Delicious - http://delicious.com
- Technocrats - http://technocrats.com
- Blogtronics - www.blogtronic.com
- Collectivex - www.collectivex.com
- Bebo - www.bebo.com
- My space - www.myspace.com
- Tagworld - www.tagworld.com
- Town crossing - www.towncrossing.com
- Meetup - www.meetup.com
- Linked in - http://in.linkedin.com

- Face book - www.facebook.com
- What's up - www.hotsapp.org/whatsup

8.6.8. Twitter

Twitter is one of the useful web 2.O tools for conveying small messages on the web. Till recently twitter message was limited only up to 140 characters. However, now the length limit is increased to 280 characters. This facility has some social background. It makes it possible to remain continuously in contact between individuals. And also one can control message communication with twitter. With twitter it is possible to obtain people's opinion on a latest topic, event, news and exchanges messages about new concept. Since it began with small message it is easy to communicate with group or collect response from people on the important social issues. It is the best tool to push out messages. It can be used as an individual or social platform to talk to people. In twitter we can see collective effects of instant messaging, micro blogging or social networking technologies. Twitter is seen as an alternative to costly SMS services of mobile networks. In twitter technology message is known "tweets". In 2006 Jack Dorsey first invented the concept of twitter. There are websites which provide tweeting facility. One can visit such site, register, open one's own profile and start tweeting. Then onwards you can start sending tweet messages to the people who are also registered users of twitter. For tweeting there is a famous service available by its site named http:/ / dev.twitter.com. There are many media channels who keep in touch with their audience. They get responses from them which make a live discussion on various current topics of social and political concern. Example could be given of NDTV's famous anchor Vishnu Som who is available with his twitter ID as @vishnuNDTV. Library can also host its twitter site to remain in contact with its readers to get their live feed back.

Website - http://dev.twitter.com

8.6.9. Social Book Marking

Like social networking there is a book marking technology available under web 2.0 but it is more useful for the individuals. It is the general practice of web browsers to save a list of web sites which they frequently visit. It is normally done by saving site addresses in the "favorite" facility available on screen of any web browser. However, problem here is the favorite saved list is specific to the PCs of people which cannot be accessed when they are away from their PCs. Web 2.0 has given very good solution to this. It provides facility to save our favorite website address list online which would be available universally. There are several book marking sites available today in which prominently includes sites such as spurl or delicious, which are favorite by most of the users. Out of these furl or Perl is available free of cost, where one can work with user's own PC. Delicious web tools is other most favored web tool for bookmarking which allows us to save our list of web links on the site of delicious site itself available on the web .This facilitates users to access their list of web link where ever they are; at any remote corner of the world. In addition to saving web links it also facilities saving URLs or blogs or reviews and use them from anywhere. In the library also readers can use the facility of social book marking to save their list of web links which they frequently use such as web links of e – journals, e- books or open access journals.

8.6.9.1. List or Web tools available for Book Marking

- Furl - www.Furl.net
- Delicious - or del.icio.us -www.deliaious.com

  To search websites where book marking is saved the websites are available as:
- http://populicio.us/fulltotal.html
- http://delicio.us/recent or popular

  For the library users twitter tool is- http://del.icio.us/sanmatelolibrary/

  Other web tools for social book marking are:
- Cite- u - like -www.citeyoulike.org
- Connote/Nature for Pub group)
- Diigo-www.diigo.com
- Blinklist-www.blinklist.com
- Spurl - www.spurl.net
- Yahoo! - my web http://myweb.yahoo.com

8.6.10. Flicker & Mash up

Flicker is another web tool available under web 2.0 technology especially for saving and exchanging photos or pictures. Flicker is also useful for preserving maps or geographic information related digital collection which could be exchanged with others.

There is another similar web tool available e.g. mashup where one can have collective effects of blogs, wikis, streaming media, instant messaging, tagging and social networking. For example readers can exchange their library OPAC facility with changed metadata as per their convenience with others.

8.6.10.1. Web Tools to use flicker

In order to create flicker one need to open an account on their site www. flicker.com, where one can store his / her photo collection. Flicker helps in searching a particular photo. There is an advance technology available with flicker e.g. www.flicker.com/ search/advanced. We can save links of other websites in flicker by which one can do their mapping {www.flicker.com/ map.flicker}.Such mapping could be effectively used in library e.g. library tours, events, local history, community and publicity.

8.6.11. Start page

Whenever we open our computer and look for internet we get a browser screen like Firefox, Internet explorer, opera or fedora. When we are a part of any organisation we use its home page. In both these types of opening screen are called start page. However, these things have now become old and people feel boring seeing same type of browser again and again and they need something new. In web 2.0 environment we get freedom of creating our own start page. If any one sees the following things on the front page of browser then it becomes interesting such as:

- E - Mail link
- Links of news paper site which are frequently visited
- Links of Weblogs
- Links of alert /RSS feeds
- Icons of search engines
- Links of URLs
- Icons of Games and
- Other links

If a start page in configured and the above links are seen as soon as browser is opened then anybody would be certainly happy. Normally we try to make things suitable to us through the use of favorites or book marking but it is difficult to bring links on front page.

One can create his / her start page by writing it with HTML language if one has the expertise to do it, but it is difficult for others. There are web tools available to create one's own start page without having the knowledge of web programming, and such tools are available freely. In this process one can create a default start page which can be accessed from anywhere with login and password. Library readers can also create their own start page where they can get link of library OPAC search on the front page along with the favorite links like library and other RSS Feeds. This brings a lot of convenience in using with self created browser page which is found time saving although there are advantages in having own start page but there are also some disadvantage and risk in it. This is because we might put our personal and confidential information on the front screen like our internet banking details recorded in transactions, credit or debit card numbers. As such the information may go into hands of strangers and hackers who may misuse it. In spite of all these risk factors people choose to create and use one's own start page as it is attractive and convenient to use.

8.6.11.1. Web Tools for creating own start page

- www.pageflakes.com

  This is one of the well known site to create own start page
- www.netvibes.com
- http://live.com (for ms windows)

  Other web tools :
- Eskobo - www.eskobo.com
- My web desk top - http://mywebdeskop.net
- Protopage - http://protopage.com/
- Start - www.start.com
- Favoor - www.favoor.com
- Magnato - www.magnato.com
- Goowy - www.goowy.com

8.6.12. Managing own search Engine

In the internet age there is a lot of significance in using search engines. It is very difficult to know which web page what information is available. However, search engine does this job very easily. This happens because search engine has a large index of hyper links under which all the web pages are connected. As we post a query, search engine takes us to a particular page in which needed key words are located. Today a number of search engines available has reached almost 50 in number. Google, Yahoo, Bing and MSN are the prominent among them. In spite of all it is still difficult to search the information on internet platform. Normally when we search an information with a set of key words it assumes the string by joining the words by AND/ OR operators and carryout the search. Some search engines work smartly. They provides list of search terms in the order from containing maximum search words to minimum. We see the search link hits in lacs. However, such search is very vague. One can go for advanced search mode by using Boolean Operators like AND OR and NOT however, we are not much satisfied with it. Thus we do find difficulty in getting specific or pin pointed information as the search engines are not reliable. Now question comes in mind, whether there is any alternative than to depend on search engines. The solution to this problem is to manage our search engine and by making own search engine. The main reason behind the failure of search engine is that they do not use good information retrieval techniques. So we need to select the reputed search engine and select proper search terms. Web 2.0 technology is ready to provide such technique to us. It can be achieved with the following tools :

- Rollyo - www.rollyo.com
- PSS - www.pssdir.com
- Yahoo! search builder http://builder.searchyahoo.com
- Eurekster - swiki - http://swiki.eurekster.com
- Google custom search engine
  http://google.com/coop/cse

Many of the above tools are available for free. The process of using these web tools is like this: -first visit these sites and register your account. Then list the search terms and then also register 25 links of search engines and preserve such data. We get the research on our search terms which is far specific than we get normally from a normal search engine. So one can manage one's own search arrangement especially it would be useful for researchers. While searching information through library web site one can very well adopt this strategy to get good search results.

8.6.13. Podcasting

In web 2.0 technology one more available excellent tool is 'Podcasting' .Podcasting gives us the opportunity to listen the author's work in his / her own voice. Literature in printed medium is most sought by the readers as it gives us processes of reading, thinking, cognizing and meditation, which is automatically done. However, in the process we do not understand author's real emotions behind the words. However, they could be understood if we listen to pronouncing the words in the author's own voice. Words with voice tones have very close relations with the emotions behind the words. This specific technique is used in the podcasting technology. Podcast is the literature of an author recorded in his / her own voice which we can listen with the help of computer or any reading device. It can be stored in MP3 files and one can hear at any time. We recognise the voice of author which is called podcast and this entire process is called podcasting. We can realize how podcasts are popular on YouTube by seeing hits or likes for them. Creating a podcast is very easy and hearing it is still easy. The convenient part is that one can hear it while doing any other job or even doing computer programming. One can connect to podcast playing device with headphones and continue listening it while doing our daily activities or one can hear it while on tour with MP3 devices. This technology has long back accepted by BBC TV and radio stations.

New Oxford American Dictionary included first time key word of podcasting in 2005 in it. In library collection podcast is emerging as important information source. There is a search facility on web for searching podcasts e.g. http://podcastyahoo.com. It is a very powerful tool to search podcasts. Once we get a link of a particular podcast just by clicking it we can start hearing it. It is possible to download and save in MP3 File. There is a easy tool available to do it for a small cost. There are tools like Apple-I tunes or singing fish with which we can search audio video literature and save it on our iPhones or tabs to listen whenever we feel to do so :

There are tools to create podcasts in web 2.0 technology

8.6.13.1. Web Tools for Creating Podcasts

- singing fish - http:// search.singingfish.com/sfw/home.jsp)
- Podzinger - http://podzinger.com

There are other sources to search podcasts e.g.

- Blog Digger - http://blogdigger.com/media/index.html
- Podscope - www.podscope.com
- Podcast directory - www.podcastdirectory.com
- Podcast network - www.thepodcastnetwork.com

Making podcast is not difficult but to search the specific author's voice and recording it is a bit difficult. Care needs to be taken that there would not be mixing in it. When we listen to radio programmes we do not see actual faces of speakers who present the programme but we certainly recognize them by their voices. The same thing is expected when we hear the podcast work. So we understand that at both times while recording and listening podcast mike is essential. Now days we get mike cum head phones. There are some packages available for creating podcasts e.g.

- Audicity - http://audicity.soruceforge.net
- flashkit - www.flashkit.com/loops
- Lame MP3 - http://audicity.sourceforge.net/help/lame.mp3

Podcast are uploaded using web tools like:

- www.ourmedia.org

- http://odeo.com

Podcasting technology can be very well used for library user education programmes like library audio tour with head phones, library instruction guides, library events or by providing list of podcasts available.

9
Open Source Systems & Open Access Resources

9.0. INTRODUCTION

In LIS literature we often come across two terms 'open source' and "open access" which sounds us very similar as in both of them have "open" word. As such it always creates confusion about their understanding. However, as a library professional one must have a clear understanding about these two terms. With this need in mind the author felt it necessary to include the chapter on "Open Source Systems and Open Access Resources" in the book.

Computer technology as a platform and as softwares have progressed in a speedy manner. Initially the technological platforms or the operating systems have attracted us. Operating systems provides a lot of convenience to the user. However, there are many difficulties in using them; especially because of their ownership issues, it becomes tedious to adopt them. Considering these constrains many computer experts came together, did some research and invented open source technology as an alternative to the windows a commercial system. Moreover, it further grew as a movement to develop open source technology which resulted in designing many open source platforms and applications for use.

These systems are now widely accepted. There was another concept emerged with the same "free" philosophy. e.g. "open access". It is a general opinion that the every knowledge source should be freely available to the readers especially to the researchers, which was the main social objective behind the concept of open access. These two concepts are entirely different. The difference is like this - open source is the open source platforms, which facilitates to have open source software tools, where as open access means the information sources which are freely available.

9.1. OPEN SOURCE SYSTEMS

Now let us first try to know what the open source concept is and what is its background, definition and about open source initiative.

9.1.1. What is Open Source System?

Whenever we buy any software or download it, it comes in a compiled form which is ready to use. When any programmer designs a software he creates a source code to it, which is the secret code, only a programmer knows it and the computer understands it, which is invariably kept hidden. This source code is never given to a software purchaser and it does not accompany with it. For all the commercially designed softwares this is the common thing to experience. As far as open source system is concerned it is done in exactly opposite manner. In case of open source software the source code is provided to software user. Moreover open source software is not distributed on commercial terms and is provided free of cost.

The programmers who design open source softwares feel confident that those who have knowledge to improve or repair software if source codes are provided, it would help in removing bugs and more advanced software would emerge. However they should remember the following expectations that -

- The software should be freely distributed
- Each software copy should possess source code
- Everybody has the freedom to change or improve the software by using the source code.
- User need not have the license to use the software.

Now let us understand how the open source concept has emerged.

In 1991 Linus Torvalds a student of Helsinki University at Finland designed a new Minix named operating system based on UNIX. He named it further as LINUX. He made its 0.02 version available as a general public license. Many programmers across the globe downloaded it and started working on it. They made the changes in the source code as they liked it. After some time Linus the originator obtained software back from the programmers. Then he incorporated all changes done by the programmes in his original software and brought out new 1.0 version of LINUX in 1994 and made it available to all. However, at that time it did not have any technical support and the users were not confident without the support. Red Hat software came forward with the warranty to LINUX which is now available everywhere free. Only one has to pay a little amount for technical support. Like Red Hat there are several companies which provide LINUX with its different flavor names. There are other open source platforms available like LINUX. Such as:

Mozilla (Netscape) Operating System

Apache - Web server

PERL - Web scripting language

PNG - Orphic file format.

9.1.2. Open Source :Historical background

Open source movement in real sense started somewhere in 1997. The discussion begins with the publication of an article, "The Cathedrals and the Bazaars"(subsequently published as paperback), Written by Erik S.Raymond in Perl conference organised by O'Reilly Media. Netscape opened its browser software. This event gave strength to open source movement. The concept of open source first came into existence in 1998. Immediately after that, Open Source Initiative (OSI) Organisation was established. In the same year another "free software summit" organised by O'Reilly approved it.

In this summit along with other software like LINUX, Sendmail , Perl, Python and Apache were presented and got recommended. In 1998 Erik Raymond became the first Board of Directors of OSI organisation. In 2005 OSI got international status in which representatives from Europe, South America, Japan and India joined the organisation.

9.1.3. Open Source Definitions

Definition of open source benefited with several technical explanations. Open source concept is not limited only to source codes. They are as:

(a) **Free Distribution :** Any software or one or many parts of it (Comprising of small programmes) when it is distributed a by one to others would not require any license or no royalty would be charged while distributing it further.

(b) **Source code :** It is mandatory to pass on source codes prepared for softwares to the user so that next recipient should be able to make changes in the software using those source codes.

(c) When improvised version of the original is prepared then also license for distribution would not be mandatory.

(d) When improved version of old software is further distributed, it is not necessary to maintain old name and it can have new name.

(e) While distributing original improved software or improved parts of it then there should not be any discrimination in distributing it to individual or the organisation.

(f) Original Software to be distributed along with improved ones.

(g) Originality of software to be attached with the software or its parts and it would not bring any restrictions on other softwares.

(h) Originality of design should be same everywhere and should not be biased towards technology style or interface.

While referring the above definition we find that care is taken to give explanations to small technical issues also.

9.1.4. Open Source Initiative (OSI)

Open source initiative organisation was established in 1998 to support open source movement and popularise it. Erik Ramond was the first director of OSI who worked as the Director until 2005. To promote free software movement was the prime objective of OSI. It provided technical definitions of open source concept. Subsequently free software foundation was also established. Now both these organisations are jointly working in support of open source movement.

Generally people who have expertise and knowledge of correcting the software or improving them are called Hackers community. OSI does the important work of providing support to open source softwares or software tools. OSI emphasises on promoting and publicising open source concept worldwide, organise training programmes and creating awareness about the importance of open source softwares among the users. OSI has organised several international conferences to bring software designers and users on one platform to discuss about open source technology, about its licensing and benefits of open source movement.

OSI has its headquarters at San Francisco, (Po Box 410990, 256 San Francisco CA - 941114 - 0990 USA) It has its website at http://opensource.org/osi. OSI provides registrations to new open sources software and provides license to them. It involves two parts as licensee by name and license by category. However OSI has its rules and conditions for giving licenses. They are available under open standard requirements for software where rules and conditions are listed. Some of them are as below:

1. No international secretes
2. Free availability - without any cost.
3. Even if software is patented no royalty to be charged on its distribution.
4. There should not be any agreement for use of software
5. For Open source use no other technology should be required.

Whenever open source software is distributed it is necessary to mention that it is distributed as per open standard compliance so that it would not become obligatory to an individual or by an institute who receives it.

9.1.5. Open Source Tools

There are various software tools available under open source category as open source operating systems, packages or full softwares or parts of it.

9.1.6. Open Source Operating Systems

There are various version or flavors of Linux such as :

- UBUNTU - Linux
- UBUNTU - Studio
- Fedora - Linux

So also available as PC - based Unix, desktop BSD Linux and Firefox browsers such as:

- Unibozu. net
- Customized Google. Firefox
- stumble upon
- G - mail manager and G - mail notifier
- Yahoo mail notifier
- Cookie Pre

9.1.7. Open Source Programming Languages

There are as many as 80 open source programming languages, some of well known are as follows:

- Beta Bigwig
- C, C++
- Eiffel
- Java
- Lua
- Mono
- Perl, PHP
- Python
- Ruby
- Small talk squeak

9.1.8. Open Source Softwares

9.1.8.1. Open source softwares for digital library development

With the help of the following open source softwares digital libraries could be developed e.g.

- Greenstone
- Sourceforge
- DSpace
- E - Print
- Fedora
- Kate
- Ibiblio

9.1.8.2. Open Source Softwares for library computerisation

There are various open source type integrated library management systems(LMSs) available today which are useful for library computerisation such as:

1. Evergreen : Prepared in 2006 by Georgia Public Library Services. It can be downloaded free of cost from website: http://evergreen-lis.org download/ php.

2. Koha : Koha is the first open source LINUX based software which was made available in 1999. It is designed by Horowhenna Library Trust at New Zealand. It was actually brought into use in 2000. Its current version is V 3.16 website: http://koha.org

3. Newgenlib : It is Indian made open source software for library computerisation. It was made available jointly by Verus Solution Pvt. Ltd. and Kesavan Institute of Information and

Knowledge Management, Hyderabad website - http://verussolutions.biz/web

Current version is 2.x

4. PMB (Php my bibli)

It is deviced by a French Co in 2002

5. Liblime : For more details about open source type library management systems one can visit web site as OSS4lib http://oss4lib.org/node/365

9.1.9. Open Source servers

In order to host LMS and other software applications there are different open servers available today as:

- Apache
- Mamboserver
- Zimbra Email server
- Zupe
- Red 5
- Ubuntu

9.2. OPEN ACCESS RESOURCES

We have understood that open source technology relates with softwares, operating systems and tools. Whereas open access is about e – resources which are freely accessible on web. Now let us understand what the open access is.

9.2.1. What is open access?

Open access concept is about the literature which is in digital form and available on internet platform. The special characteristic of open access is that it is accessible free of cost, secondly it won't carry any ownership issue. It becomes possible because the authors who believe in the concept of open access and make their ownership right of their literature available to the website owners. Generally most of scholarly journals do not give royalty to their authors. However, with publishing their literature in such journals they get name and fame. In such situation royalty issue is treated as secondary. Now the trend of open access literature is emerging. There are two ways of making literature available to readers having open access facility e.g. 1. Open access archive 2. Open access journals.

9.2.1.1. Open Access Archives / Repositories

When an author makes own literature available on his/her own website is called open access archive or also called as self archiving. He/she would also include his/her preprints on such site. Normally literature published on open assess archives is not assessed, reviewed or referred to or cited, which is possible in case of journal published in a commercial way. Repositories are normally published by institutes or organisations, universities or laboratories. The authors can publish their preprint articles on such repositories. However in publishing reprints on local repositories publishers may raise some copy right issues. Some publishers allow it but such examples are very few. It is expected that open access archives or repositories would comply with open access initiatives (OAI). The readers would also be able to access it through open access search engines which are based on Open Archives Initiative (OAI) protocol for metadata harvesting (OAI PMH). The main expectation of open access archives is that it should be as par metadata harvesting rules. The other way of publishing open access literature is open access journals.

9.2.2. Open Access Journals

These days many quality journals are published as open access. One need not have to pay subscription to get such journals. Directory of Open Access Journal (DOAJ) website provides an exhaustive list of open access journals subject wise along with their web links.

Open access journal publishers also get them peer review before they are published. Publishing such journals requires some expenses and if authors voluntarily own this expense then it is not passed on to readers unnecessarily. Some universities provide funding to publish open access journals, by getting some sponsorship and advertisements, the needed expenses could also be recovered. The main objective behind doing all these efforts is to make scholarly literature available to the readers free of cost.

9.2.2.1. The definition & characteristics of open access journals

- Open access type of literature is generally published online in a digital form and available on internet /web.
- It is freely available without having any copy right restrictions which also does not require licensing.
- Open access concept sets aside the cost barrier.
- It would have restriction on redoing or republishing in a commercial way
- To make literature available free of cost in full text form is the main objective of open access movement.

There are two main ways to publish open access journals e.g.

- 1 - open access journals Gold OA
- 2 - open access archives Green OA

Open Access Definitions

- Freely available without any restrictions is an open access.
- The definition made by Budapest Open Access Leadership is as below.

"Open access to the literature we (Budapest OA) mean it is freely available on public internet permitted by any reader to read, download, copy, distribute, print, search or link it to full text of these articles, crawl them for indexing, pass them as data to softwares or use them for any of the law full purpose without financial, legal or technical working other than those inseparable from gaining access to the internet itself. The only constrain of reproduction and distribution and only role for copy right is, this domain should be to give authors control over the integrity of their work and the right to be properly acknowledged and cited".

According to open access conference of Budapest (Feb. 2002), Bethesda (June 2002) and Berlin (Oct 2003), it is said that the authors to surrender copy rights of their literature to the publishers. In all the above conferences the above definition of open access got the confirmation.

9.2.3. Open Access Initiative (OAI)

We have read about open source initiative in the first part of this chapter. Similarly there is a concept of open access initiative (OAI) and its protocol. Let us understand it with some details. Open access initiative is a common understanding or a protocol. It is related with handling of scholarly literature published in open access journals and also about handling of data files from open access archives with common metadata structure. This means whenever open access type of literature is searched under open access protocol literature in open access archives is also searched with similar metadata structure. In technical language it is called as metadata. Harvesting protocol supports interoperability. There are three organisations which support open access initiative technology e.g.

1. Budapest open access Initiative
2. Bethesda statement publishing
3. Berlin declaration on open access to knowledge in the science and

Humanities.The activities of these organisations about open access initiatives are as:

9.2.3.1. Budapest Open Access Initiative (BOAI)

In 2001 Open Society Institute (OSI) established Budapest Open Access Initiative (BOAI) Organisation out of organisations which support open access protocol to science and scholarly journal literature. BOAI has international status. The meeting in this concern was held in Budapest hence it is named as Budapest. The main objective of BOAI was to have coordination among the organisations which work for the same cause. Out of these protocols open access initiative is related with journal literature, whereas open archive initiative is related with open archives resources. Budapest Open Access Initiative is not limited only to science fields but it is related with all fields. BOAI protocol is equally applicable to open access journals and individual archives. BOIA emphasises on promoting scholarly literature (Peer reviewed research literature). These protocols however are not applicable to software, movies and cinemas. In BOAI point of view is that the free availability of literature depends on authors surrendering their intellectual copy rights to the publishers. In this concern there are specific rules regarding author's licensing and their copyrights.

9.2.4. Creative Commons and open content licensing

Creative common license is an organisation which facilitates providing copy rights to authors to use their literature as open access by the users. Its motto is "to share, remix, reuse legally." This portal works on no profit making principles (http://creative commons.org). It is available free for authors and is very easy to use. This organisation works to provide open access rights to authors for their literature.

Open Content License : This is another website which also provides open access rights to authors for their literature. By using this, authors themselves can obtain open access rights for their literature. http:// www.opencontent.org / open pulls

9.2.5. Creating Open Access Resource

So far readers have revealed that open access literature need to be presented as per open access protocol. It is also necessary that once literature is published by using open access creating tools users should be able to search, which means source must respond to OAI - PMH open access archives initiative protocol for metadata harvesting type search engines so that users can retrieve such literature without any difficultly. Open access type of literature is published in two ways i.e. open access journals and open access archives. There are tools available to publish open access type of literature especially for publishing open access journals such as:

- Biomed central
- Public Library of science
- Pubmed central
- Scielo
- Open journals system

There are also tools available for open access archives or repositories by which open source digital libraries are also developed e.g.

Greenstone

D space

Fedora

G.N.U E-prints

In developing countries especially in agriculture and health fields there are open access literature publishing tools like AGORA and HINARI. Once open access literature creation process is complete then they are registered at portals like creative commons and open content license in order to receive open access rights for the literature. Among them creative common is generally preferred.

9.2.6. Open Access Literature Searching tools

Any literature published as open access as per OAI protocol then it should adopt appropriate searching tool. These searching tools or search engines must be developed as per OAI PMH protocol. Which means its contents should able to search as per open access initiative Metadata Harvesting protocol. There are OAI - PMH category of search engines available for use e.g.

- Brog digger
- Cite base
- Google scholar
- OAIster

- PEP(Perspective in Electronic Publishing)
- Scirus

9.2.7. Open Access Resources

Currently a large quantity open access type of literature is publishing. It is too difficult to list them out here. However, the author has tried to present a short list of secondary sources for open access literature as:

(A) Bibliographies

- Open Access Bibliography: Liberating Scholarly Literature with e – Printing and open access journals

  (http:// info.lib.nh.edu/cwb/oab.pdf)
- Scholarly Electronic publishing bibliography

  (http://info.lib.uh.edu/sepb.html)

(B) Directories

- Directory of mathematics preprint and e - print servers
- Directory of open access repositories
- E - print networks
- Institutional Archives Registry
- Virtual Tech Report centre
- Directory of Open Access Journals (DOAJ) www.doaj.org

  Published by Lund University Libraries; in this directory there are open access journals pertaining to various subjects. It contains links for 1500 open access journals. For library and information science there nearly 80 open access journals.
- Free full text (http://freefultext.com)
- SPARE Publishing Resources association of Research libraries has brought out this directory www.orl/spare.resources/pubres.htm

(C) Serials

- Ariadne - www.ariadne.ac.uk
- ARB Bio-monthly report on research libraries: Issues and actions from ARL www.arl.org.newsltr/index.htm
- Cites & Insights -http://cites.boisestate.edu
- D - Lib magazine
- High energy physics libraries
- Information world review
- Learned publishing
- Science Development net -www.scidevnet/scider/net

(D) Digital Libraries in Library information field

- Million Book project
- Project Gutenberg
- E - LIS
- INDEST
- Librarians, Digital Library(OpenDOAR)
- Digital Library of India
- Wikipedia- Free encyclopedia

Like the above there are several dictionaries and encyclopedias available on web as open access. In short trend of publishing open access type journals, archives and digital libraries are growing day by day. When libraries cannot afford to subscribe costly journals or they cannot participate in library consortia for the want of funds there is nothing wrong in publishing quality and scholarly open access journals for the benefit of their readers. Concern librarians need to take necessary initiatives in this direction.

REFERENCES

Open Source

1. Directory of electronic journals newsletters and academic discussion lists (Annual) first published in 1991 Washington: Association of Research Libraries
2. Open source initiative -http://www.opensource.org
3. What does open source mean: http://www.how stuff works.com(Accessed on 2nd July,2016)
4. The Cathedral and the Bazar Essaysby Eric S.Raymond,O'Reilly Media Inc. 1999

Open Access

1. Ho,Adrain k. and Biley Sr. Charles W. : Open Access webliography Reference service Review vol. 33 (3) Sept.2005 pp. 346-364
2. Suber, Peters: Open Access Overview 2007 http://www.eartham.edu/mpeters/fos/overviw. html) (Accessed on 29th January 2016)

10
Semantic Web

10.0. INTRODUCTION

Semantic web is an advanced stage in the internet technology development. In the previous chapters we got an introduction of internet and web 2.O technologies. We have also noted the various generations of internet / web technology : e.g.

1. Web 1.0 (It is a character '0' and not zero)
2. Web 2.0
3. Web 3.0

Semantic web could be termed as next advanced generation of web technology. World Wide Web (www) technology is now over 45 years old. During this development there has been many progressive evolutions in it. Initially only textual material was transmitted with the help of hyper link technology. Subsequently it was possible to send digital photo, video clips and data. We further saw availability of search engines and today we see advances like social networking and semantic web. The main purpose of semantic web is networking data available on web and creating a situation so that this comprehensive source could be available on web openly and would be used by anybody looking for it.

We know on web, information is segregated in various servers around the globe however there is no interlinks among them. There are databases in the fields of medical, pharmaceutical, government etc. and more and more new databases are being created. However, all these resources are commercially owned and handled. If all these web resources are interlinked and made them available in machine readable form that too free then many things could be achieved out of it. Now what would happen if these databases are networked and how they could be networked? The answer to these questions is the new ideology of semantic web. In semantic web the emphasis is on reading and handling data by machines. There would be intermediate agents to give the query based instructions to semantic web platform pertaining to users requirements as they put across in their own way. Up till now people are using internet for various purposes like online shopping, making travel plans, or to carryout day to day work in personal life. However, we experience various limitations in doing this. These activities are done at individual level. Although they facilitate us with fast and easy actions but there are lot of botheration for us in handling the technology. It is expected that semantic web would certainly bring revolution and change in using web technology.

In this chapter, we are going to understand- what is semantic web technology? How it works, what is the state of art of this technology and what opportunities it will bring for us? However, before touching upon this core theme of the present chapter we are first going to review the historical development of web and then we are going to know about semantic web as it is easy to understand semantic web after having good background about the current web technology.

10.1. WEB TECHNOLOGY: HISTORICAL DEVELOPMENT

Internet technology was invented by Tim Berners-Lee in 1969 at the institute CERN where a team of technocrats under his leadership took a lot of research efforts and finally got the success. They worked on the problem of scientists not able to exchange scientific information while they are at different locations. A solution to this problem was first found by creating database of scientific information in the form of hyper text and making it available with the help of hyperlink on network. It was never thought that such a thing was possible but researchers like Tim Burners-Lee proved it. Subsequently in order to make the data available to scientific community several methods and tools were explored - like http, web pages, browsers. These developments facilitated to make web technology available for use by everybody. There onwards use of web increased tremendously. The earlier browsers were not so advanced, as users were facing a lot of constrains in accessing the information. Afterwards better browsers like Cello or Netscape were added. In 1994 Lee formed World Wide Web consortium (w3c). This organisation worked for the main task of liberlising web technology as it was necessary to make general public aware of it. The situation still was not conducive to use web. Due to different formats, there was no uniformity. There also was no unanimity in HTML technology. The first internet protocol Gopher was made available but this led to set a war of formats. While founding Internet Tim Berners-Lee never accepted ideology of going for financial profit out of internet. The only idea was to create a basic foundation to facilitate flow of information and mostly free flow of information among scientific community. HTTP protocol invented by Lee was freely available worldwide as Lee thought about it..

However, further development of internet Lee's assumption about internet was left aside and in 1996 people started using internet for commercial purpose with availability of dot.com technology. Websites with a group of webpages facilitating financial use began to proliferate. However, in 2001 world share market collapsed and so called balloon of dot.com technology got burst. The news about limitations of internet technology was first time widely spread around the world. Actually internet at this stage helped a lot to companies in advertising their product on internet to outreach wide customer population. Customers could see products of day to day use free of cost on internet web sites. However, this set to increase expectations of companies tremendously. They became panic to get more and more benefits out of internet publicity.

After dot.com market crashed people started realizing if the internet technology was going to die. Many companies were bankrupted, they lost their existence and assets.

However, it is interesting to see that some companies like e-bay, Amazon & Google in that situation also survived and not only they further prospered till today and they are there with strong capital base.

Around this time social networking technology began to emerge. My space like utilities came into use and became famous in the the society. Now the same concept is available as face book utility and today we see it is much settled and widely used. It was the second generation of web technology known as web 2.0. In web 1.0 generation of internet most of the web pages were created by web masters. The scene was such that web users were numbered in lakhs against few thousands web creators. The need was to revolutionise it. In web 2.0 technology it was the age of collaborative or group efforts to generate web products or put data on web. The concept of wiki emerged. Wikipedia is one such online encyclopedia created by many people collaboratively. There were many such utilities that came into existence in web 2.0 technology like blog, flicker and YouTube etc. You tube is a collection of videos created by people and by sharing their contributions. Today the video collection in You tube is numbered 700 million videos. If one tries to view consolidated data on web then in 2007 it was 289 billion gigabytes (280 Exabyte) and it was estimated that by 2015 it is estimated as approx 1000 Exabyte. We can understand its quantum and comprehensiveness by looking into its growth.

10.2. DEFINITION AND CONCEPT OF SEMANTIC WEB AS LEE THOUGHT

We all are convinced with the fact that the internet in the dreams of Lee is still to emerge completely and he is much concerned about it. The internet technology which we know and use is different than one as Lee thought, as it has not been developed in that way. However,Lee never lost his hope and always persuaded his research. He kept on telling the world and writing about his ideas about internet in true sense. Right from beginning he thought of internet like semantic web only. He finally in 1998 presented his clear vision about semantic web. It is interesting to note his definition about the semantic web. He says that, "It is my dream that in future each and every computer on the internet would be capable to analyse data on web itself. Computer would understand web contents, links, costumers and they would also understand the transactions they do about sales and purchase things on internet." If we critically think about the present internet and capabilities of computers on web find that any task done today is not done by the computer itself but as users direct to computers. Lee confidently says that in semantic web it is possible once the semantic web technology is fully emerged the computers on web would understand meaning of each trading done or they would also understand meaning of tasks done by customers in their daily life. They would talk about user needs among them and come forward with solutions to their problems. It is also expected that intelligent web agents would be available for user's assistance. Now let us try to understand a little more about semantic web.

10.3. WHAT IS SEMANTIC WEB?

If one wishes to understand semantic web then it is necessary to accept the concept of semantic web as it is "a web of data." Today we assume that the information on web is in the form of documents and we search them through search engines. Once we get web pages or documents we need to read ourselves to understand their meaning or to find out the specific contents in those pages. Although all the information is presented using current web technology and computers, however they do not understand anything in the webpage or contents in the document. In order to understand the limitations of the present day web let us take an example as: A user wishes to find out about the Everest i.e. the Mount Everest. Suppose he gives search word as "Everest" then the result would be as below:

- Everest shopping Mall
- Everest club
- Everest Tours or Travels
- Everest Airlines
- Everest Society

and so on a long list of unwanted things

As the user does not get the desired topic he gets frustrated. His search topic would be there somewhere in the junk retrieved by the search engine. This happens because computer does not understand meaning of word "Everest" or anything about Mount Everest.

So with the current web capabilities the computers and systems fail to provide user with exact information by understanding various meanings of words put into search window. However, with semantic web it is possible. Semantic web would interact with user and get correct description that the searcher having in his mind or user gives a few more words or a string in support of his queries, which would be clearly understood by web computers, such as:

1. Everest is a tallest mountain
2. It is in Nepal

Having understood the meaning of these set of queries intelligent computers would certainly provide the specific information: Let us take an another example to understand the concept of semantic web.

Let us consider some words known to us very well, Dashrath, Rama, Sita, Laxman, Bharat and Shatrughna.

As we read these words we known that these are personalities / characters from Ramayana period. When we as humans read these words our logic recognises not only meaning of these words but about relations among them, that:

Rama, Laxman, Bharat, Shatrugnh are 4 brothers.

Dashrath is the father of these 4 brothers.

Sita is the wife of Rama

However, the computer does not understand the meaning of these words or about the relation of each one has with others. In semantic technology capable computer would understand meaning and relations of such words exactly as we understand. Now let have another complicated case:

Suppose a person stays in one of the suburbs of Mumbai, have two kids and a wife in the family. Imagine that his marriage anniversary approaching near. He wants go to Mulund with his family, he wishes to see a comedy film with his family, then he wishes to have vegetarian food in a good hotel and finally he wishes to return his home.

Now in this set of queries there are various questions as:

1. In which theaters at Mulund currently comedy films are screened?
2. How far the theater is from the person's home in suburb?
3. Whether tickets for 2 + 2 are available?
4. Where to book the tickets?
5. Which good vegetarian hotels are there near to cinema hall?
6. While returning from Mulund at night what would be situation on the road?
7. How much time it would take to return home covering certain distance?

Now question is that in a present day web search can we get answers to the above questions in one single attempt? The answer is clearly No! In current web technology we need to take up question one by one and whether can we analyse result of each search and get the desired conclusion? It seems it is a difficult task. However, semantic web technology would make it feasible to record entire set of question and finally get one exact result as expected, which would be prompt and instantaneous. Moreover the system would expect one single query and it would seek further clarifications from the information seeker in a interactive way. This is the success and characteristics of the semantic web.

Computers in semantic web technology would understand the complexity of queries and would provide the answers to them. Now let us understand how it happens with semantic web technology.

10.4. HOW SEMANTIC WEB WORKS?

World Wide Web consortium, known as W3C, is a web technology standardising organisation founded by Tim Berners-Lee. W3C assumes task to design and issue international standards which would helps further growth and progress of web technology. They have already prepared protocols relating to internet like HTTP and www. W3C has also prepared standards and protocol for linked data about ontology useful in semantic web technology. W3C has also prepared guideline to link open databases on the web known as RDF (Resource Description Framework), which is the significant part of semantic web. RDF facilitates inputting metadata and the resources uploaded on web. Having such metadata of resources computers on web can know the existence of the resource and can also understand meaning of metadata elements. Now let us try to know how data resources on web are interlinked.

As W3C has prepared the protocol for semantic web named RDF they have also prepared guidelines for web ontology. Ontology represents key terms. Ontology is a method to describe / explain concept of any resource through set of key elements. Subject, predicate and object with relations among them are interpreted through ontology.

Definition of key terms and their relations with various fields helps computers to understand identity and characteristics of any resource, enabled by ontology method. Let us see an example as:

Suppose as a person I wish to create RDF of my identify on web by noting my specific characteristics as an individual then I need to input metadata about my profile on web as:

My full name	:	Dattatray Narayan Phadke
My Mail ID	:	dnphadke@gmail.com
My Field	:	Library information technology

By using standard key terms (ontology) as the above computer can very well understand my identity on web.

Ontology guidelines help to classify key terms or concepts for interpreting relation among set of key terms relating to any field by which data integration process is carried out. If there is any complexity of inter term relation or if there is a problem about clarity of the meaning of key terms, then efforts are made to bring uniformity among them. For example while specifying RDF of various individual, sometime mailbox or "E-mail ID" terms are used synonymously. In such case with the help of ontology term relation is interpreted as

Relationship : "e-mail" is the same as "mailbox". This is the simple example of ontology script. Sometimes ontology is complex in nature then tools like RDF schemes are used to integrate it.

There are various ontology tools like:

- SKOS (Simple Knowledge Organisation Systems)
- OWL (Web Ontology Language)
- RIF (Rule Interchange Format)

We have seen the concept and purpose of ontology used in semantic web to create metadata about resource, field or an individual and input it. There are guidelines to ask query about web resource. In order to frame query there is another guiding tool named SPARQL. By making use of the query language one can search and retrieve the information about any web resource. SPARQL is a specific tool for metadata specified by RDF, which facilitates searching data about web resource on http or SOAP platform, which is presented in a table form and such tables are uploaded on another website. This data table is used in web designing, to mesh up the site or can also be used as search engine. This process is called data streaming in semantic web technology.

10.5. HOW SEMANTIC WEB IS USEFUL TO US?

It is expected that semantic web technology would bring total change in our web accessing. It is also expected that with semantic web technology internet surfing would be easy and comfortable. It is estimated that since zero internet usage has increased to 380% and now internet has become our lifestyle to use with much confidence. Although we use computers to do repetitive tasks still we need to take a lot of efforts in doing our tasks. With semantic web it is expected that it would become easy than before. Now while working we need to click several links but it is certain that with semantic web the number of clicks would be decreased and still one would be able to fetch the expected data. It would also be consider all your expectations and choices. However, we need to use specific search engine for this. It is confirmed that whatever is done with TWINE software would be possible here. The system would provide agents or software assistance in retrieving expected data. If you are going to prepare travel plan then one can use agent like Triple and with just one site you can do booking available on multiple sites, so one can get the expected data without any problem.

There would be great opportunities for government companies as well as commercial traders. Banks can too get the data of their account holders without much hurdles and there would not be difficulty in understanding customers banking activities. Financial institution would easily judge risks in financial transactions. For pharmaceutical companies it would be economical and would reduce cost of production of medicines as they can interface their own data with the open data available as linked open data on web. It can make customers as well as employees happy.

Semantic web environment can help in national security systems as well in preparing for disaster management, in case of natural calamities. It would also help in the military actions during war or military action in disaster management. Semantic web could help in handling situations more efficiently as the Govt. and defense can use open geographic data for their actions, as Govt. offices collect a lot of data on their own which would be supplemented with free data available from same service providers, making it more comprehensive database.

10.6. WHAT IS NEXT AFTER WEB 3.0

If we critically review the development and progress of web technology then we find that every web technology generation or phase has founded the base for the next advanced generation. As we have seen, web 1.0 laid the foundation of web 2.0. We see in web 2.0 facilitated emerging of social networking application. In web 3.0 computers are empowered to interpret semantics of data.On this background the question comes to our mind then what is next to web 3.0? If we consider and assume that if life span of each web generation is roughly 10 years, then it is expected that there would be web 4.0 after web 3.0 and its tenure would be between 2020 to 2030. It is also predicted that web 4.0 would be a technology like web OS and there would be agents available to help us in using this technology. The web at that time would be like an operating system and it would also be intelligent web or so called emotional web which would understand the human emotions too. If we consider the current pace of web development then it is expected that by 2029 web 4.0 technology must have stabilized and used optimally by people with the assistance of software agents.

10.7. TECHNICAL BACKGROUND OF SEMANTIC WEB TECHNOLOGY

Out of our discussion in previous paras we understand that semantic web is web of data (s) which includes individual, financial or data relating to several fields like pharmaceutical industry and others. The special characteristic of these data bases is that, they get a format of open linked types, once they uploaded on web. There is special technology available to link and extract as per need by combining local available databases. The semantic web technology makes use of RDF and OWL protocols.

Tim Berners-Lee while inventing semantic web technology prepared a set of rules for it. They are also known as "Linked Data Principles". Under these guidelines the data is published on web in such a way that with the collection of various linked data it becomes a global data space. This data is used as raw data for semantic web, which could be inter connected as per required needs to retrieve output of desired information. In semantic web technology the old concept of URL (Universal Resource Locator) is used with new concepts of Universal Resource Identifier, in short it is called as URI. In this the concept the following guidelines are used to publish data on web.

1. For small, small parts of website URIs are used.
2. While publishing data on the web one should use combination of HTTP-URI, so that it would be easy to search data on web.
3. While constructing URI, RDF protocol is used with XML and SPARQL is used query language to search it.
4. For one main URI it is better to have many sub-URIs so that searcher can get additional allied information. In order to make it feasible it is necessary that people submit their raw data on web, which would be available as open data. Efforts are being taken to inspire submission of such data on web. Many international universities, industries have uploaded their raw data in open data form on semantic web.

In the TED conference organised in 2009 wherein Lee appealed to the world participants to upload their raw data on web. The response was positive and as a result many submitted their data on web, which was free and open type. Scientists used such data and results were really surprising to all. One of the examples of it is as given below :

We remember there was an earthquake at Haiti in Fiji in 2010, which caused havoc in that country. In order to handle post quake rescue operations it was thought to use Google map to map the destructions. However, Google map was not found suitable for this. Understanding this problem Geoeye - a satellite imaging co. offered to provide geo images data of Fiji and they uploaded the data on web in open format. This facilitated world to see the locations of destruction sites due to earthquake, which facilitated many to forward the aids to that country. It should be noted that with web 2.0 technology tool e.g. social networking tool (twitter) was possible to first spread the breaking news about this earthquake on network across the world.

10.8. LINKED OPEN DATA PROJECT

Linked open data (LOD) project was initiated by Tim Berners-Lee in 2007. The main purpose of the project was to get information about data bases uploaded to web with open license method and by interlinking them. For linking these databases RDF/XML protocol is to be used and data would be published as per link data principles guidelines. After 2007 with its initial start open data started growing the on web. The companies who submitted their data on web with open license include US Government, BBC, Flicker and New York Times. Since the database available on web is of open license type, available free of cost and there would be facility to link them with database of organisation or company, which could led to generate new data or information useful for commercial purpose. The growth of such data is considerable and one can judge how the future

Fig. 10.1. Linked Open Data Cloud Picture
***Courtesy*: Linked Open Data Cloud Diagram**
http://lod-cloud.net

semantic web would be growing. Actual photo of Debipedia open data cloud is shown in figure - 22.1 on over leaf. In this graphics we can see how each data set inter linked with each other as seen by lines drawn among them. It gives an idea how to interlink useful datasets available on web to get desired new data set and information relating to it as many are benefited by this.

10.9. IMPORTANT PARTS OF SEMANTIC WEB TECHNOLOGY

Semantic Web Technology contains following important parts:

1. URIs
2. URI ref
3. XML
4. RDF
5. OWL
6. FOAF
7 SPARQL

Let us see the details of these parts.

10.9.1. URI (Uniform Resource Identifier)

In semantic web environment we surf on web with URI instead of URL. As a part of Uniform System of Identifies each and every small part of source has a separate URI, which facilitates identification of source as a whole. In old internet technology URL was indicating only the web address, which was helping us to search that particular web page. However, it never helped us to identify or search any item, point or theme in the page content. Where as in semantic web each and every important contents bears a URI and they can be independently searched on the web easily, and to search routine document or image on the web is not difficult, as they are subjective.

In old web technology concepts like individual, institution, a book in library or author do not exist independently. In semantic web each of these and many like them do exist on web independently and this is the specialty of semantic web technology.

10.9.2. URI ref

In order to support URIs on semantic web another string is used, known as URIref. In this there is facility to incorporate URI fragment in the main URI. This is done by using symbol #. For example:

Reference http://www.example.org/index.html # section - 2

In this string section - 2 is an another fragment or part of main URI is attached. The purpose of both URI and URI ref is to unite fragment or part source with the main source and to facilitate them to identify independently.

10.9.3. XML

XML is a web language, which enables uploading of document on web. While doing this anyone would format the document to be uploaded, by creating the markup to facilitate identification of that document on the web. Such mark ups could be read by computer and with suitable software computer could also understand the exact meaning of them. This is the main functionality of the semantic web. There are various types of softwares available which make it possible. However, the process needs usage of XML and RDF technologies together and it is not possible only with XML.

10.9.4. RDF (Resource Description Framework)

RDF or Resource Description Framework is a special web language, which facilitates description of data on web. RDF is the significant technology of semantic webs wherein description string is linked to URI. Now let us understand the process of RDF. Suppose we want to describe:

"Abhishek the Website Creator" on the web.

1. "The first part is subject i.e. the thing described is "website" The second part is the "Predicate"
2. The description of work i.e. "website creator".
3. The third thing is proper noun i.e. actual name of the person - Abhishek

In above three parts of description is subject, predicate and proper noun or name.

This way descriptions are incorporated in XML script with the help of RDF. We as humans so we can very well understand above but the computer does not understand these terms and relations among theme.

We need the following two things to achieve this:

1. A system of Machine Processable Identifiers
2. Machine processable language

The technologies makes it possible to know words, their meaning and relations as referred in the above example i.e. entity subject as web, about the entity, about the web as web creator and finally name. The words used in this description with the above technology are understood by computer or they can interact among them about it.

The description written in terms of XML markup along with RDF computers can understand it. In semantic web it is possible with the combination of XML and RDF. In the above example and in other descriptions the words used as subject, predicate and names are collected together in a dictionary. In semantic web this dictionary is called ontology. The collection of terms is also called metadata.

Task of incorporating such metadata is carried out on web page. The ontology of description words are inserted in XML structure and such web pages are made available for semantic web. Such semantic web enabled websites with their ontology and data sets are available and one can choose such data sets suitable for obtaining desired information by creating links among them. Such data is called linked data. Since such data is freely made available on web it is also termed as "open linked data". There are agents who take up the task of searching suitable datasets with such category, link them as per requirement and make such system available for use. The agents, however, work on commercial basis. As the data is freely available agents service to link data sets is not that costly. In short we can review the process as: with joint use of XML and RDF the words are used to describe URIs. The interpretation of meaning of the words and relations among them is done by making use of ontology language software.Now let us try to know about the ontology language.

10.9.5. OWL - Web Ontology Language

In semantic web environment in order to get additional information or to know relations among various URIs uses of vocabulary or ontologies are made. This facilitates data integration, for example a provision can be made so that different terms in various data sets are used with same meaning. If we would go little deeper in ontology then we should refer guidelines issued by W3C, which means one should refer OWL protocols.

Web ontology language in short is called as OWL. We have seen that ontology language is used to convert normal web pages into semantic web pages, which facilitates interpretation among the web contents or relations among them. OWL is one of the computational logic based language. This language has significant feature of knowledge expression and computer can interact with this facility through the language scripts to understand the knowledge expression of any data set. The special feature of this is that ontology used with OWL in one web page can also interact with ontology used in another web page of semantic category.

It is said to be a tedious task of creating semantic category of web pages by specifying following:

1. Specifying thing on web page in terms of subject, predicate and names e.g. individual or institution, relation and their names.
2. Specify or interpret relation among these subjects, predicates and names.
3. Specify synonyms relating to these things or terminology.
4. Additional information about the things on web.

Looking into the difficulties in assigning ontology about web contents many prefer to label or tag the objects. These tags can classify these objects. We know that web 2.0 technology provides tagging facility. Especially various contents of a research paper could be tagged and tags can be indexed or arranged logically to create tag group. In flicker utility individual can tag photos as per their convenience. Google Image Labeler facility of Google is also used for tagging. Secondly, tagging done by one person can be used by others due to open access characteristics of tagging. It is expected that tagging facilities of web technology would be supportive to web 3.0 technology also.

10.9.6. FOAF (Friend OF A Friend)

FOAF or in full form Friend-of-a-Friend is another ontology software which computers can read word context. FOAF is an important part of Linked Data Project. It is also a technological tool for social semantics. Any individual can create his / her own FOAF profile. It gives unique identity description entity which does not require any central data background, which can participate in social networking on semantic web. A computer can prepare a list of individual and their friends using FOAF profiles.

10.9.7. SPARQL

If we consider developments of semantic web technology then we assume that it would form a big collection of resources on semantic web. As small things on web, individuals, institutions, books, authors each of these would get unique identity and existence on web. Naturally there would be need of a capable search tool or query language tool to search such specific information contents on web: There is such capable search engine or query language tool available known as SPARQL.

We use SQL query language to retrieve information from databases having relational database management systems. In case of XML structured database there is a query language called XQUERY to search the information, so similarly for information to be retrieved from semantic web resources people use SPARQL query language. By assigning query term one can search data from http or soap type of domains. In semantic web SPARQL is used along with RDF, as we define data while storing it in the same way as it is retrieved.

In case of SPARQL a different query formation is adopted, the process works in three ways and called triple pattern RDF. Additional features of things to be queried are recorded one by one.

This triple formed query is submitted and if database has information satisfying all 3 queries then exact answer is displayed. This process ensures searcher of getting exact expected answer.

While if searching data using SPARQL search tool system prompts searcher to record 3 types of inputs while submitting a search query by which the individual or things attributes are specified. The query submitted on SPARQL platform system, makes efforts to match 3 query inputs to that of databases on web resources having RDF pattern and data matching exactly with query, if found, is retrieved. Let us have an example to know how it works :

Suppose if searcher wishes to look for books by S. R. Ranganathan in semantic web environment, them see how the triple action query is formed in this case:

1. What is to be searched is "books" which is subject.
2. In books what the searcher is looking for is the author which is predicate.
3. What is exact name of another the searcher is trying to get i.e. Books of Ranganathan.

Now let us see how query is written in SPARQL

PREFIX query <http://www.w3.org./2014/02/19-rdf-syntax-na#>

PREFIX OWL : <http://www.w3.org./2002/7 owl#>

PREFIX Books: <http://www.listbooks.com/book# SELECT? title

Where? bookrdf : type books : books?

books: author

http:/s.ranganathan.in/foaf.rdf#me/bookdc:title ?title

Ordered by title

The result of this query would be list of books by Ranganathan arranged by titles.

The above example gives us an idea how semantic web technology facilitates to get right answer to the query, where as in present web search a lot of junk is presented to a searcher, which really frustrates him/her.

Now we are going to learn how web 3.0 has emerged from web 2.0 technology.

10.10. ROAD TO WEB 3.0 TECHNOLOGY THROUGH WEB 2.0

We agree that web 2.0 technology got much publicity as it provided many collaborative tools to the society. However, still web 2.0 technology has not been utilized fully by the people. Especially in developing country like ours we have not yet started using web 2.0 in various fields.

Web 2.0

If we go into the historical facts about web 2.0 we know that Dale Dougherty and O Reilly brought web 2.0 technology in reality. Many criticize on web 2.0 by saying that web 2.0 technology was developed keeping in view commercial benefits. However, there are many others who admit and highly appreciate development of web 2.0. They plead web 2.0 for its following significant characteristics. Web 2.0 has given many useful utilities for all of us :

1. User can post their ideas on web eg. people can post book reviews on Amazon online book store.
2. Media like social networking as well as Facebook people get connected with each other, form a group and discuss things together.
3. YouTube is the example of able platform for sharing videos. It is fast developed and is found most capable. It is now possible to upload a video created in any corner of the world within an hour's time for browsing by the whole world.
4. One can register for RSS feeds to get updates of RSS enabled web pages in our mailboxes continuously. Example: contents pages of journals.
5. Internet browsing has not remained limited to desktops or within a LAN environment but it is now browsable on tabs, iPods or smart phones. Video games are freely available in cyber cafe. The day is not far to browse internet on television screens. There are many dedicated sites for sports events or for online music.

It we consider over all the web development we can sum it in the following way:

- We may call web 1.0 of library, which facilitates searching information. However, it was difficult to contribute or add any information into it.
- With web 2.0 collaborative development of web resources became possible eg. Wikipedia. People got connected with each other.
- Social Networking : People get connected with each other.
- Web technology did no remain limited to home or office computers but we can take it with us to any place where we go.
- In web 3.0 it is expected that we need not take efforts, retrieve information ourselves but we can tell systems to work for us and to give desired information.

  For example: Suppose a searcher looks for following information :

A family wishes to go on tour having budget of Rs. 50,000/- They wish that :

1. They want to go at good place
2. Wish to have affordable tour cost.
3. Look for maximum returns from their budget

If the searcher uses the current internet portals then he has to go to several sites, get the information, compile it and after doing a lot of home work probably one may get some consolidated information. However, one may not be fully satisfied with this. If the searcher opts to use web 3.0 or semantic web then he can submit the query with series or inputs corresponding to above expectations. Then making use of some intermediary agent he could get exact information without much effort i.e. the specialty of semantic web. Even if one put ups a query as :

Local vacation with Rs. 5000/- for a family of four. The system would provide you with various options for choosing a right one.

Now let us have an idea about how search process works on normal platforms and on semantic web platforms. One main difference is that on normal (current) platform it is human oriented search. Where one plans to write search queries, look for various resource websites and gets the information with one's laborious home work. In this type we do search on Google with simple and advanced search. In Google platform it has index created out of key words, which are used generally by the searchers. From this index we can search the web pages and not the contents of web pages and as such specific search mode from broad to specific we may not get anything ,which is normally categorised as "OR" category of search. Event we try to use other operators like AND or NOT then probably we may fail to get the exact information.

However, in case of semantic web type search it is mainly categorised as application oriented. The search is directed by search software, where in other related relevant attributes of search items are also considered. This includes objects; concepts, individuals or institutions are considered and also plus attributes of exact documents. The search is done multifaceted way. It being a software related search it uses linked data available and the search is done with higher level query formation.

10.11. EXAMPLES OF SEMANTIC WEB PRODUCTS

By now we have got a fare idea about semantic web, its concept and the technical features. Semantic web is a web of data. Any individual or institution can create their own profile in RDF/ XML structure. By using own ontology software, one can support it with appropriate ontology and upload it on web. People can upload their data as free / open linked semantic web enable data on web. Several open linked data in various fields are forming clusters by interlinking within the data sets. Anyone who wishes to extract such data from group of linked open data relevant to his/her own data. They can either try to link them or get the help from agents to establish link among them relevant to own data and would try to retrieve information as new set of data for using individual on business needs. This was in short how semantic web would be new, different, innovative and more useful technology than the older internet world.

Having this brief interpretation about semantic web now let us try to review some information products available in semantic web environment to get a feel about this technology.

10.11.1. Health-base - Medical Field

Health-base is a source like your doctor. The source facilitates to search information on semantic web relating to health relating information on three levels i.e. symptoms, treatment and drugs. While searcher searching the web instead of health literature, articles, books or advertisements, which may not be of direct use but gives pin pointed information on health problems. In health-base there are over 10 lacs health related papers. The source relates database like WebMD as well as yahoo health. The information retrieved through this source is not like normal search output but is available in a classified manner, which is not screamed with adds and animations. This happens because health-base does not have its own database but the information on health queries are answered using other open linked databases to which the source is linked. However, the retrieval process gives feel to the searcher like live sites.

10.11.2. DB Pedia

DB Pedia is an open linked software. It is a joint venture of Leipzig and Berlin University. The purpose was to look for structural information within Wikipedia, connect the structure with outside linked datasets and present this advance source on web with semantic web technology. We know that Wikipedia itself is an open type very useful important database vulnerable for semantic web. It contains over 2. 9 Lakh. topics which gives information collaborated by many contributors. The wiki source would be interlinked with other similar data sets like Freebase, Geo-names and World fact books to form a comprehensive source with banner as DB Pedia.

With the above interlinking the DB-Pedia project would present a broad based source comprising of:

- Information on individual profiles number 292000
- Information about 33000 places around the world.
- Information about 130000 species of animals.
- 8000 music albums
- 44000 films
- 15000 Video films
- Information about 119000 institutions
- Information about 4400 diseases and remedies

The above statistics speaks about the comprehensiveness of DB Pedia source. DB Pedia is now growing with a pace as Wikipedia is advancing.

We normally perform keyword search in Wikipedia. However, in DB Pedia one can search life stories of musicians of 18th century. DB Pedia also facilitates to perform advance search by refining in semantic point of view to get pin pointed exact information. One can find and view old films like "The Departed" and "The Aviator"

10.11.3. Music Brainz

UK based news channel also broadcasts musical concerts of well known music artists. BBC has enormous data of artists, their profiles and music concerts. It has now adopted semantic web technology to broadcast the music programs by innovatively inter linking music data in such a way that music lovers get an opportunity to listen music which they rarely get to hear. Some of those artists may not exist today. Semantic web technology has facilitated to unfold the special features of music treasure.

BBC has not only used the music data it has but semantically it gets interconnected with music dataset available with another database having music collections like Music Brainz and DB Pedia (As seen in previous example) Music Brainz has collection of 400000 music collection and DB Pedia has records of 8000 music albums. Interlinking all three resources has created numerous music database consisting of artists, their biographical features and their archived concerts. Ref: http:// musicbranze.org.

10.11.4. E-Tourism

Today web has become showcase for tourism. People make use of enormous data on tourism in planning their tours. There is a competition among travel & tourism companies in attracting tourists towards worldwide tourist cities backed with their information on internet world. These days tourist prefer week end tour, short breaks, sports tourism, social and health tourism. A city named Zaragoza in Spain has grabbed the opportunity of attracting tourists from all over the world towards the city. They have developed tourism app called cruiser, which makes use of expert knowledge systems and ontology software. The system provides tailor-made package to each tourist based on their liking added with their preferred places to visit. Sometime tours are organised attached with famous sports events. There are special attractions about beautiful beaches also.This is an excellent example of using semantic web in tourism.

10.11.5. Every Block-Mash up Site

Mash-up is such a website which facilitates linking its own data with other relevant open linked type data in providing information service to the society. It is UK based source called "Every Block". It concerns with civic kind of information. Linked data emerged with this banner is very famous in UK. It comprises of information from buildings, their locations, surroundings along with information about availability of community centers, their inspections are also backed up with information published in local news papers about problems faced by the citizens. This data is further linked with the data of flicker of photo collections. It has also connections with the programs of local radio stations and blocks concerned with social event and problem. The information retrieved from this entire source cluster is presented with geographical digital data so that anyone can find out what is happening around us - and nearby. The source is well known in family as well as social security point of view. The web sources use semantic web search engine. This important database is linked with government data making it dependable, authentic and meaningful.

10.11.6. Other Examples of Semantic Web

10.11.6.1. Guardian Data Stores

Guardian Data Store is related with Guardian, which is an UK based organisation which works in journalism fields. The facts available with them are on data blog. Launched in 2010 Data store is an online directory providing a selection of datasets on topic of public interest (govt. data, education, culture and population and other tools to explore), along with demonstration of original guest visualization of the data sets. Resulting guardian data-store is growing database of open data sets used by guardian and available for download in a variety of forms. It supports active community engagement and sharing of how data sets are being used and reused.

Ref: http://guardian.co.uk/data_store

10.11.6.2. Open Street Map

Open Street Map (OSM) is a collaborative project to create a free editable map of the world. It has been created with the concern of constrains and restriction of map information of the world and the advancements of in expensive portable satellite navigation devices. OSM was created by Steve Coasts in UK in 2004. The idea of creation was success of Wikipedia and preponderance of proprietary map data in UK and elsewhere. OSM provides free worldwide geographical information such as maps. This site uses creative commons licensing Global Community. OSM facilitates active community engagement and sharing.

Ref : http://wiki.openstreetmap.org/wiki/main_page

10.11.6.3. OS Open Data

OS Open Data offers range of quality assured, regularly updated products that enable one to analyse for self use. The data build in interactively with the websites which could create stunning visuals. In such situation system facilitates to have free access for this support of OS-open data product which could take you right down to street level to have details of happening of any untoward things. They include backdrop maps, boundaries, post codes and more. As long as data user and credit to open data user is free, they can use the products in any way as long as user wishes so provided that is not against the laws. As we start our open data journey there is an active community of knowledgeable people ready to offer useful advice. Example OS open data provides a selection of open ordnance survey mapping datasets of Great Britain, in addition, an open API (OS open space) also allows the integration of OS open data to incorporate with creative commons to enable the recombination of data.

Ref:http://www.ordanancesurvery.co.uk/oswebsite/opendata/index.html

10.11.6.4. BBC Backstage

BBC Package is a collection of open BBC data feeds and APIs available for remixing and mash-ups. The site aims to "encourage participation and support creativity through open innovation". There are some license restriction (mainly about its commercial use) which are clearly defined on the site Ref: http://ideas.welcomebackstage.com/data

Conclusion : In short the discussion in this chapter leads that we looked into historical developments of web technology in general and semantic web or web 3.0 in particular. We then understood the concept of semantic web; usefulness of semantic web to us, about future of web 3.0, technical features of semantic web; about linked open data project, about w3 guidelines and various examples of semantic web. By now author feels that readers have got fare knowledge about semantic web technology. In simple way to review it again, it could be in the lines as said by W3

The semantic web provides a common framework which allows data to be shared and reused, across one's application, enterprise and community boundaries. It is a collaborative effort led by W3C and it is based on the resource description framework (RDF). W3C defines main goals of semantic web as :

Semantic Web : The semantic, unlike current internet is a web of data and not the documents. The vision of semantic web is to extend the principles of the web from document to data. In it data should be accessed using the general web architecture with URIs, Data should be related to one another just as documents are related. Semantic web considers creation of common framework which allows data to be shared and reused across the web, to be processed automatically by tools as well as manually, including exploring new relationships among pieces (or URIs) of data.

In order to facilitate these goals, it is required to define and describe the relation among the datasets on web. This does not refer to usage of hyperlinks which just concerns with the current semantic web and such relationship could be established between any two named resources or values and the relationship itself (i.e. the Linux) is also described.

In tradition web a link is not named like this. The naming and defining those relations on semantic web, explicitly enables better and automatic interchange of data. RDF provides fundamental building blocks in semantic web. The formal definition about that interchange is given in w3c guidelines (http://www.w3.org/2001/sw/SWAQ) which says that:

The ability of dynamically describing complex and evolving concepts, resources and relationships, which could have profound impact on how we all access and use web data.

Semantic web technology makes use of standards such as :

Uniform Resource Identifier (URI) (http://ietf.org/rfc/rfc2396.txt)

RDF vocabulary description language 1.0 RDF schema

(http://www.w3.org./TR/relf-schema/)

SPARQL Query language of RDF (http://w3.org./TR/rdf-sparql-query/)

OWL 2 web ontology language:(http://www.w3.org./TR/owl2-overview)

Rule interchange format core dialect:Simple knowledge organisation system

Semantic Technologies : Enables machines as well as people to understand, share and reason with them at execution time.

Linked Data : In order to make semantic web or web of data is a reality, it is necessary to have a large volume of data available on web in a standard, reachable and manageable format. In addition to these it is also necessary to have relationships among the data available for access. This collection and inter-related data on the web can also be referred to as linked data. Thus linked data lies at the heart of semantic web for the large scale integration of and reasoning on, data on the web can be referred w3c-

(http://www.w3.org/standards/semantic web/data)

11
E-Publishing Technology in Library

11.0. INTRODUCTION

With the development of digital media the publishing of e - resources has started growing gradually along with printed literature. As compared to printed form readers are yet to receive acceptance to e-form of literature fully. However, there are advantages in publishing literature in electronic form. In order to preserve valuable and rarely printed literature, process of digitizing them is widely welcomed. Many publishers are publishing their books and journals in both forms e.g. printed as well as in e-form. However, publishing literature only in electronic form has just started. Number of e-books and e-journals have started growing in the library collection. The situation for electronic form might vindicate that library should publish its own literature for the readers in electronic form. With this background and need we are going to understand e–publishing, its concept and technology.

11.1. E–PUBLISHING – A CONCEPT

E-publishing means storing and publishing literature in electronic form. It is expected that e – publications to be available online to the users through computer as offline or CD format is becoming obsolete. E - publishing method is adopted by the publishers to attract the new authors. E - publishing gives opportunity for authors to proliferate their literature worldwide without much effort. In the present knowledge economics e - publishing is the most important development. Secondly, it is a cost saving method of publishing as it is done with minimum expenses. Electronic publication comes generally in digital form only. However, it needs to go through all the publication process as it is done in case of printed literature such as:

- Preparing manuscript, data entry and validating
- Editing
- Converting into digital form and saving
- Designing cover page and preparing book layout
- Preparing E - book

- Publishing it on Publisher's website
- Registration for ISBN
- Establishing copy right certificate
- Marketing and selling

11.2. TYPES OF E-PUBLISHING AND FORMS

E - Publishing enables getting e-literature published immediately e.g. online E - publishing helps in bringing innovation in publishing industry. Newer and newer technology is emerging in this area. The different types of E - publishing and forms are as follows:

- E - book publishing
- E - Journals Publishing
- Print on demand
- Digital Content
- Electronic Ink
- E - Mail Publishing
- Web publishing etc.

11.2.1. E-Books

E - Book is an electronic form of a normal book which is available for the readers online or in a CD from or on reading device like Kindle. For reading e - book other than computers there are several reading devices available today. There are standards available for e - books publishing. Open e - book standard is one of them. e - Books are published in different formats like adobe-PDF or online form on internet or they are published in XML / SGML based web formats. Although today readers are reluctant to read e-books, they are aware that there are several advantages in buying e - books and reading them anywhere at their convenience.

Actually there are lot of opportunities and future scope for e - book publishing. Now it is seen that instead of storing printed books in cupboards young readers prefer to store many e - book in their e - book readers and read them whenever they feel or read them in journey or while on tours. These days hand-held e - book reader costs just around $50=00 or cost of kindle in Indian is from Rs 6,000/- to Rs.14,000/- and it is definite that the cost would reduce in future. When the e - book readers would be available at still reduced cost then probably e - book reading will grow very fast without much difficulties, may be readers need to wait little more. In fact using e - books is very easy, moreover it is attractive and very much convenient. They look like normal books, such as cover, title page, preface, contents page, chapters and at the end the index. One can reach them very quickly. There are icons for these book contents. One can reach a particular page quickly, one can place a book mark as you stop reading on a particular page and next time one can open e - book and reach where one has stopped previously. One can go forward or backward to scan the pages. One can also turn the pages with a finger as we do with normal book in a virtual way. One can also download part of few pages of e – book.

E-book is fully digitized cover to cover and each word on each page is searchable and it takes us to the word or string quickly. Some authors publish their e - books as open access or as free online on internet. All the priced and free e - books are available on internet.

Publishers sale e-books against yearly subscriptions. Libraries and individual readers buy e - books by paying the respective subscription amount. E - Books are made available on publisher's website or online book stores or on e - purchasing portals like Amazon, flipkart, Bookganga etc. Individual readers buy e-books to read one to one where as libraries buy them in network version to put them on intranet by paying additional charges. They need to sign license agreement giving access conditions, access modes and IP address of machine. Cost of e - books vary with access conditions and on other technical constrains.

In order to continue accessibility, library or individual need to renew subscription every year by making payments. Amazon.com portal provides many e - books to be read on their own reading device i.e. kindle. Some e - books are available on CDs. Google book store is a gallery of e- books

11.2.2. Print on Demand

Print on demand is a modern method of printing books. Instead of printing 500 or 1000 copies at a time, publishers choose to print a number of copies as per demand. Method of printing the small no. of copies makes it affordable for the publishers. Technology required for this includes complex laser printing system and electronically formatted text. Presently this technology is costly but expected that its cost would be reduced. Probably this could be the future publishing way. Print on demand is one of the processes of entire publishing printed books industry and if the electronic media is popularised among the readers then print of demand method may lag behind.

11.2.3. Digital Content

Digital content type is mainly connected with electronic form of novels or pocket books which are size wise smaller or nonfiction documents. Many publishers make such publications available to readers which are comparatively smaller in size in the form of digital contents. They also allow readers to download on their handheld readers. For publishing such contents technologies like adobe-PDF, XML, HTML, WAS (Wireless Application Protocol) are required. However, for such publications it is difficult to provide security from copying unauthorizedly as it is very easy to copy and share the contents. However, publishing contents via wireless content method, on phone, on hand held reader or though microwave method(like WIFI) has a good future opportunities for publishing industry.

11.2.4. Electronic Ink

Electronic Ink is a new innovative technology emerging today. If this technology becomes successful then it would leave a long lasting impact on publishing industry. It is expected that it would be initially used for news paper publishing or anywhere The wonderful process in this type is that the contents once published get updated automatically like bill board publication. Its projection could be seen on wall or on cloth in home. This technology is very useful to add media as the text or contents in adds would get changed to attract the customers as well as others. This type of publishing would be certainly beneficial for the ad companies.

11.2.5. E-Journals

Along with publication of printed journals; journals are also published in electronic form, called "e – journals". About the process of obtaining e – journals, getting their access that too in different modes we have already discussed in the chapter no. 07. "E - Resources Collection Development" at length. Once the e - journal is obtained by the following procedures it is made available to users on internet PCs. They are listed on the web page of library and by clicking the title link one can go to the journal website. When we see the front page of journal normally we see the content page of current issue of the current volume. In the content page all the articles are listed in the order of page number. If we click the title we would get full text of article. There are links for old volumes given in your left side chronologically.

E - Journals are available after paying the subscription to publishers and one would continue to access by renewing subscription every year. If library makes the arrangement to keep the access to previous year's journal continued i.e. perpetual access by making additional payment.

11.2.6. E - Mail Publishing

E - Mail Publishing or making a publication in E - mail form is a modern way of promoting literature. Many readers like it, if they get a news paper in their E - mail box. Such publication includes small newsletters. This is the most preferred way and a large number of news letters are mailed to their readers. Some authors also publish their literature on e - mail which is found most attractive to the readers.

11.2.7. Web Publishing

With the development of internet technology publishing literature on web is not a new thing. For web publishing web languages like HTML are mostly used. There are many mark-up languages emerged today which helps in stabilizing web publishing. The main advantage in web publishing is that publication is made available on any portable device or a reader. People use desktop, palmtop, hand held devices or mobile for reading web publications. Like HTML literature is also available in PDF from.

11.3. WAYS AND MEANS OF E - PUBLISHING

E - Publishing is done in many ways and it is done in the following main ways :

1. On commercial basis
2. Subsidised publication or print on demand
3. Free or open access publication
4. Individual e - publication

11.4. ADVANTAGES OF E – PUBLISHING

There are certain advantages in e-publishing such as:

- E - Publishing process works faster and once author submits his / her manuscript, in a few weeks it gets published. It happens only in e–publishing; in traditional way of print publishing takes it several months.
- Cost of E - publishing is less or minimum. E - Publishing does not require large funds.
- Relations between authors and e- publishers are always cordial as it is not difficult to incorporate changes in the text, and even accommodating new figures and charts even at the last moment. Secondly it is also not difficult for author to revamp his publication with the help of publishers.
- Once the literature is published it is possible to make correction or bring improvement subsequently and it would not be costly affair.
- Every commercial publication gets ISBN No. so it is easy to buy e –publication from the distributors or sellers.
- Author can get bigger percent of royalty on e-publication as e – publishing does not require much money and the royalty in this case could be up to 70%
- Although author gives his publishing rights to publisher to publish his material in e - form he can maintain copy right of e - publication with himself/herself
- Since readers easily accept literature in e- form it gives many opportunities to new authors. The readers judge the reputation of author in literature while selecting the e - publication. New authors too get many opportunities being new in the publishing.
- Although author publishes his / her literature at local level it is not difficult to reach to national or even international level.
- Literature once published in e - form remains in print for long time and situation like out of print does not arise in case of e - publishing.
- It is not expensive to maintain e - book in the collection by the readers.

11.4.1. Disadvantages of E - Publishing

1. Sale of E - Publication is very less as compared to printed publications. The reason is that general readers are not much aware about availability of e - publications and they prefer printed literature than e - publications
2. It might happen that responsibility of marketing of e - publication is left to the author. However, in e - publishing authors do not get any idea about how many readers are actually reading their literature.
3. Authors of e- publishers do not get royalty in advance e.g. before publishing e – publication, as royalty depends on sale of the same.
4. There is more threat of piracy of e – publications, as it is easy to obtain a copy of e - publication and it is also possible to republish e-publication by making little change in it with a new name and author.

11.5. CARE TO BE TAKEN BY AUTHORS IN SELECTING E - PUBLISHERS

Nowadays many e - books are coming in the market. Nearly over 100 e - publishers are active in publishing e – literature. Since this is new and emerging field it is necessary for the authors to select E - Publishers very carefully. There are some criteria on which e - publishers could be judged and authors should consider them while selecting as :

1. Whether e - publisher has his own informative and dynamic website?
2. Whether the front page of their website is attractive? Else readers would not look for it and it would affect the sale of e - publication hosted by them?
3. Whether the e- publisher is reputed one and has wide publicity?
4. Whether the e - publisher is a register member of publishers association?
5. Whether they have received any awards for their e - publication work and their books have been well reviewed by the good reviewers?
6. Whether they previously have signed any agreements with the authors and if such information is available on their website?
7. Whether the publisher insists the copy right of the work to be published from the authors, whether they have established royalty percentage, royalty policy and definite royalty percentage to authors. Whether, they allow authors to cancel the agreement?
8. Whether the e - publication you are going to publish through the publisher has long tradition to publish that type of e - publication or the subjects?
9. Whether the prices fixed by e - publisher are affordable by the readers to buy e-books?
10. Whether they publish diverse type of e- forms like PDF, HTML, Palmtop, iPod etc ?
11. Since how long the publisher is in e - publication business and if their status is established in publishing trade?
12. Whether e - publisher has renowned editors in their editorial panel?
13. Whether e - publishers has his own marketing network?
14. Whether e - publishers try to get their e - book reviewed from the renowned subject expert and whether they submit the new book for their review before they are published?
15. Whether e - publishers makes e - book available for sale with online book stores like Amazon.com or bookganga.com etc?
16. Whether publisher makes an arrangement to get ISBN Nos. for newly published books?
17. Whether the publisher is easily available for contacting and if they properly attend you?
18. Whether you as author would feel proud in publishing your books from them?

So author may assess credibility of e- publishers on the above criteria and make the selection of e - publisher for his/her e - literature.

11.6. E-PUBLISHING BY LIBRARY : A NEW CONCEPT

With speedy progress in developing electronic media speed of e - publishing is growing tremendously. E - Publishing business is also becoming famous and attractive. Number of e-Publications like e – book, e - journals, e - news letters are growing very fast. Gradually readers are also showing their acceptance towards them. We see considerable impact of e - publication on functioning and services of libraries. This impact can be analysed in the following three levels.

1. Making e - publication available to readers in the library : In this level mainly libraries are expected to organise e - publications in a better way and arrange to make all types of e-publications available to the readers. We have already read various aspects of e - Resources Collection Development in previous chapter of this book. In addition to this it is also important to see how e - publications could be used in providing Virtual Reference Service.

2. Developing Digital Libraries : There is a good progress in developing digital libraries by the libraries. Digital library is a powerful tool to publish digital literature locally. Institutional repositories and digital archives are becoming common in the institutes. As out of local intellectual assets creating e - literature and making it available to students without having any copyright constrains, is helping students to get opportunity to read literature relating to their curriculum / syllabus. There is also a separate chapter on digital library development in this book.

3. Publishing e- publication by the library : This is the new and emerging topic which is much in discussion in LIS literature these days. Before going into understanding the new concept, let us consider some of the complimenting facts on the part of library which states how libraries are helping world literature and their authors as:

- Many renowned authors are always in touch with the library
- Libraries try to preserve works of various authors with honor and dedication just as a service to society without any bias.
- As a result author's works find a safe heaven in the library
- The authors have great faith in library
- Librarians take care that no one would try to copy the literature in uncontrolled way and no one is trying to violate the copyright of the authors. This faith in libraries is seen universally.

Due to progress in digital media and due to ease in using the technology author strongly feels that there is definite a right situation for libraries to come forward to enter into e - publishing activity. With this need in mind e - publishing by library is being discussed here at length.

Library association like ALA is doing contributory work of e- publishing. Directory of Electronic journals, Newsletters and Academic Discussion List (Annual) is a good example of it. "Colorado by numbers" is another example to see how libraries are working on projects on publishing of social and economic data in country like US. Some research institutions working in specific subjects, their libraries are publishing research articles by scientists working in that organisation. In addition they also invite researches from other research organisations which are working in the similar field to publish their research output with them.

It may so happen in future that researches would prefer publishing their literature in the e-journals published by library of research institutions than contributing them to e-journals published by the commercial publishers, as literature published in e – journals by a library of a research organisation has professional status in that subject literature. Authors world not only get the same name and fame as they were getting it by publishing their literature in commercial journals but they would get more royalty than the publishers were giving them. Over and above libraries would do such work with the same enthusiasm and honor that they give the author's work available in library and at the same time they would help in proliferating scientific communication worldwide. Author is confident that in near future libraries would be equipped with required information technology needed to publish e - journal on their own and conducive situation would be created so that researchers need not have to go to commercial publishers at all for publishing their intellectual works.

11.6.1. Reasons Behind Libraries Publishing e - Journals

There are various reasons for why libraries should turn towards e - publishing. The main reasons are that the literature publishing in commercial journals is clumsy , complicated and there are stringent legal bindings in it. Secondly, a large amount of published literature is in the hands of commercial publishers, as such availability of scientific literature freely for readers to read is almost nil. If we look into the various stages of scholarly knowledge creation we would realise the problems associated with today's publishing process such as:

1. Authors undertake research on newly emerging ideas, they collect necessary data for it, with citing of previous concepts and data with author's new concepts and data they produce new knowledge based on conclusions and they try to share it with their peer groups.
2. The research group discuss the output and decide whether to publish it or not.
3. Author contacts the publisher of a journal who is active in that field and presents the papers for publication. The editorial board evaluate the submission and okays for publishing. If referees feel necessity of improvements the author is advised accordingly. The article is put into journal publication process and in subsequent issues the article is finally published. The author might get some royalty or may not get anything but the satisfaction, that his / her article has been published is an international or reputed journal. Sometimes cost of publishing is also recovered from the author for this gain. Once the article is published the publishers gets its copyright ownership. The author also does not get freedom to use it subsequently.
4. Publishers gets research based articles almost free. Publishers convert those intellectual materials into money. The institute in which the author undertakes the research has to purchase the output of authors research in the form of journal issues.

The readers of the institute have to use the literature with so much binding and copyright constrains. It is a vicious cycle and author gets trapped in it. He is compelled to buy his own things and author is almost robbed in the so called scholarly publishing process. The authors are so much exploited that author cannot do anything but bear it. Today the subscription cost of scholarly journals, especially in e-form is in crores in developing country like India. The author is not allowed to publish his own already published literature, in digital library of his own institute which is really a tragedy of scientific communication in the world. Due to too much commercialisation of journal literature especially of scholarly literature the authors and ultimately libraries are sucked from all sides. The subscription rates of journals are constantly increasing every year as they have to impress the prices of their shares in share markets. Libraries are however ultimately get crushed in the process of increased subscription rates ,which is the soar truth. The library tries to find some temporary solution to the inflation problem as:

1. By discontinuing highly costing journals
2. Reducing purchase of books
3. Stop subscribing high cost databases.
4. Depend on inter library loan for getting required material
5. Going for cooperative collection development
6. Increase funding for library.

In contrast if libraries choose to go for long term measures it would not only help in saving funds but it would also help in proper communication of intellectual assets among the researchers and other readers. The measures could be as:

1. Get back copy rights of own authors from the commercial publishers.
2. Find new ways of knowledge dissemination
3. Promote or inspire for open access method in knowledge creation
4. Establish digital depository for the institute and
5. Library to publish peer reviewed scholarly e-journals

We find that instead of temporary solutions if institute goes for long term solutions then there would be transforming change in knowledge communication. After considering the concept of e-publishing by library and the reasons behind it, now let us turn towards actual method of e - publishing by the library as e - publishing is easy and most economical.

11.7. LIBRARY E - JOURNALS PUBLISHING METHODS

There are two main methods of publishing e - journals

1. As commercial way e - journals are published in the same way library can publish it's own e-journal on no profit no loss basis.
2. Publishing e - Journal by open access method.

Even for publishing e - Journals as open access way there are different methods. In the current situation e - Journals publishing is generally done by open access method due to the following reason:

1. It is economically viable method of publishing e - journal in open access and it could be remedy for inadequate library funding.
2. The Institute would get publicity and name
3. It helps in improving research process as use of scholarly literature increases in the research.

There is one more hurdle that commercial publishers show reluctance towards articles on too narrowed subject. Open access journals can publish such articles very happily.

4. New data bases created in the publishing process by the research can be put into use by new-researchers
5. It helps in developing inter disciplinary branches of subjects.
6. It is possible to regain control on intellect or knowledge dissemination

11.8. OPEN ACCESS E - JOURNAL PUBLISHING

Let us try to understand the process of publishing open access literature through the following model :

E-Publishing with Boston College with the help of **BePress package** to publish e - journal by open access method. The model works like this. :

- The main server is Apache with the help of MOD-Perl or CGI script its subparts work such as:
  1. User interface
  2. Literature submission
  3. Management and editing by peer review process
  4. To develop new website or web page
- In prostgre - SQL database contains details such as manuscript and various versions, their metadata, authors' reviews, editorial board members and subscribers
- E - Journal generally comes in PDF version with full text indexing facility.

E-publishing with the help of Edikit software e - journal publishing process is as below :

1. Authors submit their literature online; the system converts it into PDF
2. Authors and editorial member communicate through E – mail, decision whether to publish the material or not is taken based on the reports of referees.
3. The editorial board has full control on e - journal publishing
4. It is feasible to search articles in full text as it is fully digitized.
5. It is possible to keep statistics of use of contents of e - journal
6. It is also possible to provide alert service about publishing of forthcoming issues.

11.9. TOOLS FOR OPEN ACCESS E - JOURNALS PUBLISHING

- Article system
- D - Pubs Cornel University
- E - First XML (Openly informatics)
- E - Publishing Tool Kit (Max Planck society ZIM)
- Open journal system (Pkp@simon-Fraser University)

Other systems for e – journal publishing

- Allen Track (Allen PRESS)
- Author-2- Author (Vist. Intl.)
- Bench Press (High wire press)
- Edkit (Berkeley Electronic Press)
- Editorial Express (Uni. of Maryland)
- Editorial Manager(Aries Sys. Corp.)
- E - Journal Press
- E - Press
- E - Publishing Service
- Erud it
- E -spere
- E - Stack

Some Other Tools of E - Publishing are as below :

- All academic Journals Services
- Journal Soft
- Open Access Journal Publishing (Biomed Central)
- DSP Rey (National Research Council, Canada)
- Rapid Review
- Roquade
- Scholarly Exchange
- Small Publishing
- Temple Peer Review Manager (Temple University)
- X press Track

CONCLUSION

It is possible to publish e journals by the libraries. Now there is a need for all intellectuals and librarians to come together and throw away crèches of commercial publishers and opt for alternative to free our intellectual assets in real sense and make them freely available to readers and researchers to strengthen their research out puts.

REFERENCES

1. E - Journal Publishing Tools Services -http://library.queensuca/webir Planning /queensuca/ ejournal publishing support html (Accessed on 24th September 2015)
2. Kovas, Dianek .Electronic Publishing in Libraries : introduction Library Hi-tech Vol. 17, No. 1 1999 pp 8-9
3. Rapple, Brendan, Caprio, Mark &Gerrity Bobs The Librarians as Library Agent Establishing a library's scholarly publishing programme for faculty of students NER comp 2006 Project from slide share site (Accessed 20th Dec 2015).

12
Cloud Computing

12.0. INTRODUCTION

Since twentieth century, computer technology is on the progress ride. Even at the mid of twenty-first century, computer technology is still progressing, evolving and innovating further. Whenever and in what form this technology was available it was used extensively. It finds its application in most of the fields. While it was progressing whatever changes or innovations emerged time to time have been happily accepted and adopted. Moreover, older computer technology kept on replacing with its newer form. In spite of all these developments the use of computer technology remained confined to a work place or within institute buildings. At every location of use of computer it was equipped with required software, servers, client machines, word processing and other licensed softwares. All these hardware and equipments were specially acquired. We are seeing this picture with almost each and every institution as it was essential. After looking into time, efforts and money in maintaining systems, computer machinery and peripherals a question was raised by many experts, whether it is necessary to spend so much on information technology infrastructure? Is there no alternative solution to this? How to control the expenses on computer technology for getting computing facilities by every institution? While thinking on these issues a bright solution came forward in the form of new concept of hiring computing facility available elsewhere e.g. "**Cloud Computing**". Although this emerging concept is still to satisfy its application, it is growing very fast, being a most convenient technology for every individual and institution. Now let us try to know the meaning and concept behind the term "cloud computing", as just by looking at it we do not get the clear idea.

12.1. WHAT IS CLOUD COMPUTING?

Before we try to understand cloud computing concept, let us know about the words computing in its terminology. Computing means all the tasks which are carried out with the software, as well as tasks of word processing through the computers. In the application of information technology computer, communication and internet technologies are collectively used. Generally computing is done in network environment. Every institute possesses computer network (LAN) in the form of intranet. All the internet related computer jobs are carried out within the intranet, where contacts with the outside world are established via internet. Every LAN intranet is equipped with the servers, and client machines. It is seen that all the required computer infrastructure exists within the institute, which consists of various softwares, their servers, and operating systems, licenses of word processing utilities like Microsoft. Now considering this background let us try to understand the concept of cloud computing.

Cloud computing means instead of using computer infrastructure for all computing tasks of any institute, use the computing infrastructure of the third party located at some remote place outside the institute. In other words it is about using servers and computing resources available with cloud. In that case the institute would have only client machine through which servers are accessed via internet connectivity and institute need not create computing infrastructure within the institute or it need not maintain them.

Basically cloud is a service provided by a cloud computing companies. They create the entire necessary computer infrastructure including CPUs, servers, operating systems, application software, storage, bandwidth and word processing licensed utilities of Microsoft, which would take care of all the computing needs of any institute. Cloud facility is created at some remote location and computing services are made available to needy institutes through internet connectivity but at a cost.

There are various cloud computing service providers in the world, which are competent, secured, well known and reputed ones, and also there are several organisations that have opted for cloud computing services. Leading cloud service providers include Amazon Web Services(AWS); Microsoft Azure, IBM/ soft layer and Google compute engine.

Cloud computing promises several attractive features to institutes, business organisations and to end users. These cloud services could be characterised into the following three:

1. Self service provision : End users can utilise computing resources for all most any type of computing workload on demand.

2. Elasticity : Users can increase the computing needs when needed and also decrease when demand is decreased

3. Pay Per use : Computer resources are made available rationally allowing users to pay only for the resources and workloads they use.

12.2. NEED OF CLOUD COMPUTING

Up till now information technology is being accepted as modern technology. When we adopt any technology especially information technology it is an expensive thing. However, in adopting any technology for modernisation then by comparing cost with benefit one may not earn anything. Whenever we try to modernise any service system like library & information services comparing cost with benefit would not be a proper assessment. It is necessary to consider and accept indirect or notional benefit. We generally accept that the benefits of adopting technology would not be direct but indirect which are measured in terms of customer satisfaction or in terms of effectiveness

However if we try to assess expenditure on creating computing infrastructure in business point of view then decisions have to be taken whether there is any alternative to the expenditure? The main reason behind accepting cloud computing technology is saving in establishing computing facilities/ infrastructure and incurring cost in maintaining the same. If we jot down the details of traditional way of creating computing facilities they are as:

1. Cost of planning of computing
2. Infrastructure cost of software and cost of their renewals
3. Expenses on hardware setup
4. Cost of purchasing servers and cost of maintaining them
5. Cost of up-gradation of hardware
6. Cost of operating systems and their licensing plus the renewal
7. Cost on human resources required
8. Cost of data security and systems and re evaluating the computing set up.

Going for Cloud computing is a solution to conserve the cost of creating and maintaining computing facilities. Having this market needs many service provider companies, which try to provide computing services through their clouds, have emerged these days and the trend is seen that many organisation and the individuals are adopting cloud computing.

12.3. HOW CLOUD COMPUTING WORKS?

We obtain information from the internet based resources. In order to handle that information to process and store it, we need to have adequate computing facilities; we also need information handling tools. We know that browsing internet with client server system and cloud computing work in all together different way.

Under the cloud computing system whatever computing facilities subscriber needs are provided by cloud service provider. In this arrangement user only needs PCs with internet browsing capability. Even they need not have to install a cloud server client. Responsibility of cloud service provider is to fulfill all the computing needs of an individual or an entire company. In return they get money from the cloud facility user. However, it is found that the expenses incurred on seeking cloud facility is certainly less that the expenses required to create same facilities in the company. Cloud server has full control on all the tasks and management relating to computing of that company. Cloud provider gives all the facilities like operating systems, their licensing, application softwares, storage space and finally access to their software and the data bases.

Although cloud computing is still evolving, its technological functioning is divided into 3 major service categories :

1. Infrastructure as a service (Iaas)
2. Platform as a service (PaaS)
3. Software as a service (SaaS)

12.3.1. Infrastructure as service (IaaS)

IaaS providers such as AWS supply a virtual server and storage as well as application software that allows users to migrate workloads to virtual machines at the cloud. Users are allocated with storage capacity access, configuring the virtual machine and the storage as they wish. Iaas provider offer small, medium, large or extra large memory of computing levels; in addition they customise their allocated set up for different work load needs.

12.3.2. Platform as a service (PaaS)

In the paas type providers host development tools on their infrastructures. Users can access those tools over the internet using web portals or gateway softwares. PaaS is used for general software development and many paas providers host the software after it is developed. Common paas providers include salesforce.com, force.com, Amazon Elastic, Beanstalk and Google's App Engine.

12.3.3. Software as a service (SaaS)

Saas is a distribution model which delivers software applications over the internet and these are called web services. Microsoft office 365 is a saas offering for productivity software and email services. Users can access saas application and services from any remote locations using a computer or mobile device which has internet access.

Not necessary that all the categories of the above services would be provided by one single cloud service provider but there are different service providers which may be specialised in one of the above categories.

If we carefully look at the computing facilities which are provided by the cloud providers we find that they are sufficient and competent to take care of your entire requirement. They are same as we try to create locally by investing huge funds.

We can hire a server, develop and host own software or adopt open source software, customise it, put your databases on cloud, make the system operational and use it just by accessing the services thorough Internet. One can use programming language and develop programmes and make them available for the users. One can work also use MS utilities (word, access, excel or PPT) and do your word processing work. Individual can keep their files, music files, cinemas, videos, book marks, games in cloud serve or host a mail server on cloud and provide mail facility to the employees. Following figure (no. 12.1) gives clear picture of various types of cloud services.

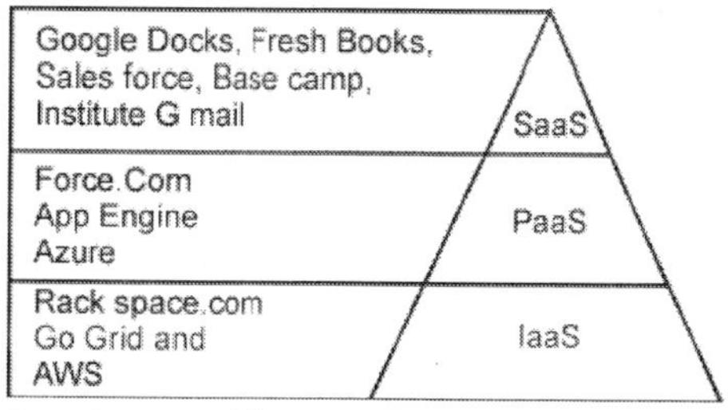

Fig. 12.1. Cloud service types (*Courtesy* : The Gadget square www.gadget.com)

There could be still a longer list of cloud services such as of storage as services (STaas) Security as a service (SEaas) Data as a service (Daas) Test environment as a service (TEaas) Desktop as a services (Daas) and API as a service (Apiaas).

12.3.4. How cloud operates?

Cloud user needs a pc, laptop, desktop, I-pad or a smart phone devices which have internet access. Whenever user wishes to use cloud facility he/ she need to login for cloud services. Cloud provides its services tools and data to the users. The output is seen on users monitor. User can use MS utilities available with cloud to created word document. After making necessary changes one can save the documents on the storage of cloud. One can also get back the document whenever needed for reading, editing or improvement or one can send it to someone by e - mail.

The performance of cloud depends on the strength of internet access, its speed or on its reliability. It can depend on the information handling capacity of the user machines also. Since cloud services are web based facilities they can work on the various platforms also, such as Windows, LINUX or Macintosh. As all machines of an institute or company are interconnected on LAN all such machines can access cloud computing facilities together and they do not face any difficulties. Cloud server also works with pooling of machines in the organisation and it can perform all other tasks like data backup, maintaining security of the data and maintain utility or update software versions automatically. Any single organisation would find it difficult to handle the entire computing load; cloud does it very easily and conveniently.

12.4. NIST DEFINITION OF CLOUD COMPUTING & CLOUD COMPUTING TECHNOLOGY

12.4.1. National Institute of Standard and Technology,

NIST defined cloud computing as :

"Cloud computing is a model for enabling ubiquitous, convenient and on demand network access to a shared pool of configurable computing resources (e.g. networks, services, storage, application and services) that can be rapidly provisioned and released with minimal management efforts or service provider interaction."

This cloud model is composed of five essential characteristics as below:

1. On demand self service
2. Broad network access
3. Resource pooling
4. Rapid elasticity
5. Measured services[1]

---

1. The NIST Definition of Cloud computing. http/csvc.nist.gov/Publication/pubs sps. html#800-145 (Accessed on 20-12-2017)

The details are as:

Consumer can unilaterally choose to use computing capabilities such as server time and network storage as needed automatically without requiring human interactions with each service providers.

Capabilities are available over the network and accessed through standard mechanism that promotes use of heterogeneous thin or thick platforms (e.g. mobile phones, tablets, laptops and work stations)

The service provider's computing resources are pooled to serve multiple consumers using a multi-tenant model with different physical and virtual resources assigned to consumer demand. There is a sense of location independent in that the consumer generally has no control or knowledge over the exact location of the provided resources but may be able to specify location at a higher level of abstraction (e.g. country, state or region) the examples of resources are included with storage processing memory and network bandwidth.

Capabilities can be elastically provisioned and released in some cases automatically, to scale rapidly outward and inward commensurate with demand. To the consumer the capabilities available for provisioning often appear to be ultimate and can be appropriated in any quantity at any time.

Cloud systems automatically control and optimise resource use by leveraging a metering capability at the same level of abstraction appropriate to the type of service (e.g. storage, processing bandwidth and active user account) Resource usage can be monitored, controlled and reported providing transparency for both the provider and consumer of the utilized service.

12.5. TECHNOLOGY OF CLOUD COMPUTING

Cloud computing services are provided on commercial terms with involvement of experts, higher level technology and infrastructure. In cloud computing service user get an interface or a virtual computing source as an agent. This is the top most state of internet technology which enables to give need based services. It is a web based computing tool. It works like electric supply grid, wherein whenever electric energy is needed it is switched on in the same way one can get computing power in cloud computing.

Cloud computing services are provided through a server at cloud through internet media under normal internet protocol. While doing so confidentiality for the business institutions is fully ensured so that they can access needed software databases or software tools as if they themselves have installed at the cloud for the required computing task. In cloud computing screen sharing technology like (Cicatrix-Xen-Apps) are used where various computing sources are integrated. Generally business institutions required all applications are provided by cloud with technology like AJAX (Asynchronous Java Script and XML) similar to web based technology. As such cloud computing technology is a consolidation of various computing services where infrastructure, storage and software services are included.

Different cloud service providers try to provide different forms of computing resources (models) for the customers which are provided under various protocols as :

HTTP: Hyper Text Transmission Protocol

SOAP - Simple Object Access Protocol

REST - Representational State Transfer Protocol.

XML - Extensible Markup Language

In cloud computing various concepts are made available together.

- Grid Computing ASP (Active Server Pages)
- Server Hosting
- Utility computing and virtualization

We know that cloud computing services are available on the basis of their basic models as:

1. Iaas - Infrastructure as a service
2. Paas - Platform as a service
3. Saas - Software as a service

12.6. CLOUD COMPUTING SERVICE PROVIDERS

Cloud computing technology is still constantly evolving. There are a large number of companies which try to provide services to the customers. The list of prominently known companies are as :

- Akami
- Amazon cloud
- Areti Internet
- Enki
- Fortress ITX
- Joyent
- LayedTechnology
- Rackspace
- Salesforce. Com
- Terremark

Along with the above there are routine service providers like IBM, Google and Microsoft.

12.7. CHARACTERISTICS OF CLOUD COMPUTING SERVICES

Basically cloud computing services have been emerged to limit the expenses incurred by the business organisations for creating computing facilities within the organisation. As an alternative to create internal computing, establishment cloud computing technology and their service provider companies are available today. Cloud computing companies provide services to the customers with the following characteristics such as:

- **Self Management** of computing arrangement

- **Client server model :** They are ready with convenient systems for the providers and receivers for any distributed application.
- **Greed computing :** With the integration of distributed and parallel, super and virtual computing network cluster, it gives collective effectiveness and as such with simple connected terminal it is possible to retrieve high level computing work.
- **Mainframe Computing :** Large scale and high level computing
- **Utility computing :** Integration of different computing facilities
- **Peer to peer :** Direct relationship between service provider and consumer
- **Service Oriented computing :** service as it is needed.

12.7.1. Significance of cloud computing in service provider's point of view

Service providers feel confident in delivering their services that :

1. With well equipped capacity at cloud it can increase computing strength of business organisation as per consumers need.
2. With availability of application programming interface (API) and with availability of capable interface it is possible for a normal client machine to very well communicate with cloud server. Most of cloud computing systems provide interface bases on REST system.
3. Cloud computing certainly helps in saving expenditure on creating computing facilities within the organisation and it also saves expenditure incurred in maintaining them as there is no maintenance cost at all.
4. Since cloud computing is available at independent location, consumer can get its services from any where
5. Since cloud is multi tenancy service, all consumers need to use cloud resources cooperatively and the expenses are divided and centralization infrastructure facilities are created in less expenditure. It also helps in increasing peak load. Cloud tries to bring more convenience with increased capacity of computing.
6. Since Cloud systems are most reliable, one can very well depend on them.
7. Since cloud services are available 24 × 7, one can use it optimally which ultimately helps in increasing computing capacity of organisation.
8. One can very well have control on computing tasks by using cloud services
9. Since business organisation are hosting their software and uploading their data on cloud it is the first responsibility of cloud provider to secure confidentiality of computing work of companies so that they can rely on cloud without any worry.
10. Cloud itself maintains software, databases, database management system, search tools, and thus, consumer need not have to do anything special to look after them as things are automatically updated.

12.8. CLOUD COMPUTING : ARCHITECTURE

If you look into the architecture of cloud computing we find it very easy. It contains two main components.

1. Front End and
2. Back End Systems

These components communicate with each other through internet. Front end is the user's part called user interface or clients. The client is PC with internet connectivity plus possessing application interface to get access to the cloud services. At the back end there would be various machines like servers, data storage devices, softwares and various tools of computing and word processing utilities. All these make a cloud of services. There would be everything from computing to games. In addition to these there would be a central server for administration of cloud services. It performs tasks like traffic management to attend to request coming from consumers and to see whether all the cloud functions are smoothly running. Back end admin server also maintains all necessary protocols/ rules so also softwares like middle wares. Job of middle ware is to act like liaison between cloud and user and it helps to keep proper communication between them.

If cloud computing company has several users then everyone need to be allotted with storage space. It is also necessary to store data of user's computing in more than one machine so that if data is damaged or lost, one could get it back from other computer. This process is called redundancy management. Considering all the above infrastructure architecture of cloud computing could be like as shown in the following Fig. 12.2.

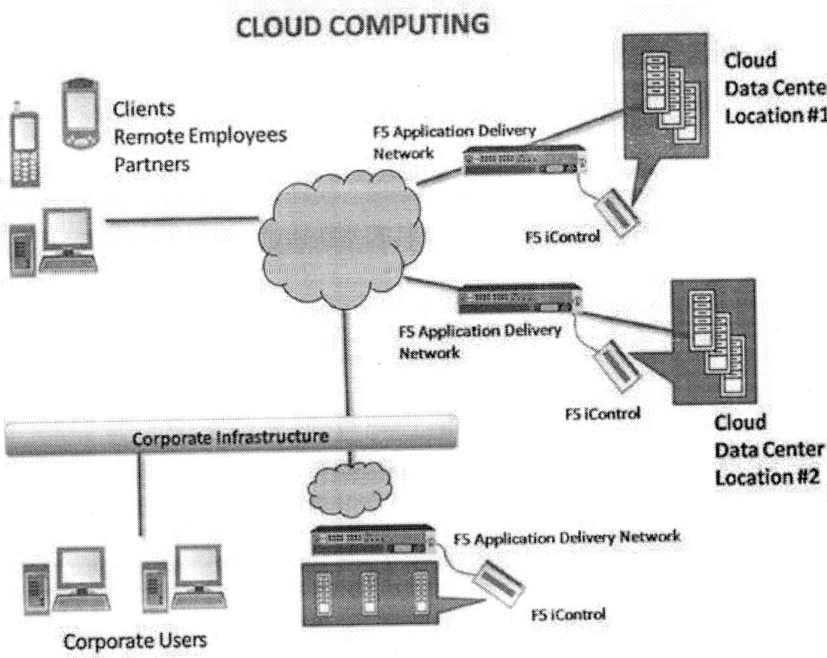

Fig. 12.2. Cloud Computing Architecture

12.9. TYPES OF CLOUD

Depending on the ownership and community trends there are four types of cloud computing technologies such as:

1. Private Cloud
2. Public Cloud
3. Community cloud and
4. Hybrid Cloud

12.9.1. Private cloud

Means using a cloud infrastructure (Network) solely by one customer/ organisation. It is not shared with others still it is remotely located. If cloud is externally hosted then the companies have an option to choose on premise a private cloud on premises which may be more costly but they do have full physical control over the infrastructure and computing. When a company opts for a private cloud it ensures high security and control level.

12.9.2. Public cloud

When we talk about public cloud it means that the whole computing infrastructure is located on the premises of the cloud computing company which offers cloud services. The location- Since the location remains separate from the customer and thus companies would not have physical control over the infrastructure.

As Public clouds use shared resources they are optimally used in performance. However, they are vulnerable to various security threats.

12.9.3. Community cloud

Represents an infrastructure which is shared among the organisations, usually who shares data and data management systems. For example a community cloud can belong to any national government the community cloud can be located both on and off campus.

12.9.4. Hybrid cloud

It is the combination of public and private clouds depending on their purposes such as public cloud can be used to interact with the customers while keeping their data secured through a private cloud.

Some organisations for their routine computing function can have their own infrastructure and use cloud services when there is a pick load. This is called **cloud busting;** like cloud busting there is another concept which has been recently emerged called **inter cloud**. Inter cloud means the interconnected international cloud cluster. This is also termed as **cloud of clouds**. The concept emerged in 2007 is still emerging. Such inter cloud contain several servers with inter communicating mechanism. The main objective behind this is that every cloud cannot fulfill all the needs of all consumers. Secondly, if a cloud reaches to a maximum limit of his capacity then its growth stops, in such situation in order to fill the gap inter cloud services are involved.

12.10. IMPORTANT ISSUES OF CLOUD COMPUTING

Cloud computing technology has been proved to be boon for any organisations so that every organisation desires to have it. This is because someone bears the entire responsibility of computing and one can use cloud resources with their facilities whenever they are required. However, while using these resources one still feel about dangerous things especially about security. There are so many issues which create a doubt about this new technology such as :

1. Confidentiality and security
2. Restrictions and rules
3. Threats in using open source technology
4. Other issues

Now let us discuss these issues with more details.

12.10.1. Cloud Computing Confidentiality & Security.

12.10.1.1. Confidentiality

If data of communication facility provider companies or financial transaction is done with e - business or data about terrorism or data about criminal confidentiality are handled by cloud computing then it is a matter to worry about whether the cloud can safe guard the confidentiality in such risky information environment. However, reputed cloud computing companies try their maximum extent to maintain the confidentiality; for example US - EU -Safe Harbour Harbor or Amazon which provide unique Speciality of choosing safe zone. In spite of all these measures confidentiality issues are not fully controlled. In fact this is a challenge before cloud computing service provider companies. Especially business organisations worry whether anyone would hack their confidential matters.

12.10.1.2. Security

The other worrying issue of cloud computing is about the security of information uploaded to cloud. Business institutions try to avail the benefits of cloud computing facilities. We also know that cloud is located anywhere within or outside of countries at any remote place. In this situation if the details or some top secrets of the business organisations are kept on cloud server then those organisations certainly feel at risk in doing so. There are several issues concern to cloud security such as:

- Sensitive data access
- Data segregation
- Privacy
- Bug exploration
- Data recovery
- Accountability
- Malicious insider

- Management console security
- Accounts control
- Multi tenancy issues

However, now it is possible to control some of these issues by adopting some measures provided by the cloud providers especially due to cryptography.

In such uncertain and insecure environment it is always advisable to go for different clouds computing facilities of different companies instead of depending on one single cloud provider. This method is called particular public key infrastructure. Today due to APL standardisation it has become possible to have control over these problems to a maximum extent if not 100%

12.10.2. Protocols Restrictions and Rules

Considering various threats and dangers in using cloud facilities many cloud service provides insist consumers to accept certain protocols or compliances. For example in USA and European Union counties many such compliances have been issued such as: FISMA, HIPPA or SOX which are concerned with data security. Especially for the financial transactions which are carried out with credit card there are restriction of using PCS- DSS rules.

Considering these restrictions business organisations are not left with any alternative but to go for private or community or even hybrid cloud computing systems. On this back drop it is observed that cloud services provided by Google have been successful in fulfilling government Departments. Even Amazon cloud service provider has won the certificate of SAS-70 Type II Standard.

12.10.3. Use of open source and open standards

In cloud technology new trend is seen using more and more open source standards. In relation to open source is concerned it is considered to use standards like Hadoop framework, after General public license, GPLU-3 Whereas as far as open standard is considered for APIS - OGFS -open cloud computing interface is used so also there are standards like OCC - Open Cloud Consortium are available.

12.10.4. Other issues of cloud computing technology

Even after considering the above issues of cloud computing, still there are some more issues left such as:

1. Continuous function and availability of cloud services.
2. Cost and time required for using data. Since data is kept outside the organisation it is necessary every time to download it. There is also seen impact on internet service providers on use of data from clouds.
3. There is always threat from the hackers who try to hack and steal confidential data from cloud computing systems and it becomes necessary to have additional protective measures to ensure safety from such dangers.

12.11. APPLICATIONS OF CLOUD COMPUTING

Computer and internet technologies have jointly influenced most of the fields. From simple computerisation to advanced application of information technology laid the foundation of automation and modernisation in all fields and services. Advances of internet technology like web 2.0 and further versions have provided many useful tools which have made our life interesting. Web 2.0 technology has added many tools which work on collaborative principles. It has helped communities to create many services and resources. In fact web 2.0 has laid the foundation of cloud computing. Examples of web 2.0 tools like wikis, cooperative development of web sites like open map, writing papers collaboratively, creating own search engine has proved it. Similarly web 2.0 has helped creating and using book marking sites, social networking (delicious), creating video collection on YouTube, PPT -slide sharing, Google docks or drop box and web based e - mail or storing mobile data in cloud storage service are the examples of how we are using cloud computing like services in our daily life. All these processes have already brought cloud technology in use. Business organisations are extensively using cloud computing services in handling their huge tasks of computing. Only thing we do not get chance to closely look at how they utilize cloud computing in the business work. However, we can closely look at how cloud computing is being used in library computerisation.

12.11.1. Application of cloud computing in library management

Cloud computing is now being used in libraries for storing information, retrieval data sharing, hosting software and other application tools. The computing power of cloud is being collectively used by many libraries.

Many libraries are using Amazon cloud computing services for computerising their activities especially when they use Koha like open source library management system. Many service providers today are offering all the expertise of using cloud computing technology in computerising library activities. At this juncture it is worthwhile to review the services of Amazon cloud services available for libraries.

12.11.1.1. Amazon cloud computing services

Amazon Web Services (AWS) is a subsidiary company of Amazon.com which offers a package of cloud computing service which helps in fulfilling demands of computing platform. AWS service operates from 12 geographical regions across the world.

The most important and best known of these services include Amazon elastic computing cloud known as EC2 and Amazon simple storage service known as S3. AWS now provides more than 70 services which take care of wide range including computing storage, networking, database analytics, application services, deployment, management, mobile, developer tools and tools for the **Internet of Things (10T)** (This is the new terminology W3C user used to represent Internet) It is said that AWS provides services of large computing capacity quicker and cheaper.

In 2006 Amazon Web Service (AWS) began offering its IT infrastructure service to business on cloud. Amazon launched this service so that companies could gain from the rich experience of

Amazon in cloud computing. Which runs a large scale distributed transactional IT infrastructure. AWS today provides a highly reliable, scalable, low cost infrastructure platform in the cloud that helps hundreds and thousands of businesses in 190 countries across the world.

AWS Organises it services as

- A large business organisation deploys new internet applications such as HR solutions, pay roll applications, inventory data and online training programmes
- e - commerce hosts its website
- A pharmaceutical research firm execute large scale simulation using computing power provided be AWI
- Media cos. serve ultimate video music and other media to worldwide customers

AWS is popular because of its characteristics like

- Cost Effective
- Flexible
- Scalable or Elastic and
- Secured

AWS is a comprehensive cloud service platform which offers computing power, storage, content delivery and other functionalities that organisations can use for following computing applications :

- Application hosting
- Website developing and hosting
- Backup and storage
- Enterprise IT Applications
- Content delivery network
- Databases creation and maintenance

12.11.1.2. Amazon Web Service Pricing

To begin with AWS provides free trial to enable you to get hands on experience with AWS cloud services. The AWS free trial is available for the first 12 months following with your AWS sign up as well as additional services offered which do not automatically expire at the end of 12 months period. Once you create your AWS account you can use any of the products and services listed below for free:

- Infrastructure software – Cent-OS
- Developer tool - GIT
- Business software - Word press
- Lamp stack
- Bugzilla

- Magneto
- Cloud-base
- App dynamics
- Sugar CRM

Amazon AWS features products (Priced)

1. Amazon EC2 - 750 hours per month of LINUX, RHEL or SLES. 12 micro instance usage, Validity 12 month.
2. Amazon S3 Data storage infrastructure - 5 GB standard storage, 20,000 get requests, 2000 put requests, validity 12 month
3. Amazon RDS Reliable databases services for My SQL, Postgre SQL, Maria DB, Oracle BYOL or SQL- 750 hours, 20 GB storage, 20GB for backup, 10,000,000 Input/ outputs, with validity 12 moths
4. AWS IOT Content devices to the cloud - 250,000 messages per month,validity: 12 months
5. Amazon E2 Container store and retrieve docked images - 500 MB per month, validity 12 months

Amazon cloud front pricing is on the basis of pay only for what you use. There is no minimum fee. One can estimate one's monthly bill using AWS simple monthly calculator

Just to get an idea some price details are given as below.

1. On demand pricing for regional data transfer out to internet (Per GB)

   First 10TB $0.140 per month for India
2. Regional data transfer out to origin Per GB

   All data transfer $160 per month for India
3. Request Pricing for all HTTP methods (per 10,000)

   HTTP requests $0.0090 for India/ month.

   India is placed in price class of 200

REFERENCE

1. Amazon cloud computing -http://aws.amazon.com/cloud
2. What is cloud computing : www.searchcloudcomputing.techtarget.com
3. cloud-computing.wikipedia -http://en.wikipedia.org

13
Big Data : An Introduction

13.0. INTRODUCTION

We have so far understood many new and emerging concepts in information technology through the previous chapters like, data database, data-mining and warehousing, linked data, raw data, and database management systems etc. All these terms have their own significance and concepts. These terms continue to exist and would evolve further also. In this entire process the basic component e.g. data is constantly evolving and expanding further. It is expanding in terms of volume, variety and velocity. As such in order to handle data in newer form it needs faster data processing tools. The new concept of Big Data is the currently evolved form of data. Big data is a future challenge for technocrats to think about how capable technological tools and analytics would handle emerging voluminous data.

In this book if we do not discuss Big data concept then the book would not be a complete. The author therefore, felt it necessary to discuss the same in this book. So we are going to understand the new and emerging concept of 'Big Data' here onwards, which would certainly enrich the knowledge of the readers

13.1. WHAT IS BIG DATA?

Big data is the data in terms of extremely large data sets, which may be analysed computationally. Big data term therefore corresponds to datasets that are so large or complex that traditional data processing tools are found inadequate. The challenges in handling such data include analysing, collection, registering, sharing, transferring, visualizing, querying and about its information privacy.

As time passes, data sets are growing rapidly as they are being gathered by information sensing devices like mobiles, remote sensing devices, software logs, cameras, microphones and by wireless sensors or even by radio frequency identification devices.

If we consider increase in information creation and storing capacity we get an idea about of quantum of big data. It is found that data storing capacity is doubled in every 12-18 months since 1980 s. It was estimated that in 2012 the 2.5 Exabyte (2.5X 1018) data was created.

We find that it is a challenging job to handle, analyse and store such an enormous data. It is also found now that the age old relational database management systems, statistical visualizing packages are finding difficulties in handling the big data. It might require a large number of softwares along with tens, hundreds or even thousands of servers. The big data is increasing with capability of users and their tools. It is found difficult to handle big data by expanding capacities of prevailing tools. Some organisation like Facebook or Amazon or goverment departments are facing problems with hundreds of gigabytes of data to manage with.

Bigdata prompts to use predictive analytics, or use of other methods to extract value from the data. It is predicted that the accuracy in big data may lead to more confident decision making, which could result in greater operational efficiently, cost reduction and reduced risk.

It is also felt that the analysis of big data could help in finding new correlations to know new business trend, to prevent diseases etc. It is found that scientists, business experts, medicinal practitioners, advertising agencies and government bodies find difficulties with large data sets in terms of internet search, business information, scientific work like meteorology, genomics, connectomics (study of brain's structure), complex physics, simulations biology and environment research. Since 2012 onwards size of data is constantly growing. In 2012 it was a few dozens of terabytes to many petabytes. It is worthwhile to compare how quantum of data is measured.

Bytes (8bits), Kilobyte (10^2 bytes) Megabytes (10^6 bytes), Gigabyte (10^9 bytes), Terabyte (10^{12} bytes), Petabyte (10^{15} bytes), Exabyte (10^{18} bytes), Zettabyte (10^{21}bytes), Yottabyte (10^{24} bytes), Xenott bytes (10^{27} bytes), Shiletobyte (10^{30} bytes) and Domegemegrotte bytes (10^{33} bytes).

The bigdata currently available is in terms of Petabytes or even Exabyte, which gives us an idea how the big data is really big. It is beyond the ability of commonly used software tools to handle the big data. So far our systems were capable to handle data size in the range of gigabytes (GB) or at the most terabytes. Secondly, the data available for analysis was coming from sources in a structured form but bigdata as we get from the various sources, it comes mostly in unstructured form making it difficult to analyse, store and further handle it.

13.2. CHARACTERISTICS OF BIG DATA

We can imagine from the following graphical picture how big data is expanding in terms of data volume, data variety and data velocity (Speed of data processing) Fig. 13.1.

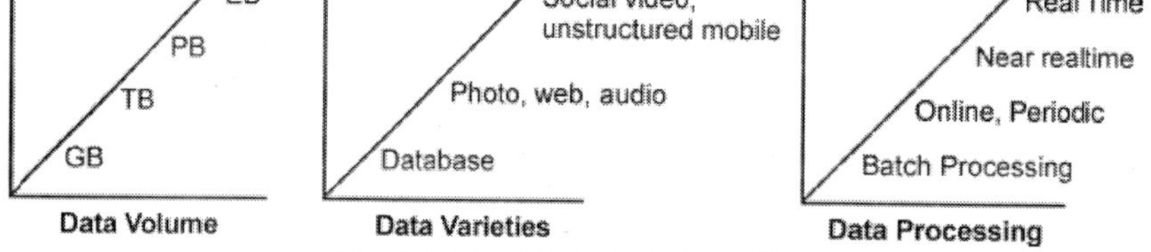

Fig. 13.1. How Big Data is Expanding

Bigdata would need too much time and cost to handle and analyse by traditional relational database methods. Now new approaches to store and analyse data have emerged which depend less on data schemes and data quality. Now raw data with extended metadata is aggregated in data lake and machine learning techniques as well as artificial intelligence programmes use complex algorithms for pattern analysis in data mining. Bigdata is generally associated with cloud computing as it requires bigger platform to analyse large data sets in real time environment. New platforms like Hadoop is used to store large data sets across a distributed cluster and map-reduce to coordinate, to combine process big data received from multiple sources and in unstructured form

13.3. BIG DATA EVOLUTION, EVENTS AND USAGE/APPLICATION

Usage and applications of big data :

Bigdata has increased demands of information management specialists. Many IT industries are gearing up to make themselves prepared to develop expertises in handling big data. For example software AG, Oracle Corp., IBM, Microsoft, SAP, EML, HP and Del have spent near about some billion dollars in creating expertise in handling big data and on specializing data management and analytics. It is estimated that in 2010 this industry was worth of more than billion and is growing steeply with the rate of 50% per year.

It is seen that in developmental economies are prompting in increasing use of data intensive technologies. Such as:

- There are 4.6 billion mobile phone subscribed worldwide.
- Around 1-2 billion people access the internet as more and more people become IT literate resulting information growth.
- World's effective capacity to exchange information through telecommunication networks was 281 Petabytes in 1986, which has raised to 65 Exabytes in 2007
- The internet traffic was estimated to increase nearly 567 Petabytes annually by 2014
- It is also estimated that globally stored information is in the form of alpha numeric text and still there would be image data which is the most big data applications. In addition there is large unused data in the forms of audio and video.

Applications of Usage of Big Data

Using big data in government processes is beneficial and found effective in terms of cost productivity and innovations such as:

USA

- In 2012 Obama administration announced the big data research and development initiative which is composed of 54 different big data programmes.
- Big data analysis played a significant role in successful re-election campaign-of Barack Obama in 2012
- U.S federal Govt. owns six of the most powerful super computers of the world

India

- Big data analysis was responsible for BJP's victory in 2014 general elections

- Indian goverment is using numerous techniques to assess how electorates are responding to goverment actions and policies.

UK

- United Kingdom is using big data in public services, in medicine and in health care areas.

Corporate Use of Bigdata

- **e–bay.com** uses two data warehouse of 7.5 Petabytes and 40 PB as well as Hadoop cluster to search consumer recommendations and marketing.
- **Amazon.com** uses the technology which Amazon is running in Linux based and they had world's three largest LINUX databases with capacity of 7.8 TB, 18.5 TB and 24.7 TB
- **Face Book** handles 50 billion photos from its user's base
- In 2012 **Google** was handling 100 billion searchers per month. Application of big data increasing in manufacturing cyber-physical models, in health care and education media.
- **Internet of Things (IOT) -** Big data and internet of things together application of Big data is also growing in retail industry, real estate, science, research and sports etc.

Now let us look at Bigdata Technologies and Bigdata Analytics

13.4. BIG DATA TECHNOLOGIES

Bigdata topic is broad and involving many trends and new technological developments. Dr. Kaur has reviewed these technologies in her book, "Inter Transitioning Embedded Systems To Intelligent Environment"[1] she has presented 10 emerging technologies which are helping users in handling big data in a cost effective manner.

13.4.1. Column Oriented Databases

It is found that traditional row oriented databases fall short on query performance as the data volume grows and when data becomes unstructured. Whereas column oriented databases store data with focus on columns which allows huge data compression and very fast query performance.

13.4.2. Schema less or NOSQL databases

We find several database types which fit into this category, such as key value stores and document stores. They focus on storage and retrieval of large volume of unstructured, semi structured and evenly structured data. They achieve more performance gain by doing away with some of the restrictions traditionally associated with the conventional databases such as read-write consistency in distributed data processing.

NoSQL : No-SQL was originally referring to as "non SQL" or "non relational" database which provides a mechanism for storage and retrieval of data which is modified in ways other than the tabular relations used in relational databases. Such databases have been existing since the late 1960s, but did not obtain the "NoSQL" monitor for quite some time till Web 2.O companies such as Facebook , Google and Amazon.com functioned. NoSQL databases are increasingly used in big

1. Satwant Kaur : Transitioning Embeded systems to intelligent Environment create space Independant pub, 2013

data and real time web applications. NoSQL systems are also sometimes called "Not only SQL" to emphasize that they may support SQL-like query languages.

13.4.3. Map Reduce

This is an algorithm which allows massive job execution scalability against thousands of servers or clusters of servers. Map reduce implementations performs two tasks.

1. Map reduce task where in an input dataset is converted into a different sets of key / value pairs or types.
2. Reduce task where in several out puts of the mapping tasks are combined to form a reduced sets of tuples. Hence it has got a name as Map Reduce

13.4.4. Hadoop

Hadoop is a software for implementation of map reduces which is an open source platform for handling big data. It is flexible for multiple data sets. e.g. aggregated multiple source of data or even reading data from a database. It is useful for large scale data processing or in order to run process intensive machine learning jobs. It has several applications but one of the most is for large volumes or constantly changing data such as location data from weather or traffic sensors, web based solar media data or machine to machine transactional data

13.4.4.1. Hive

Hive is a SQL like bridge which allows conventional BI (Business Intelligence) applications to run queries against Hadoop cluster. It was originally developed by Facebook. However, now it is opened as open source which us used as higher level abstraction of Hadoop frame work, which enables to make queries against data stored in Hadoop cluster.

13.4.4.2. PIG

PIG is another bridge which makes Hadoop useful to business users. PIG consists of Perl like language which also allows query execution over data stored on Hadoop cluster instead of using SQL. PIG was developed by Yahoo! and now available as open source.

13.4.4.3. Wibi Data

Wibi Data is a combination of web analytics and Hadoop which is built on top of Hbase, which acts like a database layer on top of Hadoop. Wibi Data allows websites to better explore and work with their user data which enables real time responses to user behavior such as personalised content recommendations and decisions.

13.4.4.4. Platfora

Platfora helps in overcoming limitation of Hadoop as it is low level implementation of Map Reduce which requires extensive developed knowledge to operate. Platfora is a platform that turns user's queries into Hadoop jobs automatically thus creates an abstraction layer that anyone can exploit to simplify and organise data sets stored in Hadoop.

13.4.4.5. Store Technologies

As data volume grows it needs effective storage techniques. The main evolutions in this case are related to data compression and storage virtualization.

13.4.4.6. Sky tree

Sky Tree is a high performance machine learning and data analytics platform used for handling big data. Machine learning in turn is an essential part of Bigdata as the massive data volume makes manual exploration or even conventional automated exploration methods unfeasible or too expensive.

13.4.4.7. Big data in the cloud

Technologies associated with big data handling make use of cloud. Big data and cloud computing go hand in hand and therefore, cloud computing enables companies of all sizes to get more value from their data with fast analytics at reduced cost.

13.5. BIG DATA ANALYTICS

The basic goal of big data analytics is to help companies to make more informed business decision by enabling data scientist to analyse large volumes of transactional data as well as other types of data which is untapped by conventional business intelligence programmes. It would include data like web server logs, internal click stream data, social media contents and social network activity report, texts from customer e-mail and their feed backs to surveys, mobile phone calls detail records and machine data captured by the sensors connected to the Internet of Things.

Big data can be analysed with the software tools as a part of advanced analytics disciplines such as predictive analytics, data mining, text analytics and statistical analytics. Main stream business intelligent software and data visualisation tools play an important role in the analysis process. As semi structural and unstructured data do not fit in traditional data warehouses based on relational data bases. Considering difficulties of traditional tools many companies are going for new class of technologies which includes Hadoop and related tools such as- Yarn, Map Reduce, Spark, Hive and Pig as well as NOSQL databases.

13.6. HADOOP

Hadoop is an open source framework which allows to store and process big data in a distributed environment across clusters of computers using simple programming models. It is designed to scale up from single server to thousand of machines offering local computing and storage. It provides massive storage for any kind of data with enormous processing power and ability to handle virtually limitless concurrent tasks. It has been developed by Apache and it is open source software.

One of the top reasons why organisations turn to Hadoop is its ability to store and process huge amount of data - with any kind of data quickly. With data volumes and varieties constantly increasing especially from social media and internet of things which is key consideration. The other benefits are:

- Computing power
- Flexibility
- Fault Tolerance
- Low cost
- Scalability

13.6.1. Components of Hadoop

There are four core modules in Hadoop in its basic framework from the Apache foundation.

1. Hadoop common

   Libraries and utilities used by other Hadoop modules

2. Hadoop distributed file systems

   It is a java based scalable system that stores data across multiple machines without prior organisation

3. Map Reduce

   A software programming model for processing large sets of data in parallel

4. YARN

   It is a resource management frame work for scheduling and handling resource request from distributed applications. YARN is an acronym for 'Yet Another Resource Negotiator'

There are other software components that can run on top of alongside Hadoop and have achieved top level Apache Project status such as:

- Pig
- Hive
- HBase
- H-catalog
- Ambari
- Cassandra
- Chukwa
- Flume
- Oozie
- Sqoop
- Spark
- Soir
- Zookeeper

13.6.2. Use of Hadoop

Hadoop takes users beyond their original goal of searching millions of web pages and returning relevant results. Many organisations are looking towards Hadoop as their next big data platform. Its popular use includes:

- Low cost storage and active data archive
- Staging area for a data warehouse and analytics store
- Data lake creation
- Sandbox for discovery and analysis
- Recommendation system

13.6.3. Hadoop - Brief History

The genesis of Hadoop came from Google file system paper that was published in October 2003. The paper initiated another research paper from Google -Map Reduce simplified data processing on large clusters. Development started in Apache Nutch project but was moved to new Hadoop sub project in January 2006. The first committer added to the Hadoop project was Owen O'Malley in March 2006. Hadoop 01.0 was released in April 2006 and further continued to evolve by many contributors to Apache Hadoop project. Hadoop was named after one of the founders toy elephant.

In 2011 Rob Bearden parted with Yahoo! to establish Horton works with 24 engineers from the original Hadoop team including founder Alan Gates, Arun Murty, Devraj Das, Mahadev Konor, Owen O'Malley, Sanjay Radia and Suresh Srinivas. The current version of Hadoop is 3.0.3 released on 31 May 2018.

Website : http://hadoop-apache.org

REFERENCE

- Search Business Analytics
  www.searchbusinessnalysticstecharget.com
- Bigdata - Wikipedia
  http://en.wikipedia.org
- Techrepublic
  www.techrepublic.com/bigdataanalysis

14
Introduction to BIBFRAME : The Future Cataloguing Standard

14.0. INTRODUCTION

Libraries have progressed through different walks of professional phases e. g. from traditional to non-computerised to computerised and now they are in digital age. Bibliographic data of the materials they hold in their collection has also gone through various revolutions. Initially they created registers/list of books to handwritten catalogues cards which subsequently changed to computerised catalogue. In one of the phases of generating catalogue cards and computerised cards the emphasis was on style e. g. AACR or AACR – II cataloguing rules. When libraries started converting their catalogue data it was done in various ways e. g. through formats like Access, Excel, FoxPro, dbase, CDS ISIS and C- programming language platforms. Need of bibliographic communication prompted libraries further to adopt communication formats like MARC, UK, US-MARC, UNIMARC, CCF etc. These formats were further rationalised in one format named MARC-21 or advanced Z39. 2 / MARC. Most of libraries now insist to have data in their LMS only in MARC 21 Format. However, in the semantic and linked data age, MARC - 21 format has become obsolete. The main reason for advancement of libraries from their local and non-web invisible status was to have web visible libraries by adopting linked data design. The project based on linked data and semantic web technology initiated by Library of Congress (LOC) known as BIBFRAME is about bringing the revolution in library bibliographic data assets. In this chapter, we are going to understand about the concept behind the BIBFRAME.

14.1. HISTORICAL BACKGROUND OF BIBFRAME

Up till now libraries were working for standardisation of bibliographic data structure much needed while creating the library database in respectively adopted library management systems (LMS). In the process, each librarian has common bibliographic standard structure format in mind e. g. MARC or to be specific MARC - 21 format. This is because MARC facilitated exchange of bibliographic data among the libraries and it also helped smooth conversion of library bibliographic data while migrating from one LMS to another. However, these developments were okay in the pre-web environment. When there was a revolution in the use of information technology in libraries and about use of semantic web and related linked data model librarians started envisaging future possibilities for libraries and cultural heritage institutions. Although MARC facilitated libraries to exchange bibliographic data among the libraries and related communities the data remained invisible for the web world. MARC or so called technically Z39. 2/MARC served libraries for almost forty years but now it looks like older technique for data management, as it has become obsolete in the programming style of today. Looking into this situation Working Group of Future Bibliographic Control recommended Library of Congress to take action in devising a new format for bibliographic control, which would suit in the current web development and would work with the library and other interested communities to specify and implement a new carrier for bibliographic information, which could be capable for representing the range of data of interest to libraries and to facilitate the exchange of such data both within the library community and also to open it for communities through the web platforms. In US, National Agriculture Library, the National Library of Medicine and Library of Congress conducted a survey-cum test on 26 participating library community which also revealed the same opinion that the MARC format used for several years is now showing limitations/ shortcomings and for having full capabilities of RDA (Resource Description and Access) a new bibliographic framework is necessary. Readers to note that RDA is the revised guidelines or up-gradation of our old AACR–II rules. With strong recommendations from Working Group of Future Bibliographic Control and result of RDA test, Library of Congress initiated the project "Bibliographic Framework (BIBFRAME)" in collaboration with libraries, bibliographic standard experts and IT technologists, expecting that it will serve the library community in a better way in the future to come.

It is worthwhile to remember the benefits of MARC standard at this juncture. The MARC has been responsible for the creation of millions of bibliographic records around the globe. The MARC was created in the late 1960 and early 1970. Librarians along with computer experts decided to take a revolutionary step to share bibliographic data. This resulted for an individual library to become a node in the larger network of libraries for adoption of MARC which yielded in reducing cost of cataloguing. On this backdrop, it is expected that the newly thought bibliographic framework will certainly broaden library participation in the network of resources, at the same time librarians would also be able to link their patrons to bibliographic resources of all kinds (from library and also from many other resources) at the affordable cost.

14.2. WHAT IS BIBFRAME PROJECT ?

Bibliographic Framework or BIBFRAME : This project is the initiative launched by Library of Congress(LC) which intends to provide new means for capturing and sharing of bibliographic data. The initiative further expects replacement of the age-old MARC format used for exchanging bibliographic data among the libraries. The BIBFRAME project is based on the recommendations of 2008 report of LC's Working Group of the Future of Bibliographic Control, which has been the outcome of discussion undergone in librarian's community. The new format, would reinforce the data infrastructure, developing information technology and would comply with changing patterns of resource description, which has suggested a transition to a more current and futuristic data creation and interchange environment. The developments of semantic web and its related Linked Open Data (LOP) model has provided many future possibilities for libraries and cultural heritage institutions.

The MARC series based data infrastructure has been extensive and flexible to a limited extent with changing technology. However, a quantum effort is needed to create a competitive data exchange instrument which would be based on the current set up and expected to give future shape of data interchange. In order to ensure a new environment which will allow the reuse of valuable data and remain supportive to current one, in-addition to innovating it, there are certain requirements which could provide a basis for this work. These requirements have been discussed in the library community, which have been considered while beginning the transition to a new bibliographic framework. The initiative of bibliographic framework indicates an environment rather than a format. The requirements are as:

1. Broad Accommodation of Contents : Rules and Data Models – Libraries use different cataloguing rules. Different rules are used by various communities for different aspects of data description. Various guidelines have been created in different eras, and some metadata are not rule based. The BIBFAME initiative expects to have rational to accommodate all these variations. The accommodation of RDA (Resource Description and Access) will be a key factor in the development of data elements as other mainstream library archive and cultural community rules i. e. AACR - II and its predecessors as well as DACS (Describing Archives a Content Standards) VRA(Visual Resource Association) core, CCO (Cataloguing Cultural Objects) have been doing.

2. Provision for the types of data that logically accompany or support bibliographic description : The types of data here include such as holdings, authority, classification, preservation, technical rights and archival metadata. All these types could be accommodated through linking technological components in a modular way with standard extensions and other techniques.

3. Accommodation of textual data in linked data with URIs instead of text and both.

4. Consideration of the relationship between and recommendations for communications format tagging record input conversions and system storage manipulation.

Up till now the bibliography data management was seen in library cataloguing point of view. However, future bibliographic framework would be handled less by cataloguers than the current MARC Format. Internal storage, display of communicated data and the input screens are unlikely to have the close relationship to a communication format which was visualized in the past.

5. Consideration of the needs of all sizes and types of libraries from a small public to the large research library.

Although the MARC format became a key factor in the development of systems and services of different types and sizes of libraries, which have tried to implement services according to the local needs of their patrons and with their resources. The new bibliographic framework would continue to support simpler needs in addition to those of large research libraries too.

6. Continuation of Maintenance of MARC data no longer necessary.

It is expected that during migration in the near future of a large segment of library community from AACR-II to RDA will be needed to have RDA adapted MARC format. So, the changes required in old MARC format in new RDA point of view are only necessary and thus there is no need to maintain the entire MARC data which would save the time and energy of library community.

7. Compatibility with MARC based records

8. Provision of Transformation from MARC - 21 to a new bibliographic environment

It would require a software which could transform data from MARC - 21 to the new bibliographic framework and back to old which would facilitate experimentation, testing or other activities.

It is important that library of congress (LC) and its partners e. g. Zepheira and others are interested in bringing change in bibliographic environment which will further facilitate library community to progress into the future form with a more robust, open and extensible handler for our rich bibliographic data. It would further accommodate the library community's new cataloguing rules i. e. RDA. Efforts would also be on both i. e. evolving new system and maintenance of MARC - 21 systems while testing of new model. It is expected to happen in a cost saving manner.

14.2.1. Think-tank behind BIBFRAME Concept

Think-tank of web inventor, Tim Burners Lee and his revolutionary concept i. e. web of all things, is now greatly influencing the new way of representing the data e. g. linked open data. Lee argues that web should use the basic principles of the web more directly to data (contents of our traditional data bases) and that we should not be shy about making links to non-computer resources such as people, tangible and abstract things, places and so on to our data. In his view this expansive linking is called "the web of data", which forms the basis of linked data.

In the Lee's point of view the BIBFRAME draft is to provide framework for modeling future resources and bibliographic assets also which traditionally are encoded in MARC-21. This pattern will shape as common descriptive framework which would achieve the following objectives.

1. To integrate the existing bibliographic resources and
2. To provide a road map for moving forward towards further refinement.

Library community has been doing pioneering work of creating bibliographic assets, its management, organisation and collaborative utilization of the data of works of our culture. All these efforts has led to evolution of library data interchange format i. e. MARC -21. This data asset is proving now as specialised market for bibliographic modelers. The enormous amount of high quality data available with library community has been successfully utilized in providing library services to their patrons. Now this same data has become valuable assets to take it beyond the traditional library boundaries. By restructuring MARC-21 format to linked data model it is expected to expand the utility and value of the data as well the community which would be served. In remodeling the MARC-21 format as a Web of Data it is important to deconstruct and then reconstruct the information assets. In doing so the following primary functions of MARC-21 are the most important for its evolution to the new framework.

1. Data relating to the intellectual essence of work
2. Data relating to the actual instance of the work, which you hold in your hand retrieved from an electronic source network.
3. Record metadata such as control numbers, record handling codes and other annotations.

The deconstructing of the data elements corresponding to these functions, one can begin to materialize the concept embedded in these data element sets as linkable information resources. These MARC based data resources then to be resembled into a coherent architecture which provides the basis of new bibliographic framework and allow for cooperative cataloguing as it was done in shared cataloguing in the OCLC model. However, now the co-operative cataloguing would be of more granular level (persons, places, subjects, organisations). Then whenever updates to these MARC resources would occur (as someone adds new information about the existing person, new mapping relating to subject etc.) notification could be sent to system to automatically update the resources. Having these innovations these information assets can now be more effectively utilized at a granular level to provide a richer substrate to local collection, special collections and third party data can be easily annotated with library contents to be utilized co-operatively.

BIBFRAME : Library of Congress along with its partner institutions are working to create a new cataloguing standard to replace the existing standard i. e. MARC-21. The new standard named BIBFRAME would facilitate linked data model to enable library collection bibliographic data to integrate with web. The following paras would cover the details of the newly evolving standard BIBFRAME.

14.2.2. New Approach of BIBFRAME Project

The new BIBFRAME project has focused on web environment, linked data principles/ mechanism and the RDF (Resource Description Framework) as basic model. The idea behind linked data is to open the scope for bibliographic data from a library to web as it would have association with substantial related resources even beyond the cultural heritage sector. It is expected that with the use of RDF model and with other W3C (Worldwide Web Consortium) developments bibliographic data which was otherwise locked in library system would enable integration of library data and other cultural heritage data existing on web there by providing wider user access to the information.

With availability RDF model as recommended and emphasised in W3C recommended method, it has facilitated conceptual description or modeling of information. Now RDF data could be serialized or written out in various syntax formats, such as XML (Extensible Mark-up Language). RDF data can also be used in relational database manner as most library data exists in the computerised systems in the form of MARC–21. RDF would also facilitate triple stores mechanism which would be readily available in the new model which would further facilitate library community with more options about how to store and retrieve its data in the future. It is further expected that the common exchange technique (web and linked data) and broadly adopted data model i. e. RDF/ XML will transform the current library technological environment away from being a closed market into itself to the one more readily understandable by the current and future data creators, data modelers and software developers. It is anticipated that all these considerations taken together, will result in greater cost saving for libraries.

14.2.3. Need of BIBFRAME

Before we discuss BIBFRAME we need to know why new standard is needed. In-order to find this we should look into past development of standardising bibliographic data held by library community.

Libraries since their inception have been maintaining structured information about their collections. The purpose was to help library patrons to find information they needed. It was done by providing them access to key information about the collection i. e. title, author and the subjects. The very first method of recording these bibliographic details was to record them serially in a book catalogue. Then card catalogue emerged. The card catalogue with its dictionary and classified form could establish relation between the information provided in the catalogue cards, so also it is used to help readers to find interested document on the shelf. The card catalogue method of describing data of library holding worked for quite some time.

However, as library collection grew it was necessary to improve efficiency of catalogue card production (as they were manually written or typed on typewriters). In the late 1960 Henriette Avram at Library of Congress developed a new method of encoding bibliographic information. This facilitated to create data which was readable by machines (Machine Readable catalogues) and the same further facilitated to print catalogue cards by automating the process. It is seen that during the last half of 20th century and first half of the 21st century libraries were rushing to computerise their functions and they used stable foundation of MARC records. Most of world wide LMSs have adopted the MARC - 21 format in building their databases.

14.2.4. BIBFRAME - "The project Review"

Before we elaborate further on BIBFRAME let us try to review about BIBFRAME initiative and about some important points and terms associated with it as appended below:

- Library of Congress contracted with Zepheira (2012 through early 2014)
  - To develop the model and the model description that kick started the BIBFRAME project
  - Produced a model for profiles and use cases
  - Opted to pursue active hands on experiments
- Involvement of Library of Congress, National Library of Medicine, George Washington University, British National Library, Princeton University, the National Bibliotheca, OCLC, Zepheira.
- All parties continue to experiment and move forward the evolution.
- Working Group of Future of Bibliographic Control and Resource Description and Access (RDA) test / survey outcome (RDA would be new style of MARC) Recommended to go for

new / future bibliographic structure i. e. BIBFRAME

- **RDF (Resource Description Framework)**

  It is a common model for creating web data

- **Linked Data** a term used to describe recommended best practice for exposing, sharing and connecting pieces of data information and knowledge and the semantic web using URIs and RDF (http://en. wikipedia. org/wiki/linked_data)

14.2.5. Aim of BIBFRAME Project

The aim here is to take library bibliographic data from its invisible status to linked data platform on web through RDF and restructured it through RDA, (reformatted from AARC-II), which would be visible to web world and open to harvester to use it for fruitful purpose.

14.3. REPLACING OLD MARC WITH LINKED DATA

Libraries were depending on MARC based data systems for bibliographic communication storage and demonstration of their bibliographic data. The MARC era worked for quite some time. However, in course of time when web technology is evolving speedily MARC based systems started showing their limitations. There is no doubt it helped to automate the catalogue card production in libraries and the MARC was so structured that it helped libraries to create reliable and stable data. However, on the other side libraries started realizing that the MARC based data is only with library and not visible to world at large especially in the web world, as MARC cannot integrate or link with world wide web. It was so happening that on oneside libraries were investing their time, efforts and money into building computerised data based on MARC but on the other side web technology was born and was further progressing very speedily which changed the concept completely how we express and share information. Web was conceptualized one time as web of documents but now has evolved to form a new concept of data on the web or "web of data". Now with the common Internet standards we are in position to use the web to share, reference and store data. The new innovative form of web/Internet is known as linked data which is everywhere on the web. At this juncture libraries also started feeling that they need to replace old styled MARC with linked data so that library data could be integrated and engage with wider information seeker community i. e. on the web.

Libraries built all their systems, processes and work flows around the MARC. No doubt it served them very well but it had only quality of machine readability but it did not possess machine actionability. The old web was a fun technology but now we realise that it was a dumb. It contained a lot of unstructured and unorganised data in terms of documents. However, in the new and modern form of Internet i. e. in semantic web, the web understands data and can make connections and links, if the things are encoded correctly to express relationships. Semantic web facilitates relationship between things through structured data which expresses explicit relationship so that machines and humans can understand them in the same way.

The bibliographic assets of world literature are available with the library community but it is invisible to web world and it just cannot remain isolated with libraries. Thus, the bibliographic data with library community encoded in age old MARC structure badly seeks its visibility in the web which would be looking further for integration and for expression relationship with machines & humans. So, the next objective of library should be to replace MARC with linked data and facilitate its integration with web environment and link library data with wider information community to make MARC machine actionable than only to be machine readable. So, the replacement of MARC with linked data was essential in modern web technology.

14.3.1. Visualizing Bibliographic Data in Semantic web

We have understood in early chapters of this book how Internet has evolved from its first generation to third generation i. e. semantic web. We also had introduction to semantic web. Now let us try to revisit our MARC based bibliographic data in semantic web and let us know benefits of it.

Now we say Web of Things rather than just Internet. Semantic web is the real web as Tim Burners Lee visualized. Semantic web brought new way of structuring data called "Linked Data". (As lectured by Lee in- Ted talks http:// www. ted. com/ talks/Tim-Burners Lee on the next web language-en) Now there is new method/ tool available to encode data in RDF / XML. There are four rules to represent data in linked data format as:

1. Use URIs to indicate things
2. Use HTTP URIs so that the things can be referred to and looked up on web (Re-referenced)
3. Provide other useful information about things when it's URI is re-referenced using standards like RDF (Resource Description Framework) and SPARQL (Sparql Protocol and RDF Query Language) RDF entry relationship model is the foundation of linked data.

   [RDF is a model for encoding semantic relationship between items of data so that their relationships can be interpreted computationally. SPARQL is an RDF Query Language means a semantic query language for databases which is able to retrieve and manipulate data stored in RDF format]
4. Include links to other related things (Using their URIs) when data is published on web.

We can imagine if linked data pattern is also used to structure bibliographic data then local library holdings would be displayed in search engine results like it happens in Google search. Linked data emphasises all about building and encoding relationship between things so that computers can make sense of data and relationship in it. The same would be with bibliographic data if linked data encoding is also applied for building of bibliographic data held by libraries.

Now let as visualize an example of Google search for well known personality: Paul Outlet - in normal Google search and the linked data form displayed on your right side on the monitor, (see Plate 14.1).

14.3.2. Significance of Linked Data in BIBFRAME

If the library integrates its catalogue in linked data format the google search would also display additional information about your local library holding. Finally, we understand that linked data tells us about building and encoding relationship between things making computers to sense the data and its relationship.

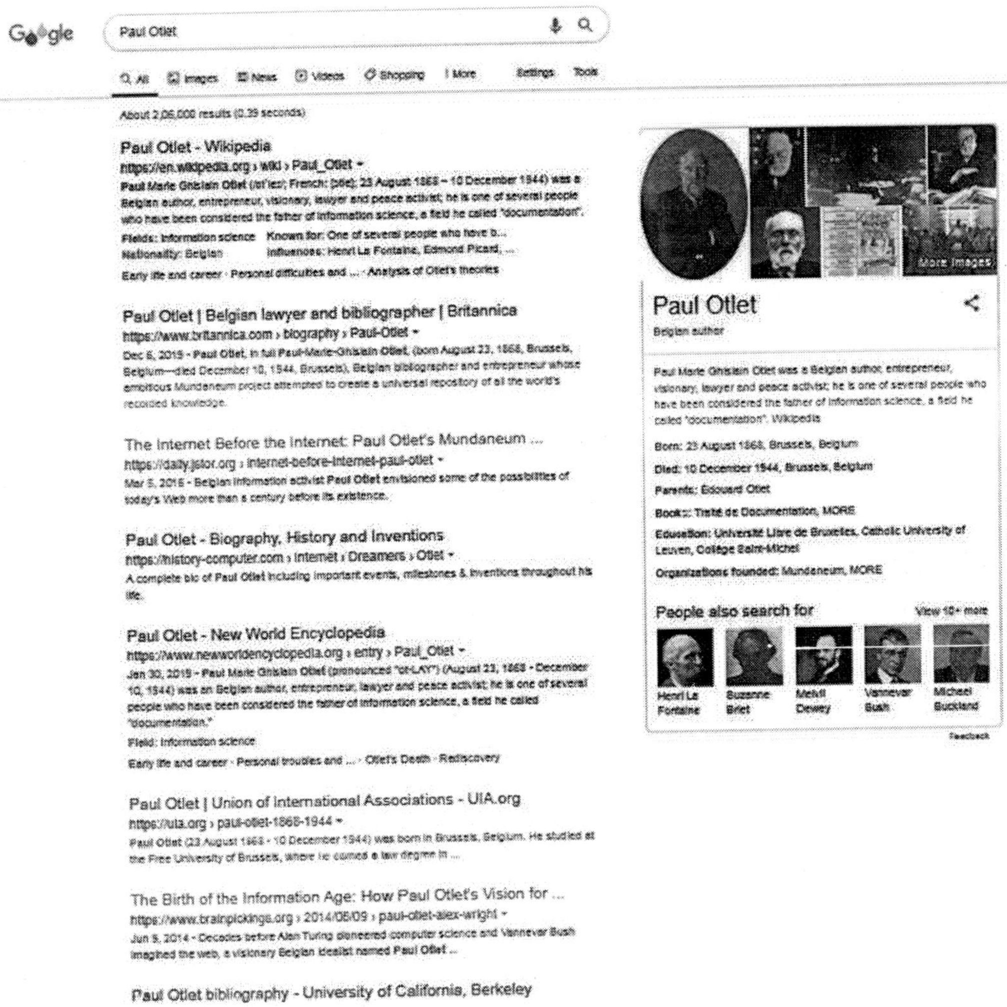

Plate 14.1

Let us now explore the concept further as:

14.3.2.1. RDF Foundation

Thus, RDF is the foundation of linked data as:

1. Data is encoded in RDF structure
2. RDF is a standard model used for data inter linking on the web.
3. It facilitates creating the relationships between things on the web.

Now let us try to know more about RDF. RDF expresses relationship through a structure called "triple" of things i.e. Subject + Predicate + Object. We can very well compare this method with the way we interpret library data e.g.

An author is the creator of work} = subject

so, it is the }

The subject/title of book is the = object

We express their relationship = Predicate

So, the relation can be shown as

Subject —— Predicate ——— Object

Now if we take an actual example of one book and its bibliographic details we can see how the triples could be represented, see Fig. 14.1.

Author : Ranganthan, Shiyals Ramamrita

Title : Five laws of library science

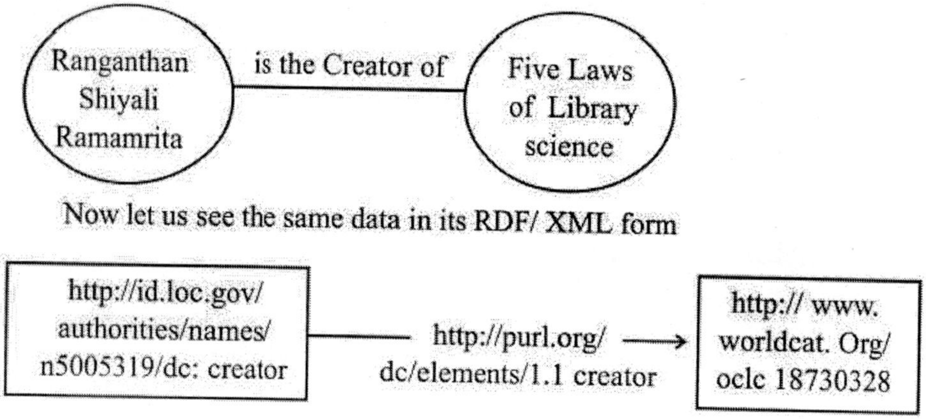

Fig. 14. 1

Advantage here is, if bibliographic contents instead of structured in just text form if it is described in RDF form then web understands it and if any one searches or enquires with SPARQL it could be retrieved on the web also. In structuring RDF form we get the help of its ontology and vocabulary. We can take another example of bibliographic data of a book and see how it is structured in RDF / XML form:

Bibliography in Catalogue Entry Form

Example : The Budha walks into the office: A guide to livelihood for a new generation by LodroRiazler. Boston; Shambhala Publications: 2014

This bibliographic data when we see it in RDF / XML form it looks like as below:

<rdf: RDF Xmlns: rdf = "http://www. w3. org/1999/02/22-rdf

Xmlns: dc" http://purl. org/dc/elements-rdf-syntax#ns>

<rdf: Description rdf : about = "http://www. worldcat. org/oclc /8636325305>

<dc: titles >The Buddha walks in the office: a guide to livelihood for a new generation / dc:title>

<dc: Creator> http:// id. loc. gov / authorities / name/ n2011023258. html </dc creator>

<dc: publisher > Boston: Shambhala< dc/: publisher>

<dc: data > 2014 </dc: data >/rdf : RDF

The above example is an example per say and it is not complete in all respect.

14.3.3. Inter linking Bibliographic Data

There is another advocacy behind recommending linked data/rdf structure for bibliographic data is that, libraries have been considering relational databases keeping OPAC point of view and hierarchical data bases while thinking thesauri in mind however they have never thought about Graph form of bibliographic data bases. In Graph Databases, arbitrary object relationship is considered which is the most flexible in describing relationship among bibliographic contents i. e. among objects or nodes not only of one object but different objects also could be linked in graph data structures. This is however achieved with the help of linked data structure.

Let us try to understand the above graph data structure concept by considering following example Fig. 14.2 as below :

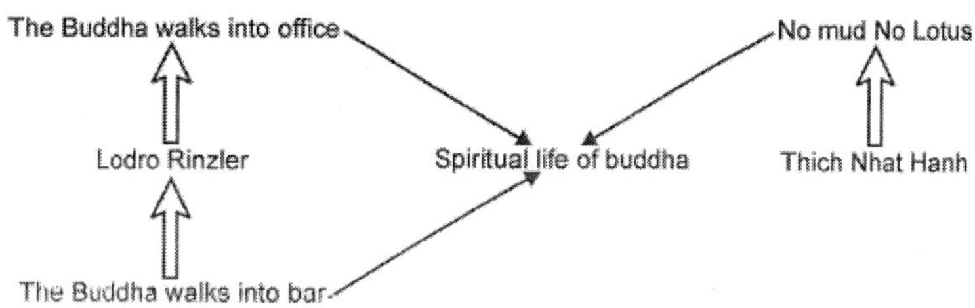

Fig. 14.2. Showing linking two objects with a graph data structure

One more supporting evidence put forth towards new bibliographic framework model is-

With linked data, we would be able to take Rules of Dictionary Catalogue as Outlined by CharlesAmmi Cutter to the next level. Recording relationship between bibliographic entities to organise resources and promote enquiry has been core of the cataloguing work but we are still striving to achieve objectives of dictionary catalogue, even today.

It is strongly expected that it would be achieved in adopting linked data framework. It is also expected and argued that linked data or new BIBFRAME framework will help libraries to follow Cutter's dictionary catalogue rules better than catalogue cards or MARC format. BIBFRAME is essentially a framework or structural standard for expressing bibliographic meta data and the relationship between bibliographic entities. BIBFRAME is developed primary to replace MARC. The main objective of linked data technology is to express and expose relationship between bibliographic entities within library environment and beyond. The advantage in converting framework from MARC to BIBFRAME is that linked data and library meta data can integrate with and could reach to wider information community than before. It is envisaged that new method of describing library data, libraries could return to age of Cutter's dictionary catalogue. This relationship within bibliographic entities somehow was lost in the course of library automation and during data conversion/ uploading it to LMS in the MARC form.

14.3.3.1. Interlinking Data : Graphical Mode

Now let us take further and see how different bibliographic objects could be inter linked with first in text from then in triple structure method, then graphical mode and finally in script of machine readable forms as shown in table 14.1 and Fig. 14.4.

Subject	**Relation**	**Object**	**Field**
Paul Outlet	Creator of	Traite de Documentation	Library Sc.
S R. Ranganathan	Creator of	Five laws of library science	Library Science

Table 14.1

Example - 01 : Triple Structure Mode

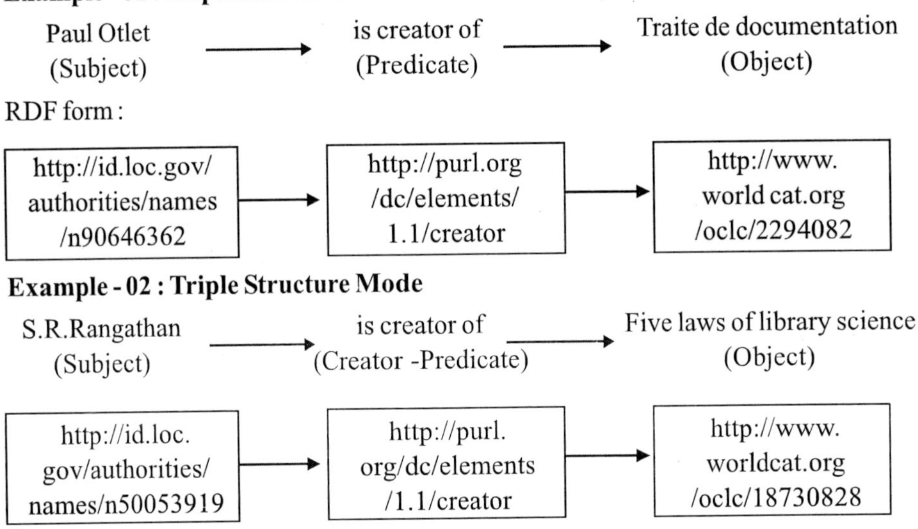

Fig. 14.4. Linked Data Expression Relationship in Graph form

Showing bibliographic contents in graph mode has been facilitated in using linked data expression which was not possible in our traditional cataloguing method see the following Fig. 14.5.

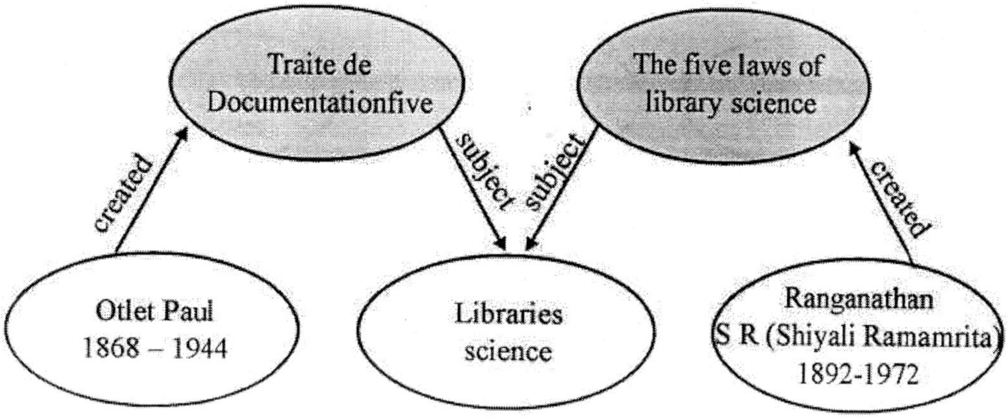

Fig. 14.4

Linked Data Expresses Relationships in Machine readable format as shown in Fig. 14.5.

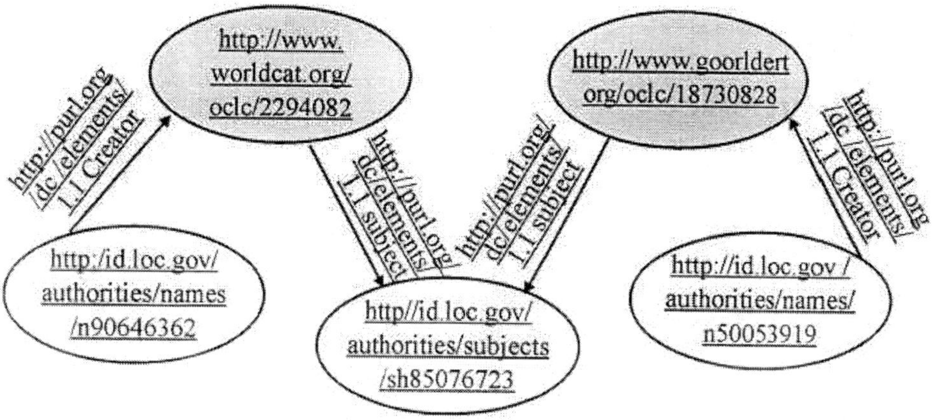

Fig. 14.5

Linked data always facilitates more relationship in various bibliographic objects considering some common attributes among them. Let us see a graphical view of such relationship in the following Fig. 14.6.

With reference to the above figures it is differentiated as :-

In our Library bibliographic environment or in library science section two bibliographic entries could be seen. However, while describing same objects in linked data environment it gets additional textual information. The potential of such relationship can go far more in linked data which we could never imagine.

After knowing the significance of linked data and its constituting elements i.e. **Universal Resource Identifier (UDI)** which represent every smallest content of bibliographic data and finally shows data structure used to encode the contents i.e. RDF / XML. Let us see how the entire data relationship discussed in previous example is represented in RDF / XML which computer can understand in the following script.

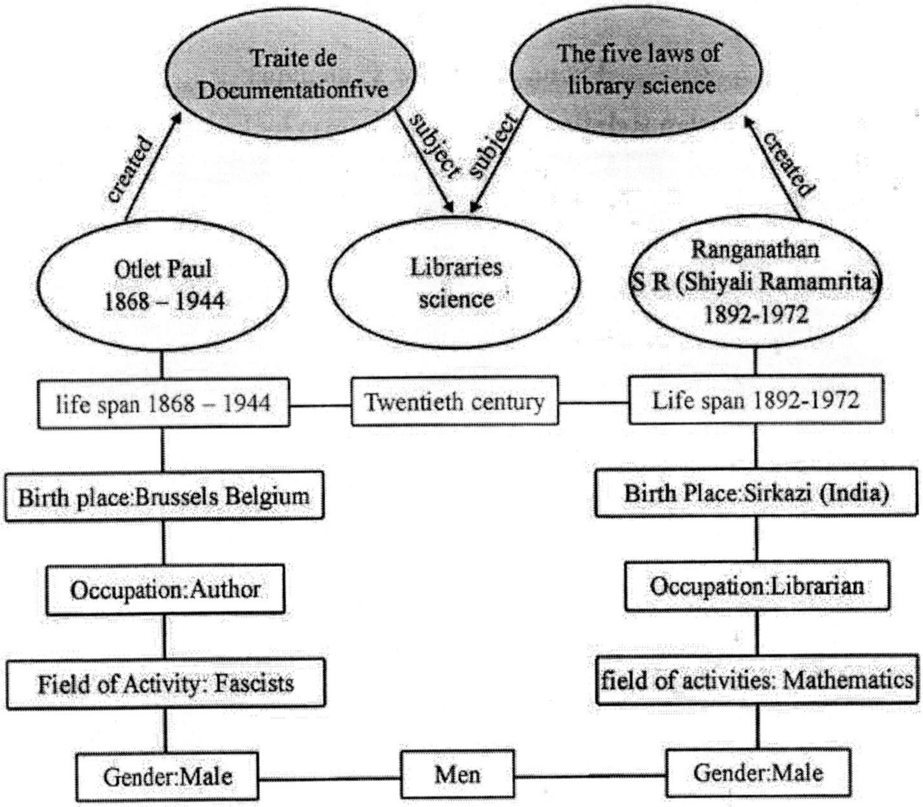

Fig. 14.6. Comprehensive Relationships in Bibliographic Objects.
Courtesy : **(Fig. 14.4 - Fig. 14.6) BIBFRAME Basics by Amber Billey, Columbia University Libraries You Tube Presentation on 12-08-2015**

RDF Triple in XML

<? xml version = '1.0'?>

<! Doctype rdf: RDF Public

"-//DUBLIN CORE//DCMES DTD 2002/07/31//EN"

"http://dublincore.org/documents/2000/07/31/dcmes-xml/dcmes-xmldtd.dtd">

<rdf:RDFxmlns: rdf = "http://www.w3.org/ 1999/02/22 - rdf - syntax-ns#" xmlns:dc = http:// purl.org / dc / elements 1.1/">

<rdf: Description rdf: about =

"http://www.worldcat.org / oclc / 2294082">

<dc: title>Traite de documentation: le lure surlelivre, theorie et practique</dc:title>

<dc: creator> http://id.loc.gov /authorities/names n90646362 < /dc: creator>

<dc: publisher>EditionesMundaneum<dc : publisher>

```
<dc: data > 1934 </dc: date>
<dc: subject> http://id. worldcat.org / fast /997916 < /dc: subject>
        <rdf: description>
<rdf: description rdf: about = "http:/ www. world cat.org/ oclc / 18730828">
<dc: title> the five laws of library science </dc. title>
<dc: creator> http: //id. loc.gov/authorities /names/n50053919 </dc : creator>
<dc: Publisher>Asia pub. House </dc: publisher>
<dc: data>1963</ dc: date >
</dc: date>
<dc: subject> http://id.worldcat.org /fast/997916 </dc: subject>
        <rdf: description>
        </rdf:RDF>[1]
```

As linked data is encoded using RDF / XML structure there are other RDF like encoding languages such as RDFJ and JSON and Turtle. When we see the above script written in RDF/ XML we might feel it is very laborious task but it is not so. For most of subjects, objects etc. there are readily available URIs which could be picked and incorporated in the script. Secondly, for the common nouns like, "subject" or predicates like "creator" their URIs are available in the vocabulary/ dictionary. These tools can very well be used to create RDF / XML script for any item in the content of bibliography. RDF validator is used to create the graph. (http://www.w3.org/RDF/validator)

Another speciality of linked data method is that, one can also structure each and every content of data and it can be described with a Unique Resource Identifier URI which is structured in RDF. Linked Data technology also further facilitates to encode the relationships among the unique URIs and it can utilize external metadata available in open data domain i.e. web, thereby enhancing bibliographic relationship beyond cataloguing limits, as seen in the Table 14.4 with unique URI of each attributed.

Table 14.4

Subject	Otlet, Paul http://id.loc.gov/authorities/ names/n9064362	Rangnathan,Shiyali Ramamrita http://id.loc.gov/ authorities/names/n50053919
Predicate	Creator of http://purl.org/dc/ elements/1.1 creator	Creator of http://purl.org/dc/ elements/1.1 creator
Object	Traite de documentation http://www.oclc.2294082	Five laws of library science http://www/worldcat.org/ oclc/18730828

Table 14.4. Contd...

1. Courtesy : BIBFRAME Basics by Amber Billey , Columbia University Libraries You Tube Presentation on 12-08-2015

Authorities subject predicate	http://purl.org/dc/elements/1.1/subject	http://purl.org/dc/elements/1.1/subject
Authorities object Library Science	http://id.worldcat.org/fast/997916	http://id.worldcat.org/fast/997916
Life Span	1898-1944	1892-1972
Birth Place	Brussels (Belgium)http/id.loc.gov/authorities/names/n79013830	Sirkazhi (India) http/id.loc.gov/authorities/names/n80672712
Occupation	Author http://id.worldcat.org/fast/821688	Librarian http://id.worldcat.org/fast/997301
Field of activity	Pacifists http://id.worldcat.org/fast/1050133	Mathematics http://id.world cat.org/fast/101212163
Gender	Male http://rdaregistry/ins/termlist/gender/1002	Male http://rdaregistry/ins termlist/gener/1002
Men	http://id.worldcat/fast/1015978	Common

As mentioned above RDF linked data can be expressed/ serialized/ marked up in a variety of syntaxes / languages such as :RDF / XML (http://www/w3.org / TR / rdf - syntax grammar RDFS - https://en.wikipedia.org/rdf schema. http://www.w3.org/2001/ sw / wiki / RDFS)

When we try to mark RDF to be functional and useful, it must adhere to the standards(agreed upon) vocabularies and ontologies. Linked data vocabularies are used to outline various elements (classes and properties) used to describe things. Author hopes that with this understanding of linked data methods to encode and describe the relations among various bibliography contents gets clearer to the readers. Now we would try to understand BIBFRAME model and what it is in the following paras.

14.4. BIBFRAME MODEL

The main objective behind development of BIBFRAME is to replace the MARC with new data structure to provide bibliographic relationship model. RDF / XML structure or standard is used to encode bibliographic data to convert our MARC based data to web or computer actionable format i.e. linked data format. So, the constituting parts of BIBFRAME model are:

1. Structural standard - BIBFRAME. It is upgradation of old MARC format and similar to ISBD,FRBR, Dublin Core, EAD, MODS, VRA-Core, CIDOC etc.
2. Content standard = RDA (Resource Description and Assess). It is a revised standard of AACR- II and similar to CCO and DACS
3. Encoding standard = RDF / XML. It is an upgradation of MARC, CVS, XML and JSON or similar to our old 3x5 catalogue card.

4. Value standard = RDA Vocabularies and is similar to LCSH, NAF, LCGFT, RBMS Thesaurus.

BIBFRAME vocabulary contains classes and properties. The classes are type of things (subject or objects). The properties connect or relate resources to each other called predicates.

Now let us look into what BIBFRAMEorganisation is :

14.4.1. BIBFRAME Organisation

The Organisation of BIBFRAME has 4 main classes:

1. works
2. Instances
3. Authorities
4. Annotations

Creative work : A source reflecting a conceptual essence of the cataloguing item. So, it would be subject and object. In case of book it would be creator and created item or title of the book.

Instance : A resource reflecting an individual material embodiment of the work

Authority : A resource reflecting key authority concepts that have refined relationships reflected in the work of instance. This includes people, places, topic, organisations etc.

Annotation : A resources that decorates the BIBFRAME resources with additional information example of annotation include library holding information, cover art and review.

So, there is creative work and instance, authority and annotation are the other resources key authorities and additional supplementing information resources.

Now let us see the graphical representation of the BIBFRAME model and the relationship among main BIBFRAME classes in the following diagram. Fig 14.7.

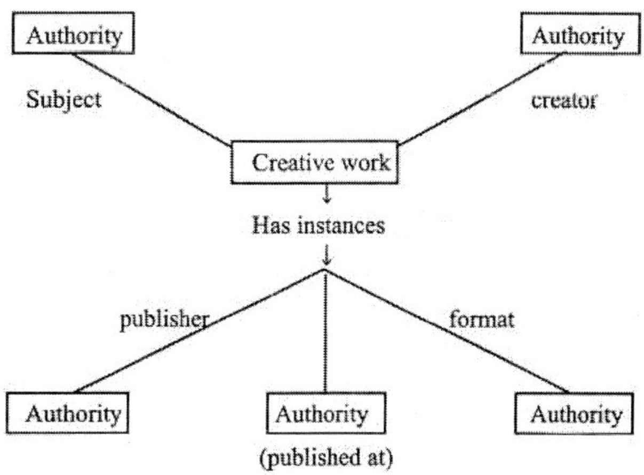

Fig. 14.7. BIBFRAME model in graphical from

***Courtesy*: BIBFRAME Basics by Amber Billey, Columbia University Libraries You Tube Presentation on 12-08-2015**

After seeing the core BIBFRAME model now let us see the model with a definite illustration in mind in Fig. 14.8.

Modern fairy Tale

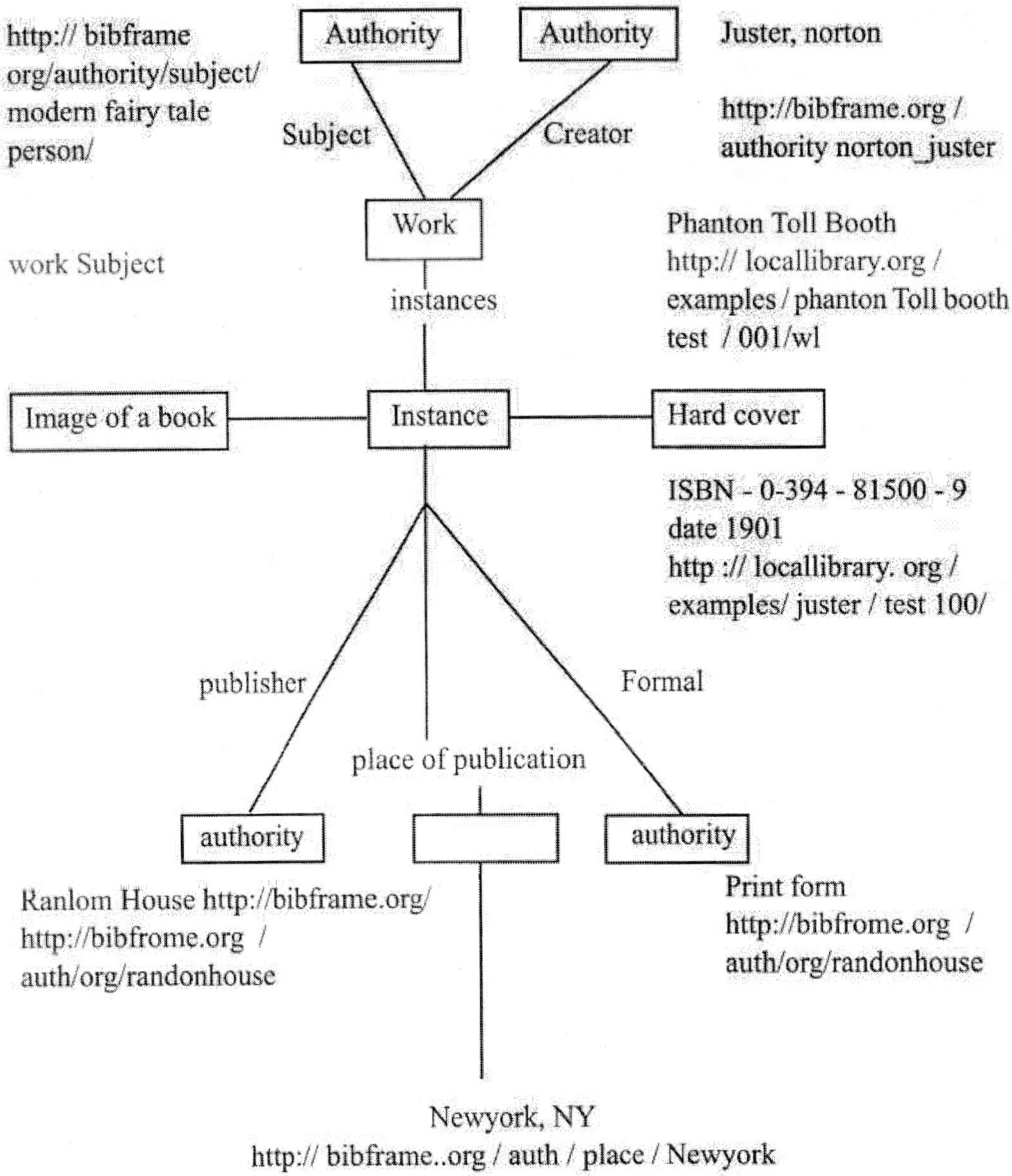

Fig. 14.8. BIBFRAME Model

Courtesy : **BIBFRAME Basics by Amber Billey, Columbia University Libraries You Tube Presentation on 12-08-2015**

Above graphical model (Fig 14.8) explains the relationships among the main BIBFRAME classes and it is displayed just for our understanding. Inorder to convert the contents of a relationship to a machine identifiable presentation it needs following actions:

1. A system of machine processable identifiers to identify BIBFRAME classes (OR A system of identifiers which can be processed by machine) to identify BIBFRAME classes.
2. A machine processable presentation of the model.

In linked data environment, it provides form of identifier called the Uniform Resources Identifier (URI) for each bibliographic content. The process involves creating BIBFRAME primer document to XML serialisation of the RDF data model. In XML sterilization, the particular work is encoded in its corresponding instances and associated authority information. With this background let us visualize another work in terms of BIBFRAME structure as given below.

The document name is: Functional Requirement of Bibliographic Record - A final report.

The work has three instances (one physical print, one PDF and one HTML website). It possesses authority information as (subject, author, publishes etc.) The links in this example would appropriately/actually encoded in RDF / XML structure, which is not appended but we would again see it in the graphical example as Fig. 14.9.

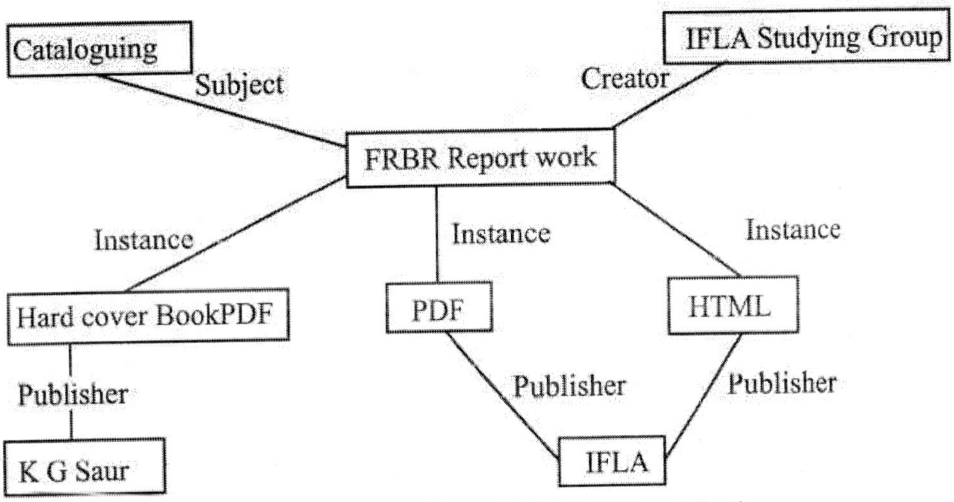

Fig. 14.9. Shows RDF model associated with XML serialization
Courtesy : **BIBFRAME Basics by Amber Billey, Columbia University Libraries You Tube Presentation on 12-08-2015**

The report in question possesses 4 authorities and 3 instances associated with 2 publishers.

Subject or creator.

Formats - Hard cover, PDF or HTML

Publishers - K.G. Saur and IFLA

14.5. HOW TO BIBFRAME?

After having understood the BIBFRAME project, its framework and about the BIBFRAME model, now let us try to know how library MARC data could be converted in to open linked data and then incorporated in BIBFRAME structure, which would be searchable with the web search tools. Logically the MARC to BIBFRAME conversion involves procedure of gradually converting library bibliographic data into a final BIBFRAME format. The purpose is to use the existing MARC data assets and try to convert them into a new format.

There are various ways available for libraries. Some expert say that we need to follow four building blocks for cataloguing systems to work i.e. content standards (RDA like AACR – II), schema, serialization and exchange systems.

The BIBFRAME has been designed to replace MARC (our current schema) by breaking the information which currently comprises of our bibliographic records into atomic units which can then be reconfigured using RDF / XML structure into various URIs.

As presentation given by Amber Billey in her speech "BIBFRAME Basics" she has mentioned the following steps to achieve the conversion as:

- code
- scribe
- customise
- transform
- Store and
- Deliver

The above steps she expects to work as:

1. Code : Create hand codes of existing information data units of existing MARC data into BIBFRAME compatible RDF / XML structure

2. Scribe : For this there is editing tool available provided by Zepheira as per contract given to them by LOC to design BIBFRAME model 1.0. This tool works as a native link data editor tool to create bibliographic description as endorsed by BIBFRAME. There is test site or sandbox of zepheira scribe process.

3. Customize : Then create a custom profile for editors to meet cataloguing experience or needs say one only wants to see the classes and properties associated with book data.BIBFRAME profiles allow for custom editor interface presently locally hosted installs can be customised.

4. Transform : To use LC- MARC to BIBFRAME Transformation tool to convert data into BIBFRAME (BIBFRAME Editor). BIBFRME editor is an open source tool for creating BIBFRAME metadata. Available to test data on web and can be downloaded at http://bibframe.org/ /tools. In transformation of MARC to BIBFRAME services, one need to supply URI to MARC data or one can paste MARC / XML data in BIBFRAME editing tool (http://bibframe.org/tools/ transform/start).

5. Store : Store BIBFRAME -RDF data in a triple store (Similarly as we do with any RDF linked data). Open linked Data can be stored in nosql database in triplestore. Zepheira is stills working on it.

6. Deliver : To deliver BIBFRAME RDF linked data using linked data publishing software and by using Library of Congress demonstration data sets (http:// www.loc.gov/bibframe/ implementation)

While the task of chapter writing was in progress, the author had e-mail conversation with Amber Billey. Amber Billey is the Metadata Librarian at Columbia University Libraries and posses 10 years experience of cataloguing and digitization. She is Zepheira Alumna. The author found her presentation (webinars). 1 : Essentials of BIBFRAME and 2.BIBFRAME BASICS were very informative. Author felt that if the e-mail communication with Amber Billey is incorporated in the form of Questions and Answers it would help the readers to understand the topic and would help in refining their idea about the theme.

Q. How to BIBFRAME? – 28 Feb 2017 —*Amber Billey wrote on 1st March 2017*

A. In : How to BIBFRAME I have described steps as:

Core : To hand code BIBFRAME data.

Scribe : This is the tool developed by Zepheira. It is a native link data editor tool to create bibliographic descriptions using BIBFRAME RDF data…

She explains further BIBFRAME steps as:

Customise : To create custom profiles for editors (scribe) to tailor one's cataloguing needs.

Transform : To use LC-MARC to BIBFRAME transformation tool to convert data into BIBFRAME.

Store : To store BIBFRAME data in triple store.

Deliver : To deliver BIBFRAME linked data using linked data publishing software or use LC's demonstration data sets…. Amber Billey

Q. The significance of BIBFRAME Initiative of LC is to provide vision for future of library cataloguing. The main theme of BIBFRAME is to bring library catalogue in the middle of the web search domain, so if one googles a title/author then one would know the entire open linked data about it and one would also know availability of item in nearby library. Is it not so? …… 28th Feb2017

A. Being able to find bibliographic information through an internet search engine is just one main theme of BIBFRAME. Perhaps the most important purpose of BIBFRAME is to migrate bibliographic data into a (new) standard syntax that is primarily used and governed by the web and W3C. The first step is bibliographic data in BIBFRAME, and then we will need to figure out the functional and transaction work flow (Acquisition, holdings and circulation) in the linked data environment. In an ideal situation (I agree that) one would be able to know availability of a book in a nearby library based on bibliographic linked data. Moreover having bibliographic data freely available on web makes you question the necessity of proprietary platform like worldcat. Many American Libraries view BIBFRAME and library linked data efforts as a possible solution to being locked -into a single vendor a handful of vendors.

Amber Billey.. Wrote on 20th March, 2017.

Q. What has been done at Columbia University Libraries about the implementation of BIBFRAME? Have your patrons been benefited by it? ..... 2nd March 2017

A. Columbia is currently testing BIBFRAME. We have not implemented it into ILS or OPAC. So our patrons have not experienced any BIBFRAME data yet. We do use linked data technology for our digital collections and our patrons are benefiting from the linked data infrastructure through that interface..... Amber Billay...20th March2017.

Q. Do you know any LMS which has already incorporated BIBFRAME data structure in it facilitating development of new database in library in IBIFRAME format directly? ...... 2nd March 2017

A. The only ILS/LMS that I know of that is incorporating BIBFRAME is Casalini's Share Catalog. It is in experimental development stage. They have version available to test out http://share.vde.org/sharevde/clusters... Amber Billey......

Q. Finally in your view how do LIS professionals in US look towards BIBFRAME developments?

A. Introduction of Linked Data concept and BIBFRAME to LIS professionals in US and third world countries has equal importance. To make real world wide web of linked data and therefore the semantic web, we will need the entire world to participate in creating linked data using standard ontologies like BIBFRAME-even third world countries. BIBFRAME is where IT and LIS colloid. Our experience in US has shown that introducing these concepts to LIS professionals (at all levels) increases their understanding and enthusiasm for linked data...Amber Billey.......22nd March 2017

14.6. BIBFRAME DEVELOPMENTS (IMPORTANT MILESTONES)

14.6.1. BIBFRAME-Pilot

At the stage when the BIBFRAME development reached to a saturation level it was tough time to take-up BIBFRAME Pilot (BIBFRAME 1.0). It was organised from 8th September 2015 to 31st March 2016. A network development of MARC standard office (NDMSO) and Co-operative Instruction Programmes Division (COIN) of the Acquisition of Bibliographic Access Directorate planned and developed a pilot to test the efficacy of BIBFRAME. The pilot was organised by Library of Congress. The pilot actually begun in October 2015, by this time it was yet to see the full functionality of BIBFRAME but BIBFRAME model and vocabulary was fully developed. The next phase of pilot was named as BIBFRAME - 2.0

Around 40 staff as mixed of cataloguers and services specialists were chosen as the participants for the pilot. The participants were responsible for processing monographs, serials, cartographic materials, music (annotated), sound recording, movie images and two dimensional artifacts (prints and photographs). They were also told to process the materials as they do normally in library. They were told to catalogue materials in MARC - 21 first and then in BIBFRAME format.

Training Programme : At the beginning participants were given exhaustive training of semantic web, linked data and use of BIBFRAME editor. The participants then began using the BIBFRAME editor. They entered data both in LC-LIS (voyager) and BIBFRAME editor. They created MARC - 21 records in voyager first and then in BIBFRAME. The experience of trainees and suggestions were used to refine and upgrade the BIBFRAME editing tools.

While training was in progress searching was available to primary datasets on the LC linked data service. Authorities vocabulary web site (http://id.loc.gov). There were LC / NACO Authority file and LCSH. In BIBFRAME both these datasets were accessible. The enhancements were made to the searching mechanism to improve the retrieval.

The outcome of training Requirements was found as:

1. Good understanding of RDA is essential for working in the BIBFRAME editing environment. So, the emphasis must be on RDA terminology than MARC coding.
2. Participants were seen curious about RDF sterilization. They found seeing and analysing BIBFRAME RDF sterilization in the pilot as it was first time live experience about using linked open data.

14.6.2. BIBFRAME Vocabulary

In MARC exchange environment one identify data elements with content designation. It is like:

- Tags to group and identity
- Subfields to identify
- Serialized with ISO - 2709 and further with XML, whereas, in BIBFRAME we use RDF conventions such as:
- Classes to group and identity
- Properties to identify and relate. They are with initial in lower case (Names have first letter in capital case.)
- Serialized with use of RDF triple.The list of classes properties and their attributes are the BIBFRAME Vocabulary. It is comprised of the RDF properties, classes and relationship among them.

BIBFRAME vocabulary is the key to the description of resources like MARC formats has a defined set of elements and attributes, where in classes identify type of BIBFRAME resource and properties serve to further describe the resource.

Version 2.0 of the vocabulary for BIBFRAME was released in April 2016.BIBFRAME vocabulary is available at home website http://bibframe.org/vocab. In this home page, there are three different views as :

- Model view
- Category view
- List view

Class is defined as a "type of things" while properties represents relationship between entities. Any term i.e. class will be the subject or object of RDF triple, whereas any term that is the property be the predicate of triple. In BIBFRAME model "Resource" is the top most class. Every other class is a subclass of resource. Domain and range terms are provided for properties which are reflected in terms of RDF triple. Domain is the subject; the property is the predicate and the range is the object. An easy way to decide whether a term is class or properties then remember that class always begins with caps and properties always begins with a lower-case letter. In a consolidated manner BIBFRAME model is described as shown in Fig. 14.10.

BIBFRAME model -

Four Main Classes
- Creative work
- Instance
- Authority
- Annotations

Fig. 14.10

There are total 53 classes and 289 properties. There is no need to actually enter the data in RDF templet but data is readily available and from other vocabularies like LOC, Worldcat, OCLC and Dublin Core can be searched and incorporated directly.

14.6.3. Zepheira

Zepheira has played a significant role in designing BIBFRAME a new bibliographic standard. Zepheira was technological partner in developing BIBFRAME model as it has been contracted by Library of Congress to bear this task.

Zepheira is a leading provider of software and services designed to help clients across industries to make information available more prominently on web. Founded in 2007, Zepheira has extensive experience of creating products and solutions focused on the modernisation of library information systems. Zepheira linked data readiness assessment has provided guidance and concrete steps for libraries to adopt open linked data and semantic web technologies in converting MARC to web actionable bibliographic format i.e. BIBFRAME. Zepheira was responsible to develop BIBFRAME 1.0 model and created linked data vocabularies for addressing the web visibility of library and similar organisations. It launched a new Linked Data Readiness Assessment (RA) product. In 2012, US Library of Congress selected Zepheira to architect BIBFRAME a new web friendly linked data format for library data to replace MARC-21. Zepheira has also facilitated to provide training to librarians in adopting BIBFRAME model for their catalogue data.

website : http://Zepheira.com. Its website on linked data library solution is as -

http://Zepheira.com/solution/library26.6.3.1 http://zepheira.com solution library

14.6.3.1. Zepheira's Training Program

Zepheira has designed a programme for academic library people who intend to go for early adoption programme and who wish to accelerate their team's education around the BIBFRAME standard and to participate in LIBHUB initiative by converting, contributing, linking and publishing up to 1000000 of their MARC records.

Zepheira is providing these training services to Academic Library teams since December 2015. They are delivering following services on an agreed upon schedule as:

- Zepheira's Practicals consists of linked data and BIBFRAME essentials. Training series is generally for 1-10 participants with conversion of 100 MARC record samples.
- Linked Data Readiness Assessment and converting up to 1000000 MARC record.
- Finally, conversion of up to 1000000 MARC records
- Transforming and connecting BIBFRAME contents publishing on the web.
- Collaborating in making additions and deletions to the web.

The libraries who purchase early adopter programme would get status of LIBHUB initiative as "Early Adopter" on the libhub.org website. LIBHUB initiative aims to raise the visibility of libraries on the web by actively exploring the promise of BIBFRAME and linked data. The following shows the list of libraries who are early adopter of LIBHUB initiatives.

- Denver public
- Dallas public
- Arapahoe library district
- Edmonton public
- Sno - Isle public
- Douglas county
- phoenix public
- Calgary public
- Anthric
- Worthington public
- Multnomah county
- Hamilton public

14.6.4. LIB-HUB

On 2nd September 2014 at Columbus, Ohio USA founding sponsor Zepheira introduced LIBHUB initiative to create an industry wide focus on giving collective visibility of libraries and their resources on web. Before BIBFRAME development was under taken by Zepheira the situation was that libraries had rich bibliographic contents resources that the web cannot see or use. The LIBHUB initiative aims to find common ground for libraries, providers and partners to publish and use bibliographic data with non-proprietary web standards. The libraries therefore could communicate in a way web application understand and web users can see them using enabling technology like linked data and share vocabularies such as schema.org and BIBFRAME.

The LIBHUB initiative emphasised on linking of these newly exposed library resources to each other and to other resources across the web.

Denver Public Library took the first lead in taking LIBHUB concept further by purchasing Zepheira's solution for libraries. They implemented the BIBFRAME model to convert their bibliographic data to linked open data.

Michelle Jeske, Director of Collections, Technology Innovation Centre at Denver Public Library expressed his feelings about this innovative library initiative as:

> "Libraries need to find new ways of reaching out and demonstrate that they truly are where their people need them, which includes Google and other search engines. When they would be able to showcase their rich collection and fabulous Western History and Genealogy resources more readily on the web, it is really an exciting."

About LIBHUB initiative Vailey Oehike, Director of Libraries for Multnomoh County Library and the President, Public Library Association on early LIBHUB initiative supporter said that:

> "Libraries have long been the greatest free source of information in each country. However, as people increasingly turn to Google and other search engines for their information needs we see that libraries' role is diminishing That is because our data is largely dark to the Internet and held in proprietary cataloguing systems which creates barriers in discovery. The LIBHUB initiative offers the possibilities for making library holdings discoverable directly through search engines like Google"
>
> Zepheira helps libraries to tell their stories on their web as News Break Information Today. http://newsbreak.infotoday.com.newsbreak.
>
> http://zepheira.com

14.6.5. Linked data for Libraries (LD4L)

It is a project designed to explore how libraries can use linked data and the semantic web to improve discovery / search and access to scholarly information. In 2014 Stanford University, the Harvard library- innovation lab and Cornell University were awarded a Mellon foundation grant to create Scholarly Resource of semantic information store model. The project has been named as Linked Data for Libraries (LD4L) with website : http://wiki.duraspace.org/pages/viewpage.action?page id=41354028/.

In this project, it has been attempted to link three large resources of data about scholarly resources, bibliographic data, person data and usage data and to connect library resources with institutional and other data on the web. LD4L also intends to provide a transparent mapping from the MARC records which currently housed much of this information to source via BIBFRAME. It is also expected that the project would produce an open source LD4L ontology compatible with BIBFRAME and other OLD efforts. An open source LD4L semantic editing ,display and search system and a project Hydra has compatible interface to LD4L.

14.6.6. BIBFLOW

It is a development to set a roadmap for migrating essential library work efforts to a

BIBFRAME/ linked open data ecosystem. It is believed that libraries on their own cannot adopt the modern technologies in their current work flow constrains being the complexity and dependencies on a large ecosystem of data software and service provider. It is a two years' project funded by IMLS of the UC Davis University Library and Zepheira. It's official title is, "Reinventing Cataloguing"- Model for the future of library operations. The University is investing the future of library technical services (cataloguing and related work flow) in the light of modern technology infrastructure, such as the web and new data models and formats such as Resource Description and Access (RDA) and BIBFRAME, the new encoding and exchanging format in development by the Library of Congress. The university hypothesis behind starting BIBFLOW project is that while these new standards and technologies are essentially needed to help the libraries community to avail the benefits and efficiencies that the libraries cannot remain far from modem developments of open linked data. However due to complexity of this technology and the constrains of libraries due to their current library standards i.e. AACR - II and MARC the research is therefore needed on how research libraries should adapt new practice, workflow software systems and partnership to support evolution of new standards and technologies.

BIBFLOW is expected to take up this agenda and set these activities to modernise library community understanding of the resource description landscape the current and desire future state. This university world begins to develop a roadmap that the library community can be ready for planning investing and changing over the coming years.

The BIBFLOW project would focus on Academic Library technical services/ processes, including acquisition, licensing, cataloguing, technical processing, digitization etc. in the light of new bibliographic standard BIBFRAME. Ref Blog: - http://www.lib.ucdavis.edu/bibflow.

14.7. LIBRARY SOFTWARES READY WITH BIBFRAME STRUCTURE

As Amber Billey has mentioned in her mail correspondence that then software named - casalini is available now. Let us see what it is.

14.7.1. What is Casalini's Share VDE (Virtual Discovery Environment) project?

Casalini's share VDE project is a prototype of a virtual discovery environment where BIBFRME's three layer architecture (person/work, instance, and item) has been established through the individual process of analysis, enrichment, conversion and publication of data from MARC-21 to RDF. It is expected to work with the context of libraries with different systems.

Share virtual discovery in linked data is a platform which allows the browsing of library collection organized as per BIBFRAME standard. The portal (www.shar-vde.org) to share VDE project is equipped with navigational tools with three layers of BIBFRAME as :

Person/Works : This level facilitates to enrich to get data from external resources with a view to extend the research potential.

Instances : At this level it tries to aggregate the resources of various editions, works with different languages of one creator and try to connect them with the overlaying person/work.

Item : With this instance the publication is linked to the information contained in a data set of the local library OPAC.

Now let us visualize how search in Virtual Discovery Environment seen in linked data. Share VDE is a experimental platform for searching and accessing bibliographic resources according to BIBFRAME data model which is available in some important libraries like:

Stanford University, University of California, Berkeley, Yale University, LC University of Chicago, University of Michigan, An Arbor, Harvard University, MIT, Cornel University, Columbia University Library, University of Pennsylvania, Texas A & M University and University of Toronto.

The search page looks like this: Fig. 14.11.

The search has the further options as :

- Refining search
- Advanced search
- Browsing the Index and
- Finally where to access the resource, where one can export bibliographic records with choice of desired format. One can alternatively access the OPAC of the library where the resource is held.

Ref. Share Virtual Discovery Environment in linked data : Brief user guide

Courtesy: www.shar-vde.org (Share VDE is a CasaliniLibri and@ Cult partnership)

14.8. HOW TO GET INVOLVED IN BIBFRAME MOVEMENT

Now it is the question how world libraries, librarians and LIS professionals would get themselves involved in this modern development. It could be done by:

- Following BIBFRAME related projects and experiments.
- By exploring BIBFRAME tools
- By participating in BIBFRAME discussion LISTSERVE groups
- By attending sessions at ALA

One can also attend live session like as:

1. MARC Transition Interest group sessions: Saturday between 3.00 to 4.00 with focus on BIBFRAME tools
2. BIBFRAME updates Sunday at 10.00

- Zepheira offers a Linked Data/BIBFRAME training class with access to ongoing alumni group http://zepheira.com/solutions/library/training.

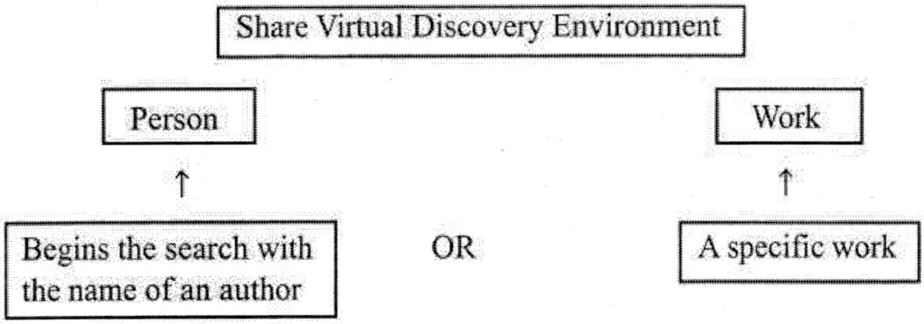

The result page of person will show the following information.

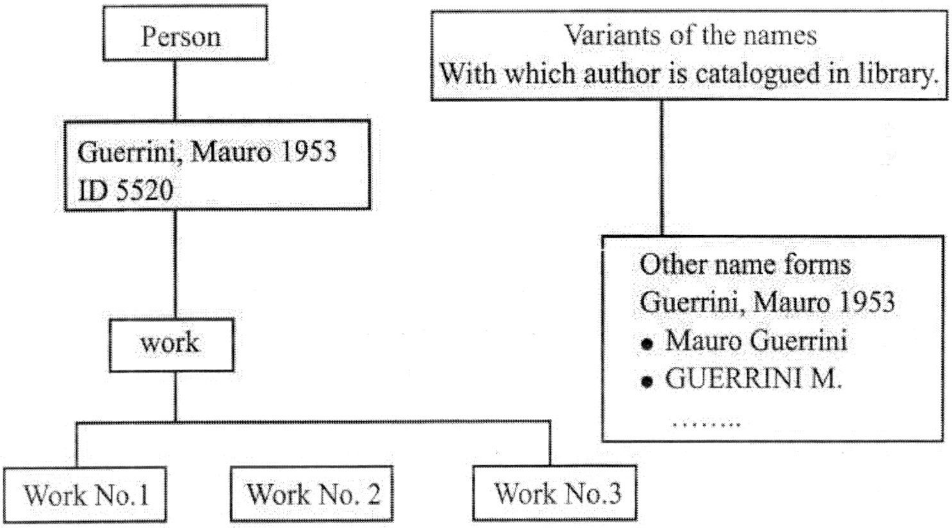

(List of work in a alphabetical order)

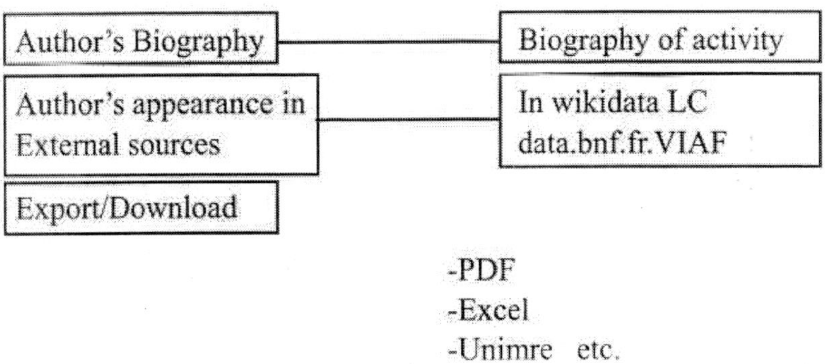

Fig. 14.11. Casalini -Share video project design

REFERENCES

1. ALA: From MARC to BIBFRAME: An Introduction: Webinar: Carolyn Hansen http://www.ala.org/alcts / confevents/upcomingwebinars/051315. (accessed in February 2017)
2. BIBFRAME bibliographic framework initiative (Library of Congress) http://www.loc.gov.bibframe. (accessed in February 2017)
3. Over view of BIBFRAME 2.0 modelhttp:// www.loc.gov/bibframe/docs/bibframe2.model html.
4. http://bibframe.org
5. Zepheira :http://zepheira.com.
6. Linked Data for Libraries (LD4L) :http://www.ld41.org
7. Libhub :www.libhub.org/join/
8. Bibflow :http://www.lib.ucdavis.edu/bibflow
9. Amber Billey(Metadata Librarian) :Essentials of BIBFRAME; Columbia University Libraries http:// www.youtube.com/
10. Amber Billey : BIBFRAME Basics Academic commons Columbia University Libraries 12/08/2015
11. Amber Billay about your Presentation on BIBFRAME : E-mail response date 01.03.2017 amber.billey @columbia.edu

15
Green Library

15.0. INTRODUCTION

Importance of library has been admired in all the fields worldwide.Until non-print material was yet to be entered into library's collection, libraries have been growing in terms of their sizes and collections. Thanks to Atkinson's zero growth concept,which had tried to limit the growth of libraries by introducing weeding of old and obsolete items from the collection.When print journal resources started transforming into digital form weight of bound volumes or back volumes might have reduced to some extent, however, the books and old bound volumes of journal still remain to be present as the majority part of library collection. The libraries continued to be heavier as weight of stacks was becoming unbearable to the upper library floors. This has put a limit on verticals growth of library buildings, making it essential to put the stacks on the ground level or in the basements. In maintaining traditional library buildings the cost of operating has been huge. Especially the cost of electrical energy used to illuminate the library premises and the cost of air-conditioning, which ware really significant, posing threat to funding needed for building operating and maintenance.

As green technology emerged in almost all aspects of building construction, it was obvious that libraries would also start thinking of constructing new green libraries or adopting greening aspects in renovating the old library buildings. There are plenty of advantages in adopting green library technologies. It was the first time in 2007 that libraries started taking part in green library initiatives. In adopting green library technology we try to support the concept of sustainability and environmentalism, which is the most needed to protect the global ecosystem. In this chapter we are going to discuss all the aspects of green library technology in detail.

15.1. WHAT IS GREEN LIBRARY ?

When librarians talk about green libraries they usually have in mind the green library buildings. The California Integrated Waste Management Board defines a green or sustainable building as, "a structure that is designed, built, renovated, operated or reused in an ecological and resource effective manner." Interest in green library was actually intensified sometime in December 2007, when Library Journal Design Institute hosted the seminar on "going green" in Chicago Illinois.

In this seminar the architects, city planners and librarians came together and shared their ideas about the latest developments and solutions in adopting green library technology (Library Journal 2007). The LEED (Leadership in Energy and Environmental Design) brought the certification system to rate the green libraries, which was initiated by US Green Building Council. It has become the US national standard for commercial and institutional buildings as their performance standard.

Library becomes green when it tries to adopt the green technology, which is prominent in building construction now a days. These days most of the fields talk about green concept as we all have realised several threats to our environment or to the eco system of our planet earth.

The Oxford English Dictionary defines the word,'Green'as , "pertaining to or to help the environmentalism". The environment always comes along with sustainability. The sustainability relates to our economic activities and culture which do not lead to environmental degradation anyway. These measures consider reducing footprints of carbon and also reducing generation of greenhouse gases causing holes in the ozone layer around the Earth.The library can also become green when it allows green design in its architecture plan.Adopting green concept could be in constructing new building or in renovating the old one. It further becomes significant part in its operation or reuse it in an ecological resource efficient manner.

15.2. CHALLENGES BEFORE GREEN LIBRARY

It is found that green library design also has special challenges like in green building design.In green library the major challenges are posed by the needs of materials and the patrons. In spite of proliferation of Internet technology and availability of digital resources through the same, the printed books are still dominating their existence in the library collections. Since libraries still need to stock a large number of books, which brings responsibility of processing ,managing and preserving them. In addition the library need to bear the weight of book and bound volume collections.

If we try to accommodate weight factor in organising library collections then it brings limitations in adopting multi floor construction,which favors in green technology. Secondly, when we think of preserving book collection the main concern would be to protect them from direct sunlight or ultraviolet rays of sun and from the extreme temperatures. Where as green building recommends maximum use of natural day light.Like the library book collections same is the case of patrons as they also need to be protected from the extreme environmental conditions like temperatures and ultraviolet rays of sun. Now let us see how and why the libraries are becoming green in spite of above challenges.

15.3. BROAD OBJECTIVES BEHIND GREEN LIBRARY

Broadly the Green Library design works towards minimising impact on the natural environment and to maximise indoor environmental quality by selecting the site carefully, by using natural construction materials, by using degradable products/ furniture and furnishers, by giving priority to conservation of resources (energy, water and paper) and by adopting responsible waste disposable (recycling) techniques. Adopting green design in library is an integrated process of many broader issues such as:

1. Site Selection
2. Water Conservation
3. Energy Conservation
4. Building Materials
5. Indoor Air Quality

Now let us elaborate them a little.

15.3.1. Site Selection

The selection of the site for the building is the major concern in green library planning. When any new library goes into planning proper site selection, then it seeks some queries broadly on how library would be eco friendly. The LEED has provided many guidelines which provide many tips for library site selection.There are various question highlighted relating to the site selection, given in their specifications such as:

- What kind of impact it would have on the local environment ?
- Will there will be erosion? Whether the site is already green?
- Whether the library would be located in the populated area and most of the service related buildings are easily approachable?
- If good public transport facility is available to the site and whether there is enough parking facility available for the people to park their energy efficient vehicles?Overall it should not add to the pollution
- If library's hard surfaces are covered or shaded through heat island effect e.g. by adopting Green Roofing etc.

15.3.2. Water Conservation

There are many ways and means to conserve the water resource in the library. It can be achieved by adopting following measures:

- By installing water recycling and reusing plant
- By adopting rainwater harvesting system which could be used for toilets and irrigation.
- By installing device which extracts water from the atmosphere which could be used for drinking purpose (Nero project at IIT Madras)
- The wastage of water could be prevented by using low flux bathrooms fixtures and by installing waterless urinals.

15.3.3. Energy Conservation

Having the energy-efficient buildings is the most important factor in adopting green library technology. LEED rating system has, therefore, given maximum significance to it. In energy consideration the importance is given on the following aspects:

1. How to reduce cost of heating and ventilation (air conditioning, cooling and heating).

2. How to reduce the cost of illumination of the library premises through artificial lighting.

As for as the cost of ventilation is concerned it can be achieved by adopting the following innovative technologies:

- Green roofing and
- Geothermal cooling and heating system.

Regarding illumination of library premises the following measures help in saving cost of electric energy consumption :

1. By fitting energy-saving fans and lights e.g.by adopting energy efficient lights (Led lights) and cost saving fans.
2. The efforts need to be taken to make use of natural sunlight to-the maximum possible extent and to create good balance between natural and artificial lighting.
3. Using renewable energy sources like wind and solar power generation systems certainly help not only in reducing the power bill but it can also turn a power generating source.

15.3.4. Green Furniture

In progressing towards green library the major obstacle is about how to reduce the construction waste. Most of the present furniture and fixture items bound to end up in adding to the construction waste. The solution to this problem can be achieved by using furniture and fixture items,Which are made out of reusable or recyclable materials. Biological degradable materials like wood, linoleum, bamboo and cork can also be used in making furniture and flooring. Using cork material for flooring can greatly prevent creation of the construction waste.

15.3.5. Healthy Indoor Quality

In maintaining indoor quality or atmosphere having the healthy and pleasant environment is also an important factor in marching towards green library. The efforts are always made to provide air conditioned air quality inside the library premises. However, due to faulty AC equipments it could lead in generation of toxins. Secondly, CO_2 exhaled by the people (worker and patrons) who spend their considerable time inside the library could also create threat in raising carbon level inside the library. In order to improve and maintain the good air quality the efforts are made by bringing in materials having low Volatile Organic Compounds (VOC), which generate ozone toxins and by installing CO_2 monitors to maintain safe CO_2 level. These materials not only help in maintaining the environment but it can also helps in taking care of health of people present inside.

15.4. SPECIFIC FEATURES TOWARDS ACHIEVING GREEN LIBRARY

After discussing the broader issues concerned to the Green Library let us look at some of the specific issues. As Brown says, "Green library plan considers need of a library as the sustainable design and real cost saving in energy consumption together." The overall objective of green building is to adopt sustainable energy efficient approach in its construction, maintenance and look at overall life of the structure. Brown has further identified the following green design features to be adopted in the green library building. The most of writers have also endorsed these elements in green library design as :

1. Using Daylight : Light shelves
2. Green material/ furniture
3. Green roofing
3. Raised floor system
4. Energy efficiency
5. Natural ventilation
6. Green power and renewable energy
7. Indoor environmental quality

15.4.1. Innovative Technologies for Green Library

While going through the special features of different well known green libraries the author found that there has been use of many innovative technologies in achieving green status of the libraries.The innovative technologies could be listed as:

- Light Shelves
- Green Materials
- Green Roofs
- Geothermal Heating and Cooling Systems
- Rainwater Harvesting
- Waterless urinals etc.

Now Let us discuss these technologies along with their technical backgrounds.

15.4.1.1. Light Shelves

Use of sun light inside the library and providing access to natural lighting for illuminating the library premises has a lot of significance in adopting green library concept. Getting direct sun light once upon a time was creating a serious problem as it was posing health hazards for the people present inside the library (workers and patrons) due to ultra violet rays and heating due to direct sunlight was also not conducive for preserving of the printed collections. However, with progress in glass technology now all those bad effects are filtered and clean day light could be easily made available, which neither allows ultraviolet rays nor raises the temperature inside the library building, which was causing the health hazards to the people present inside the library. Moreover, National Library of Singapore has developed new means to bring in as much as sunlight as possible, wherein light shelves are used with a technique to pair the daylight with artificial lighting leading to reduce the energy cost to a considerable extent.

The architect of the library Ken Yeang has designed an innovative way of bringing as much as possible sunlight through light shelves.A light shelf is a horizontal surface that reflects daylight deep into the building. Light shelves are places above eye level and have high reflectance on upper surface, which reflects day light on to the ceiling which facilitates traveling sunlight deeper into the building premise. In this design the building has two blocks separated from each other by an atrium. The atrium is fully day lit and semi enclosed close to drive light into various parts of the building and also helping and facilitating ventilation. The bridges in the atrium acts like linkage between two blocks. The bigger block of the library accommodates the core library which is located over it with naturally ventilated civic plaza, which is open to the sky. The smaller curved part which houses all the noisy activities like exhibitions, auditorium and multimedia space, thus providing noiseless and quiet atmosphere both in the main library premises, at the same time it allows people to undertake creative activities simultaneously.

Another special feature of the building is that it is orientated from east-west axis to avoid exposure of the afternoon sun, whereas from south-west wall remains to stop sun rays to get into the building. Sun-films have been fitted all over the glass panels, which prevent heating and glare of sun rays .This allows only natural light to come in even to the deeper parts of the library and use of artificial lighting is minimised to a maximum extent, which has been proved to be the great energy saving measure.

15.4.1.2. Green Materials

The second important factor to reconsider in achieving Green Library is the use of green materials. Furniture and fixtures available in the library consist of computers and hardware materials, furniture and furnishers. Out of these computer hardware when becomes useless is termed as e-waste or electronic waste and it can be destroyed with a certain method. There is trend of using green material in constructing or manufacturing the furniture. As consumers these days tend to look for furniture which is made out of green materials, similarly librarians are also considering environmental factor while buying the furniture for the library. Green material or green furniture normally symbolised by a tree. The products that use materials from sustainable forests, which have low toxic material levels, which is also locally manufactured and durable enough to last a long time. Metals like steel and aluminum are also durable type of materials which can be recycled. Bamboo is a super sustainable material. Cork is also extremely versatile material which can be used into making flooring. Green furniture can also be made from recycled metal, reclaimed wood and other safe materials.

15.4.1.3. Green Roofs

Green roof is the roof of a building that is partially or completely covered with vegetation and a growing medium, planted on a waterproofing membrane. Green roof consistent of different layers such as root barrier, drainage and irrigation systems. There are various advantages of having green roof such as absorbing rainwater, providing insulation and creating a habitat for birds. It could also help in decreasing stress of people around the roof by providing a more aesthetically pleasing landscape, helping to lower a temperatures round the building and creating the heat island effect. The term green roof is also be used to indicate that made from green technology such as roofs with solar collectors or photovoltaic panels. Green roofs are also referred to as eco-roofs, vegetated roofs or living roofs. Green roofs are preferred to maintain temperature inside the building cool and pleasant. Membrane roofing is another type of roofing system used to create watertight roofs to protect the interior of the building.Membrane roofs are made from synthetic rubber, thermoplastic or modified bitumen. Membrane roofing technology is mostly used to protect the building from water seepage, however it may not be on the lines the green roofs which are specifically used in green building.

15.4.1.4. Geothermal Heating and Cooling

Geothermal heating and cooling systems are now becoming popular because of their energy saving capability. It is a better alternative than to use direct electricity for heating and cooling which is more expensive. Geothermal heat pumps work exactly like normal heat pumps. In normal case when heating is needed thermal energy is transferred from outside to inside building where as in case of geothermal heating and cooling system geothermal heat moves from the ground or earth in the building. The mechanism here is like this that if we dig about 3 meters below the surface we can gain stable temperature of 10°C therefore, one can make use of this stable level of temperature for maintaining a desired temperature in the building situated above. When heating is needed then required heat energy is drawn from the Earth through heat pumps and when cooling is required excess heat is transferred to earth. In both cases the earth's sync is used. Geothermal heating and cooling system can handle multiple loads for the community. Geothermal HVAC (Heating, ventilating and airconditioning) can bring the building in harmony with the earth by taking advantage of subterranean temperature to provide heating in winter and cooling in summer.

15.4.1.5. Rain water Harvesting

If we try to store the rain water in reservoir when it is actually raining and use it suitably when needed, it becomes the rainwater harvesting system.Such water can be used for car washing, gardening or for toilets. In Rajasthan people try to store the rain water in a clean manner so that such water storage can be used even for normal drinking. In multi storage library we need water for different purposes from drinking and for toilets. As this system is most recommended to achieve water conservation then we essentially need to have the rain water harvesting system, if we want to create the green library.

15.4.1.6. Waterless Urinals

Waterless urinals do not require water for flushing , which can be installed at homes, institutions or even in libraries.Waterless urinals not only saves water energy but it also tries to harvest urine as a resource. Waterless urinals work like a conventional urinal in design. However, they do not require water for flushing and this results in saving water in a large quantity per urinal per year.In waterless urinals urine flows down the bowl ,urine then passes through a sealant liquid, usually a specially made oil base or even an ordinary vegetable oil. The urine being denser than the oil it sinks through the liquid at the bottom leaving oil always on top which prevents bad smell.IIT Delhi has undertaken a research project on this innovative systems

15.5. GREEN LIBRARY MOVEMENTS, RATIONAL, SPECIFICATIONS AND STANDARD

These days there is growing concern of the sustainability of libraries in general. In a very complex situation and in adverse environment the librarians continue to carry out thankless job of preserving print as well as digital collections. They try to adjust themselves with the changing information technology and networking infrastructure. They always try to provide free service to the reader; they try to meet the growing cost of maintenance of building. However, doing all these essential functions and duties it was all leading in lowering the ecological foot prints. The challenge before the libraries is therefore, issues of sustainability of libraries and to identify the ways on how to opt for sustainability strategies in their functioning and making them eco-friendly. Naturally the popular rational in this direction is how to go for greening the libraries. The paper by Maria Anna Jankowska and James W. Marcum on sustainability challenges for academic libraries: Planning for future has taken a detailed view on Green Libraries. Now good amount of literature is available on, Green Library, which says that people are now concentrating on greening of libraries. The greening of libraries is not only process but it is a state of mind asking for action reciprocating as we take care of environment it takes care of us. American Library Association (ALA) has taken a pioneering steps in that direction and has established a Task Force On the Environment (TFOE), Which has helped in initiating the green concept in librarianship .With these initiatives it has now become possible to:

- Make libraries and public aware of diverse environmental information sources
- One window solutions to green concerned and practices in library
- Organising ALA greening conference
- Educating librarians and public by organising special programs to focus on environment
- Provide open access platform for scholarly environmental communication with publishing electronic green journal.
- ACRL organised 14th ACRL conference at Seattle to consider Green as a major theme.

Past 1990s topics on green has been popular in terms of terminologies like Green Academic Sectors; Greening College; Green Librarian; Green Librarianship and Green Blogs and Go Green. The literature and the topics are also addressing issues like recycling, noise, paper, environmental user education and environment literacy. There is website on Green Libraries www.greenlibraries.org which works as a directory.

Now green library building theme discusses architectural design, which considers sustainability solutions in building new libraries and in renovating old ones. So far it has been the fact that the traditional libraries use significant quantity of electricity, water, energy as well as threes for paper. These libraries also have been seen producing significant amount of solid waste (Now e-waste). In Green Library concept all these actions work against the environment and therefore there is great need to relook towards them with green point of view. US Green Building Council formed LEED which disseminates code and standard for green certification to be awarded for new as well as renovated green libraries. In 1990 many public libraries in the US and Europe adopted green concept in their buildings contradicting to their traditional library's bad environmental impact. The green buildings are always energy efficient; they use non toxic recycled content materials and furniture; they make optimum use of day light; they make use of low flow toilets or use waterless urinals and try to reduce the maintenance cost as much as possible. The green design project initiated by LIBRIS provides a detailed design, planning and documentation on green building. It has considered the aspects from acoustics of libraries through interior finishing, library technology to infrastructure design. The Green Library concept is now trying to emphasise designing library premises to facilitate new role of the library as a research and learning centre rather than, its traditional role, as the preservation and depository. With giving importance to green building efforts are made towards making libraries more sustainable with building interior and exterior which could promote sustainable use of renewable and non renewable resources to create healthy and pleasant conditions not only for library users but also for the collections and services. There may not be specific standards only for the green library buildings

15.5.1. Specifications and Standards for Green Libraries

Green building is purely a civil engineering concept. Green Technology in construction has become popular in the last two decades. Many specification and standards have been emerged and used as the guidelines by the professionals .The standards therefore only for green library may not be there so it would be mix of general and specific standards for green libraries.

Before we actually discuss standards for green libraries let us take a note of the pioneering work done by some organisations as follows:

15.5.1.1. Specification

1. USGBC- U.S. Green Building Council : It is co founded by Mike Italiano, David Gottfried and Rick Fedrizzi in 1993. It is a private non-profit organisation which promotes sustainability in building design, construction and operation. USGBC was well known for its forming a green building certification rating system known as Leadership in Energy and Environmental Design (LEED). The certification is available for variety of levels pertaining to green building status. USGBC also holds international conference and expo dedicated to green building. US GBC has also its role in founding World Green Building Council.

2. Leadership in Energy and Environmental Design (LEED) : US GBC initiated formation of LEED. it is a program which provides third-party verification of green buildings. The LEED rating system considers variety of buildings such as commercial building ,homes, ,healthcare, schools and libraries as well as considers every phase of building lifestyle including design, construction, operation and maintenance. Any project depending on its achieving the certain level of green building specification can earn rating certification such as certified, silver, gold or platinum depending on number of points or credits earned within the specification. LEED has also established its hubs in different countries, which provides ratings certifications locally.

In collaboration with USGBC IGBC (Indian Green Building Council) carries out the activities in india. Similarly LEED's local hub in India is known as LEED-India, Which issues certifications for green buildings in India.

In addition to LEED – in India there is another green building rating system known as Green Rating for Integrated Habitat Assessment (GRAHA) initiated by TERI (Tata Energy and Research Institute), New Delhi, which carries-out further the green building movement in india.

15.5.1.2. Standards for Green Building

The following Green building standards are in use:

(a) Chicago Illinois Standards

(b) Brown Green Standards

(c) IGBC — Indian Green Building Council

(a) Chicago Illinois Standard : Chicago is the fist city to apply environmental practices in construction of public buildings which finally succeeded in bringing out Chicago Illinois green building standard. This standard is on the lines of LEED's green building rating system. The green building and sustainable building concepts both refer to have minimum impact on environment in design and construction. The green building comprises all phases of construction like design, material selection and construction including life-cycle analysis and energy efficiency.

(b) Brown Green standard : Governor of California Jerry Brown has emphasised the emerging trend of green libraries and predicted that many libraries were on the verge of adopting Green design. So the new or renovated state buildings having area of over 10000 sq.ft. have to the level of US Green Building Council's LEED silver certification and would have to accept clean energy generation methods.

(c) IGBC Indian Green Building Council : Since 2001 IGBC the counter part of USGBC in India started functioning with the support of Confederation of Indian Industries and as result IGBC has got authority to award LEED's Green Building rating certifications.

15.6. ROLE OF LIBRARIANS IN AGREEING LIBRARIES

Librarians play very significant role in greening the libraries. Moreover, in planning, designing, constructing and operating green libraries, participation of librarians has to be there. Although the green building is purely a civil engineering concept librarian may not take part as an expert but since librarian and all library staff need to be associated in operating the green building once the building construction is completed and handed over to the library management. It is always good if librarian is actively engaged in each and every aspect of green building as he along with his staff is fully aware of the purpose and objective of green library so that they can share the same with other library professionals. It is like librarian's participation in the process of library computerisation.

15.7. WORLD FLAGSHIP GREEN LIBRARIES

15.7.1. Anythink Brighton: Brighton

It is known to be the first green library ,which achieved carbon positive Library in USA. It has been recorded that in 2009 the library was offsetting 17621 pounds of carbon dioxide. The second achievement in greening is, it has installed 108 KW photovoltaic system which generates almost 1/3 rd of buildings power requirements, yields in saving almost £30000 a year of energy cost. The building heating and cooling is taken care of by the thermal heating and cooling system, the most natural and economical way of indoor air quality.

15.7.2. The National Library of Singapore

The Singapore National Library is said to be the greenest library building among all on the planet.The building was meticulously designed by Ken Yeang, which was inaugurated in July 2005.The special characteristic of this building is new and innovative use of light shelves with a view to make use of natural sunlight even to the deepest part of library along with artificial lighting, which resulted great saving on illumination cost. Another speciality is that it is the first green library for kids

15.7.3. Blair Library, USA

It is the first green public library in USA. Registered with U.S. Green Library Council In October 2004. The construction began in October 2014 and was completed in 2006. The other speciality of this green building is that it has adopted rainwater harvesting system and the stored water is being used for irrigation purposes. Another speciality in adopting green technology in the library is the flooring made of cork material.

It also uses recycled material for furniture and fixtures. Use of waterless urinals,low VOC finishes and fabrics.The library has received certificate lEED Silver NC certificate.

15.7.4. Spanish Peaks Library, Wilson Berg, UK

In this library use of geothermal heating and cooling is the special feature of green building, which is the most natural and economical air-conditioning system. The library is the recipient of Stephen H. Rechard Award got in 2010.

15.7.5. Fayetteville (AR)Public Library

This green library was inaugurated in 2004. It is known to be the first building in Arkansas to registered with US green building council. It also received the silver LEED certification in 2006. In this building green roof technology has been used, which results in saving of about £4000 per year cost of energy.

The library's reading areas and circulation desks are situated in such away that it could use maximum natural light without over loading the air-conditioning system, which has resulted in saving of 25 to 30% of the cost of building's energy consumption.This special architecture design makes it possible to reach sunlight to 75% of library's public spaces.

15.7.6. Minneapolis Public Library

Another exemplary of green library is the Central Branch of the *Minneapolis Public Library*, which was designed by *Cesar Pelli*, and was inaugurated and opened in May 2006. The special features of this library is having *green roof*. The green roof is planted with vegetation that does well in Minnesota's peculiar climate. With adopting green roof it reduces rainwater runoff, reduces the building's heating and cooling load, which creates the buildings *heat island effect*. It has added green space to the downtown cityscape.

15.7.7. Public Library of Charlotte and Mecklenburg County

The next flagship green library is the Joe and Joan Martin Center is the first public building in Charlotte and Mecklenburg County, which has certified by the US Green Building Council. In 2006 the library was awarded with LEED certification at the silver level

15.7.8. Children's Museum of Pittsburgh

This is the first museum which has successfully adopted the green concept. When The *Children's Museum of Pittsburgh* planned extensive expansion and renovation in 2004 incorporated many sustainable techniques and guiding principles in redesigning it with green concept, which resulted in earning silver LEED-certification. This is one of largest museums in the Pennsylvania USA to receive this designation. This is the first children's green museum in America.

15.7.9. University of California, Merced Colligian Library

This is another well known green library which was opened in August 2005, UC Merced's Colligian Library got a prestigious Gold LEED Certification in 2007. The special characteristics of this green library having combination of glass-and-concrete which achieved saving of 42% less water and 50% less energy than the comparable buildings. The building's carpet contains 37% recycled material. The another special feature of this green library is that its acoustical ceiling tiles contain 66% recycled content that includes telephone books and newspapers. Secondly, it has used nearly 30% of the materials in construction manufactured locally, resulting significant saving on transportation and energy cost.

The list of green libraries is growing with the time, which shows the new trend in library building construction.

REFERENCES

1. Maria Anna Jankowska and James W. Marcum: Sustainability Challenges for Academic Libraries: Planning for the future. *College and Research Libraries*,vol.71,No.2(2010) ,PP 160-170
2. Anindya Bhattacharya : Green library and its utilities in modern day library service: A study. *International Journal of Next Generation Library and Technologies* (IGNGLT), August 2017 Vol. 3, Issue 3, pp 1-11
3. Brown, Bill : The new green Standards, *Library Journal*,128,61-64, 2003

   In- Anindya Bhattachrya op.cit
4. Monika Antonella : The green Library Movement : An overview and beyond. Electronic Green Journal 1(27),2008
5. Light shelves design in Natural Library of Singapore : *http://www.archute.com/national-library-in* - singapore by - ken-yeang In -Architecture/Library/public Facilities/sustainability – by Ian Mutuli

1. Licensing breaches and piracy: This basically deals how to track pirated transactions from the proxy server while using the resources.
2. Virtual Reality:It is about providing virtual reality product in library through use of Google cardboard as VR platform which is combined with mobile app like Google expeditions for creating virtual reality trips.
3. Video streaming using multiple methods.
4. Decline of the printed books? not so fast
5. Visionary tech
6. Affordable media labs
7. Tech soup resources

He further mentions about how under Lenovo discount programme the public libraries are getting IT equipments at discounted prices

16.1.5. Top library trends : American Library Magazine (*http://americanlibrariesmagazine.org*)

This is a contribution of Alison Marcotte in the American Library Magazine in 2017. In her view she has presented following new trends for the future libraries as,

1. Take patron on a virtual library tour
2. Make google cardboard sets (for VR Tours)
3. Go on google expedition
4. Teach with gamification platforms
5. Get coding with code schools
6. Make circuits with tech loving students
7 Teach patrons with private browsing
8. Create strong password with a roll of the dice
9. Streamline with data driven development
10. Develop your own applications

16.1.6. Predicting the future: Library technology to keep in mind (*http://www.tandfonline.com*)

It is the submission made by Kenneth J.Varnum in which he has discussed new trends like virtual reality, augmented reality, Internet of things(IOT) and about adoption of a systems " buy the data ,build the interface" approach to make service provision.

16.1.7. What is future of library technology (*http://edtechnology.co.uk*)

It is the post published by Ed. Brown in July 2017. In this she has generally compared future library technology as we upgrade our smart phones. She has emphasized innovating library with use of RFID security technology, which includes facilities like self checkouts, check in and renewal.

However, these facilities are already being used in many modern libraries.

16.1.8. Other articles and sources relating to future of library technology

Author found following two articles relevant to the present chapter theme:

1. Future of public libraries : Technology perspectives by Leif Petersen in, *Public Library Quarterly,* Vol. 35, 2016, Issue-4

2. Smart buildings : An introduction to library of the future by Mathew B. Hoy, *Medical Reference Service Quarterly* , Vol. 35, 2016- issue 3

These papers talk about (1) use of energy efficient networked sensors data recording in exciting ways and (2) in space planning future library building.In this author suggests that future public libraries should also think of providing services like career development and lifelong learning techniques in addition to social changes related aspects.

3. A New BOOK : There is a new book about to be released on the theme similar to this chapter is on, "*Emerging Technologies in Libraries: It's not just for geeks*", by Ida Joiner published by Elsevier which is available in both E-book as well as in soft copy form

In total author found that there is long list of new technological concepts or innovations waiting to enter into library environment and it is difficult to explain each and every of them. So after reviewing above literature the author felt it appropriate to elaborate on the following future library technologies and invite readers to understand the concepts behind them:

1. Bigdata
2. Virtual Reality
3. Augmented Reality
4. Digital interface for printed books
5. Blockchain Technology
6. Internet of things(IOT)
7. Robots and Drones
8. Library utensils
9. Library Mobile Apps
10. Intelligent Library Guide and Bookmark
11. Maker-space programmes
12. Application of Artificial Intelligence in Library
13. Data harvesting
14. Use of Biometrics ,Digital Signature and Smart cards in Authentication
15. Digital Preservation
16. 3D Printing Technology

At this juncture author would like to share the perception of Piotr Kowalczykas mentioned in his blog,"Library of the Future"which is exactly matching with the current chapter theme as":

"Libraries lead the way to digital citizenship. They should be first place where most advanced technologies are implemented. Today, libraries are not only about lending books. They are creative spaces for the individuals. They are economic incubators and learning hubs. Most of all, the libraries are the entry points to the digital world. They are the ways to embrace technology and avoid digital exclusion. Therefore, to improve technological literacy of local communities libraries should be equipped with relevant technology."

Now let us elaborate on above technologies in the following paras.

16.2. FUTURE LIBRARIES WITH FUTURE TECHNOLOGY

16.2.1. Big Data

The data that libraries held in their systems is about:

1. Patron data (Their personal data)
2. Collection data (Including collections of library materials in different formats)
3. Transaction data (Materials issued, returned, reserved and lost)

This refers the data concerned with basic or physical entities. We may also consider the data of the patrons when they are present on the library WebPages and browsing various web resources and links. If we consider data on all above points then we find that the total data becomes very large, may be called it a bigdata. Although the libraries face problems of storing and preserving this data, however, there is advantage of having such data in finding behavior of patrons or use the library services by them. We can analyse these databases by applying data mining techniques and analytical tools and the results are found very fantastic. It can throw light on future marketing strategy of library services. We have seen this topic in detailed in the respective chapter on **Big Data** in this book itself. Now let us refresh it in short. We know the library data is held in library systems or in LMSs. We also know that it is organized in the systems in MARC format rather specific in MARC-21 format.This format is now more that 40 years old. The main limitations of this data is that it is not visible in web world and remain isolated in library systems. With initiatives of Library of Congress new format like BIBFRAME is available. It is expected that in future world libraries would convert their MARC data to this new format and they will also share their library catalogue data as Open Linked Data to others. So that one could search availability of a particular book in the specific library directly through Google search and read it after obtaining the same. It will also be helpful to readers not only in finding a book but with open linked data they can also search books in combination of various subject heading and get more comprehensive catalogue search on web similar to as they search books in their own library catalogue. In a way Tim Berner-Lee's dream of real internet would be fulfilled through the future library data assets in the new format.

These are some flagship examples of using big data but having relevant skills and knowledge, storage and analysis of large datasets it could be real advantageous for librarians, so that they can make use of these massive resources of information to turn into knowledge.

16.2.2. Virtual Reality

With new and conducive environment in library readers enjoy both e.g.reading books and accessing e-resources.Now it is possible to make readers life in library more attractive by adding innovative gadgets and formats. With Virtual Reality (VR) sets readers can play to learn and explore other places while seating in their own library. The VR tools can also be used to bring library closer to patrons by devising virtual tour sets. Moreover, by adding this facility more readers could be attracted to come to library. There is no need to do a lot to create VR tools in library as getting VR headsets can start this supported with a few computers which are powerful enough to power the headsets. Google cardboard boxes are also useful in creating this facility in the library.

16.2.3. Augmented Reality

Augmented Reality looks like it would be the future of the communication technology. Apple has already announced that their future iPhones would be equipped with AR using facility. People are now more curious to see this in reality. There are many apps in android as well as iOs mobile softwares available, which have started giving feel of this new technology. Like in mobile technology this innovation is going to extend to other various domains from medicines to gaming.Now let us try to understand what it is. There is more news about use of AR in library but there are very few examples to actually see it. There is a video in YouTube based on *articles on the "eBook friendly" website, wherein Piotr Kowalczyk which gives a few examples of new technologies*(Courtesy : *https://ebookfriendly.com/library-future-technologies/*).It gives a facility how one can locate a book on library shelves.Augmented reality is an interactive experience of real world environment whereby objects that resides in the real world are "augmented" by computer generated perceptual information. It is the technology which superimposes a computer generated image with the real world images, which can provide a composite view. It can also be used as path finder for user in the library. There is another video in YouTube about use of AR in library under title "Design for Augmented Reality : Library application" by Moon-Hwan Lee, which wonderfully explains how the library use will be drastically changed with use of AR tool in the library.

16.2.4. Blockchain Technology

Blockchain is the current buzzword in advancement of information technology. Where-in we have heard about use of crypto currencies like BITCOIN and other currency in doing e-business. On face of it we do not understand about this new concept. It is said that blockchain is decentralized database which keeps records of pseudonimised digital transactions secured and it is visible only to concerned ones within the network of people who involve in the respective transaction. Now efforts are done if this technology could be used to build an enhanced metadata systems for libraries. Blockchain promises a new, decentralized way of recording and storing data. Potential use of blockchain has been so far identified in fields like business (e-Commerce), law and education. However, it also finds use in every situation, where data and transactions or sources and values are existing. The concept of blockchain was recently discussed in a conference. There was a presentation by, Institute of the Future, as referred in Blockchain in the library... by Jessica Leigh Brown, as she mentions in her article that" I heard about blockchain at a conference about two years ago, wherein

Sue Alman, the project's co-principal investigator and a lecturer at San Jose State University who teaches a course on emerging technologies who gave presentation in the *Institute for the Future*". (Courtesy: *https://www.edsurge.com/news/2018-02-01-blockchain-in-the-library-researchers-explore-potential-applications#*). It is now clear that using blockchain means credentialing e.g. creating one authenticated source where an individual could store all their metadata. Author thinks, it wouldn't be great if a libraries or information centers could use blockchain technology so that libraries/patron could store their credentials there. So the Blockchain is all about credentialing e.g. creating one authenticated source where an individual can store all his/her credentials.

In other words it could be said that presently we normally share our personal information on internet and when we try to transfer values of anything we revert ourselves to centralized financial institutions like banks or wallets. Secondly, whenever we try to purchase things online may be through Paytm or Bhim apps we require bank details to transfer money to them or when we pay through debit/credit cards or internet banking we need bank accounts. Where as in Blockchain technology we try to bypass all these middle gets by carrying out the financial tasks through financial service organizations, which comprise of recording transactions, establishing identity and by establishing contacts. It results peer to peer transactions like Bittcoin. Blockchain allows anyone to send values wherever in the world where blockchain profile can be accessed. Each blockchain is essentially just an online database, stored in a distributed, peer to peer fashion among its users. Cryptography takes care that users can only edit the parts of the chain that the individual owns by processing the private keys necessary to edit the transaction file. In the process giving private keys which you own to someone else, one can effectively transfers the value of whatever is stored in that particular section of the blockchain[(1)]. Now with at most security many financial service providers are switching to this new technology while giving services to their clients. Now not only in financial sectors it is proving that blockchain can be used to store any kind of digital information. Speciality of blockchain is that it created "smart contacts", which are so self secured for any kind of threat and they are automatically signed off as certain assigned conditions are met. Such as an invoice received online in the blockchain system can be automatically paid if the set conditions are met. It is assumed that blockchain technology could support to prosper internet of things. For example a blockchain home devices could automatically pay the energy or telephone/mobile postpaid bills if the set conditions are met. In is believed that blockchain technology could be one of the most powerful data handling development in the coming years. If we look into logic of the applications. At the moment other that its use in e-commerce or to be specific in Bitcoin we do not see the live examples of blockchain to get feel of advantages of bockchain in most of other fields or in our daily life. As far as its application of blockchain technology in library and information field is concerned author envisages the following advantages of its application :

1. Protecting collection metadata, transactional data as well as system software.
2. In protecting users authentication or credential rights
3. Library can create smart contracts for library borrowing as well as visiting users.

---

1. Bernard Marr: Data Strategy. London: Kogan Page; 2017, PP 15-16

4. Providing safety to online resources from misusing by the unauthorized users.
5. Providing secured extranet access to library patrons from any remote corners of the world to access their own library resources /services, computing facilities as well as their book accounts to avail online fine payment and reissuing of library materials without visiting library.
6. Library operations would be faster as patron need not provide their identity /barcoded/ smart cards etc.
7. System supported with blockchain can take care of subscription work and payment tasks automatically by setting prior conditions. It can also send reminder automatically of non receipt of journal issues.In general blockchain can further automate library functions and serve users with prompt actions.
8. Patrons can use bitcoin or similar crypto currency to pay library dues.

It is uncertain when blockchain technology would enter into library management but once it enters it will come with abundant of advantages.

In our daily life also blockchain technology is going to bring drastic change. It will take care in clearing our utility bills automatically. We can set to pay our dues of income tax automatically. In education field too blockchain finds many applications. Foreign university have already accepting tuition fees through bitcoins. It would be interesting to see when this technology arrives in developing country like India.

16.2.5. Library and Internet of Things (IOT)

It is seen that internet of things or IOT is receiving good attention like RFID.ITO considers possibilities of connecting devices and transferring data among them.It is thought that IOT can improve access to materials and services by the library patrons. IOT technology allow for remote monitoring, data transmission and control. It can help in tracking room usage and library skills teaching or information literacy programme attendance. It can also monitor environmental data of special collection preservation area in the library. Using this technology Hillsboro Public library introduced the Book-O-Mat, a self service book kiosk in a crowded area away from the main library with stock of new and popular books and movies.The usage of this workstation is being monitored from the library to know usage and to get alerts for restocking of reading materials.ITO applications can be used in library operations as well as teaching tool.

16.2.6. Library Mobile Apps

We have read about creating library website for mobile in a separate chapter in authors another book. It is observed that young readers spend more time on using mobile apps than using their browsers. Considering this trend nowadays libraries tend more on creating library apps which could be downloaded in mobiles and used whenever needed. Normally library mobile websites are accessed in the intranet or in the institute premises in WIFI zones. However, library mobile apps can also be accessed outside the physical boundaries. Library mobile apps can provide functionalities like library OPAC, interactive library guide or a library's virtual tour plus library calendar and library events. There is a list of nearly 50 ideas for creating library mobile apps presented by Nicole Henning in his blog (*http://nicolehenning.com*). By using these ideas one can create variety of library apps to promote library usage among the readers.

16.2.7. Drones

Nowadays use of flying devices or Drones and controlling them with remote control is increasing. Using Drone for delivering Pizzas is becoming innovative facility for foodies. Libraries thinking of use of drones to deliver books at doorstep of readers will not be an exception, so that library can reach to readers where it is not possible to serve readers. In addition to delivering books it is found that Drones could be used for creating contents for library or for collecting data as referred in blogs of Princh (courtesy :*http://princh.com*) and of Piotr (courtesy: https://ebookfriendly.com/library-future-technologies/).The Australian startup Flirty has made its first demonstration of delivering books e.g.book rental service called Zookal which can be viewed in video at (courtesy: *http://latimes.com*).

These days drones find several applications from transporting human organs needed for emergency life saving surgeries to deliver of pizzas to the customers.It is certain that future libraries would use Drones to deliver books at the doorstep of readers. In scientific term drone is known as UAV(Unmanned Aerial Vehicle).Although there is ban on use of drones in India but in advanced countries one can get drones easily in any electronic shop.Drone technology finds its origin in 1917 when Right Brothers experimented taking off kitty Hock, the first winged plane without a pilot. Further it was known as UAV. However it got its real name as 'Drone' due to its noise like honey bee(masculine bee).

Drone earned its' first success on 1 st May 20019 when a donors' kidney was successfully transported for emergency kidney transplant surgery to be performed at Maryland Medical Centre, USA. Where the transfer of kidney was done within a five minutes time. The life of 44 year old patient suffering from kidney disorder was survived. This was the first life-saving use of drone. On the other side we have recently seen how drone was used for destructive purpose where Saudi Arabia's oilfields was attacked to destroyed it,Which has resulted in 50% cut in oil production of the Saudi Arabia. Drone's military applications for spying enemies territory is well known. However, there are plenty of useful applications of drone and they are growing day by day. There are various special characteristics of drone technology such as:

1. Drones are always unmanned . It can be used to transport anything portable except an human
2. Drones are controlled from ground cockpits.
3. Since its flying is controlled from the ground it earns limited range. It permitted up to the sight of the controller. The drone has only two components 1.The drone itself and 2.the control unit.
4. Drone works almost like helicopter but without a pilot.
5. The drone are equipped with vision sensor, ultrasonic, infrared and dioder, which are used to identify the handles in the path and to avoid collision.

6. With the gyroscope equipment drone is kept stable while flight, which also facilities its smooth take off and landing.
7. Personal use of drones are available in three types : fixed wing, single and multi-rotor.

Although drone finds well-known use for military applications or use as toys but it has wonderful applications applications such as in :

- In event management, Drone cameras in taking live visuals for live sports commentary.
- Transporting retail items or delivering food item orders to the customers.
- Monitoring wildlife and in assessing forest fires.
- For aerial photography
- In entertainment industry
- In the medical field for transporting human organs from the donors to the site of emergency surgeries.
- In future the libraries would also use drones to deliver books at the door of readers located at remote places.

16.2.8. Robots

Libraries always try to apply newer and newer automated technological tools to make life of users easy and helpful. We now can imagine if robots can be used in functioning of libraries is possible. Yes there are good examples of use of Robots, where they are used in storing and retrieving library materials from the shelves. There is another example of use of Robot in library in Connecticut's Westport library, where library has recently acquired two robots named Vincent and Nancy which are being used in intelligent work of teaching coding and computer programme skills to students. Thus they can also be used to train library users in learning library and information literacy skills.

16.2.9. Digital Interface for Printed Book

We have seen new technology e.g. Augmented Reality by combining digital and real world situations. We are waiting to see the development/technology, which considers use of actual physical object also. People expect a technology which facilitates to use a particular page of physical book and also try to see the same page in respective e-book. Finger Print is a prototype of such technology developed by Fujitsu, which promises to use digital functionalities on a printed book. There is showcase video of this at You Tube (Courtesy : *https://www.youtube.com/watch?v=Mmcc Ee6JAcA*). The system here facilitates to detect the user's finger and what it is touching so one can create an interactive touch screen where one can select the corresponding part of e-book he/she wants to copy and mails to his/her mailbox in a digital form.

16.2.10. Intelligent Library Guide and Book Mark

Intelligent library bookmark is the device user can use in navigating needed materials on book shelves. In a large library users find it difficult to trace the book on the shelves as tracing books by

Dewey Decimal classification number becomes a tedious task for book searchers. They generally look for personal assistance or a device which can help them in navigation. The user can first check code of the a particular book in the device and set for navigation the same in library. With the device in hand user follows turn by turn directions/instructions given by device so that device takes the user to a particular shelf where the interested book is shelved without much tension and in a shortest time. Such device proves as invisible helping hand for the user. The operation is visible in link: (courtesy:*http://itechfuture.com/library-guide*). Similarly, it helps when users find it difficult to remember book return policy of the library and about remembering loan duration of the materials they have borrowed. For this there is concept of having book mark for library borrower devised by Chinees design company Toout .This tiny device is same as regular bookmark. However, having navigation features one can use library with ease.(Courtesy: *https://ebookfriendly.com/library-future-technologies/*)

16.2.11. Maker-Space Programme for Public Library

This development or technology is completely different than technologies we have discussed so far.It is assumed that knowledge is easily accessible in highly digital form. However, it is seen that interest in diverse technologies which motivates creating, learning and puzzles solving, is growing. It is observed that there is a demand that such technology hub or so called "Makerspace" be made available in public libraries. It is now proved that this concept is attracting users of all age group. The term Makerspace indicates broadly to a workshop where one can create his/her own design. The concept Makerspace attracts people who are generally not visiting library frequently. For example at Ballerup Library with establishment of makerspace has resulted in increasing in number of male visitors in addition to children, entrepreneurs, artists, senior citizens and technology enthusiastic. Author feels this would be really an innovative addition to the library. In order to create such a place or workshop in library it requires a lot many thing to consider, but once it is created it proves to be bonanza for creators, artists and designers. People who come here and use available facilities may be successful or not but such comprehensive framework for working creatively with the concept and designing could provide a real option in the library. Many technology libraries (as it is easy for them to create) could think of attaching the makerspace with library in order to increase footprints of visitors in library as many of them especially in developing countries are struggling to have more readers in library these days. For detailed review of makerspace concept can be read in the following linkL (Courtesy: *http://modelprogrammer.slks.dk/en/challenges/zones-and-spaces/-makerspace/*)

16.2.12. Library Utensils

As compare to costly technology like finger links there is cheaper alternative available known as Library Utensils. With this library could offer small utensils for using in reading room. The utensils are manufactured by Ivy Guide. They can put on very well on tip your pen, which is used for translating words found in pink book. The device helps readers to digitally highlight the required text. The concept is like this, the digital highlighter could be connected to computer. When one tries to highlight just by moving along the text in a pink book, which will appear in computer monitor.

The highlighted text part would be converted in a single text document. Once the entire work of highlighting is finished the collected text could be mailed to your mail address. In addition to carry out this simple task the device Ivy guide can also be used to scan the words for translation. It is also used to understand you new language in a better way. The device is rechargeable via USB and can easily adapts to your grip on pen. The concept is described by Pitro in his blog,(Courtesy *https://ebookfriendly.com/library-future-technologies/*) When more and more students go abroad for further education this device comes to their rescue to cross the language barrier. One can see more features of this device referred in the article on, "Pen translators for better understanding", written by Radhika), as cited in the reference.

16.2.13. Applications of Artificial Intelligence in Library

Artificial intelligence or AI is one the important branches of computer science. AI focuses on creating machines or systems which can be engaged in the operations like human intelligence. The AI system development generally involves the following areas of computer technology:

1. Expert system
2. Fuzzy logic
3. Artificial neural networks
4. Evolutionary algorithms
5. Case based reasoning
6. Image processing
7. Natural language processing
8. Speech recognition
9. Robotics

These techniques are not separate and in many intelligent systems two or more such techniques contribute in developing the expert systems in order to solve the complicated problems. Now AI techniques /tools are used in many areas such as business, management, medicine, military and so on. The idea of making use of artificial intelligence in library functions was initiated in 1990. Now it is established that intelligent library systems provide knowledge based services to the library clientele . AI or expert systems and intelligent agents are the complex areas of study and development which is difficult for non-specialist to understand. AI ultimately promises to create computer based systems which could replace the human intelligence. AI has now good prospects in applications in librarianship.

Now there is enough literature available which describes use of AI applications in library management such as:

1. Classification
2. Descriptive catalogue
3. Acquisition including online purchasing
4. Technical services

5. Collection development
6. Subject indexing
7. Virtual reference service
8. Database searching and information retrieval
9. Document delivery systems

While reviewing the literature on AI applications it is found that many authors have dealt with the underlying design issues of knowledge representation and natural language processing, whereas others have provided detailed and in-depth review of AI technologies. There is also considerable research and developmental efforts undertaken relating to library functioning based on study of major models of human intelligence. Basically the AI applications in library management refers to development of expert systems. Due to developments in computer technology and AI programming techniques it has become possible to develop expert systems needed for various intelligence related functions in library management. Developing a Robot Librarian is not a far from the reality

Expert systems : Artificial intelligence is utilised in creating intelligent machines or so called expert systems through intelligent programming, by which it has become possible to replace the process how human brain handles the problems and provides the solution. In reality the expert system get the questions from the user and respective answers as the input. Using this input the knowledge based system is built and and used subsequently.

Application of AI/ ES and Intelligent systems : Up till now libraries are making use of computerised management systems, which take care of all the routine, repetitive type of housekeeping functions. In these systems the simple conditioned based logic is used in designing them like yes or no. However, other than these routine tasks there are number tasks which are handles by only intellectual thinking by the expert individuals. For such tasks libraries need expert systems or the intelligent agents. In expert systems there are two major components:

1. Knowledge base
2. Inference engines

Normally humans use their knowledge base and intellectual skills in taking decisions. The information in the knowledge base are the rules. As compare to human intelligence expert systems can make much better decisions as the knowledge base could be of team of experts.

While preparing knowledge base for library tasks all the related concern rule are taken into account. In each rule there are two phases e.g. 'If' phase and 'Then' phase. If phase consists of conditions and then phase consist of results. In designing expert systems for a particular task, the if conditions are correlated with results through a inference engine. This way the ES try to simulate human decision making artificially. As we have seen the efforts are made to prepare ES for number of tasks by creating exact simulation of human decision making process in solving problems relating to those tasks. In case of library management there are following tasks where we need expert systems such as:

1. Acquisition including cooperative acquisition and online purchasing
2. Classification
3. Subject indexing
4. Virtual reference service
5. In semantic Web search and retrieval system we need intelligent agents
6. Helping the users while the browse on internet if they face any difficulties
7. Robot librarians
8. Information retrieval in digital libraries.

All these experts or intelligent systems are right now in developing stage and as time passes these would be available to the librarians for using them actually in providing services to the user. We therefore, need some more time to see them in reality

16.2.14. Use of Biometrics, Digital Signatures and Smart Cards for Authentication

In library management especially, in computerised circulation systems we need to authenticate patrons for issuing books and other materials. Use of identity cards or bar coded cards are the normal methods used to authenticate the patrons. In digital age face and eyes recognition are also used for authentication purpose. In such cases either systems fail to recognize or many people might forget to bring such cars along, as such authentication become difficult or time consuming. Sometime code/pin numbers or signatures are also used for authentication. However, these things are also not found so effective and it needs much time in identifying the individuals, therefore we need to have fast way of authenticate the patrons. The biometric recognition found these days very useful, accurate, economical and the fast method for this purpose. Biometric recognition refers to automatic recognition of individuals based on their physiological and behavioral characteristics. Biometrics can be used to identify the patrons at counter. In order to implement biometric method one needs to create biometric data, e.g. scanned images of finger prints. Secondly, the authentication system needs a scanning device interfaced to input systems. In actual operations biometric system is found very much convenient to use.

Like biometrics, digital signatures are also used for authentication .In this case data regarding digital signatures is collected beforehand which is interfaced to the system. Whenever any transaction is done the used is asked to sign on device screen with digital pen and then the signature is tallied with the signature available in the database, if it tallies then the transaction is completed, else it is not allowed.

There days instead of ID cards or bar-coded cards smart cards are also used to authenticate the users. Basically smart card is like RFID tag created to represent a book. Smart card consists of a microchip in which all the details of the reader/ user including photo image are pre recorded. When user gives books and smart card to counter staff. The smart card is inserted in the computer card reader slot whereby the details are read and then tallied with data existing in the system database. If it matches the transaction is allowed to complete.

16.2.15. Digital Preservation

In the age of changing, progressing and evolving information technology tools preserving digital contents poses a great challenge especially for libraries and archiving institutions. In digital preservation includes all practices which ensures safety of information. Threats to digital contents are emerging due to medium failure, as well as obsolescence of software and hardware devices which hold the digital contents. In the digital age preserving information products involves not only backing up the contents but maintaining the storage media on which the valuable data is stored. The digital information is more significant as the digital form is the most suitable form to store documents as compared to fragile paper or microfilm media. However, digital media is also subject to danger of vanishing due to continuous changing behavior of the information technology which has provided the better medium to preserve the information. We see normally two types of digital materials[1]. 1. Digitally born and 2. digitized materials. The contents which are only made available digitally need more digital preservation efforts. Digital preservation becomes necessary because of challenges faced by the digital information due to storage media obsolescence, storage medium failure, and software obsolescence or up gradation. The methods of preservation data included actions like:

- Refreshing data and transferring it to fresh or new media of same type to prevent data loss in transferring process
- Migration(transferring all together on to a new medium) and preventing data loss due to hardware obsolescence
- In the case of software obsolescence emulators are used to render contents. These emulators then become the part of what need to be preserved
- Organized and disorganized piracy also play a part in digital preservation. Pirates may provide redundant copies of the best quality digital contents
- Multiple backups also helps in preserving the digital documents and data. File sharing software such as Bit Torrent, which facilitates distribution and geographically separate backingups.
- Digital Library software found helpful in preserving contents of digital libraries for a long time as it collects comprehensive meta data including details of data formats.
- The efforts to protect the interests of IP holders in some way also necessitates the digital preservation

16.2.16. 3D Printing Technology

3D printing is basically an additive technology. It is used to manufacture products in 3D form directly. Here additive refers to successive adding layer by layer which are very thin which creates the products. With 3D technology one can create toys, mould for manufacturing products in a large scale or human organs (3D bones and skins) or even constructing the actual house. All 3D technologies work in similar way as objects are created layer by layer.

How 3D prints works

The process of 3D printing is described in the following steps:

First Step : Before printing 3D objects its' 3D digital file is created using CAD software or 3D scanner or one can download it from 3D market place

Second Step : In this step one needs to actual do the 3D printing of the object or actually creating the one. In this step the system decides the properties of material knowing properties of the final product. There are variety of materials used for this, generally materials such as plastics, ceramics, resins, metals, sand, textile, biomaterials and the glass etc. The finishing of products thus created is done further to get the fine design as one imagines while preparing its digital picture.

Third Step : In this step the created finished products are applies with paints to give it a final look.

The 3D printing process is about actually manufacturing a product through the photo polymerization, which involves solidification of photo sensitive resins by using ultra violet lights.

Applications of 3D printing

3D printing is used for creating moulds for jewelry or even making actual jewelry. It is popular in customizable gift manufacturing industry or even 3D printed chocolates can be prepared using food materials. One can also prepare a model of an house or even construct the actual house.

The main characteristics of 3D prating is making solid three dimensional objects layer by layer from a digital file. It is achieved through additive process. One can use appropriate materials needed knowing the properties of the final product. Another name for 3D printing is Fused Deposition Modeling(FDM). The file formats for 3D printing used are STL and VRML.STL is stereo-lithography. The 3D printer was first created by Charles W. Hull in 1980s. Now cost of the consumer grade 3D printer is roughly $700/- and professional type 3D Printers cost $10000 or more.

How can Library Provides Assistance in Using 3D Pinging Technology

Considering high cost of 3D printing technology libraries can very well provide the same in its Maker Space branch of the library so that designers and creators can enjoy the using and learning the very new technology. This is good way to attract the readers towards the library in a large number. With this we complete the first part of this chapter wherein we discussed the future technologies in the library.

Now in the following paragraphs we are going to review the new terminologies emerged in the field of library information technology.

16.3. EMERGING TERMINOLOGIES : A REVIEW

16.3.1. Repositories-ROAR, DOAR-Open DOAR, SHERPA and SHERPA - RoMEO

All the above terms are conceptually closely related to each other. Now let us first look at their full forms:

ROAR= Registry of Open Access Repositories

DOAR=Directory of Open Access Repositories. Open DOAR is repository of repositories which provides access to repositories around the world DOAR through its portal.

SHERPA=Securing a Hybrid Environment for Research Preservation

SHERPA RoMEO=SHERPA Rights Metadata for Open Archiving

SPARC=Scholarly Publishing and Academic Resources Coalition

Now let us try to elaborate them further.

ROAR (Registry of Open Access Repositories) : It is concerned about creation ,location and growth of open access repositories and their contents. ROAR is a searchable international database indexing system. It is a product of E-Print initiated at Southampton University in UK (2003). It started with the name as Institutional Archiving Registry, which was further renames as ROAR (2006). As on 2015 it has registration of over 3000 institutional and cross institutional repositories.

Along with ROAR there is another similar directory known as DOAR (Directory of Open Access Repositories) also available in UK. These are two leading open access directories worldwide. As mentioned above Open DOAR is repository of repositories which provides access to repositories around the world. Although Open DOAR is based in UK, it lists repositories from America, Canada, Asia, France, Germany, Spain, Oceania and Australia. Out-of ROAR and DOAR, ROAR is the larger directory and allows direct submissions of any new repository to this directory, whereas DOAR or Open DOAR controls submission of materials and depends on the direction of its staff. Open DOAR is responsible or looks for open access of scholarly or academic materials. ROAR on the other hand allows all the other types of materials to be included in the registry. ROAR provides facility of filtering by country, type of depository. It also allows searching and sorting by repository names.

Open DOAR is maintained by University of Nottingham under the SHERPA umbrella of services, which was developed in collaboration with Lund University. The Open DOAR project is funded by Open Science Institute JISC (Joint Information System Committee),the Consortium of Research Laboratories (CURL) and SPARC Europe together.

SHERPA : it is known as Securing a Hybrid Environment for Research Preservation and Access. Originally was established in 2002, it is an organisation to run and manage the SHERPA project. It started with a view to support the establishment of number of open access institutional repositories in UK universities and said to be act as an umbrella for open access repositories of the world. Stephen Pin-Field was the first director of SHERPA (2002) who continued until 2012.

SHERPA RoMEO : It is known for the services by SHERPA to show the copyright and open access self archiving policies of academic journals.The database uses the colour coding scheme to classify publishers according to their self archiving policy such as:

Green : Can archive pre-print and post prints or publishers version in PDF

Blue : Can archive post print or publishers version in PDF

Yellow : can archive pre-print or pre- referring

White : Archiving not formally supported.

SHERPA Juliet : Is an online database of open access mandates adopted by academic funding bodies. It is also a part of SHERPA suite of services around open access and is run by JISC

SPARC : is known for Scholarly Publishing and Academic Resources Coalition .It is an international alliance of academic and research libraries developed by Association of Research Libraries ((1998). It promotes open access scholarships. It currently includes 800 institutions from North America, Europe, Japan and Australia. Richard Johnson served as the first director of SHARP (1998-2005).Heather Joseph further became the executive director (2005).

16.3.2. Internet Terminologies-HTTP, HTTPS,FTP, SMTP, TCP/IP, URL and URI

HTTP : It is known for Hypertext Transfer Protocol. It is the basic technology of Internet or foundation of data communication for the World Wide Web. WWW includes hypertext documents where with the help of hyperlinks in documents one can click them using mouse to browse web pages successively. Technically It is an application protocol for distributed, collaborative, hypermedia information systems available on Internet world. HTTP was developed to facilitate hypertext and www. It bears the international standard name as RFC 7230.HTTP was developed by successively initially by CERN then further by IETF and W3C.The development of http initiated by Tim Berners-Lee at CERN in 1989.

HTTPS : its full form is Hypertext Transfer Protocol Secure. Basically it is extended version of HTTP. It is used to secure safety for private transactions on Internet. The purpose behind having this protocol is to provide proper authentication on the accessed websites and to maintain the privacy and integrity for the data exchanged while making important transactions especially the financial transactions. The protocol tries to provide protection from hackers and individuals attempting to make bank frauds. In https the communication protocol is encrypted using Transport Layer Security (TLS)

FTP : FTP (File Transfer Protocol)- is a standard/ basic network protocol used generally to transfer files between client and server on the Internet over tcp/ip connections. In a network it works on a client – server model architecture using separate control and data links between the client and server. FTP is a way to transfer files online. Normally we transfer files by using attachment facility of any email box. However, one can also transfer files while working on internet either we can send contents we choose to ftp server or if we down load something then one can send it to server by using file transfer protocol. The server is accessible to the user across the network , one can access the server from any computer which is a part of network and can use the files in a client machine.FTP is the oldest protocol used today to move files conveniently. Under FTP system a server is created using users authentication keys .It can also provide a directory or sub directories which are used as destination while transferring the files .User get connected to server through a client machine .A small software lets one to download the files from server to the client machine or it can also used to upload the file from client to server. However, It is also possible to get connected anonymously to ftp server if the server permits so. In the secured transmission protection user name and passwords is provided while encrypting the contents ftp is always secured with SSL/TLS.

How to activate FTP Server

1. Use windows keyboard short cut to open the power user menu and select programme and features

2. Click the turn windows features on or off link
3. Extend Internet information service and check the ftp server option
4. Expand FTP server and check FTP extensible option
5. Check web management tools with the default selection
6. Click ok to begin the installation
7. Click close

How to access the ftp server

1. Use windows keyboard short cut key to open the power user menu and select control panel
2. Open administrative tools
3. Double click Internet Information service (IIS)Manager
4. Expand sites
5. Select the FTP site and double click authorisation rules.

SMTP: It is Simple Mail Transfer Protocol. This protocol is used for sending e-mail messages between the servers. In most of the e-mail boxes send the messages over the internet use SMPT protocol to forward messages from One mail server to other. Such messages are then retrieved by e-mail client machines by using either POP up or IMAP

TCP/IP: It is Transmission control Protocol / Internet protocol. TCP?IP is the basic protocol to get any PC or computer connected to internet. While installing every new computer it needs to be configured with TCP/IP. Normally it comes as a default internet software whenever a new system is bought.

URL : URL(Uniform Resource Locator) is known for unique web address of any web page available on the internet.URL is governed by internet protocol (http) or Hypertext Transmission Protocol. In worldwide web (WWW) technology web page address always begins with www. All these web pages are essentially uploaded on the internet .The web pages which are only uploaded on intranet, do not begin with www in their web page addresses. They are written as *http://library.iitb.ac.in.* Normally URL refers to a web page but it can also be used to refer the file transfer(ftp),email(mailto) etc. We can see the URL of the web page we are browsing displayed in the address bar of any web browser screen. The URL has the structure as:

http://www.example.com/index.html

In this address the different parts are seen as:

http= It represents internet protocol

www.example.com = It represents the host or domain name

index.html= Represents the file name

URL or Uniform Resource Locator has been defined in a standard RFC 1738. It was invented by Tim Berners-Lee the inventor of www (World Wide Web). Different extensions are used to indicate type of website as:

.com= Commercial Website

.edu =Educational website

.org= Institutional(non profit making) website

.gov = Government website

Web site can also represent geographical location as:

http://www.example.com/state/city.html

Unless specified all web addresses refers to USA and for other countries specific extensions are used such as:

.in Indian website

.uk United Kingdom website etc.

URI : URI is represented for Uniform Resource Identifier. It is a string of characters which identifies a particular resource on the internet. It came into light in the third generation of internet e.g. web 3.O or in semantic web. In normal internet browsing e.g. in web 1.O or web 2.O the web pages are known by their web addresses or know as URLs. Whereas in Semantic web we surf URIs instead of URL.The special characteristics of URI is that it refers even to every smallest part of resource on web having unique URI for each of them. The combination of various URIs can represent a resource as a whole. In old internet technology URL was indicating only the web address, which was helping us to search a particular web page on the internet. However, it was never helping us to search any item, point or theme of that web page/content. In semantic web we can independently identify and search each and every important contents with the help of URI on web easily such as a particular document or image.

In old web technology concept like individual, institution or book in library or person as author were not existing independently or rather they are not recognized by the computers. In semantic web each of them do exist on web independently and recognized by the computers .Now let us understand how URI is created and presented. Basically it contains the linked data, which means data in terms of its attributes.Like HTTP the W3C has prepared protocol for linked data in terms of its ontology, which is useful in semantic web. There are guidelines or structural describers to Link Open Database on the web known as RDF (Resource Description Framework).RDF facilities imputing metadata of a resource and upload it on web.Now one can create RDF structure of any item or resource. Suppose I wish to create the RDF of my identity on web by creating metadata about my profile . For example:

My full name : Dattatray Narayan Phadke

My mail ID : *dnphadke@gmail.com*

My field : Library Information Technology

By using standard key terms (ontology) I can create RDF and upload it on the web. Now in semantic web environment if anybody tries to search for me the computer can exactly show my profile.There is difference in search strategy in web 1.O and web 3.O or the semantic web. In semantic web computer very well understands what is what.It not only understands the exact meaning of words represented in data but it also understands the relation amongst the words, which was not possible in the old internet versions. For example normal computer will never understand the meaning of words Ram, Lakskman, Bharat, Shatrughan and Dashrath (we very well known these names are from Ramayana epic) but in semantic web computer understand that Ram, Lakshman, Bharat and Shatrughan are the brothers and Dashrath is their father. We will discuss this further when we discuss more about RDF in the nest para.

16.3.3. RDF and RDFs

RDF (Resource Description Framework) : RDF is one way of creating metadata of a source on internet. The meta data recorded here is in a structured form with a set of attributes. It is also used for inputting open linked data. This concept is from semantic web technology or from Web 3.O. RDF is the foundation of linked data. It is a method to encode data in a structured form.It is a standard model used for interlinking data on web. RDF facilitates way of recognizing and expressing relationships between the data elements on the web.It uses prominent structure called "Triple" e.g. Subject+Predicate+Object. Now let us use this method to understand bibliographic data in library database as follows:

(a) An author is creator of work so it is the 'Subject'

(b) Subject of book is the ,'Object' so it is an Object

(c) When we express their relationship ,is the ' Predicate'

Now let us understand with an example:

S.R. Rangnathan———— Is the Creator of————— Five laws of library science
(Subject) (Creator-Predicate) (Object)

If one writes or encodes the same in terms of RDF then it looks like:

(S.R.Ranganathan) (Five laws of library science)

http://id.loc.gov/authorities/http://http://www.worldcat

purl.org/dc/elements/ names/n500539191.1/.org/oclc/18730828creator

The computers universally recognise and understand the meaning and relationship as seen in above example

There is ontology or the dictionary available which is used to create such data structure in RDF.

RDFs (RDF Schema) : It is the terminology from the semantic web. RDF Schema (RDFs) is the Resource Description Framework Schema which also refers to various abbreviations as RDFS, RDF(s), RDF-S or RDF/S. It is the set of classes with certain properties used for RDF extensible knowledge representation data models, which provides basic elements for the description of ontotologies, else called RDF vocabularies intended to structure RDF of a resources. In RDF the resource is structured in triple-store as referred above. These structured models can be searched by a special language called SPARQL

Protégé : Protégé is a free ,open source software which provides software developer community with a set of tools to construct the domain models and knowledge based applications in developing ontologies.

16.3.4. Cataloguing Standards and Protocols- ISO 2709, Z39.50, Z39.71 and Z39.2

ISO 2709 : ISO-2709 is an ISO standard for bibliographic description concerned with titled information and documentation. This is a bibliographic format used as transitional format in information exchange. This format is used to transfer data to various formats. When library goes for migration of software and while doing so data of an old system need to exported to the new format then first data is ported in ISO 2709 format and then it is converted into a desired format as ISO 2709 is compatible to most of the other bibliographic formats.

Z39.50 : Z39.50 is an international standard client server application layer communication protocol. It is used for searching and retrieving bibliographic data from library database over the internet. It is covered by standard ANSI/NISO standard Z39.50 and ISO standard 23950. It is maintained by Library of Congress. Z39.50 is widely used in creating library catalogues or bibliographic databases in integrated library systems. Any catalogue created using this protocol also called as an open access library catalogue, which is open for other libraries to directly download the desired catalogue entries in adopting them in their database while building the catalogue. The example is Library of Congress catalogue which is used by any library in creating library database or in retrospective conversion of library database, where one can get complete bibliographic information just by matching entry by its ISBN number

Z39.71 : The ANSI/NISO Z39.71 is an international standard for bibliographic data of serials holdings display standard, which is a combination of two types e.g. conceptual holdings elements and nine principles for recording the holding elements. This standard supersedes the standards Z39.44-1986 serials holding statements and Z39.57 -1989 for non-serial items.

Z39.2 : ANSI/INSO Z39.2 1994 is an international standard for information Interchange Format. This is the basic for MARC (Machine Readable Catalogue) record. This standard specifies the requirements for generalised interchange format which can be used for communication of records in any media.

16.3.5. Bibliographic Record Formats and Standards – ISBD, MARC 21, CCF, RDA, FRBR, Bibframe

ISBD : It is International Standard Bibliographic Description (ISBD). It is used for describing bibliographic in any type of catalogue. It produced by IFLA and published by De Gruyter Saur in 2011. It helps in maintaining consistency in cataloguing of various resources like books, maps, serials, sound recordings, computer files and other electronic resource into a single text.

MARC-21 : MARC is machine readable catalogue format and MAR-21 is the latest version of it.This format is generally adopted in creating database format in various library management systems (LMSs). Basically it is the combination of USMARC and CAN/ MARC. MARC is based on the INSO/ANSI standard Z39.2 standard. Speciality of this standard is that it allows different database to communicate each other in exchanging bibliographic records.

CCF : CCF is Common Communication Format is a structure format for creating bibliographic records and for exchanging records between various libraries .UNESCO organised an international symposium in Taormina, Sicily in April 1978. Outcome of this symposium UNISCO/PGI formed the ad hoc group on the establishment of Common Communication Format. Several countries especially SARC countries adopted this format for exchanging and creation of bibliographic records at national level. It is as per ISO-2709 format.

RDA : It stands for Resource Description and Access (RDA) is a content standard which provides a set of guidelines for formulating data to support resource discovery. RDA is a revised version of AACR 2. Basically it a style for encoding various bibliographical fields in a database. RDA is based on FRBR (Functional Requirements for Bibliographic Record) and FRAD (Functional Requirements for Authority Data). RDA standard in electronic form is now available and Many libraries have started adopting it in creation and conversion of bibliographic databases. OCLC has taken initiative to implement it worldwide.

FRBR : FRBR-Functional Requirement For Bibliographic Records is a-conceptual entity relationship model developed by International Federation of Library Association and Institutions (IFLA) which is about how user to access and retrieve in online form the library catalogues and bibliographic databases from user's point of view. It provides more comprehensive approach in accessing and retrieving the records as relationship between the entities, which provides links to navigate through the hierarchy of the relationship. This model is more useful because it is separate from cataloguing standards like AACR2 or ISBD. It was created as an entry relationship for way the bibliographic universe should operate.The FRBR model consists of entities, relationships and attributes which are used to describe the resources. There are 3 groups of entities

Group -1 Consists of works, Expressions, Manifestation and Items

Group-2 Persons, Corporations, and families These are responsible for group-1.

Group -3 Is the subject oriented and consists of concepts, objects, events and places

All these entities are directly mapped to library user's search activity and rationalised the way that data is organised and presented to the searchers. The important factor behind the FRBR model was an attempt to allow library systems to create better relational databases from the bibliographic records.

BIBFRAME : BIBFRAME (Bibliographic Framework) is a data model for bibliographic description. Bibframe was devised (Library of Congress) to replace the age old MARC standard/ format.Linked data principles have been used in designing it to make bibliographic data more useful both in within the library premises as well as outside the library through the internet.In MARC type data format the catalogue was restricted to be used only within the library and was not visible to web world. The Bibframe is expressed in RDF structure which is further based on three categories of abstractions (work, instance and items). Bibframe provides the foundation for the future of bibliographic description, both on the web and inside the library OPACs. It is created on linked data techniques. A major focus of the Bibframe initiative is to determine a transition path for the MARC format while preserving a robust data exchange process thereby saving the time, efforts and money. One can refer the 14th Chapter on IBFRAME included in this book to gain thorough knowledge on it.

16.3.6. Data Harvesting

Data harvesting is somewhat similar to data mining. The data harvesting process is used to extract and analyse the data collected from online sources. Data harvesting could be similar to web mining, data scrapping and data extraction or web scraping. The term data harvesting is derived from the agriculture process of harvesting, where good is collected from the renewable resource. The data found on the internet is also like a renewable resource, as every day new data is generated. In order to extract the data online some relevant and previously selected websites are targeted for data extraction or harvesting. The data thus obtained could be pretty good as harvester expected. The one method to harvest the data online could be through an automated bot. Data harvesting may not be easy always, as the respective website managers could impose restrictions to prevent data in order to protect it from harvesters. Generally websites use Application Programming Interface (API) as used by Twitter and Facebook managers to protect the data. Most of the time the data harvesting task is got done from the third party being a professionals job. Through data harvesting one can get very useful information and insight which could influence the business decisions, especially in knowing the prospective consumers and competitors. Since the vast amount of data is available on the internet and every day new data is added the data harvesting has become popular and somewhat necessary tool for the companies which are very much interested in knowing the market places, the consumers and the competitors to improve the business

16.3.7. Social Mobile Analytics and Cloud (SMAC)

SMAC or Social Mobile Analytics and Cloud is a new concept emerged at the backdrop of BIG data development, which relates to transition from e-business to digital business. It is the convergence of four technologies viz

- Social Media Platforms
- Mobile Technology Platform
- Data Analytics
- Cloud Computing Platform.

It is now fact that these four technologies together help in improving business operations by bringing companies closer to customers with minimum overhead expenses at the same time maximum reach. It has become possible due to proliferation of data (structured and unstructured) or due to availability of big data created by mobile and wearable devices, sensors, social media and website browsing, which is facilitating creating new business models built on customer generated data. Instead of considering these individual technologies it beneficial if integration of social, mobile, analytics and cloud, which creates competitive advance and new business opportunities.

The concept of SMAC has been evolved since 2011/12 as a result of consumerisation of information technology. The enterprise computing has been strengthened by adding mobile and cloud technologies to the existing one to one communication and hardware software systems. International Data Corporation has referred SMAC as the third platform. Where in first platform is the large computing systems, the second platform is TCP/IP client server model that is internet and third platform is SMAC, which combines the incumbent technologies like social networking, mobile, analytics and cloud technologies and now IOT Internet of things, which is providing a new way to allow business to accelerate their digital transformation. The third platform is futher accelerated by considering six innovative technologies including augmented and virtual realities, AI systems and robotics as referred by IDC.

Now SMAC has provided a new foundation for doing business in digital economy, where data analytics, and information technology work like backbone.The major vendors like Amazon, Face book and Google are already availing benefits of SMAC concept. One can earn greatest value in SMAC where all the concern technologies are used together. The key here is to integrate these complex technologies on the backend and to provide an easy to use customer or employee interface on the front end.

The suggested framework for SMAC includes selection of proprietary or open source to build hybrid stacks. The Technologies could include No SQL and machine learning for analytics as used in handling big data, cloud services such as integration platform as a service (iPaaS) to integrate services and applications, as well as the technologies which facilitates machine to machine communication such as near field or blue tooth to transmit data from a connected devices to cloud, web APIs can be used to connect social media outlets and cloud services to the platform. The integration of the technologies require clear policies and guidelines as well as management tools which can automate business process.

The media company NETFLIX is set to be the best example which has successfully availed the benefits of SMAC. The story could be like this, when NETFLIX members stream TV show of Netflix cloud to their I-pads, they are given option to give the multiple feedback by signing with face book's social login after viewing the shows. They can also rate the contents with stars, write reviews and share the contents they watched with their friends on face book or twitter. Netflix try to use social media only to build and promote its brand. The company creates original contents and by releasing an entire series of show episodes at once triggers a social media buzz which inspires customers/viewers to talk among about the show which builds up a fan base for NETFLIX automatically.

16.3.8. Intrusion Detection System

An Intrusion Detection System (IDS) is a system which takes care of any suspicious or malicious activity while monitoring the traffic on the network and gives alert if it notices the same. The anomaly detection and reporting is the primary function of any IDS. Some IDS are capable to take actions against such activities on their own, including blocking such signals or messages from entering into the systems sent from originating IPs. Like IDS there are Intrusion Prevention Systems which monitors network traffic /packets for potential generally damaging activities. However, IDS actually responds to malicious traffic navigation found in the traffic and issuing the warnings.

Different Types of Intrusion Detection Systems

There are different types and methods available in IDSs such as:

A Network Intrusion Detection System (NIDS) : When deployed at strategic point on the network it can monitor incoming and outgoing traffic to and from all the devices existing in the entire network.

Host Intrusion Detection System(HIDS) : It takes care of all computers and devices in the network having direct access to internet browsing and downloading activities. It not only takes care of malicious activity detected entering from outside but it can also detect such activity if generated within the system and if NIDS failed to detect it. Some times malware is generated within the host system and likely to spread across the system where HIDS takes care in detection and alerting.

Signature Based Intrusion Detection System : This monitors each and every packets that travelling all over the network and compares them against a database of signatures or attributes of known malicious threats similar to antivirus software.

Anomaly based intrusion detection systems : This monitors the compares which is normal and abnormal malicious activity with respective to bandwidth, protocol, ports, and other devices and alerts the administrators about potential malicious activity.

Like different types of Intrusion Detection Systems there two major types such as passive and active IDSs. Passive type of IDS detects the activity ,alerts but do not take any action to destroy it, whereas the active IDS not only detects and alerts but it also takes action to deal with it. The main function of any IDS is to protect the network and provide the security against damaging the network and systems from malicious activities.

REFERENCES

1. 12 Innovative technologies to implement in the library of the future: (*http://princh.com*)
2. Library of the future: 8 technologies we would love to see. (*https://ebookfriedly.com/library-future-technologies/*)
3. How technology is changing future of libraries (*http://hub.wiley.com*)
4. Library trends for 2018 (*www.techsouplibraries.org*)
5. Top library trends :American Library Magazine (*http://americanlibrariesmagazine.org*)
6. Predicting the future: Library technology to keep in mind (*http://www.tandfonline.com*)
7. What is future of library technology (*http://edtechnology.co.uk*)
8. Blockchain in library? Researchers explore potential applications by Jessica Leigh Brown (https://www.edsurge.com/news/2018-02-01-blockchain-in-the-library-researchers-explore-potential-applications) (All the above web resources were accessed on 07-09-2018)
9. Radhika Seth. Pen translator for better understanding : The designers are Shi Jian, Sun Jiahao and Li ke: (*http://www.yankodesign.com/2013/01/21/pen-translator-for-better-understanding/*)
10. Bernard Marr: Data Strategy. London: Kogan Page; 2017, PP 15-16
11. Asefeh Asemi and Adeleh Asmi : Artificial Intellignece (AI) Applications in Library System in Iran : A Taxonomy Study University of Nebraska-Lincoln Library Philosophy and Practice (e-jounal) winter 2-5-2018 (*http://digitalcommons.unl.edu/libphiprac/1840*)

Index

D

F

G

H

I

K

L

M

O

P

Q

R

S

T

U

V